Dawn

Volume Five

Based on the edition by
Giorgio Colli and Mazzino Montinari
First Organized in English by Ernst Behler

Friedrich Nietzsche

Dawn

Thoughts on the Presumptions of Morality

Translated by Brittain Smith
Afterword by Keith Ansell-Pearson

STANFORD UNIVERSITY PRESS

STANFORD, CALIFORNIA

Stanford University Press
Stanford, California

Translated from Friedrich Nietzsche, *Sämtliche Werke: Kritische Studienausgabe*, ed. Giorgio Colli and Mazzino Montinari, in 15 vols. This book corresponds to Vol. 3, pp. 9–331.

Critical edition of Friedrich Nietzsche's *Sämtliche Werke* and unpublished writings based on the original manuscripts.

Printed in the United States of America on acid-free, archival-quality paper

CIP data appears at the end of the book.

Contents

A Note
on This Edition

This is the first English translation of all of Nietzsche's writings, including his unpublished fragments, with annotation, afterwords concerning the individual texts, and indexes, in nineteen volumes. The aim of this collaborative work is to produce a critical edition for scholarly use. Volume 1 also includes an introduction to the entire edition, and Volume 19 will include a detailed chronology of Nietzsche's life. While the goal is to establish a readable text in contemporary English, the translation follows the original as closely as possible. All texts have been translated anew by a group of scholars, and particular attention has been given to maintaining a consistent terminology throughout the volumes. The translation is based on *Friedrich Nietzsche, Sämtliche Werke: Kritische Studienausgabe in 15 Bänden* (1980), edited by Giorgio Colli and Mazzino Montinari. The still-progressing *Nietzsche Werke: Kritische Gesamtausgabe,* which Colli and Montinari began in 1963, has also been consulted. The Colli-Montinari edition is of particular importance for the fragments and variants comprising more than half of Nietzsche's writings, many of which are published there for the first time. Besides listing textual variants, the annotation to this English edition provides succinct information on the text and identifies events, names (except those in the Index of Persons), titles, quotes, and biographical facts of Nietzsche's own life. The notes are numbered in the text and are keyed by phrase. The Editor's Afterword presents the main facts about the origin of the text, the stages of its composition, and the main events of its reception. The Index of Persons lists the dates of birth and death as well as prominent personal characteristics and includes mythological figures. Since the first three volumes have appeared, important corrections to the 1980 edition of the *Kritische Studienausgabe* have been noted, and these corrections have been incorporated into the translation that appears here.

Ernst Behler and Alan D. Schrift

Dawn

*Thoughts on the
Presumptions of Morality*

"There are so many dawns that
have not yet broken."

Rig Veda

Preface

1

In this book you will find a "subterranean" at work, a tunneler, miner, underminer. Provided that you have eyes for such work of the depths, you will see him — how he makes his way forward slowly, deliberately, with calm relentlessness, scarcely betraying the hardship that accompanies every lengthy deprivation of light and air; even in his work in the dark, you could call him content. Doesn't it seem that some faith[1] guides, that some comfort recompenses him? That he perhaps wants to have his own long darkness, his incomprehensibility, concealment, enigma, because he knows what he will also have: his own daybreak, his own salvation, his own *dawn*? . . . Certainly he will return: don't ask him what he's up to down there; once he has "become human" again, he will tell you himself, this apparent Trophonius[2] and subterranean. One thoroughly unlearns how to keep silent after having been, for as long as he, a mole and alone—

2

Indeed, my patient friends, I will tell you what I was up to down there, tell you here in this belated Preface,[3] which could easily have become an obituary, a funeral oration: for I have returned and — I have also escaped. You needn't worry that I will summon you to the same perils! Or even merely to the same solitude! For whoever travels down such paths of his own encounters no one: such is the nature of "own paths." No one comes to help him along the way; he alone must contend with all the danger, chance, malice, and bad weather that befall him. He has his path *for himself*—and also of course his bitterness, his occasional vexation over this "for himself": part of which includes, for instance, his knowledge that even his friends cannot discern where he is or where he's going and that, from time to time, they ask themselves, "What? Is he even going at all? Does he still have—a path?"—Back then I undertook something that might well not be for everyone: I climbed into the deep; I tunneled into the foundation;[4] I began to investigate and to dig away[5] at an ancient *trust*[6] upon which, for the past few millennia, we philosophers have tended to build as if it were the securest of foundations—time and time again, although every building heretofore has collapsed: I began to undermine our *trust in morality*. But you don't understand me?

3

Previously, thinking has been at its worst with regard to good and evil:[7] that was always too dangerous a subject. Conscience, reputation, hell, and, if necessary, even the police allowed and continue to allow no candor. As with every authority, in the presence of morality one precisely *should* not think or, even less, speak one's mind; here, one—*obeys*! As long as the world has existed, no authority has ever willingly permitted itself to become the object of critique; and even to think of criticizing morality, to consider morality as a problem, as problematic: what? was that not—*is* that not—immoral?—But morality has at her command not merely every type of terrifying bogey to keep critical hands and instruments of torture at a distance: her security rests even more surely in a certain power of enchantment in which she is well skilled—she knows how to "inspire."[8] She succeeds, often with a single glance, in laming the critical will, even in luring it over to her own side; there are indeed cases where she manages to turn the critical will against itself: so that, like the scorpion, it plunges its sting into its own body. From time immemorial, morality has been well skilled in every devilry of the art of persuasion: there has never been, even these days, a single orator who does not solicit her assistance. (Just listen, for instance, to the way even our anarchists speak: how morally they evince in order to convince![9] They even go so far as to end up calling themselves "the good and the just.") From the beginning of time, as long as people have evinced and been convinced, morality has proven herself to be the greatest mistress of seduction — and, as far as we philosophers are concerned, the true *Circe*[10] *of philosophers*. Why is it that from Plato to this day all philosophical architects in Europe have built in vain? That everything they themselves honestly and earnestly held to be *aere perennius*[11] is threatening to collapse or already lies in ruin? Oh how false is the answer to this question that, even now, one keeps ready and waiting: "because they all had overlooked the prerequisite, an examination of the fundament, a critique of reason in its entirety"[12] — that disastrous answer of Kant's, with which, without a doubt, he failed to entice us modern philosophers onto a more solid and less deceptive ground![13] (— and, come to think of it, wasn't it somewhat strange to demand that an instrument should critique its own excellence and usefulness? That the intellect itself should "apprehend" its own worth, its own power, its own limits? Wasn't it even just a bit contradictory? —) Actually, the right answer would have been that all philosophers, Kant included, have been building under the seduction of morality — that although their proposed aim seemed to be certainty and "truth," actually they have sought "*majestic moral edifices*": in order to use once again Kant's innocent language, we recall that he designated it to be his own task and labor, which was "less resplendent, but certainly still meritorious" "to render the ground for these majestic moral edifices level and suitable for construction" (*Critique of Pure Reason* II, 257).[14] Alas, we now have to admit that he did not succeed in his efforts, quite the opposite! With such a rapturous goal, Kant was indeed the true son of his century, which, more than any other, may be called the century of rapturous enthusiasm;[15] as, fortunately, he also remained with regard to his more valuable sides (for example, the healthy bit of sensualism[16] that he took over into his theory of knowledge). He too had been bitten by that tarantula of morality Rousseau, he too held in the very depths of his soul the idea of moral fanaticism whose executor yet another disciple of Rousseau's, namely Robespierre, felt and confessed himself to be, when he longed "*de fonder sur la terre l'empire de la sagesse, de la justice et de la vertu*" (address from 7 June 1794).[17] With such Frenchified fanaticism at heart, one could not, on the other hand, have acted more un-French, more profound, more thorough, more German—if the word "German" in this sense is still permissible these days—than Kant acted: in order to create room for *his* "moral realm,"[18] he found himself obliged to posit a nondemonstrable world, a logical "Beyond"—expressly to this end did he need his *Critique of Pure Reason*![19] Or to put it another way: *he wouldn't have needed it*, if one thing had not been more important to him than everything else: to make the "moral realm" unassailable, better yet, inapprehensible by reason—he felt too powerfully the very assailability of the moral order by the forces of reason! In the face of nature and history, in the face of the fundamental *immorality* of nature and history, Kant was, like every good German from way back, a pessimist: he believed in morality, not because it is manifested in nature and history; rather, he believed in spite of the fact that nature and history constantly contradict it. In order to understand this "in spite of," one might perhaps recall a related passage in Luther, that other great pessimist who, with all of his natural audacity, once remonstrated to his friends: "if we could grasp through reason how God, who shows so much wrath and malice, could be merciful and just, then why would we need *faith*?" Nothing, of course, has ever made a deeper impression on the German soul, nothing has "tempted" it more than this most dangerous of all conclusions, which, to every true Mediterranean, is a sin against the spirit: *credo* quia *absurdum est*[20]—with this conclusion, German logic makes its first appearance in the history of Christian dogma; but even today still, a millennium later, we Germans of today, late Germans in every respect, catch the scent of—something like truth, like the *possibility* of truth behind the famous real-dialectical axiom with which Hegel in his day procured for the German spirit a victory over Europe—"Contradiction moves the world; all things contradict themselves"[21]—we are, through and through, even in our logic, pessimists.

4

Logical value judgments, however, are not the deepest and most fundamental to which our valorous suspicion can descend: faith in reason, according to which the validity of these judgments stands or falls, is, as faith, a *moral* phenomenon . . . Perhaps German pessimism must still run its final course? Perhaps it must yet one more time, in a terrifying manner, juxtapose its *credo* and its *absurdum*? And if *this* book is pessimistic even over into morality, over into and beyond the trust in morality—wouldn't it be, for this very reason, a German book? For it does indeed present a contradiction and does, in no way, shy away from it: this book gives notice to trust in morality—but why, you may ask? *Out of morality!* Or how else should we name what occurs in the book—and in us? For in accordance with our taste, we would prefer more modest words. But there is no doubt that to us also there still speaks a "thou shalt": we also still obey a strict law set over us—and this is the last morality to which we also still attend and by which we also still know how *to live*; in this, if in anything at all, are we also still *people of conscience*: namely, in that we do not want to go back once more into *what* we deem outlived and decayed, into anything at all "unworthy of belief," call it God, virtue, truth, justice, or love thy neighbor; in that we allow ourselves no bridges of lies to old ideals; in that we are inimical to the core to everything that would like to appease and to interfere with us; inimical as well to every present type of faith and Christianness; inimical to the half-and-half of all Romanticism and fatherland-fanaticism; inimical as well to artists' love of pleasure and their lack of conscience, which would like to convince us to worship where we no longer believe—for we are artists—inimical, in short, to the whole of European *feminism* (or idealism if that sounds better to you), which eternally "draws us upward"[22] and, precisely for that reason, eternally "drags us down"—only as people of *this* conscience do we still feel ourselves related to the millennia-old German integrity and piety, albeit as its last and most questionable descendants, we immoralists, we godless ones of today, yes, even, from a certain understanding, as its heirs, as executors of its innermost will, a pessimistic will, which, as I said, is not afraid of negating its very self because it takes great *pleasure* in negating! Fulfilling itself in us is, in case you want a formula—*the self-sublation of morality.*[23]— —

5

—But ultimately: why should we have to proclaim what we are, what we want and don't want, so loudly and with such fervor? Let us view it with a gaze more cold, more distant, shrewd, lofty; let us speak it as it may be spoken among ourselves, so furtively that the whole world pays no attention to it, that the whole world pays no attention to *us*! Above all, let us speak it *slowly* . . . This Preface comes late, but not too late; what difference, after all, do five or six years make? A book, a problem such as this, has no hurry; besides, both of us, I just as much as my book, are friends of the *lento*.[24] Having been a philologist is not for nothing; perhaps you remain one, a teacher, in other words, of slow reading—in the long run, you end up writing slowly as well. Nowadays it is not only a matter of habit for me, but also one of taste, a malicious taste perhaps?—To write nothing more that would not drive to despair every sort of person who is "in a hurry." Philology is, namely, that venerable art that requires of its admirers one thing above all else: to go aside, to take time, to become still, become slow—as a goldsmith's art and connoisseurship of the *word*, which has nothing but fine, cautious work to take care of and which achieves nothing if it does not achieve it *lento*. But for exactly this reason, philology is today more necessary than ever, by exactly this means, philology attracts and enchants us most powerfully in the midst of an age of "work," that is to say, of precipitateness, of unseemly and sweating overhaste that wants at once to be over and done with everything, even with every old and new book: — philology itself is never so easily over and done with anything whatsoever; it teaches to read *well*, which means to read slowly, deeply, backward and forward with care and respect, with reservations, with doors left open, with delicate fingers and eyes . . . My patient friends, this book desires for itself only consummate readers and philologists: *learn* to read me well! —

Ruta near Genoa,[25]

in the Autumn of the year 1886

Book One

I

Retroactive[1] rationality. — All things that live a long time gradually become so saturated with reason that their lineage[2] out of unreason thus becomes implausible. Doesn't virtually every exact history of an emergence[3] strike us as feeling paradoxical and outrageous? Doesn't the good historian, at bottom, continuously *contradict*?

2

Scholars' presumption. — It is an accurate judgment[4] on the part of scholars that human beings of every epoch thought they *knew* what was good and evil, praise- and blameworthy. It is, however, a scholars' presumption that *we know it better now* than in any other epoch.

3

Everything has its day. — When human beings first ascribed a gender[5] to every single thing, they did so in all seriousness, believing they had gained a profound insight — only very late, and perhaps to this day not yet fully, have they admitted to themselves the enormous scope of this mistake. — In just the same way, humans have conferred on everything that exists a relationship to morality and have laid upon the world's shoulder an *ethical significance*. One day this too will have just as much, and no more, value as the belief in the masculinity or femininity of the sun[6] has today.

4

Against the imaginary disharmony of the spheres. — We must oust from the world anew the many types of *false* grandeur, because they go against the justice that all things are entitled to demand of us! And to that end, it is necessary not to want to view the world as more disharmonious than it is!

5[7]

Be grateful! — The greatest achievement of humankind to date is that we need no longer be in constant fear of wild animals, barbarians, the gods, and our dreams.

6

The conjurer and his contrary.[8] — What astonishes in the sciences is directly opposed to what astonishes in the conjurer's art. For the latter wants to coax us into seeing a very simple causality when, in reality, a very complicated causality is at work. The sciences, on the other hand, compel us to relinquish our belief in simple causalities at the very moment when everything seems so self-explanatory and we are being the fools of what is before our very eyes. The "simplest" things are *very complicated* — one can't marvel enough at that!

7

Learning a different sense of space. — Have real things or imaginary things contributed more to human happiness? It is certain that the *breadth of space* between highest happiness and deepest despair has been established only with the aid of imaginary things. Accordingly, the influence of the sciences is constantly diminishing *this* type of spatial sense: just as science has taught, and continues to teach us to experience the earth as small and the solar system even as a mere dot.

8

Transfiguration.[9] — The helplessly suffering, the bewilderedly dreaming, the celestially transported — these are the *three ranks* into which Raphael divides human beings. We no longer view the world this way — and these days Raphael would no longer *be able* to do so either: he would behold with his own eyes a new transfiguration.

9[10]

Concept of the morality of mores.[11,12] — In relation to the way of life of humankind for entire millennia, we present-day humans live in a very unaccustomed, immoral[13] age: the power of custom is astonishingly enfeebled and the sense of morality so refined and lofty that one can say it has well nigh evaporated. Hence, for us, the late born, fundamental insights[14] into the emergence of morality become difficult; when we have found them nonetheless, they stick to our tongue and don't want out: because they sound coarse! Or because they seem to slander morality! As, for instance, right away with the very *first proposition*: morality is nothing other (therefore, above all *no more!*) than obedience to mores, no matter what ilk they might happen to be; mores, however, are merely the *traditional*[15] manner of acting and evaluating. In matters where no tradition commands, there is no morality; and the less life is determined by tradition, the smaller the orbit of morality becomes. The free human being is unaccustomed and immoral because, in all things, he *wants* to depend upon himself and not upon a tradition: in every primitive state of human society, "evil" is tantamount to "individual," "free," "arbitrary," "unusual," "unforeseen," "incalculable." Judged according to the standards of such states: when an act is committed *not* because tradition commands it, but owing instead to other motives (for example, one's individual advantage), the act is always deemed immoral and is experienced as such, even by its perpetrator, even when the motives are the very ones that established the tradition in the first place: for it was not undertaken in obedience to tradition. What is tradition? A higher authority, which one obeys not because it commands what is *useful* to us, but because it *commands*. — What differentiates this feeling with regard to tradition from the feeling of fear in general? It is the fear of a higher intellect that commands through tradition, fear in the face of an inexplicable, indeterminate power, of something beyond the personal — there is *superstition* in this fear. — Originally, all training, all tending to health, marriage, the art of healing, agriculture, war, speaking and keeping silent, traffic with one another and with the gods belonged in the domain of morality: which demanded that one observe rules and precepts *without* thinking *of oneself* as an individual. Originally, then, everything was a matter of custom, and anyone wishing to elevate himself above custom had to become lawgiver and medicine man and a demigod of sorts: that is, he had to *create customs* — a terrifying, life-threatening thing! — Who is the most moral? *For a start*, whoever fulfills the law most frequently: who, thus, like the Brahman,[16] bears the consciousness of the law with him everywhere and in each infinitesimal division of time in order that he may be continually inventive in finding opportunities to fulfill the law. *Then*, anyone who also fulfills it in the most difficult situations. The most moral is whoever *sacrifices* the most to custom: which, however, are the greatest sacrifices? Depending on the answer to this question, several different moralities unfold; but the most important distinction is still the one that separates the morality of the *most frequent fulfillment* from that of the *most difficult fulfillment*. Make no mistake about the motive behind that morality that requires the most difficult fulfillment of mores as the sign of morality! It requires overcoming the self, owing *not* to the useful consequences for the individual, but in order, instead, that custom, the tradition, might emerge triumphant despite all individual benefit from and desire to the contrary: the individual shall sacrifice — so dictates the morality of mores. — Those moralists, on the other hand, who, following in *Socratic* footsteps, press upon the *individual* the morality of self-control and abstention as a means to the individual's most inherent *advantage*, his most personal key to happiness, *form the exception*— and if it seems otherwise to us, it is because we have been raised in the wake of their effect: all such proponents chart a new course, invoking the severest disapproval from all representatives of the morality of mores—as beings without mores, they detach themselves from the community and are, in the most profound sense, evil. So too did every *Christian* who "strove first and foremost for his *own* happiness and salvation" appear to a virtuous Roman of the old school—as evil.—Wherever there is a community and, consequently, a morality of mores, there rules as well the idea that the punishment for an offense against the mores falls above all on the community: that supernatural punishment whose manifestation and extremes are so difficult to comprehend and that is grasped with such superstitious fear. The community can compel the individual to compensate another individual or the community for the present damage resulting from his action; it can also take a type of revenge on the individual because owing to him and to the alleged aftereffect of his deed, the storm clouds of the gods have gathered over the community and unleashed the squall of their mighty wrath—but the community experiences the guilt of the individual primarily as *its own* guilt and bears his punishment as *its own* punishment—"mores have become lax," bemoans each member of the community in his soul, "if such deeds are possible." Every individual action, every individual way of thinking provokes horror; it is quite impossible to fathom all the many things that, through the whole course of history, precisely those more unusual, select, and original intellects have had to suffer because they were always perceived as evil and dangerous, because, in fact, *they perceived themselves as such.* Under the dominion of the morality of mores any form of originality has acquired an evil conscience;[17] accordingly, the sky above the best of humanity continues to this very minute to be cloudier, gloomier than necessary.

10

Sense of morality and sense of causality in counteraction. — To the extent that the sense of causality increases, the purview of the moral realm diminishes: for in every case where one has comprehended the necessary effects and has learned to think of them as separate from all chance occurrences and all incidental posteriority (*post hoc*),[18] one has destroyed an immense number of *fantastic causalities*, which were believed in, and believed to be, foundations of mores — the real world is much smaller than that of fantasy — and each time a bit of anxiety and constraint disappears from the world, so too vanishes each time a bit of respect for the authority of custom. On the whole morality has lost ground. By contrast, whoever wishes to extend its sphere must know how to prevent the results from being *subject to control.*[19]

11[20]

Popular morality and folk medicine. — The morality that reigns in a community is being worked upon by everyone at every moment: most people serve up example after example for the purported *relationship between cause and effect* and, by extension, between guilt and punishment; confirm this relationship as well founded; and strengthen faith in it: some others form new observations regarding actions and their consequences and extrapolate from them conclusions and laws; a very few take exception here and there and permit faith in these matters to weaken. — But they are all alike in the thoroughly crude, *unscientific* manner of their activity; whether it is a question of examples, observations, or exceptions, or a matter of the proof, corroboration, expression, or refutation of a law — it is worthless material and worthless form, as are all the material and form of folk medicine. Folk medicine and popular morality belong together and ought no longer to be evaluated so differently, as is still the case: both are the *most dangerous* pseudosciences.

12

Consequence as supplemental ingredient. — People used to believe that the outcome of an action was not a consequence[21] but an independent, supplemental ingredient, namely God's. Is a greater confusion conceivable? The action and its outcome had to be worked out separately, with quite different means and practices!

13

Toward the Reeducation of the Human Race.[22] — People of diligence and goodwill, lend a hand in the *one work* of eradicating from the face of the earth the concept of punishment, which has overrun the whole world! There is no more noxious weed! Not only has it been implanted into the consequences of our modes of behavior — and how horrible and repulsive to reason this alone is: to interpret cause and effect as cause and punishment! — but they've gone further still and, with this infamous art of interpreting the concept of punishment, they have robbed of its innocence the whole, pure contingency of events. Indeed, they have driven this madness to such an extreme as to bid us experience existence itself as a punishment — it is as if, heretofore, the phantasms of jailers and hangmen had been conducting the education of the human race.

14

Significance of madness in the history of morality. — If, despite that fearful pressure of the "morality of mores" under which all communal human beings have lived for thousands and thousands of years before the beginning of recorded time and also in our own millennium more or less unchanged until this very day (we ourselves dwell in the demimonde of exceptions or, as it were, in the evil zone): — if, I reiterate, despite that fact, new and deviant thoughts, evaluations, drives erupted again and again, they were accompanied by a horrifying attendant; almost everywhere it is madness that paves the way for a new thought, that breaks the spell of a venerated[23] custom or superstition. Do you comprehend why it had to be madness? Something in voice and bearing as gruesome and incalculable as the demonic moods of weather and of sea and thus worthy of similar awe and observation? Something that bore so visibly the sign of compulsiveness and complete lack of control as the convulsions and froth of the epileptic, that seemed thereby to mark the madman as the mask and megaphone of a divinity? Something that kindled inside the very bearer of a new idea no longer pangs of conscience but now reverence for, awe of, himself and drove him to become the prophet and martyr of his idea?—Whereas today we are still told again and again that, instead of a grain of salt,[24] a grain of madness herb[25] affixes to genius, all earlier people assumed much more readily the idea that wherever there is madness, there is also a grain of genius and wisdom—something "divine," they would whisper to themselves. Or rather: they voiced their sentiment forcefully enough. "The greatest blessings have come to Greece by way of madness,"[26] said Plato, in accord with all of ancient humanity. Let us go one step further: *provided they weren't actually mad*, all those superior people who were irresistibly compelled to cast off the yoke of any sort of morality and to devise new laws had no choice other than to drive themselves, or to pretend, to madness—and indeed this applies to innovators in all spheres and not merely those of priestly and political caste—even the innovator of poetic meter had to authenticate himself through madness.[27] (As a result, a certain convention of madness continued to adhere to writers even into much milder ages: a convention to which, for example, Solon appealed when he incited the Athenians to reconquer Salamis.)[28]—"How do you make yourself mad if you aren't and don't dare to appear so?" Virtually all significant people of ancient civilization have pursued this dreadful train of thought; a clandestine doctrine of techniques and dietary hints on the subject proliferated, together with a feeling for the innocence, indeed, the sacredness of this type of contemplation and aspiration. The recipes for

an Indian to become a medicine man, a Christian of the Middle
Ages a saint, a Greenlander an angegok,[29] or a Brazilian a pajee[30]
are essentially the same: nonsensical fasting, perpetual sexual
abstinence, going to the wilderness[31] or ascending a mountain
or a pillar[32] or "seating oneself in an age-old pasture overlooking
a lake" and thinking of positively nothing at all other than whatever can bring on the mental disorder of a rapturous trance.[33]
Who dares to take a close look into the wilderness of the most
bitter and superfluous torments of the soul in which, in all likelihood, precisely the most productive human beings of all time
have languished! To listen to those sighs of the solitary and dis-
traught: "Ah, grant me madness at last, ye heavenly hosts! Madness that I might at long last believe in myself! Grant deliriums
and convulsions, sudden illuminations and tenebrosities; terrify
me with frost and flame such as no other mortal has yet experienced, with a deafening din and roaming apparitions; let me
howl and moan and cringe like a beast: that I might only come to
believe in myself! Doubt consumes me; I have killed the law and
like a corpse before the living, the law frightens me; if I am not
more than the law, then I am the most depraved of all creatures.
The new spirit in me, where does it come from if it is not from you?
Prove to me surely that I am yours; madness alone proves it to me."
And all too often this fervor attained its goal all too well: in that
age when Christianity proved most exuberantly its fecundity in
saints and desert solitaries and presumed thereby to be proving itself, there existed in Jerusalem immense madhouses for miscarried saints, for those who had expended on sainthood their last
grain of salt.

15

The oldest means of solace. — First stage: in every indisposition
and misfortune, a human being will find occasion to make
somebody, anybody else, suffer—in the process, he becomes
aware of the power he still has at his disposal and this consoles
him. Second stage: in every indisposition and misfortune, a human being will find a punishment, which is to say a propitiation

of guilt and the means of *extricating* himself from the malevolent spell of a real or imaginary injustice. When he catches sight
of this *advantage* that goes hand and hand with the injustice, he
no longer feels the need to make someone else suffer for it—he
renounces the one form of gratification because he now has
another.

16

First proposition[34] *of civilization.* —Among primitive peoples there is a category of customs whose sole aim seems to be
custom itself:[35] painstaking[36] and ultimately superfluous ordi-
nances (such as, for example, those among the Kamchadals[37]
never to scrape off snow from boots with a knife, never with
a knife to spear a live ember, never to lay sword in fire—and
death to whosoever offendeth against such particulars!), ordi-
nances, however, that keep one ever mindful of the ever-nearness
of custom and of the continuous compulsion to enact custom,
thereby confirming the great proposition with which civilization begins: any custom is better than no custom at all.

17

Good and evil nature. —First, human beings imagined themselves into nature: they saw themselves and their kind, namely
their evil and temperamental disposition, everywhere, hidden, as
it were, behind clouds, thunderstorms, beasts of prey, trees and
plants: those were the days when they invented "evil nature."
Then along came an age in which they imagined themselves out
of nature again, the Age of Rousseau: people were so sick of one
another that they positively had to have a corner of the world
where they, with all their suffering, could not get to: they invented "good nature."

18

The morality of voluntary suffering. —Of all the pleasures
available to people in what amounts to a state of war in that tiny,
constantly endangered community where severest morality

reigns, which is the ultimate?[38] To souls, that is to say, who are powerful, vengeful, hostile, devious, suspicious, capable of the most dreadful deeds, and who have been hardened by self-denial and morality? The pleasure of *cruelty*: likewise, it is deemed a *virtue* of a soul under such conditions to be inventive and insatiable in cruelty. The actions of someone cruel refresh the community, which, for once, casts off the gloom and doom of perpetual fear and precaution. Cruelty belongs among the oldest festive pleasures of humankind. It is assumed, therefore, that the *gods* are also refreshed and festively disposed whenever one presents them with the sight of cruelty—and thus worms its way into the world the representation that *voluntary suffering*, self-elected torment, makes good sense and is valuable.[39] Little by little, custom fashions within the community a practice in keeping with this representation: with each passing day, people grow more mistrustful of any excessive well-being and more assured in all difficult and painful situations; they say to themselves: it may well be that the gods look upon us harshly when we are happy and mercifully when we suffer—by no means out of compassion![40] For compassion is considered contemptible and unworthy of a strong and dreadful soul;—instead, the gods are merciful because they are amused and brought to exuberant spirits by our suffering: for in his cruelty, the sadist enjoys the ultimate titillation, a feeling of power. Thus, the concept of the "most moral" member of the community comes to mean the virtue of copious suffering, of self-denial, the austere way of life, cruel mortification and penance[41]—*not*, to say it again and again, as a means of discipline or of self-control or of the desire for individual happiness—but as a virtue that, among the ill-tempered gods, lends the community the sweet smell of appeasement, wafting up to the immortals like a perpetual propitiatory sacrifice on the altar. All those spiritual leaders of peoples who were able to actually move something within the torpid, yet fertile sludge of their mores have needed, in addition to madness, voluntary torture in order to inspire in others belief[42]—and first and foremost, as always, belief in themselves! The more their spirit ventured on new pathways where it was, consequently, tortured by anxieties and pangs of conscience, the more they raged against their own flesh, their own desires, and their own health—as if to offer the divinity some substitute pleasure, should he happen perhaps to be embittered about the established rites that had been assaulted and neglected and about the new objectives on the horizon. Let's not be too quick to assume that we have by now altogether freed ourselves from this sort of logic of emotion! Let the most heroic souls question one another on the subject. Every one of the smallest steps along the path of free thought or in a life shaped personally has been achieved, from time immemorial, at the price of spiritual and physical tortures:[43] not only stepping forward,[44] no! above all, any stepping, movement, change has needed its countless martyrs throughout the interminable path-seeking and foundation-laying millennia, something we certainly forget when speaking, as usual, about "world history," about this ridiculously tiny slice of human existence; and even in this so-called world history, which is basically just noise around the latest news flashes, there is actually no theme more important than the ancient tragedy of the martyrs *who wanted to stir up the quagmire.* Nothing has been purchased more dearly than the little bit of human reason and sense of freedom that make up the sum total of our pride today. It is, however, precisely this pride that makes it virtually impossible today for us to have a feeling for those vast expanses of time that comprise the "morality of mores" and that precede "world history" as the *actual and decisive main history that has determined the character of humankind*: back when it came into currency that suffering was a virtue, cruelty a virtue, dissimulation a virtue, revenge a virtue, denial of reason a virtue, whereas well-being was a danger, thirst for knowledge[45] a danger,[46] peace a danger, pity a danger, being pitied an insult,[47] work an insult, madness godliness, and change the thing most immoral and pregnant with destruction!—You suppose all this has changed and the human race has altered its character? Oh, you keen observers of human nature, learn better to know yourselves!

19

Morality and stupefaction. — Custom represents the day-to-day experiences of people of earlier times regarding what was perceived as useful and as harmful — but *the feeling for custom* (morality) is based not on those experiences as such, but upon the age, the sanctity, the inscrutability of custom. Accordingly, this feeling acts to prevent one from having new experiences and correcting old mores: in other words, morality acts to prevent the rise of new and better mores: it stupefies.

20

Freedoers and freethinkers.[48] — Freedoers are at a disadvantage compared to freethinkers because people suffer more visibly from the consequences of actions than from those of thoughts. If one considers, however, that both types are in search of gratification and that for freethinkers the mere conceptualization and articulation of forbidden things suffices for this gratification, then, with regard to motives, the two are of one accord: and with regard to consequences, the scale even tips against freethinkers, provided one does not — as does the world at large — judge according to whatever is most immediately and crudely visible. One has to retract a great deal of the abuse that people are wont to heap upon all those figures who broke the spell of a custom with a *deed* — in general, they are branded criminals. Anyone who has ever overturned an existing moral law has always, heretofore, passed initially for a *bad person*: but afterward when, as it happened, the law could no longer be propped up and people acquiesced to the fact, the evaluation began a gradual transformation — history concerns itself almost exclusively with these *bad people* who have later been *pronounced good*!

21

"Fulfillment of the law."—In the event that obedience to a moral precept yields, after all is said and done, a result other than what was promised and expected and, contrary to expectation, unhappiness and misery set in instead of the vouchsafed happiness, then the conscientious and fearful always have at their disposal an escape clause: "something was overlooked in the *observance*." In the worst-case scenario, a profoundly remorseful and crushed humanity will even decree, "it is impossible to observe the precept properly; we are frail and sinful to the core and in our heart of hearts incapable of morality and hence we have no right to happiness or success. Moral precepts and covenants were intended for better beings than ourselves."

22

Works and faith.[49]—To this day Protestant theologians continue to propagate the same fundamental error: that everything depends solely on faith and that from faith alone works must necessarily follow. This is positively not true, yet sounds so seductive it has already befuddled intellects other than Luther's (namely, those of Socrates and Plato): even though the evidence of every experience of every day speaks against it. The most certain knowledge or faith cannot supply the energy or the talent to perform a deed; it cannot replace the workings of that subtle and multipartite mechanism, which must occur before anything whatsoever can be transformed from representation into action. First and foremost works! Meaning do, do, do! The appurtenant "faith" will turn up in the long run—of that you may be sure!

23[50]

Where we are the subtlest.[51]—Because it was thought for many thousands of years that *things* (nature, tools, belongings of all kinds) were also alive and animate, with the power to

injure and to elude human purposes, the feeling of powerlessness among humans was much greater and much more common than it need have been; one felt compelled to secure oneself against things, just as against people and animals, through
the use of force, coercion, flattery, treaties, sacrifices—herein
lies the origin of most superstitious rituals,[52] that is to say, of
a considerable, *perhaps predominant*, and yet squandered and
useless component of all activity heretofore performed by human beings!—But because the feeling of powerlessness and
fear was in a state of almost perpetual excitation for so long a
time, the *feeling of power* has developed such a degree of *subtlety*
that, in this regard, humans can now compete with the most
delicate balance that measures gold. The feeling of power has
become their strongest inclination; the methods they discovered to create this feeling just about constitute the history of
culture.

24^{53}

The proof of a precept.[54]—In general, the goodness or badness[55] of a precept, for instance, one to bake bread, is proven
according to whether or not it yields its promised result, pre-
supposing that the precept is strictly observed. It is another
matter nowadays with regard to moral precepts: for here it is
precisely the results that are not discernible or else ambiguous
and open to interpretation. These precepts rest on hypotheses
of the most meager possible scientific worth; at bottom, their
proof and their refutation according to results are equally impossible:—but back in those days when the sciences retained
their original primitiveness and only meager requirements
were necessary to accept a thing as *proven*—in those days the
goodness or badness of a precept regarding custom was determined in exactly the same manner as that of any other precept
today: by pointing to the promised outcome. If the natives of
Russian America[56] subscribe to the precept, "thou shalt throw
no animal bone into the fire nor give it to the dogs," then they
prove it by saying, "if you do, you will have no luck when hunt-

ing." But then again, one almost always has, in some sense or other, "no luck when hunting." This tack taken, it is virtually impossible to *refute* the goodness of the precept, especially when a community and not an individual is deemed accountable to suffer the punishment; instead, some circumstance will always turn up that appears to prove the precept.

25

Custom and beauty. — On behalf of custom, let it be known that for anyone who subjugates the self to it completely, heart and soul, from the very beginning onward, the organs of attack and defense — physical and spiritual — degenerate: in other words, that particular someone becomes increasingly more beautiful! For it is the workings of those organs and their corresponding disposition that both sustain and increase ugliness. That is why an old baboon is uglier than a young one, and why a young female baboon bears the closest resemblance to a human and is, accordingly, the most beautiful. From this one should draw a conclusion regarding the origin of the beauty of women!

26[57]

Animals and morality.[58] — The practices demanded in refined society: scrupulous avoidance of anything laughable, conspicuous or presumptuous, the suppression of one's virtues along with one's more vehement desires, self-imposed conformance, compliance, diminishment — all these protocols thought of as social morality can be found, in crude form, everywhere, even down to the deepest depths of the animal world — and only in this depth[59] do we view the design behind all these charming precautionary measures: one wants to escape from predators and to gain advantage in capturing prey. For this reason animals learn to control and to disguise themselves in such a way that, for example, many adapt their colors to that of the environment (as a result of the so-called "chromatic function"), many play dead or assume the shapes and colors of another animal or of sand, leaves, lichens, fungi (what English researchers refer to as mimicry).[60] By the same token, the individual conceals himself in the communal generality of the concept "human being," or else in society, or he adapts himself to princes, classes, political parties, opinions of the time or place: and for all our subtle ways[61] of appearing happy, grateful, powerful, or in love, one can easily find the relevant animal likeness.[62] Even that nose for truth, which is, at bottom, the nose for safety, human beings have in common with animals: one doesn't want to let oneself be deceived, be led astray by one's own actions; one listens mistrustfully to the promptings of one's own passions; one constrains and remains on guard against oneself. The animal understands all this just as well as the human being; it also develops self-control out of a nose for reality (prudence). It too observes the effect its actions have on the perceptions of other animals and from there learns to look back at itself, to take itself "objectively"; it has its degree of self-awareness. The animal judges the movements of its enemies and friends, it learns their particularities by heart, it takes appropriate measures: it renounces battle once and for all against individuals of a certain species and also divines in the approach of many types of animals a readiness for peace and accord.[63] The beginnings of justice, as well as of prudence, moderation, valor—in short, everything to which we give the name *Socratic virtues* is *bestial*: a consequence of those drives that teach us to seek nourishment and escape hostilities. Now, if we take into consideration that the loftiest human being is elevated and refined only in the *manner* of his nourishment and in the concept of what is hostile to him, then we will not be unjustified in designating the entire moral phenomenon as bestial.

27

The value of belief in superhuman[64] *passions.* — The institution of marriage stubbornly upholds the belief that love, though a passion, is, as such, capable of duration; indeed, that enduring, lifelong love can be established as the rule. Through this tenacious adherence to a high-minded belief, even though very often, almost as a rule, it is disproved and consequently a *pia fraus*,[65] marriage has bestowed on love a higher nobility. All institutions that grant to a passion, contrary to passion's nature, the *belief in its duration* as well as the responsibility for its duration have elevated that passion to a new status: from that point on, anyone seized by such a passion no longer believes himself degraded or endangered, as was earlier the case, but feels instead exalted vis-à-vis himself and his peers. Think of the institutions and mores that, from a moment's ardent abandonment, have created eternal devotion, from the pleasure of wrath, eternal revenge, from despair, eternal mourning, from the sudden and solitary word, eternal obligation. With every occurrence this type of transformation has introduced a great deal of hypocrisy and lying into the world: with every occurrence it brings along as well, and comes at the price of, a *superhuman*, human-exalting concept.

28

Mood as argument. — What is the cause of any joyous resolve to act? — This question has kept humans very busy. The oldest and still the readiest answer is: God is the cause, it is his way of letting us know that he approves of our intention. In the old days when one consulted oracles about a plan of action, what one wanted to take home from them was this joyous resolve; and anyone who contemplated in his soul several possible actions responded to doubt by saying: "I will do what produces that feeling." Thus, one opted not for what was most reasonable, but for a plan of action, the contemplation of which filled the soul with courage and hope. Good mood was laid on the scales as argument and outweighed rationality: because mood was interpreted superstitiously as the workings of a god who promises success and allows his reason to speak through mood as the highest rationality. Now consider the consequences of such a prejudice[66] once clever and power-hungry men made use of it — and continue to make use of it! "Create the mood!"—with it you can supplant all argument, vanquish any counterargument!

29[67]

Actors[68] *of virtue and of sin.* —Among the men of antiquity who became famous for their virtue, there was, so it seems, an immense, and immensely surplus, number of them who *play-acted for themselves*: especially the Greeks, those inveterate actors, did so quite involuntarily and considered it a fine thing. With his virtue, each man was, moreover, in *competition* with the virtue of someone, or everyone, else. How could one help but apply all manner of wiles to put on a (dis)play[69] of virtue— above all, for oneself, simply for the sake of practice! What good was a virtue that one couldn't exhibit or that didn't know how to exhibit itself!—Christianity put a stop to these actors of virtue: it invented instead the nauseating grandstanding and making a show of sin; it introduced *fabricated* sinfulness[70] into the world (to this very day, it is considered "good form" among Christians).

30

Refined cruelty as virtue. —Here we have a morality that rests totally upon the *drive for distinction*—don't think too highly of it! What sort of drive is this really and what is its underlying thought, its ulterior motive? We want to make sure that the mere sight of us causes someone else *pain* and envy, arouses in that person a feeling of impotence and degradation; we want the other to taste the bitterness of his fate, as we let drip upon his tongue a drop of *our own* honey and peer intently and gloatingly into his eyes during our supposed good deed. One person has become humble and is now completely within his humility—seek those whom he has long wanted to torture with it! you will surely find them! Another displays pity[71] toward animals and is admired for it—but there are certain people on whom he has wanted to vent his cruelty with the very same pity. There stands a great artist: the ecstasy he felt in anticipation of the envy of vanquished rivals allowed his talent no rest until he had become great—how many bitter moments other souls must endure to provide him compensation for the path to greatness! The nun's chastity: with what chastising eyes she glares into the faces of women who live differently! How much pleasure in revenge resides in those eyes!—Though the theme is short, the variations on it can be countless, but hardly tedious—for it is still a far too paradoxical and almost painful piece of news that the ultimate foundation for the morality of distinction is pleasure in refined cruelty. The ultimate foundation—meaning in this case: in every instance, in the first generation. For when some distinguishing act or other becomes an *inherited* habit, the underlying thought is not part of the inheritance (no thoughts are hereditary, only feelings): and assuming it is not smuggled back in through education, even by the second generation there will be no more pleasure in cruelty: but pleasure solely in habit *per se*. *This* pleasure, however, is the first stage of the "good."

31[72]

Pride in the spirit.—Human pride, which bristles at the doctrine of descent[73] from animals and establishes a great divide between nature and humans—this pride has its foundation in a *prejudice*[74] regarding what spirit is: and this prejudice is relatively *young*. During humanity's vast prehistory, spirit was presumed to be everywhere and no one thought of honoring it by making it the privilege solely of human beings. Because, on the contrary, the spiritual (along with all drives, evils, inclinations) had been turned into common property and was, consequently, common to all, one was not ashamed to descend from animals or trees (the *distinguished* clans deemed themselves honored by such fables) and saw in spirit something that connects us with nature, not something separating us from it. Thus, one schooled oneself in modesty—and, likewise, owing to a *prejudice*.

32

The brake. — To suffer for the sake of morality and then to hear that this type of suffering is based on a *mistake*, this excites indignation. There is, after all, such unique solace in affirming through one's suffering "a deeper world of truth" than is to be found anywhere else in the world, and one would much *prefer* to suffer and, in so doing, to feel *sublimely exalted* above reality (through the consciousness that suffering brings one closer to that "deeper world of truth") than to be without suffering and thus without this feeling of sublime exaltation. Accordingly, it is pride and pride's customary means of gratification that impede the new *understanding* of morality. What force will one then have to apply to remove this brake? More pride? A new pride?

33[75]

Disdain for causes, consequences, and reality. — Those disastrous incidents that happen to beset a community—sudden storms, crop failures, pestilence—lead all its members to suspect that offenses against morality have been committed or that new rituals must be created in order to appease a new demonic power and caprice. This type of suspicion and reflection avoids the very exploration of true natural causes by assuming the demonic cause in advance. Here is one fountainhead of the hereditary topsy-turvyness of the human intellect: and the other springs up close by when one, likewise on principle, pays much less attention to the true natural *consequences* of an action than to the supernatural ones (the so-called punishments and favor of the divinity). There are, for instance, certain ablutions prescribed for certain times; one bathes not in order to get clean, but because it has been prescribed. One learns to avoid not the real consequences of uncleanliness, but the supposed displeasure of the gods over the neglect of the ablutions. Under the oppression of superstitious fear, one suspects that there must be

a great deal more than meets the eye to this washing off of uncleanliness, one concocts secondary and tertiary meanings, one
ruins any sense of, and pleasure in, reality and ends up valuing it only *insofar as it can be a symbol*. Thus under the spell of
the morality of mores, human beings disdain first the causes,
second the effects, and third reality, and they concoct all their
higher sentiments (reverence, sublime exaltation, pride, gratitude, love) *from an imaginary world*: the so-called higher world.
And even today we still witness the consequences: wherever
human feeling is *exalted*, you will find there, in some form or
other, that imaginary world at work. It is sad: but for the time
being, the man of science must distrust *all higher feelings*, so
thoroughly amalgamated are they with madness and nonsense.
Not that they necessarily or forever have to be; but of all the
gradual *purifications* awaiting humanity, the purification of
higher feelings will no doubt be one of the most gradual.

34[76]

Moral feelings and moral concepts. — It is evident that moral
feelings are transmitted through a process whereby children perceive in their parents strong sympathies and antipathies toward
certain actions and, as born apes, *imitate* these inclinations and
disinclinations; later in life, when they find themselves inun-
dated with these acquired and well-practiced affections, they
consider it a matter of decency to establish a why, retroactively,[77]
a type of justifying foundation[78] in order to authorize those
sympathies and antipathies. These "authorizations," however,
have nothing to do with either the origin[79] or the degree of feeling in people: one simply acquiesces to the rule that, as a rational being, one must have reasons for one's For and Against,
reasons that are indeed allegeable and acceptable.[80] To that extent, the history of moral feelings is completely different from
the history of moral concepts. The former are powerful *before*,
the latter especially *after* an action in view of the compulsion to
pronounce upon it.

35[81]

Feelings and their descent from judgments. — "Trust your feeling!" But feelings are nothing final or original; behind feelings there are judgments and valuations, which we have inherited in the form of feelings (sympathies, antipathies). Inspiration that stems from feeling is the grandchild of a judgment—and often a wrong one!—and in any case, not a child of your own! To trust your feeling—that means obeying your grandfather and your grandmother and their grandparents more than the gods in *us*: our reason and our experience.

36[82]

A piece of pious foolishness with ulterior motives. —What! the inventors of primeval cultures, the first fashioners of tools and measuring sticks, of wagons and ships and houses, the first observers of celestial order and the rules of two-times-two— they are supposed to be something incomparably different from and loftier than the inventors and observers of our times? The first steps are supposed to have a value with which all our travels and world-circumnavigations in the realm of discoveries cannot compete? So goes the prejudice,[83] thus does one argue for the disparagement of the contemporary spirit. And yet it is plainly obvious that, in former days, chance was the greatest of all discoverers and observers, as well as the benevolent inspirer to those inventive elders, and that these days more spirit, discipline, and scientific imagination than had ever even been present during entire earlier epochs are now expended on the most insignificant invention.

37

False inferences from utility. —Just because one has proven the highest utility of a thing does not mean that a single step has been taken toward an explanation of its origin: in other words, utility can never clarify the necessary existence of a thing. And yet, up until now, precisely the opposite judgment has held sway—permeating the most rigorous scientific fields. Even in astronomy hasn't one passed off the (supposed) utility in the arrangement of the satellites (to compensate from another quarter for the diminished light owing to the greater distance from the sun, in order that the inhabitants of the planets do not want for light) as the ultimate purpose in their arrangement and as the explanation for their emergence?[84] Whereby one is reminded of Columbus's inferences: the earth was created for human beings; thus, if there are lands, they must be peopled. "Is it likely that the sun should shine on nothingness and that the nocturnal watch of the stars should be wasted on unchartable seas and lands devoid of people?"

38[85]

Drives transformed by moral judgments. — Under the influence of the reproach that custom attaches to it, the same drive may develop into either a painful feeling of *cowardice*: or, in the event that a custom such as that of Christianity wholeheartedly endorses the drive and proclaims it *good*, into the pleasant feeling of *humility*. In other words, a good or an evil conscience is forced onto the drive! *As with every drive*, it, *per se*, has neither these nor any other moral character nor name whatsoever nor even a definite accompanying feeling of pleasure or displeasure. It acquires all this, as its second nature, only once it comes into relation to drives previously baptized as good or evil or else marked as a property of beings whom a people has already identified and evaluated as moral. — The ancient Greeks thus felt differently about *envy* than we do; Hesiod reckons envy among the effects of the *good* and benevolent Eris,[86] and there was nothing offensive in according envy to the gods: understandably, in a state of affairs whose heart and soul was competition; competition, however, had been identified and evaluated as good. Likewise, the Greeks were different from us in their evaluation of *hope*: one felt it to be blind and malicious; Hesiod offered the most violent intimation on hope in a fable,[87] something indeed so alienating that no late interpreter has understood it—for it runs counter to the modern spirit, which, owing to Christianity, has learned to believe in hope as a virtue. Among the Greeks, on the other hand, to whom access to knowledge of the future appeared to be not completely foreclosed and for whom, in countless instances, an inquiry into the future constituted a religious duty, whereas we content ourselves with hope; among those Greeks, hope, thanks to all the oracles and prophets, had, no doubt, to be degraded somewhat and so it drifted down into the realm of the evil and dangerous. — The Jews felt differently about *wrath* than we do and decreed it holy; in return, they, as a people, viewed the foreboding majesty of the individual with whom wrath showed itself connected, at a height at which a European is incapable of imagining. They created their wrathful, holy Jehovah in the image of their wrathful, holy prophets. Measured against them, the great wrath wreakers among the Europeans are,[88] as it were, secondhand creatures.

39

The presumption about "pure spirit."—Wherever the doctrine of *pure spirituality* has prevailed, it has destroyed the force of nerve through its excesses: it taught one to despise, ignore, or torment the body and, on account of all one's drives, to torment and despise oneself; the doctrine produced melancholy, anxious, oppressed souls—who believed, moreover, that they knew the cause of their sense of misery and were perhaps able to extirpate it![89] "It must be in my body! it still *flourishes* so well!"—they concluded, while, as a matter of fact, the body, through its pains, registered protest upon protest against this constant derision. A pervasive, chronic hyperexcitability was eventually the lot[90] of these virtuous pure-spirits: the only *pleasure* they could still muster was in the form of ecstasy and other harbingers of madness—and their system reached its apogee when it accepted ecstasy both as the highest goal in life and as the standard according to which everything earthly was *condemned.*

40

Ruminating over rituals.[91] — Having been gleaned fleetingly from unique, strange occurrences, any number of precepts for propriety became unintelligible very quickly; their purpose was just as difficult to ascertain with any certainty, as was the nature of the punishment to follow upon their violation; misgivings even persisted as to the sequence of the ceremonies; — but as one speculated back and forth on these matters, the object of such ruminating increased in value, and precisely the most absurd of rituals eventually metamorphosed into the holiest of holies. Do not underestimate the human energy expended on this through the millennia and, least of all, the effect of this *ruminating over rituals*! We have now arrived at the prodigious training ground of the intellect — not only are the religions hatched and nurtured here: here is the worthy, albeit ghastly prehistoric world of science, here arose the poet, thinker, physician, lawgiver! The fear of the unintelligible, which, in ambiguous fashion, demanded ceremonies from us, metamorphosed gradually into a fascination with the hardly intelligible, and where one knew not how to explicate, one learned to create.

41[92]

Toward determining the value of the vita contemplativa.[93] — As persons of the *vita contemplativa*, let us not forget what sort of injury and misfortune has befallen the people of the *vita activa* due to the various aftereffects of contemplation — in short, what accounts the *vita activa* has to settle with *us* if we parade our good deeds before it all too smugly. *First*: the so-called *religious* natures, who preponderate in the *vita contemplativa* with regard to numbers and hence furnish its lowest species, have, in all ages, striven to make the practical person's life difficult and, wherever possible, to spoil it for him: to cloak the heavens in doom, blot out the sun, throw suspicion on friends, debase hope, paralyze the active hand — all this they have known how to do, just as, for times and feelings of woe, they have had their comforts, alms, charities, and benedictions. *Secondly*: the artists, a bit less common than the religious, yet still a quite frequent type among those of the *vita contemplativa*, have, as people, almost always been insufferable, moody, envious, violent, quarrelsome: this effect must be set against the enlivening and elevating effects of their works. *Thirdly*: the philosophers, a breed in which religious and artistic powers coexist, but in such a way that a third thing, the dialectic or pleasure in demonstration, still remains close at hand; these philosophers have been the agents of the same sort of injury as the religious and artistic natures, with the addition that, given their dialectical bent, the philosophers have bored great numbers of people; on the other hand, there have never been very many of them. *Fourthly*: the thinkers and the laborers of knowledge; they were rarely out for effects, but dug quietly their mole holes. They thus created next to no vexation or discontent and often, without meaning to, lightened the load of those from the *vita activa* by serving as the object of mockery and laughter. Lately, knowledge has indeed become for everyone a very useful thing: if, *on account of this usefulness*, many more people preordained for the *vita activa* are these days hoeing the row toward knowledge under the sweat of their brow and not without brain-racking and imprecations, then the host of thinkers and laborers of knowledge bear no guilt for such hardship: it is "self-inflicted pain."

42^{94}

Origin[95] *of the vita contemplativa.* — In primitive times, whenever pessimistic judgments regarding people and the world prevail, the individual in full possession of his powers always resolves to act in accordance with those judgments, to translate representation into action by means of hunt, plunder, surprise attack, abuse, and murder, not to mention by means of the paler imitations of such actions, which are the only sort tolerated within the community. If, however, his powers decrease, if he feels weary or ill or depressed or sick and tired and, as a consequence thereof, from time to time resigned and without desire, he is then a relatively better, that is to say, less injurious person, and his pessimistic ideas are discharged only in words and thoughts, about the value of his comrades, for instance, or his wife or his life or his gods—his judgments will be *condemnatory* judgments. In this state, he will become a thinker or a prophet, or he dilates on his superstition and devises new rituals, or he mocks his enemies—but no matter what he thinks up, all ⟨his mind's⟩[96] offspring must reflect his condition, namely, an increase in fear and weariness, a decrease in his estimation of action and enjoyment; the content of these offspring must correspond to the content of these poetical, thoughtful, priestly moods; condemnation must reign in them. Later, all those who continuously behaved, as had earlier the individual, in that state of condemnation, melancholy, and inactivity, one came to call poets or thinkers or priests or medicine men—because they were so inactive, one would gladly have scorned such people and expelled them from the community; but there was danger lurking there—they had pursued superstition and the scent of godly powers, one didn't doubt for a moment that they had command over unknown means of power. This is the esteem in which *the oldest species of contemplative natures* lived—despised precisely to the degree that they were not feared! In just such disguised form, in such questionable regard, with a malevolent heart and frequently a fearful head, did contemplation first appear on the earth, simultaneously weak and terrifying, despised in secret and covered over in public with superstitious deference! Here, as always, it is a matter of *pudenda origo*![97]

43

How many forces must now come together in the thinker. — To estrange oneself from sensory perception, to exalt oneself to abstractions—at one time that was really experienced as *exaltation*: we can no longer quite get the full feel of it. To revel in the palest images of words and things, to play with such invisible, inaudible, intangible beings felt, from out of the depths of disdain for the physically palpable, misleading and evil earth, like living in another, *higher* world. "These abstractions can lead us, and we need no longer be misled!"—with that one leaped, as if upward. It was not the content of these games with spirituality but the games themselves that were "higher" in the prehistoric ages of science. Hence[98] Plato's admiration for the dialectic and his inspired belief in its necessary relation to the good, desensualized person. Not only has each bit of knowledge been discovered gradually, piece by separate piece, but the means of knowing anything whatsoever, the conditions and operations that, in humans, precede the process of knowing, have been discovered gradually, piece by separate piece, as well. And each time it seemed as if the newly discovered operation or the newly experienced condition were, not a means to all knowledge, but already content, goal, and sum of everything worthy of knowing. The thinker needs fantasy, the leap upward, abstraction, desensualization, invention, presentiment, induction, dialectics, deduction, critique, compilation of material, impersonal mode of thought, contemplativeness and comprehensiveness, and not least of all, justice and love toward everything present—but all these means were, each *separately* and at various junctures in the history of the *vita contemplativa*, considered to be the ends and final ends, and they gave their discoverers that bliss that enters the human soul illuminated by the apprehension of a *final* end.

44[99]

Origin and significance. — Why is it this idea keeps coming back to me, radiating ever more varied colors? — that *formerly*, whenever they were on the way to the origin of things, investigators of knowledge always believed they were going to find something of inestimable significance for all actions and judgments, indeed that they regularly *presupposed* that the *salvation* of humanity depended on *insight into the origin of things*: that now we, on the contrary, the closer we come to the origin, the less our interests are engaged; in fact, that all the evaluations and "interestedness," which we have projected into things, start to lose their meaning the more we head back with our knowledge and arrive at the things themselves. *With insight into origin comes the increasing insignificance of origin:* whereas the *immediate*, the around-us and in-us, begins gradually to display colors and beauties and enigmas and riches of significance, the likes of which earlier humanity could not fathom. Formerly, thinkers paced furiously about like captured animals, constantly surveying the bars of their cages, hurling against them in order to smash them to pieces: and *blissful* seemed anyone who believed he had, through a gap, caught sight of something from the outside, from the far and beyond.[100]

45[101]

A tragic ending for knowledge. — Of all the means of achieving exaltation it has been human sacrifices that have, in all ages, exalted and elevated[102] people most. And maybe a single prodigious thought could yet subjugate every other endeavor so that it might attain victory over the most victorious — the thought of a *self-sacrificing humanity*. But to whom should it sacrifice itself? One can already swear that, should the constellation of this thought ever appear on the horizon, knowledge of the truth will be the sole remaining goal prodigious enough to be worthy of such a sacrifice, because for truth, no sacrifice is too great. Meanwhile, no one has, as yet, ever raised the problem of the degree to which humanity, as a whole, is capable of taking steps to advance knowledge, to say nothing of just which drive for knowledge[103] could drive humanity to the point where it is prepared, with the gleam of anticipatory wisdom in its eye, to die. Perhaps one day, once an alliance for the purpose of knowledge has been established with inhabitants of other planets and one has communicated one's knowledge from star to star for a few millennia: perhaps then enthusiasm for knowledge will swell to such a high tide.[104]

46

Doubt about doubt. — "What a fine pillow doubt is for a well-formed head!"[105] — This saying of Montaigne's always incensed Pascal, for no one longed as powerfully as he for a fine pillow.[106] Then what was the problem?

47

The words get in our way! — Wherever primitive humans set forth a word, they thought they had made a discovery. But in truth, how different the situation was! — they had hit on a problem and, in presuming to have *solved* it, they had created an impediment to its solution. — These days, with every act of knowing one has to stumble over perpetually petrified words, and in the process one is more likely to fracture a leg than a word.

48

"Know thyself"[107] *is the entire field of knowledge.* — Only when the human being has finally attained knowledge of all things will he have known himself. For things are merely the boundaries of the human being.

49

The new fundamental feeling: our permanent transitoriness. — Formerly one tried to get a feel for the majesty of human beings by pointing backward toward their divine descent: this has now become a forbidden path, because before its gate stands the ape along with other heinous beasts, grinning knowingly as if to say: no farther here in this direction. So, one has a go of it now from the opposite direction: the path humanity *pursues* shall serve as proof of its majesty and kinship to God. Alas, this too leads nowhere! At the end of this path stands the funeral urn of the *last* human and gravedigger (with the inscription "*nihil humani a me alienum puto*").[108] However high humanity may have evolved — and perhaps at

the end it will be standing even lower than at the beginning!—
there is in store for humanity no more a transformation into a
higher order than for the ant and the earwigs, which, at the end
of their "earthly days," will not ascend to kinship with God and
eternal life. The Becoming drags the Has Been along behind it:
why should an exception to this eternal spectacle be made for
some little planet and again for some little species on it! Away
with such sentimentalities!

50

Belief in intoxication.—Owing to the contrasts other states
of consciousness present and to the wasteful squandering of
their nervous energy, people who live for sublime and enraptured moments are usually wretched and disconsolate; they
view those moments as their true self and the misery and despair as the *effect of everything "outside the self"*;[109] thus, the
thought of their environment, their age, their entire world fills
them with vengeful emotions. Intoxication counts for them
as the true life, as the real self: in anything else, be it of a spiritual, moral, religious, or artistic nature, they see the enemy
and the impediment of intoxication. Humanity has these rapturous drunkards to thank for a great deal of evil: for they are
the insatiable sowers of the weeds of dissatisfaction with self
and neighbor, of disdain for this world and this time, and especially of world-weariness.[110] Perhaps a whole hell of *criminals*
could not muster an impact as sinister and uncanny, as oppressive and ruinous of earth and air into the farthest future,
as that tiny, noble community of intractable, half-mad fantasists, people of genius who cannot control themselves and who
take all possible pleasure in themselves only at the point where
they have completely lost themselves: whereas very often the
criminal, by contrast, still gives proof of outstanding self-
control, sacrifice, and shrewdness and keeps these qualities
awake in those who fear him. Through him the sky above life
may become dangerous and gloomy, but the air remains sharp
and invigorating.—In addition to all this, these rapturists go

about with all their might planting the faith in intoxication as *the* life within life: a terrible faith! Just as the natives these days are quickly corrupted and then destroyed by "firewater," so too has humanity as a whole been corrupted slowly and fundamentally by the *spiritual* firewaters of intoxicating feelings and by those who keep alive the craving for such feelings: perhaps humanity will yet be destroyed by them.

51

Such as we still are!— "Let us be forbearing toward the great one-eyed ones!"—said John Stuart Mill: as if it were necessary to ask for forbearance, when one is accustomed to believing and almost worshipping them! I say: let us be forbearing toward the two-eyed ones, great and small—for, *such as we still are*, we will definitely not manage anything higher than forbearance!

52[III]

Where are the new physicians of the soul?— It was the means of solace that imparted to life that fundamental character of suffering in which one believes nowadays; the human being's greatest disease grew out of the battle against its diseases, and the apparent remedies have, in the long run, produced something much worse than what they were supposed to eliminate. Out of ignorance one mistook the momentarily effective, anesthetizing, and intoxicating means, the so-called consolations, for the actual remedies, indeed it wasn't even noticed that one often had to pay for these immediate alleviations with a general and profound worsening of the ailment, that the invalids had to suffer from the aftereffects of intoxication, later from want of intoxication, and finally from an oppressive, overall feeling of restlessness, nervous agitation, and bad health. Once the disease had advanced to a certain point, there was no longer any chance of recovery—the physicians of the soul, those believed in and worshipped far and wide, made sure of that.—One says of Schopenhauer, and rightly, that at long last he took humanity's suffering seriously again: where is the one who, at long last, will also take seriously the antidotes to this suffering and expose publicly the scandalous quackery with which, under the most magnificent names, humanity has treated its diseases of the soul?

53

Misuse of the conscientious. — It has been the conscientious and *not* those without conscience who have had to suffer so dreadfully under the oppression of fire-and-brimstone sermons and fears of hell, especially if they were also people of imagination. Thus, a gloom falls over the lives of precisely those most in need of serenity and pleasant images — not only for their rest and recovery from themselves, but also in order that humanity might have pleasure in them and take on a ray of their beauty. Oh, how much needless cruelty and torturing of animals has been unleashed by those religions that have invented sin! And by those people who longed, by means of it, to experience the highest pleasure of their power!

54

Thoughts about disease! — To calm the invalid's fantasy to the extent that he at least does not suffer *more*, as heretofore, from thinking about his disease than from the disease itself — that, I think, would be something! And nothing shabby at that! Now do you understand our task?

55

"Ways." — The supposedly "shorter ways" have always led humanity into great danger; overjoyed by the glad tidings that such a shorter way has been found, it always abandons its way — and thus *loses its way.*

56[112]

The apostate of free spirit. — Who has, anyway, an antipathy toward pious people secure in their faith? Quite the opposite, don't we view them with quiet respect and rejoice in their existence, with the fundamental regret that these excellent people do not share our feelings? But from where arises that deep, sudden repugnance without cause that we feel for anyone who once *had* full freedom of spirit and in the end *becomes* a "believer"? If we think about it, it seems as if we had caught sight of something disgusting that straightaway we had to erase from our soul. Wouldn't we turn our back on the most venerated person if he roused our suspicion in this connection? And indeed, not out of any moral condemnation, but from a sudden horror and disgust! Where does the intensity of this feeling come from? Perhaps someone or other will suggest that, at bottom, we aren't quite sure of ourselves? That we planted around us ahead of time thorned hedges of the most barbed contempt in order that we, at the decisive moment when age has made us weak and forgetful, cannot clamber out over our own contempt?—Frankly: this conjecture misses the mark, and whoever makes it knows nothing of what moves and determines the free spirit: how little contemptible seems to him the *changing* of his opinions as such! How, on the contrary, he reveres a rare and preeminent distinction, especially if continued into old age, of *being able* to alter his opinions! And it is his ambition (*not* his faint heart) that even reaches up for the forbidden fruits of the *spernere se sperne* and the *spernere se ipsum*:[113] let alone that he would experience before them the fear of the vain and complacent! In addition, the doctrine of the *innocence of all opinions* is as certain for him as the doctrine of the innocence of all actions: how could he become judge and hangman in the face of the apostate[114] of spiritual freedom! The sight of him actually touches him the way the sight of a repulsively diseased person touches a doctor: physical disgust at something fungal, edematous, overgrown, festering wins out for a moment over reason and the will to help. Our goodwill is thus overwhelmed by the representation of the prodigious *dishonesty* that must have held sway in the apostate of free spirit: by the representation of a general degenerateness reaching down into the very marrow of character.—

57

Other fear, other security.[115]—Christianity had added a completely new and unlimited *imperilment* to life and likewise created thereby completely new securities, enjoyments, recreations, and evaluations of all things. Our century denies this imperilment, and does so with a clear conscience: and yet it keeps dragging the old habits of Christian security, of Christian enjoyment, recreation, and evaluation along with it! Even into its noblest arts and philosophies! How stale and exhausted, how middling and awkward, how arbitrarily fanatical, and above all: how insecure this must all seem now that its dreadful antithesis, the Christian's omnipresent *fear* for his *eternal* salvation, has been lost!

58

Christianity and the affects. — Arising from Christianity is the audible sound of a great popular protest against philosophy: with their reason, the ancient sages had turned humans away from the affects; Christianity wants to *return* affects to humans. To this end it disallows all moral value to virtue as it was conceived of by philosophers—as the triumph of reason over affect—condemns rationality altogether, and categorically demands that the affects reveal themselves in their utmost strength and splendor: as *love* of God, *fear* before God, fanatical *faith* in God, as blindest *hope*[116] for God.

59[117]

Error as balm. — You can say what you like: Christianity wanted to liberate humanity from the burden of the demands of morality by pointing out a *shorter way to perfection*, or so it believed: just as some philosophers fancied they could eschew laborious and tedious dialectics as well as the collection of rigorously tested facts and refer to a "royal road to truth." Both times it was an error—but nevertheless a great balm for those overweary and despairing in the wilderness.

60

All spirit is finally becoming corporeally visible.—Christianity has devoured and thus engorged the collective spirit of countless mongers of subjugation, all those subtle and crude enthusiasts of self-mortification and other-idolization; it has, thereby, emerged from a country-bumpkinness—highly reminiscent, for example, of the earliest image of the Apostle Peter—into a very *spirited*[118] religion with thousands of wrinkles, ulterior motives, and evasions on its face; it has made European humanity sharp-witted as well as cunning, and not just theologically. In this spirit and in league with the powers that be and often with the deepest honesty of devotion, it has *chiseled out* the finest figures ever yet to exist in human society: the figures of higher and highest Catholic priesthood,[119] especially in the event that they had sprung from distinguished lineage and, from the outset, brought along grace of gesture, commanding eyes, and lovely hands and feet. Here, after a contrived way of life had subdued the beast inside the human, the human countenance attained that complete spiritualization produced by the constant ebb and flow of the two kinds of happiness (the feeling of power and the feeling of surrender); here an activity consisting of giving blessing, forgiving sin, and representing the divinity keeps constantly quickened in the soul, *indeed in the body as well*, the sense of a superhuman mission; here reigns that distinguished disdain for the fragility of the body and the weal of fortune common among born soldiers; one finds *pride* in obedience, which is the mark that singles out all aristocrats; in the prodigious impossibility of the task one finds one's excuse and one's ideality. The powerful beauty and refinement of the princes of the church have forever proven to the people the *truth* of the church; an occasional brutalization by the priesthood[120] (as in Luther's age) always brought with it faith in the opposite.—And with the end of all religions will *this* human beauty and refinement resulting from the harmony of figure, spirit, and task also be carried to the grave? And is something higher not attainable, not even conceivable?

61

The needful sacrifice. — These earnest, capable, upright, deeply sensitive people who even now are still sincere Christians: they owe it to themselves just once, for extended time, as an experiment, to live without Christianity; they owe it to *their faith* to undertake just once a stay of this sort "in the wilderness"[121] — if for no other reason than to earn the right to participate in the questioning as to whether Christianity is necessary. In the meantime they remain bound to their patch of native ground and from it they revile the world beyond it: Yes, they are ill-tempered and embittered when someone gives them to understand that beyond their patch there still lies the whole wide world! That Christianity, all in all, is really just a little corner! No, your evidence does not weigh a thing until you have lived for years without Christianity, longing with genuine fervor to endure in opposition to Christianity: until you have wandered from it far and wide. Not if homesickness, but only if *judgment* based on a strict *comparison* drives you back, only then does your return home amount to something! — In the future people will come to treat all evaluations from the past in this manner; one must *live through* them once again voluntarily, likewise through their opposite — in order, in the final analysis, to have the *right* to let them fall through the sieve.

62[122]

On the origin of religions. — How can a person experience his own opinion about things as a revelation? This is the problem underlying the emergence of all religions: each time, there was a person on hand for whom such a process was possible. The precondition is that the person already believed in revelations. Then, one fine day he suddenly catches hold of *his* new idea, and the blessed rapture of a hypothesis that encompasses

his own world and all of existence takes such powerful possession of his consciousness that he doesn't dare consider himself
the creator of such bliss and he credits his God as its cause
and, then again, as the cause of the cause[123] of that new thought:
as God's revelation. How could a human being possibly be the
founder of so great a happiness!—he questions pessimistically.
In addition, other hidden levers are at work: for instance, one
confirms for oneself an opinion by experiencing it as revelation,
thereby erasing from it any remnant of the hypothetical; one
withdraws it from critique, indeed from doubt, one makes it
holy. Thus one does, it is true, degrade oneself to an *organon*,[124]
but in the long run our thought triumphs as the thought of
God—this feeling of remaining the victor in the end gains the
upper hand over that feeling of degradation. And yet another
feeling operates in the background: whenever we exalt our *creation* over ourselves and seemingly disregard our own worth, we
then experience the exultation of paternal love and pride, which
compensates, and more than compensates for everything.

63[125]

Hatred of thy neighbor.—Supposing we felt toward someone else as that person feels about himself—what Schopenhauer calls compassion but what would be termed more accurately a single passion, a onepassion[126]—then we would have
to hate him if he, like Pascal, found himself hateful.[127] And
that is probably how Pascal felt toward humanity as a whole,
as did early Christianity, which under Nero[128] was, according
to Tacitus, convicted of *odium generis humani*.[129]

64[130]

The despairing.—Christianity has the hunter's instinct for
anyone and everyone who, by any means whatsoever, can be
brought to despair—something of which only a portion of humanity is capable. It is always chasing after them, it lies in wait
for them. Pascal attempted an experiment to discover whether
everyone, aided by the most incisive knowledge, could be

brought to despair;—the experiment miscarried, to his second despair.

65

Brahmanism and Christianity.—There are recipes for the feeling of power; first for those sorts who can control themselves and who, for that reason, are already at home in a feeling of power; and then for those others for whom this is lacking. To people of the first species Brahmanism has catered; to people of the second, Christianity.

66[131]

Visionary capability.—Throughout the Middle Ages the genuine and decisive sign of the highest humanity was considered to be: that one was capable of visions—in other words, of profound mental disturbances! And basically the medieval precepts for life practiced by all the higher natures (the *religiosi*)[132] are intended to make the individual *capable* of visions! No wonder an overestimation of half-disturbed, fantastical, fanatical, so-called persons of genius continues to spill over into our age; "they have seen things that others do not see"—indeed! and this should incline us toward them more cautiously, but not more credulously!

67[133]

Price for believers.—Whoever places such value in having people believe in him that he vouchsafes heaven for this belief—and to anyone, even a robber on the cross[134]—must have suffered under terrible doubts and have had every sort of cross and crucifixion to bear: otherwise, he wouldn't pay so dearly for his believers.

68[135]

The first Christian.—The whole world still believes in the writings of the "Holy Spirit" or else lives under the aftereffect of this belief: when one opens the Bible, one does so in order to "edify" oneself, to find, in one's personal distress, great or small, the wink of solace—in short, one reads oneself into and out of it. That the Bible also portrays the story of one of the most ambitious and importunate souls, not to mention superstitious and cunning minds, the story of the Apostle Paul—who, outside of a few scholars, knows that? Without this peculiar story, however, without the confusions and whirlwinds of such a mind and such a soul, there would be no Christianity; we would hardly have heard of a tiny Jewish sect whose master died on the cross. To be sure: if this story had been understood in time, if Paul's scriptures had been read, *really read*, not as the revelations of the "Holy Spirit" but instead, with an honest and open mind and without thinking about all our personal needs in the process—for a thousand and a half years there have been no such readers—then Christianity would long have been ancient history: so clearly do these pages penned by the Jewish Pascal expose Christianity's origin, just as the pages of the French Pascal expose its fate, as well as what will destroy it. That the ship of Christianity threw a good portion of Jewish ballast overboard, that it reached out, and was able to reach out, to the heathens—this is all bound to the story of this one person, a person very tortured, very pitiable,[136] very unpleasant, also to himself. He suffered under a fixed idea, or, more clearly: under an ever present, never dormant, *fixed question*: what is at stake in the Jewish *law*? And particularly in the *fulfillment of this law*? In his youth he himself had wanted to satisfy it, ravenous for this highest distinction Jews can possibly imagine—this people, which pushed the fantasy of ethical sublimeness[137] higher than any other people and which alone succeeded in creating a holy God, along with the idea of sin as an offense against this holiness. Paul had become simultaneously the fanatical defender and the honor guard of this God, as well as of his law, constantly in battle against, lying in wait for, the transgressors and doubters of the law, brutal and malicious toward them and inclined to the most extreme of punishments. And then he discovered in himself that he—fiery, sensual, melancholy, malignant in hate, as he was—was himself *unable* to fulfill the law, and indeed what seemed strangest to him: that his excessive lust for domination[138] was constantly provoked to transgress the law and that he *had* to give in to this goad. Is it really the carnality of "flesh"[139] that turned him into a transgressor over and over again? And not rather, as he later suspected, what lay behind it, the law itself, which *must* prove constantly its unfulfillability and which lures with irresistible magic to transgression? But at that time he did not yet have this way out. Many things lay on his conscience—he hints at enmity, murder, sorcery, idolatry, lechery, drunkenness and pleasure in dissolute debauch—and however much he tried to relieve this conscience, and even more his lust for domination, through the most extreme fanaticism in honoring and defending the law: there were moments when he said to himself, "It is all in vain! the torment of the unfulfilled law cannot be overcome." Luther might well have felt similarly when he wanted, in his monastery, to become the perfect embodiment of the spiritual ideal:[140] and as with Luther, who one day began to hate—all the more so, the less he dared confess that hate to himself—the spiritual ideal and the pope and the saints and the entire clergy with a truly deadly hate—something similar happened to Paul. The law was the cross on which he felt himself nailed: how he hated it! How resentfully he dragged it along behind! How he searched about to find a means of *destroying* it—of no longer having to fulfill it himself! And finally the redeeming thought flashed before him, simultaneously with a vision, as could only have been the case with this epileptic: to him, the raging zealot for the law, who was dead tired of it inwardly, there appeared on a lonely road that Christ, the light of the Heavenly Father streaming from his face, and Paul heard the words: "why persecutest thou *me*?" Essentially what happened there, however, is this: his *mind* had grown suddenly clear; "it is irrational" he had said to himself, "to persecute precisely this Christ! Here is truly the way out! Here is truly the perfect revenge, here and nowhere else do I have and hold the *destroyer of the law*!" Afflicted by the most injured pride, he feels himself, in one fell swoop, completely recovered, the moral despair gone, as if blown away, for morality has been blown away, destroyed—or rather *fulfilled*, there on the cross! Up until now he had considered that ignominious *death* to be the main argument against the "messianism" preached by the adherents of the new doctrine: what if, however, it was *necessary* in order to *abolish* the law!—The prodigious consequences of this sudden insight, this solution to the riddle, whirl before his eyes; with one stroke he becomes the happiest person on earth—the fate of the Jews, no, of all humanity seems to him bound together with this insight, this his instant of sudden, flashing illumination; he possesses the thought of thoughts, the key of keys, the light of lights; henceforth, history will turn around him alone! For from now on he is the teacher of the *destruction of the law*! To withdraw from evil—that is also to withdraw from the law; to be in the flesh—that is also to be in the law! To have become one with Christ—that is also to have become with him the destroyer of the law; to have died with him—that is also to have withdrawn from the law! Even if it were still possible to sin, then certainly no longer against the law, "I am outside the law."[141] "If I now wanted to take up the law again and subject myself to it, then I would turn Christ into the accomplice of sin"; for the law was there only that people might sin, it always induces sin, as the pungent humors induce illness; God would never have decided for the death of Christ if, without this death, any fulfillment of the law whatsoever had been possible; now, not only is all guilt carried away, but guilt as such has been destroyed; now the law is dead,[142] now the carnality of flesh in which it lives is dead—or at least continually dying out, as if decaying. Yet a little while in the midst of this decay!—that is the Christian's lot before he becomes one with Christ,[143] rises again with Christ, takes part in the divine majesty with Christ, and becomes "God's son," like Christ.—With that, Paul's intoxication has reached its summit, as has the importunity of his soul—with the idea of becoming-one, every shame, every subordination, every barrier is removed from it, and the untamable will to lust for domination reveals itself as an anticipatory revelry in *divine* splendors.—This is the *first Christian*, the inventor of Christianness! Up until then, there were only a few Jewish sectarians.

69

Inimitable.—There is a prodigious tension and extensiveness *between* envy and friendship, between self-contempt and pride: in the former lived the Greek, in[144] the latter the Christian.[145]

70

What a crude intellect is good for.—The Christian church is an encyclopedia of prehistoric cults and viewpoints of the most diverse origin and therefore so well suited to proselytizing: it could before, it can now, go wherever it pleases, it met and meets with something familiar to which it can adapt and onto which it can gradually graft itself. Not what is Christian in it, rather the universal heathenism of its *rituals* is the reason for the propagation of this world religion; from the very beginning, its tenets, which are rooted simultaneously in Jewish and in Hellenic traditions, have managed to transcend national and racial boundaries[146] and other subtle distinctions as if they were prejudices.[147] One may even admire this *force* that enables the most disparate elements to grow into one another and entwine: but one must not forget the contemptible quality of this force—the astounding crudeness and self-satisfaction of its intellect during the age of the formation of the Church, so as to accept, to such an extreme, *every sort of fare* and thus to digest oppositions like gravel.

71

Christian revenge on Rome.—Perhaps nothing is more wearisome than the sight of a perpetual conqueror—for two hundred years one had watched Rome subdue one people after another, the circle had been drawn, any other future seemed foreclosed, all things were arranged as if forever—indeed, whenever the empire *built*, it built with the motive of "*aere perennius*"[148] in mind—we, we who know only the "melancholy of ruins," can scarcely understand that completely different *melancholy of eternal building* from which one had to rescue oneself as best one could—through Horace's frivolity, for instance. Others sought other means of solace against the weariness bordering on despair, against the deadening consciousness that all workings of the head and heart are henceforth without hope, that the great spider was hovering everywhere, relentlessly ready to drink every drop of blood wherever it might well forth.—This centuries-old, unvoiced hate against Rome, shared by all the worn-out onlookers for as far and wide as Rome ruled, unleashed itself at long last in *Christianity* by means of compressing Rome, "world," and "sin" into *one* sentiment: it avenged itself on Rome by conceiving of the suddenly imminent destruction of the world; it avenged itself on Rome by installing a new future for itself, a future moreover—Rome had managed to transform everything into *its* prehistory and *its* present—in comparison to which Rome no longer seemed to be most important; it avenged itself on Rome by dreaming of a last *judgment*—and the crucified Jew as the symbol of salvation was the deepest mockery of the magnificent Roman praetors[149] in the provinces, for now they appeared as the symbols of perdition and of a "world" ripe for destruction.—

72

The "after-death."—In every corner of the Roman Empire, Christianity met with the representation of punishments in hell: numerous secret cults brooded over the idea with special satisfaction as the most fertile egg of their power. Epicurus[150] had been of the opinion that nothing could be of greater service to his followers than to rip out the roots of *this* belief: his triumph, which resounds[151] most beautifully in the mouth of the somber and yet clairvoyant disciple of his teaching, the Roman Lucretius,[152] came too early—Christianity took the belief in subterranean terrors, which had already begun to fade, under its special protection, and was very clever in so doing! Without this bold foray into complete heathendom, how could it have carried the day over the popularity of the Mithras and Isis cults![153] It thus won the ranks of the timorous over to its side—the most zealous adherents of a new faith! For the Jews, a people who held and hold firmly onto life—like the Greeks and even more than the Greeks—such ideas fell on barren ground: final and irrevocable death as the sinner's punishment and, as the most extreme threat, never to rise from the dead—that alone had a powerful enough effect on these unusual people who did not want to lose their body but instead hoped, with their refined Egyptianism, to rescue it for all eternity. (A Jewish martyr, whose story is told in the second book of the Maccabees,[154] does not entertain the possibility of renouncing possession of his eviscerated entrails: at the time of resurrection he plans to *have* them—that is the Jewish way!) For the earliest Christians the thought of eternal torments was quite remote; they thought themselves to be *redeemed* "from death" and expected, at any moment, transubstantiation[155] and no longer any death. (How strangely the first instance of death must have affected these expectant ones! What a mixture there of astonishment, rejoicing, doubt, shame, ardor!—surely a theme[156] for great artists!) Paul knew of no greater praise for his redeemer than to claim that he had *opened* the gateway to immortality for everyone[157]—he doesn't yet believe in the resurrection of the unredeemed;[158] indeed, as a result of his doctrine of the unfulfillability of the law and of death as the wages of sin,[159] he suspects that, at bottom, nobody has (or very few have, and then owing to grace and without individual merit) heretofore attained immortality; only now does immortality *begin* to open up its gates—and in the final analysis only a very few are chosen for it: as the arrogance of the chosen one cannot refrain from adding.—Elsewhere, where the drive for life was not as great as among the Jews or the Jewish Christians and the prospect of immortality did not necessarily seem more valuable than the prospect of a final, irrevocable death, then that heathen, and nonetheless not totally un-Jewish, supplement known as hell became an ideal tool in the hands of the missionaries: the new doctrine sprang up according to which sinners and the unredeemed were also immortal, the doctrine of the eternally damned,[160] and it was more powerful than the, by this point, expiring thought of *final and irrevocable death.* It was the advance of *science* that had to recapture that thought, and it did so by conjointly rejecting any other representation of death and any life beyond. We have grown poorer by *one* interest: the after-death no longer concerns us!—An unspeakable blessing, which is yet still too recent to be experienced far and wide as such. And Epicurus triumphs anew!

73[161]

For the "truth!—"For the truth of Christianity there spoke the virtuous conduct of the Christians, their resoluteness in suffering, the enduring faith, and above all, Christianity's growth and propagation despite all affliction"—so you keep on saying even today! How pathetic! It's time you learned that all these things don't speak for or against truth, that truth is proven differently from truthfulness, and that the latter is in no way an argument for the former!

74[162]

Christian ulterior motive.—Might the following not have been the most common form of ulterior motive on the part of Christians of the first centuries: "it's better to *talk oneself into* being guilty than into being innocent, because you never know for sure how such a *mighty* judge is disposed—you have to *fear,* however, that he hopes to find nothing but a lot of consciously guilty consciences! Given such great power, he's more likely to pardon a guilty person than to admit that someone in his presence might be in the right."—Poor people in the provinces felt the same way in front of the Roman praetor: "he's too proud for us to be able to be innocent"—how could this very feeling fail to have turned up again in the Christian incarnation of the supreme judge!

75

Not European and not noble.—There is something Oriental and something womanly in Christianity: it betrays itself in the idea that "whom the Lord loveth he chasteneth";[163] for women in the Orient view chastisements and strict seclusion of their person from the world as a sign of their husband's love and complain if these signs are wanting.

76

To think evil is to make evil.—The passions become evil and malicious whenever they are viewed evilly and maliciously. Accordingly, Christianity has succeeded in turning Eros and Aphrodite—grand powers capable of idealization—into infernal kobolds[164] and phantoms of deceit in that it aroused in the believer's conscience great torments at the slightest sexual excitation. Is it not hideous to transform necessary and normal sensations into a source of inner misery and, in so doing, to want to make inner misery necessary and normal *for every human being*! Moreover, it remains a misery kept secret and thus more deeply rooted: for not everyone has the courage of a Shakespeare to confess one's Christian gloominess on this point as he did in his sonnets.[165]—Must we then always label anything *evil* that we have to struggle to keep under control or, if need be, banish altogether from our thoughts! Is it not the way of *base* souls always to think that their *enemy* has to be *evil*! And ought one to call Eros an enemy! Properly considered, sexual feelings have in common with feelings of sympathy and worship the fact that, by doing as one pleases, one person gives pleasure to another—such benevolent arrangements are met with all too rarely in nature! And to revile[166] just such an arrangement, to ruin it by association with an evil conscience! To join like brother and sister the begetting of human beings to a guilty conscience!—Ultimately, this demonizing of Eros has taken on an ending straight out of comedy: thanks to the Church's dark secretiveness with regard to everything the least bit erotic, the "devil" Eros has gradually become more interesting to people than all the angels and saints combined: to this very day, the effect has been that the *love story* became the only real interest that *all* circles have in common—and to an excess inconceivable in antiquity, an excess that will, at a later date, elicit laughter. From the loftiest to the lowliest, all our philosophizing and poeticizing has been marked, and more than marked, by the excessive importance ascribed to turning the love story into the main story: it may be that on this account posterity will judge that the entire legacy of Christian culture is determined by something petty and foolish.

77[167]

On the torments of the soul.—These days everyone loudly decries whatever torment any individual inflicts on the body of another; indignation erupts immediately against a person capable of such a thing; we tremble at the very idea of some torment that might be inflicted upon a person or an animal and suffer most unbearably upon learning of an irrefutably proven instance of this sort. But one is a far cry from experiencing such certain and widely accepted feelings with regard to the torments of the soul and the heinousness involved in their infliction. Christianity has put them to use to an unprecedented and shocking degree and still continuously preaches this type of torture; indeed, whenever it encounters a situation in which such torments are absent, it remonstrates in all innocence against apostasy and backsliding—all with the result that today humanity still responds to this spiritual death by fire, to spiritual torments and their instruments, with the same timorous patience and indecision that it earlier felt in the face of cruelty toward the bodies of animals and humans. Hell has become, in truth, more than an empty word: and to the newly created and very real fears of hell there corresponds as well a new species of compassion unheard of in earlier times, a horrid, oppressively weighty pity[168,169] for those souls "irrevocably damned to hell,"[170] as in, for example, the pity that the stone guest displays toward Don Juan[171] and that, during the centuries of Christianity, has no doubt often moved stones to tears. Plutarch supplies a bleak picture of the superstitious person in heathendom: this picture pales to harmlessness when compared with the Christian of the Middle Ages who *assumes* that he can no longer escape the "eternal torment." Horrifying omens appear to him: maybe a stork holding a snake in its beak and still *hesitating* to swallow. Or the world around one grows suddenly pale, or smoldering colors flicker over the earth. Or the shapes of departed relatives whose visages bear traces of dreadful suffering approach. Or the dark walls in the room where one is sleeping brighten and upon them appear, in sulfurous smoke, instruments of torture and a tangled skein of snakes and devils. Indeed, what a wretched place Christianity has managed to make of the earth, merely by erecting the crucifix everywhere, thereby branding the earth as the place "where the righteous are *tortured* to death"! And when the power of great fire-and-brimstone preachers suddenly began to drive the secret suffering of the individual, the torments of the "closet," out into the public sphere, when, for instance, a Whitefield[172] preached "as a dying man to the dying," one moment weeping fervently, the next pounding loudly and vehemently, using the most trenchant and changeable of voices, without shying away from directing the entire vehemence of attack onto one attending individual, singling him out of the congregation in dreadful fashion[173] — how must the earth have seemed each and every time truly transformed at that point into the "field of calamity"![174,175] One saw then entire multitudes swept together as if under the paroxysm of a *single* mania; some were in convulsions of fear; others lay motionless, unconscious: several trembled violently or pierced the air with penetrating screams continuing for hours. Everywhere the sound of loud breathing, like people half choked and gasping for life's breath. "And in fact," according to one eyewitness of such a sermon, "virtually all the sounds that came to one's ear were those of people *dying in bitter torture*."[176] — Let us never forget that it was Christianity that first turned the *deathbed* into a bed of torment[177] and that the scenes enacted upon it ever since, with the horrid tones that appeared possible here for the first time, have poisoned for life the senses and the blood of countless witnesses along with their descendants! Just imagine a perfectly innocent person who can then never get over having once heard words such as: "Oh eternity! Oh, if only I had no soul! Oh, if only I had never been born! I am damned, damned, lost forever. Six days ago you could have helped me. But it's too late. I now belong to the devil, with him I must go to hell. Burst, burst, you poor hearts of stone! Must you not burst? What more can be done for hearts of stone? I am damned that you may be saved! There he is! Yes, there he is! Come, blessed devil! Come!"[178] —

78

Justice that punishes. — Misfortune and guilt — Christianity has placed these two things on *one* scale: such that whenever the misfortune ensuing from an instance of guilt is great, the greatness of the guilt itself is then apportioned, completely involuntarily, in relation to the misfortune. This is, however, not *antique*, which is why Greek tragedy, which deals with misfortune and guilt so often and yet in such a different sense, is one of the greatest liberators of mind and spirit, to a degree that the ancients themselves could not experience. They had remained harmless enough not to establish an "appropriate relationship" between guilt and misfortune. The guilt of their tragic heroes is indeed the tiny stone over which they stumble and, as such, the reason why they indeed do break an arm or put out an eye, at which point the antique sensibility responded: "Yes, he should have made his way a bit more cautiously and a bit less presumptuously." But it was left up to Christianity to say for the first time: "There is a grave misfortune here, and underneath it there *must* lie hidden a grave, *equally grave guilt*, even if we don't yet see it clearly. If you, misfortunate one, don't feel this way, then you are *obdurate*—you will have even worse things to go through!"—Accordingly, misfortune actually still existed in antiquity, pure, innocent misfortune; only with Christianity did everything become punishment, well-deserved punishment; it makes the sufferer's imagination also suffer so that with every malady he also feels morally reprehensible and depraved. Poor humanity!—The Greeks have their own word for indignation over someone else's misfortune:[179] this affect was forbidden among Christian peoples and has hardly developed, and they lack, therefore, a name for this *more manly* brother of compassion.

79

A suggestion.—If, as Pascal and Christianity claim, our ego is always *hateful*,[180] how might we possibly ever allow or assume[181] that someone else could love it—be it God or a human being! It would go against all decency to let oneself be loved knowing full well that one *deserves* only hate—not to mention other feelings of repulsion.—"But this is precisely the kingdom of mercy."—So is your love-thy-neighbor mercy? Your compassion mercy? Well, if these things are possible for you, go still one step further: love yourselves out of mercy—then you won't need your God any more at all, and the whole drama of original sin and redemption will play itself out to the end in you yourselves.

80

The compassionate Christian.—The underside of Christian compassion for the suffering of one's neighbor is the deep suspicion of all one's neighbor's pleasures, his pleasure in what he wants and in what he can do.

81

The saint's humanity. — A saint had fallen in with some believers and could no longer stand their constant hatred of sin.
Finally he said: "God created all things except sin: is there any
wonder he's not well disposed to it? — But humans created
sin — and they are supposed to cast out this their only child,
simply because it displeases God, sin's grandfather! Is this humane? All honor to him to whom honor's due! — But surely inclination and duty ought to speak first and foremost for the
child — and only secondarily for the honor of the grandfather!"

82[182]

Spiritual[183] surprise attack. — "You have to sort that out on
your own, for your life is at stake:" with this exhortation Luther springs upon us and thinks we feel the knife pressed to the
throat. But we defend ourselves against him with the words of
one higher and more reflective. "We are free to form no opinion about this or that matter and thus to spare our soul anxiety.
For by their very nature things themselves cannot *require* any
judgments from us."

83

Poor humanity! — One drop of blood too much or too little
in the brain can make our life unspeakably miserable and hard,
such that we suffer more from this one drop of blood than Prometheus from his vulture.[184] But the most horrible thing of all
is not even *knowing* that this drop of blood is the cause. "The
devil!" Or "sin!" instead. —

84[185]

Christianity's philology. — Just how little Christianity fosters
a sense of integrity and justice can be judged fairly accurately
from the character of its scholars' writings: they advance their
conjectures with the cheeked assurance of dogma and are rarely
at an honest moment's loss when it comes to the interpretation

of a biblical passage. Again and again they claim, "I am right, for it is written"—and then there follows such a brazenly arbitrary explication that, upon hearing it, a philologist, caught in the middle between outrage and laughter, stops dead in his tracks and asks himself again and again: Is this possible! Is this honest? Is it actually even decent?—In this regard the degree of dishonesty still practiced from Protestant pulpits, the brazenness with which the preacher exploits the advantage that no one is going to interrupt him, the extent to which the Bible is pinched and pulled and the congregation is trained in all forms of the *art of reading badly*: this can be underestimated only by someone who always, or never, goes to church. But after all: what can one expect from the aftereffects of a religion that, during the centuries of its establishment, performed such a scandalous philological farce on the Old Testament: I mean the attempt to snatch the Old Testament right from under the Jews' very noses by claiming that it contains nothing but Christian teachings and *belongs* to the Christians as the *true* people of Israel: whereas the Jews had only usurped this role for themselves. And then one submitted to a devoted frenzy of explication and interpolation that cannot possibly have been connected to a clean conscience; no matter how vociferously Jewish scholars protested, the Old Testament was supposed to speak everywhere of Christ and only of Christ and everywhere in particular of his cross; and wherever a piece of wood, a rod, a ladder, a twig, a tree, a willow, a staff turns up, that signifies a prophesying of the wood of the cross: even the erection of the unicorn and the bronze snake,[186] even Moses when he spreads out his arms in prayer. Yes, even the spit on which the Passover lamb is roasted—all allusions and, as it were, prelusions to the cross! Has anyone who claimed this ever *believed* it? One should bear in mind that the Church did not shrink from enlarging the Septuagint[187] (e.g., Psalm 96:10)[188] in order afterward to exploit the smuggled passage to support Christian prophecy. One was, after all, engaged in a *battle* and one thought about the enemy and not about integrity.

85[189]

Lack of refinement. — Do not even dream of mocking the mythology of the Greeks because it is so little like your ponderous metaphysics! You ought to admire a people who held their acute understanding in check at precisely this point and for a long time had enough tact to avoid the danger of scholasticism and of crafty superstition!

86[190]

Christian interpreters of the body. — Anything whatsoever that stems from the stomach, entrails, heartbeat, nerves, gall, semen — all these annoyances, enervations, overexcitations, the whole contingent nature of the machine we know so little! — All this a Christian like Pascal has to view as a moral and religious phenomenon, questioning whether it contains God or devil, good or evil, salvation or damnation. Oh what an unfortunate interpreter! How he has to twist and torture his system! How he has to twist and torture himself so as to stay in the right!

87[191]

The moral miracle. — With regard to morality, Christianity acknowledges only the miracle: the sudden alteration of all value judgments, the sudden abandonment of all habits, the sudden irresistible inclination toward new objects and new persons. It apprehends this phenomenon as God's plan, christens it the act of being born again, and gives it a singular incomparable worth — for a Christian anything that goes under the banner of morality and yet has no relation to the miracle, by virtue of that lack, becomes a matter of indifference and indeed, insofar as it constitutes a feeling of well-being or pride, perhaps even an object of fear. The New Testament sets up a canon of virtue, of the fulfilled law: but only such that it is the canon of *impossible virtue*: faced with such a canon, people who continue to strive morally are supposed to learn to always feel *farther and farther* from their goal, they are supposed to *despair* of virtue and then at last *to cast themselves on the bosom* of the God of mercy—only with this finale was a Christian's moral endeavor able to count as valuable, only, in other words, if it always remains an unsuccessful, cheerless, melancholy *endeavor*; as such, it could, in addition, *serve* to induce that ecstatic moment in which the individual experiences the "awakening unto grace" and the moral miracle: this struggle for morality is, however, not *necessary*, for, not infrequently, this miracle overtakes the sinner precisely when he is, as it were, leprous with sin; indeed, it even seems that the leap out of the most profound and thoroughgoing iniquity into its opposite is easier and, as obvious proof of the miracle, also *more desirable.*—Moreover, *what* such a sudden irrational and irresistible reversal, such a switch from profoundest misery to profoundest bliss, indicates physiologically (a disguised epilepsy perhaps?) is best left for the psychiatrists to ponder, as they have abundant opportunity to observe "miracles" of this sort (in the guise of, for example, homicidal or suicidal mania). The *more pleasant outcome*, relatively speaking, in the case of the Christian makes no essential difference.

88[192]

Luther the great benefactor.—The most significant thing Luther accomplished lies in the mistrust he awakened toward the saints and the entire Christian *vita contemplativa*: only from that point forward did a path to an unchristian *vita contemplativa* in Europe become possible again, and an end was put to the contempt for worldly activity and for the laity. Luther, who remained a trusty miner's son after they had locked him in the monastery,[193] where, for lack of other mines or "mineshafts,"[194] he plumbed into himself and bored out terrifying dark passageways—finally he realized that a contemplative holy life was impossible for him and that his inborn physical and spiritual "activity" would destroy him. All too long he tried to find the way to holiness through castigations—finally he made up his mind and said to himself: "there *is* no real *vita contempla-tiva* at all! We've allowed ourselves to be deceived! The saints were worth no more than the rest of us." To be sure, this was a boorish way of having his say—but for the Germans of that time the right and the only way: how edifying now it was for them to read in their Lutheran catechism: "Excepting the ten commandments there is *no* work that could *please* God—the *glorified* spiritual works of the saints are self-invented."[195]

89

Doubt as sin.—Christianity has done its utmost to close the circle, having already declared doubt a sin! Void of reason, one is supposed to be tossed into faith by a miracle and then to swim in it as if it were the clearest and most uncomplicated of elements: a mere glance in search of firm ground, the mere thought that perhaps one is not meant only for swimming on this planet, merely the lightest stirring of our amphibious nature—is a sin! At least take note that with this attitude, any need to substantiate faith and all reflection upon its emergence have also been foreclosed as sinful. What is wanted are blindness and delirium and an eternal psalm above the waves in which reason has drowned.

90[196]

Egoism against egoism. — It is remarkable how many people continue to conclude: "Life wouldn't be bearable if there were no God!" (or, as it is put in Idealist circles, "Life wouldn't be bearable were its foundation lacking in ethical significance"[197])—hence God (or an ethical significance for existence) *must* exist! In truth, the situation is simply that anyone who has grown accustomed to these ideas does not desire a life without them: that, consequently, they may well be necessary ideas for such a person and his preservation—but what arrogant presumption to decree that everything necessary for my preservation must also, *here and now*, really *exist*! As if my preservation were something necessary! What if others felt just the opposite! if, precisely under the constraints of those two articles of faith, they preferred not to live and found life no longer worth living!—And so it is nowadays!

91

God's honesty.[198]—An omniscient and omnipotent God who doesn't even bother to make his intentions understood by the very creatures He has created—is this supposed to be a God of goodness? Who allows to persist for millennia innumerable doubts and hesitations as if they were of no consequence for the welfare[199] of humanity, who again holds out the prospect of the most dreadful repercussions for mistaking the truth? Would he not be a cruel God if he had the truth and could observe how miserably humanity tortures itself in its pursuit? — But perhaps he is a God of goodness after all—and he was merely *unable* to express himself more clearly! Did he perhaps lack the intelligence[200] for it? Or the eloquence? So much the worse! Then perhaps he was also mistaken about what he labeled his "Truth," and is himself not so very different from the "poor deceived devil"! For surely he must endure practically the torments of hell itself to have to see his creatures, by virtue of their very effort to come to know him, suffer so and then continue suffering all the more through all eternity and *not* be able to counsel and to help in any way other than as a deaf mute who makes all sorts of ambiguous signs when the most frightful danger is hard on the heels of his child or his dog? A believer who comes to such an oppressive conclusion may surely be forgiven if he feels more compassion for the suffering God than for his "neighbors"—because they are no longer closest to him if that most solitary and primeval Being is also the One among all who is most suffering and most in need of solace. All religions reveal a trace of the fact that they owe their origin to an early, immature intellectuality in humanity—they all take with astonishing *levity* the obligation to tell the truth: as yet, they don't know a thing about any *duty on the part of God* to be truthful to humanity and clear in his communication—No one has been more eloquent concerning the "hidden God"[201] and his reasons for keeping himself so hidden and for emerging only halfway into the light of language than Pascal, an indication that he could never quite calm himself on the subject: but his voice sounds so confident, as if he and God had once sat together for a tête-à-tête behind the concealing curtain. He caught wind of something immoral in the "*deus absconditus*"[202] and had the greatest shame in, and aversion to, admitting it to himself: and so, like someone who is afraid, he talked as loudly as he could.[203]

92

At Christianity's deathbed. — Genuinely active people these days are inwardly without Christianity, and the more moderate and contemplative people of the spiritual middle class possess at this point only a ready-made, namely a wondrously *simplified*, Christianity. A God who, in his love, ordains everything in the long run to turn out for the best, a God who gives and takes away our virtue as well as our happiness, so that, on the whole, everything turns out fine and proper, and there is no reason to take life too seriously and certainly no reason to complain, in short, resignation and meekness elevated to the godhead—these are the best and most vital existing remains of Christianity. But one should after all realize that, as a result, Christianity has passed over into a gentle *moralism*:[204] not so much "God, freedom, and immortality"[205] have remained as goodwill and a decorous disposition and the belief that in the whole universe goodwill and a decorous disposition will rule as well: it is Christianity's *euthanasia*.

93

What is truth?—Who could not accept the *conclusion* the faithful love to draw:[206] "scientific knowledge cannot be true, for it denies God. Accordingly, it comes not from God; accordingly, it is not true—for God is Truth." Not the conclusion, but the presupposition contains the error: what if God were, in fact, *not* Truth, and if, in fact, this were proven? If he were the vanity, the lust for power, the impatience, the terror, the chilling and enchanting delusion of humankind?

94

The irascibles' remedy.[207]—Paul himself was of the opinion that a sacrifice was necessary to counteract God's extreme irascibility resulting from sin: and since then Christians have never ceased to vent their discontent with themselves on a *sacrifice*—whether it be the "world" or "history" or "reason" or pleasure or the peaceful equanimity of other people—something or other *good* must always die for *their* sins (even if only in effigy).

95

Historical refutation as definitive refutation.—In former times, one sought to prove that there was no God—today one demonstrates how the belief in the existence of God could *come into being* and by what means this belief attained its gravity and importance: thus, a counterproof that there is no God becomes superfluous.—When in former times one had refuted the proposed "proofs of the existence of God," doubt still remained as to whether better proofs might turn up than the ones just refuted. Back then the atheists were not skilled at making a clean sweep.

96

In hoc signo vinces.[208]—However advanced Europe might be in other respects: in religious matters it has not yet reached the freethinking naïveté of the ancient Brahmans, a sign that people in India four millennia ago thought more, and took care to transmit from generation to generation more pleasure in thought than is the case with us today. Those Brahmans thought, namely, first of all that the priests were more powerful than the gods, and secondly that it was in the observances that the power of the priests rested: which is why their poets never tired of praising the observances (prayers, ceremonies, sacrifices, hymns, and verses) as the true bestowers of all things good.[209] However much poeticizing and superstition may have slipped in here: the propositions are *true*! One step further: and the gods were cast aside—which Europe must also do one day! Yet another step further: and one no longer needed the priests and mediators and there appeared the teacher of the *religion of self-redemption*, the Buddha:—how far removed Europe still is from this level of culture! When at long last all observances and mores supporting the power of the gods and the priests and saviors are obliterated, when, in other words, morality in the old sense will be dead and gone: then comes—Yes, what comes then? But why play guessing games; above all let us see to it instead that Europe catches up to what was already practiced among the nation of thinkers several millennia ago in India as the commandment of all thinking! There exist today perhaps ten to twenty million people among the different countries of Europe who no longer "believe in God"—is it too much to ask that they *give a sign* to one another? As soon as they *know* one another in this manner, they will also make themselves known to others—they will immediately be a power in Europe and, fortunately, a power *between* nations! Between the classes! Between rich and poor! Between rulers and subjects! Between the most restless and the calmest, the most becalming of all people!

Book Two

97[1]

One becomes moral—not because one is moral!—Subjugation to morality can be slavish or vain or self-serving or resigned or stiflingly rapturous or without thought or an act of despair, like subjugation to a prince: in and of itself, there is nothing moral about it.

98

Morality's mutation.—There exists a perpetual transforming of and laboring on morality. This is brought about by *successful crimes* (to which belong, for example, all innovations in moral thinking).[2]

99

Wherein we are all irrational.—We still continue to draw conclusions from judgments we consider false and from teachings in which we no longer believe—owing to our feelings.

100

Awakening from the dream.[3]—Noble and wise persons once believed in the music of the spheres:[4] noble and wise persons still believe in the "ethical significance of existence."[5] But the day will come when this spherical music is no longer audible to their ear! They awaken and detect that their ear had been dreaming.

101

Problematic.—To accept[6] a faith merely because it is the custom—that is certainly tantamount to: being dishonest, being cowardly, being lazy!—And so that would make dishonesty, cowardice, and laziness the preconditions of morality?

102[7]

The oldest moral judgments.—How, in fact, do we respond to the behavior of a person in our vicinity?—First we view it with an eye for what emerges from it *for us*—we see it only from this point of view. We take *this* effect to be the *intention* of the behavior—and finally we ascribe the possession of such intentions to the person as an *abiding* trait and from now on brand him as, for example, "an injurious person." Threefold error! Threefold age-old blunder! Stemming perhaps from our inheritance from animals and from their power of judgment. Isn't the *origin of all morality* to be found in the disgraceful petty inferences: "whatever injures *me* is something *evil* (injurious *per se*); whatever benefits *me* is something *good* (beneficial and advantageous *per se*); whatever injures me *once or several times* is inimical *per se*; whatever benefits me *once or several times* is amiable *per se*." Oh *pudenda origo*![8] Doesn't this amount to: fancifully turning another person's paltry, incidental, often accidental *relation* to us into his *essence*, his most essential self, and claiming that *vis-à-vis* himself and the whole world, he is capable only of the very sort of relations we happened to experience with him once or on occasion? And still lurking beneath this genuine folly do we not find the most arrogant of all ulterior motives: that we ourselves must be the principle of good, because good and evil are apportioned according to us?

103

There are two kinds of deniers of morality.—"To deny morality," that can mean, *on the one hand*, to deny that the ethical[9] motivations people profess have really driven their actions—this is, in effect, the claim that morality exists in words and is among humanity's crudest and subtlest deceptions (namely self-deception), nowhere more so perhaps than with people most famed for their virtue. *On the other hand*, it can mean: to deny that ethical judgments are based on truths. In this case, it is granted that the motivations for an action are genuine, but that, in this manner, *errors* operate as the foundation of all ethical judgments and thus drive human beings to their moral actions. This is *my* viewpoint. Yet, I least of all would wish to fail to recognize that *in very many cases*, a sensitive mistrust such as expressed in the first viewpoint, in the spirit of La Roche-foucauld, is also justified and, by all means, of the greatest common advantage. Thus, I deny morality the same way I deny alchemy, which is to say, I deny its presuppositions, *not* however that there were alchemists who did believe in these presuppositions and acted in accordance with them. I also deny immorality: *not* that countless persons *feel* immoral, rather that there is in *truth* a reason to feel that way. As should be obvious—provided I'm not a fool—I don't deny that it is best to avoid and to struggle against many actions that are considered immoral; likewise that it is best to perform and promote many that are considered moral—but I maintain: the former should be avoided and the latter promoted *for different reasons than heretofore*. We must *learn to think differently*—in order finally, perhaps very late, to achieve even more: *to feel differently*.

104[10]

Our evaluations. —All actions may be traced back to evaluations, all evaluations are either *one's own* or are *adopted*[11]—the latter more often by far. Why do we adopt them? Out of fear—that is to say: we consider it more advisable to pretend as if they were our own—and we grow so accustomed to this pretense[12] that it ends up being our nature. One's own evaluation: that means gauging a thing in relation to the degree to which it gives precisely us and no one else pleasure or displeasure — something exceedingly rare! — But must not at least our evaluation of another, in which there lies the motive for, in most cases, our making use of *his* evaluation, emanate from us, be *our own* determination? Yes, but we arrive at it as *children* and rarely ever learn to change our view again; most often we are, throughout our lives, the dupe of the way we learned in childhood to judge our neighbors (their intellect, station, morality, exemplarity or reproachability) and to deem it necessary to pay homage to their evaluations.

105[13]

Pseudo-egotism. — No matter what they think or say about their "egotism," people, virtually without exception, nevertheless do nothing their whole life long for their ego, but instead for the phantom ego that has formed in the heads of those around them and been communicated to them — as a result, they all dwell together in a fog of impersonal, half-personal opinions and arbitrary, as it were, fictitious evaluations, one person always in the head of the other and then again this head in other heads: a curious world of phantasms that nonetheless knows how to don such a sensible appearance! This fog of opinions and habituations grows and lives almost independently of the people it envelops; within it lies the prodigious effect of general opinions about "the human being" — all these humans who do not even know one another believe in the bloodless abstraction "human being," that is to say, in a fiction; and every alteration in this abstraction brought about by individuals with power (like princes and philosophers) has an extraordinary and unreasonably strong effect on the great majority — all for the simple reason that no individual in this majority has access to any self-established, genuine ego that he could juxtapose to the common, pallid fiction and thereby destroy it.

106[14]

Against definitions of moral goals. — Everywhere these days one hears the goal of morality defined more or less as follows:

it is the preserving and advancing of humanity; but this amounts to a desire for a formula and nothing more. Preserving *what*?, one must immediately counter, advancing *where*?[15] Hasn't precisely the essential thing, the answer to this "What?" and "Where?" been left out of the formula? So what, then, can it contribute to the instruction of what our duty is other than what currently passes, tacitly and thoughtlessly, as already established? Can one discern sufficiently from the formula whether we ought to aim for the longest possible existence for humanity? Or the greatest possible de-animalization of humanity? How different in each case the means, in other words, practical morality, would have to be! Suppose one wanted to supply humanity with the highest possible degree of rationality: this would certainly not mean vouchsafing it its greatest possible longevity! Or suppose one thought of its "highest happiness" as the "What" and "Where": does that mean the greatest degree individual persons could gradually attain? Or a, by the way, utterly incalculable, yet ultimately attained average-bliss for everyone? And why is precisely morality supposed to be the way to get there? Hasn't morality, on the whole, opened up such abundant sources of displeasure that one could sooner judge that, heretofore, with every refinement in morality, human beings have grown *more and more dissatisfied* with themselves, their neighbor, and their lot? Hasn't the most moral person up to now been of the belief that, in the face of morality, the only legitimate human condition is one of *profoundest misery*?

107[16]

Our right to our folly. — How ought one to act? To what end ought one to act? In the case of an individual's most immediate and crudest needs, these questions are answered easily enough, but the more refined, extensive, and weighty the spheres of activity into which one ascends, the more uncertain, and hence more arbitrary, the answers will be. And yet it is here expressly that arbitrariness in decision making ought to be eliminated—the authority of morality demands as much: a vague fear and reverence are supposed to guide a person at once in precisely those actions whose ends and means are for him the least *immediately* clear of all! This authority of morality paralyzes thinking in matters where it could be dangerous to think *incorrectly*—in this fashion, it makes a habit of justifying itself before its detractors. Incorrectly, that means in this case "dangerously"—but dangerous for whom? Usually it is not actually the danger to the performer of the action whom the bearers of authoritative morality have in mind, but rather *their own* danger, the possible damage to their power and prestige the moment the right to act arbitrarily and foolishly according to one's own lesser or greater reason is granted to everyone—they *command* even when the questions: "How ought I to act? To what end ought I to act?" are hard enough, if not impossible, to answer.—And if humanity's *reason* grows so extraordinarily slowly that its growth through the whole course of humanity has often been denied: what bears more blame than the solemn presence, indeed omnipresence of moral commands that in no way permit the voicing of the *individual* question as to "To what end?" or "How?" Haven't we been raised *to feel pathetic* and to flee into the darkness at precisely the times when our understanding ought to function as clearly and impartially as possible! Namely, with all our higher and more important concerns.

108[17]

A few theses. Provided he wants to be happy, one ought not to give the individual any precepts regarding the path to happiness: for individual happiness springs from its own impenetrable laws; external precepts can only hinder and check it.—The precepts that one labels "moral" are, in truth, directed against individuals and are in no way aimed at promoting the happiness of individuals. These precepts are just as little concerned with the "happiness and welfare of humanity"—words completely impossible to attach distinct concepts to, let alone to utilize them as a guiding star on the dark ocean of moral aspirations. — It is not true, as the presumption would have it, that morality is more advantageous to the evolution of reason than immorality. — It is not true that the *unconscious goal* in the evolution of every conscious being (animal, human, humanity, etc.) is its "highest happiness": on the contrary, in all stages of evolution the only attainable happiness is special and incomparable, neither higher nor lower, but simply and exclusively its own. Evolution does not desire happiness; it wants evolution and nothing more. — Only if humanity had a universally recognized *goal* could one propound "such and such *should* be done": for the time being, there is no such goal. One should not, therefore, inflict the demands of morality onto humanity—that's nothing but irrationality and frivolity. — To *recommend* a goal to humanity is another matter entirely: then the goal is thought of as something that *is in keeping with our own discretion*; granted, if humanity were inclined toward the proposed goal, then it could, as a result, *give* itself a moral law—likewise, in keeping with its own discretion. Up until now, however, the moral law was supposed to stand *above* inclination: one did not so much want *to give* oneself this law as *to take* it from somewhere or *to discover* it somewhere or *to let oneself be commanded* from somewhere.

109[18]

Self-mastery and moderation and their ultimate motive. — I find no more than six essentially different methods of combating the intensity of a drive. For a start, one can avoid opportunities for gratification of the drive and through long and ever longer periods of abstinence cause it to weaken and wither away. Or else one can impose on oneself a strictly ordered regimen of gratification; by subsuming the drive in this fashion under a rule and enclosing its ebb and flow within fixed time periods, one gains intervals in which it no longer intrudes — and from that point one can perhaps proceed to the first method. Thirdly, one can intentionally give oneself over to wild, uncontrolled gratification of a drive in order to become disgusted with it and through this cultivated disgust to acquire power over the drive: provided one does not imitate the rider who drove his horse to death and broke his own neck in the process—which, unfortunately, happens more often than not with this attempt. Fourthly, there exists an intellectual ploy, namely, to yoke that gratification as such so tightly to some extremely distressing idea that, after a little practice, the idea of gratification will itself be experienced, always and immediately, as distressing (for example, when the Christian accustoms himself to feel the proximity and the derision of the devil during the pleasures of sex or eternal torments of hell for a vengeful murder or also merely the thought of the disdain that would result in the eyes of the people he admires most if, for instance, he were to steal money or, as many have done a hundred times before, a person counteracts the fervent desire to commit suicide with the representation of the lamentation and self-imprecations on the part of family and friends and has managed thereby to keep holding onto life by a thin thread—after a while, these representations follow one another in his mind like cause and effect). The same operation is in play when an individual's pride rears up, as for example with Lord Byron and Napoleon, and one experiences as an offense the dominance of a single affect over one's total deportment and over reason's regulation: from which arises the habit and the pleasure of tyrannizing the drive and, as it were, making it gnash its teeth. ("I refuse to be a slave to any appetite"[19]—wrote Byron in his journal.) Fifthly: one undertakes a dislocation of one's energy resources by imposing an especially difficult and strenuous task on oneself or by intentionally subjecting oneself to new stimulations and pleasures, thereby directing thoughts and physical energy into other channels. It amounts to the same thing if, from time to time, one favors a different drive, giving it plenty of opportunity for gratification, thus turning it into the wastrel of the very energy through which otherwise the impetuous and therefore burdensome drive would seize control. There are also

those people who know full well how to keep in check the specific drive that would like to play lord and master by offering
all their other known drives an occasional cajoling and festive
spree and bidding them consume the fodder that the tyrant
wants to have all to himself. Finally, number six: anyone who
finds it reasonable and can stand to debilitate and oppress one's
entire physical and spiritual constitution naturally achieves
the goal of debilitating a particularly vehement drive as well; as
does, for example, the person who, just like the ascetic, starves
his sensuality and, in the process, starves and spoils certainly
his vigor also and not infrequently his understanding. — So:
avoiding the opportunities, planting regularity into the drive,
generating supersatiation and disgust, effecting an association
of an agonizing thought (such as shame, dire consequences, or
offended pride), then the dislocation of energies, and finally
general debilitation and exhaustion — these are the six methods: the fact, however, *that* one *wants* to combat the vehemence
of a drive in the first place is not in our control at all, no matter
which method one falls back on, no matter whether one is
successful or not. On the contrary, in this whole process our
intellect is manifestly only the blind tool of *another drive* that
is the *rival* of the one tormenting us with its vehemence: be it
the drive for quietude, fear of shame and other evil consequences, or love. Whereas "we" believe ourselves to be complaining about the vehemence of a drive, it is, at bottom, one
drive *that is complaining about another*: in other words: any time
we perceive such *vehemence* in suffering, we can be sure that
there exists another equally, if not more vehement drive and that
a *battle* is in store in which our intellect will have to take sides.

110[20]

What sets itself in opposition. — One can observe in oneself
the following process and I wish it were often observed and
confirmed. Somewhere inside us we pick up the scent of a type
of *pleasure* we haven't yet enjoyed and consequently a new *desire* results. Now, at this point, everything depends on *what*

sets itself *in opposition* to this desire: if it is matters and considerations of minor consequence and also people who count for little in our esteem—then the new desire's goal[21] is cloaked with the sentiment "noble, good, worthy of praise and sacrifice" and the entire bequeathed moral predisposition now receives it into its rank and adds it to its store of goals that are felt to be moral—from then on we believe we are no longer striving for pleasure but for morality: which greatly enhances the self-assurance of our striving.

III

To the admirers of objectivity.—Anyone who, as a child, perceived diverse and powerful feelings on the part of relatives and acquaintances among whom he grew up without, however, their having much subtlety of judgment and pleasure in intellectual honesty—and who has consequently exhausted his best time and energy in the imitation of feelings—will notice about himself as an adult that every new thing, every new person immediately excites in him attraction or revulsion, envy or disgust; under the weight of this experience, against which he feels powerless, he admires *neutrality of sentiment* or "objectivity" as a thing of wonder, a matter of genius or of the rarest morality, and refuses to believe that it too is merely an *offshoot of discipline and habit.*

112

On the natural history of duty and right.—Our duties—these are the rights others have over us. How did they acquire them? In that they assumed us capable of contract and requital, in that they took us to be similar and equal to themselves and, as a result, entrusted us with something, educated, reproved, and supported us. We fulfill our duty—that is to say: we vindicate that conception of our power according to which everything was bestowed upon us, we give back in the same measure as was given to us. It is thus our pride that bids us do our duty—whenever we counter something others did for us with something we do for them, we are seeking to reestablish our own majesty of self—for with their deeds those others have intervened in our sphere of power and would continually have their hand in it if we did not practice, in the form of "duty," a counter-requital, in other words, an invasion into their power. The rights of others can refer only to what lies within our power; it would be irrational if they wanted something from us that did not belong to us proper. More precisely, one must say: only to what they believe lies within our power, assuming it is something we believe also lies within our power. The same error could easily exist on both sides: the feeling of duty results from our having the same *belief* as everyone else regarding the extent of our power: namely, that we *are capable* of promising certain things and of obligating ourselves to them ("free will"). — My rights: these are that part of my power that others not only have conceded to me but also wish me to maintain. How do these others come to such a point? First: through their prudence and fear and circumspection: maybe they expect something similar from us in return (protection of their rights), maybe they consider a battle with us to be dangerous or inexpedient, maybe they view every diminution of our strength as a disadvantage because we then become unsuitable as an alliance with them against a hostile third power. Then: through donation and cession. In this case the others have enough, and more than enough, power to be able to surrender some of it and to vouchsafe him to whom they donated the surrendered portion: one presumes thereby an inferior feeling of power on the part of the person who permits himself to receive the donation. Thus do rights arise: as recognized and guaranteed degrees of power. The moment power relationships shift significantly, rights disappear and new ones are established—as is evidenced in the perpetual disintegration and re-formation of rights among nations. The moment our power decreases significantly there occurs an alteration in the sentiment of those who have heretofore guaranteed our power: they calculate whether they can restore us to our former plenitude—if they don't feel in a position to do so, then from that point on they disavow our "rights." Likewise, if our power increases considerably, there occurs an alteration in the sentiment of those who heretofore acknowledged it and whose acknowledgment we no longer need: no doubt they attempt to suppress our power to its former dimension; they will want to intervene and in the process they appeal to their "duty," — but that is merely useless verbiage. Wherever a right *prevails*, a condition and degree of power are being maintained, a decrease and increase being averted. The rights of others constitute a concession by our feeling of power to the feeling of power of these others. If our power appears to be profoundly shaken and broken, then our rights cease to exist: on the other hand, if we have become much more powerful, the rights of others such as we have conceded them heretofore cease to exist for us. The "fair-minded" person constantly requires the subtle tact of a balance: in order to weigh the degrees of power and right, which, given the transitory nature of human affairs, will invariably remain suspended in equilibrium only for a short time, but for the most part will sink or rise: consequently, to be fair-minded is difficult and demands a lot of practice, ⟨a lot of⟩[22] good will, and a whole lot of very fine *spirit*.[23] —

113[24]

The striving for distinction. — The striving for distinction constantly keeps an eye on every next person coming its way[25] and wants to know his thoughts and how he's feeling: but the empathy and the being-in-the-know, which this drive requires for its gratification, are far from harmless or compassionate or benevolent. On the contrary, we want to perceive or to divine how, outwardly or inwardly, we cause this next person *to suffer*, how he loses control over himself and surrenders to the impression that our hand or even merely the sight of us makes upon him; even when the striver for distinction makes, and intended to make, a joyous, uplifting, cheerful impression, he by no means enjoys this success inasmuch as he brought joy to the person coming his way or uplifted or cheered him, but, rather, inasmuch as he *put his imprint* on the soul of that next person, altered its form, and held sway over it according to his own will. The striving for distinction is the striving for domination—be it very indirect and only sensed or even only imagined—of the other. There exists a long series of degrees of this secretly coveted domination and a complete catalogue of them would almost amount to a history of culture from the earliest, still grotesque barbarism on up to the grotesquerie of overrefinement and morbid idealism. Striving for distinction entails *for the next person*—to name only a few of the steps on this long ladder—torments, then blows, then terror, then fearful amazement, then wonderment, then envy, then admiration, then exaltation, then joy, then serenity, then laughter, then derision, then ridicule, then jeering, then dealing out blows, then inflicting torments: here at the end of the ladder stands the *ascetic* and martyr who experiences the highest pleasure precisely in himself enduring, as a result of his striving for distinction, exactly the same suffering that his counterpart on the first rung of the ladder, the *barbarian*, inflicts on the other through whom and before whom he wants to distinguish himself. The ascetic's triumph over himself, his eye trained inward throughout, beholding the human being cloven asunder into sufferer and spectator and henceforward only glancing into the exterior world in order, as it were, to gather from it wood for its own funeral pyre, this the last tragedy of the striving for distinction whereby there remains only a Single Character who burns to ash inside—that is the worthy conclusion that belongs to the beginning: in both places an unspeakable happiness at the *sight of torments*! Indeed, happiness, understood as the liveliest feeling of power, has perhaps never been greater than in the souls of superstitious ascetics. The Brahmans express this in the story of King Visvamitra,[26] who, from thousands of years *doing penance*, derived such strength that he undertook to build a new *heaven*. I believe that with regard to this entire species of inner experiences we

are rank neophytes gropingly guessing at riddles; four thousand years ago they knew more about these infamous subtleties of self-enjoyment. Creation of the world: maybe in those
days an Indian dreamer conceived of it as an ascetic procedure
that a god performs on himself. Maybe the god wanted to banish himself inside agitated nature, as in an instrument of torture, in order thereby to feel doubly his bliss and power! And
supposing it was even a god of love: what pleasure for such a
god to create people who *suffer* and, at the sight of their ceaseless torment, to suffer really divinely and superhumanly and,
by this means, to exercise tyranny over himself! And even supposing it was not only a god of love but also a god of holiness
and sinlessness: what imaginable deliriums on the part of the
divine ascetic when he creates sin and sinner and eternal dam-
nations and, beneath his heaven and throne, a monstrous site
of eternal torture and eternal groaning and moaning! It is not
totally impossible that, sometime or other, the souls of Paul
and Dante[27] and Calvin[28] and their like also penetrated the
gruesome mysteries of such debaucheries of power—and faced
with such souls one can ask: indeed, has the circle of striving
for distinction really come to an end and played itself out with
the ascetic? Could not this circle be circumscribed again from
the beginning, adhering firmly to the basic disposition of the
ascetic and simultaneously to that of the pitying god? In other
words, doing hurt unto others in order thereby to hurt *oneself*
and thus once again to triumph over oneself and one's pity and
to luxuriate in utmost power!—Excuse the excess in the consideration of all that may have been possible on earth as a result
of the psychical excess of the lust for power.

114[29]

On the sufferer's knowledge.—The condition of the infirm
who are tormented terribly and for a long time by their suffering and whose minds nonetheless remain unclouded is not
without value with regard to knowledge—quite apart from
the intellectual benefits that come with every profound soli-

tude, every sudden and licensed release from all duties and customs. From within his condition the heavy sufferer looks *out* onto things with a terrifying coldness: for him all those little deceitful enchantments in which things usually swim when regarded by the healthy eye disappear: in fact, even he himself lies before himself void of flesh and hue. Supposing that until that point he was living in some sort of dangerous fantasy world: this supreme sobering up through pain is the means to tear him out of it: and perhaps the only means. (It is possible that the founder of Christianity encountered this on the cross: for the bitterest of all utterances— "My God, why hast thou forsaken me!"[30]— understood in the full profundity with which it should be understood, bears witness to universal disappointment[31] and enlightenment as to the delusion that was his life; in the moment of supreme agony he became clairvoyant regarding himself, just as did, according to the writer, the poor dying Don Quixote.[32]) The prodigious straining of the intellect, which wants to resist the pain, causes everything he now looks at to shine in a new light: and the indescribable attraction that all new illumination imparts is often powerful enough to defy all enticements toward suicide and to make continuing to live appear highly desirable to the sufferer. He thinks back with contempt on the warm, cozy, misty world in which the healthy person lives his life without a second thought; he thinks back with contempt on the most noble and cherished illusions in which he used to indulge himself in days gone by; he takes pleasure in conjuring up this contempt as if from the deepest hell and in thus causing his soul the bitterest of suffering: precisely by means of this counterweight does he withstand the physical pain— he senses that this counterweight is just what is necessary at the moment! With ghastly clairvoyance regarding his own essence, he cries to himself, "for once be your own accuser and executioner, accept for once your suffering as the punishment you have pronounced upon yourself! Enjoy your superiority as judge; even more: enjoy your capricious pleasure, your tyrannical arbitrariness! Elevate yourself above your life as above your suffering, look down into the depths of meaning and of meaninglessness!" Our pride swells up as never before: it finds an incomparable appeal[33] in opposing a tyrant the likes of pain and in rejecting all the whisperings with which it tempts us to disparage life—and instead, in *advocating life* against the tyrant. In this state, one resists to the death all pessimism lest it appear to be a *consequence* of our state and humiliate us as one who has been defeated. By the same token, the appeal of exercising justness in judgment has never been greater than now, for now it constitutes a triumph over ourselves and over the most sensitive of all states, a triumph that would render any unjustness in judgment exculpable—but we don't want to be exculpated, precisely at this moment we want to demonstrate that we can be "without culpability." We find ourselves in veritable paroxysms of pride.—And then comes the first twilight glimmer of alleviation, of recovery— and almost the first effect is that we resist the supremacy of our pride; we call it foolish and vain—as if we had experienced anything! Without gratitude, we humble the almighty pride that had just allowed us to endure the pain and we vehemently demand antidotal venom for our pride: we want to become estranged from ourselves and depersonalized after the pain has made us *personal* too forcefully and for too long a time. "Away, away with this pride," we shout, "it was a malady and a seizure like any other!" We begin to pay attention again to people and to nature—with a more longing eye: smiling ruefully, we remember that we now have come to know certain things about them in a new and different way than before, that a veil has fallen—but it *restores* us so to view once more the *subdued lights of life* and to step out of the horrible, sober brightness in which, as a sufferer, we saw and saw through things. We don't grow angry when the enchantments of health resume their play—we look on as if transformed, kind and still weary. In this state, one cannot listen to music without weeping.—

115

The so-called "ego." — Language and the prejudices[34] upon which language is based hinder in many ways our understanding of inner processes and drives: for example, through the fact that words actually exist only for *superlative* degrees of these processes and drives — but then when words are lacking, we tend no longer to engage in precise observation because it is painfully awkward for us to think precisely at that juncture; indeed, in former times one concluded involuntarily that wherever the domain of words ceased there ceased as well the domain of existence. Wrath, hate, love, compassion, craving, knowing, joy, pain — these are all names for *extreme* states: the milder middle degrees, to say nothing of the lower ones that are constantly in play, elude us and yet it is precisely they that weave the web of our character and our destiny. Very often those extreme outbursts — and even the most moderate like or dislike that *we register* in eating a particular dish or hearing a certain tone is perhaps still, properly appraised, an extreme outburst — rend the web and are then violent exceptions, usually as a result of pent-up congestions — and, as such, how quickly they are able to mislead the observer! No less quickly than they mislead the person of action. *We are none of us what* we appear to be solely in those states for which we have consciousness and words — and hence praise and censure; we *misconstrue* ourselves according to these cruder outbursts, which are the only ones we register; we draw a conclusion from material in which the exceptions outweigh the rule, we misread ourselves in this seemingly clearest block print of the Self. *Our opinion of ourselves*, however, at which we have arrived through this mistaken route, the so-called "ego," collaborates from now on in the formation of our character and destiny. —

116

The unknown world of the "subject." — From earliest times to the present, the thing so difficult for humans to comprehend is their ignorance of themselves! Not only regarding good and evil, but regarding matters much more essential! The age-old delusion that one knows, knows just exactly in every instance *how human action comes about*, still lives on. Not only "God who sees into the heart," not only the doer who reflects on his deed—no, in addition, every other person does not doubt that he understands what is essential in the occurrence of every other person's action. "I know what I want, what I've done, I'm free and take responsibility for it, I hold others responsible, I can call by name all ethical possibilities and all inner motives that exist in the face of an action; no matter how you might act—in whatever situation I'll understand myself and you all!"—That's how everyone used to think, that's how everyone more or less still thinks today. Socrates and Plato, in this matter great skeptics and admirable innovators, were nonetheless innocent believers with regard to the most disastrous of prejudices,[35] the most profound of errors, that "the proper action *must follow* upon knowledge of what is appropriate,"—in this axiom they were still the heirs of the universal madness and presumption: that there is such a thing as knowledge regarding the essential nature of an action. "It would indeed be *terrifying* if insight into the nature of the proper deed were not followed by the deed itself"—such is the only manner of proof for this thought that those great thinkers deemed necessary, the contrary seemed to them unthinkable and insane—and yet this contrary is precisely the naked reality, proven daily and hourly from time immemorial! Is it not precisely the "terrifying" truth: that whatever one can know about a deed *never* suffices to guarantee its being carried out, that, in no single instance, has the distance between knowledge and deed ever yet been bridged. Actions are *never* what they appear to us to be! It took so much effort for us to learn that external things are not what they appear to us—now then! It is just the same with the inner world! Moral actions are, in truth, "something other" than moral truths—more we cannot say: and all actions are essentially unknown. Belief in the opposite was and is universal: we have the oldest realism operating against us; up until now humanity thought: "an action is what it appears to us to be." (Upon rereading these words, I am reminded of a very explicit passage in Schopenhauer, which I wish to quote in order to demonstrate that he too, indeed without any scruple whatsoever, was still caught up in, as well as caught up by, this moral realism: "every one of us is really a competent and perfectly moral judge exhibiting exact knowledge of good and evil, holy in that we love good and abhor evil—every one of us is all this insofar as it is not our own actions but those of others that are being investigated and we have merely to approve or disapprove, while the burden of carrying out the actions rests on the shoulders of others. Accordingly everyone can, as father confessor, completely stand in for God."[36])

117

In prison. — My eye, however strong or weak it happens to be, sees only a circumscribed distance, and within this circumscription I live and act;[37] this line of horizon constitutes, in matters great and small, my immediate fate[38] from which I cannot escape. In this way, there forms around every being a concentric circle that has a midpoint and that is unique to him. Our ear encloses us within a similarly small space as does our sense of touch. It is according to these horizons, within which our senses enclose each of us as if behind prison walls, that we now *measure* the world, we call this thing near and that distant, this thing large and that small, this thing hard and that soft: this measuring we call perception—and it is all, each and every bit, errors through and through! According to the number of experiences and stimuli we are, on the average, capable of having within a given period, we measure our lives as long or short, rich or poor, full or empty: and according to the average duration of the human being's life, we measure the life of all other creatures—it is all, each and every bit, errors through and through! If we had eyes a hundred times more sensitive to proximity, then humans would appear monstrously tall to us; indeed, it is possible to imagine organs by dint of which humans would be perceived as immeasurable. On the other hand, organs could be so constituted that entire solar systems were perceived as contracted and constricted like a single cell: and to beings of a contrasting nature, a single cell of the human body could present itself as a solar system in motion with organization and harmony. The habits of our senses have woven us into perception's wile and guile: it, in turn, is the foundation for all our judgments and forms of "knowledge"—there is no escape whatsoever, no underused or underhanded way into the *real* world! We hang within our web, we spiders, and no matter what we capture in it, we can capture nothing whatsoever other than what allows itself to be captured precisely in *our* web.

118[39]

What is our neighbor[40] after all!—What do we comprehend about our neighbor after all, other than his boundaries, I mean that by which he, as it were, inscribes himself in and impresses himself on us? We understand nothing of him except the *alterations in us* of which he is the cause—our knowledge of him resembles a *formed* hollow space. We ascribe to him the sensations that his actions evoked in us and thus impart to him a mistaken, inverse positivity. In accordance with our knowledge of ourselves, we mold him into a satellite of our own system: and when he shines for us or grows dark, and in either case we are the ultimate cause—we nonetheless believe the opposite! World of phantoms in which we live! Inverted, topsy-turvy, empty world, dreamed *full* and *upright* nonetheless.

119

Experience and make-believe.[41]—No matter how hard a person struggles for self-knowledge, nothing can be more incomplete than the image of all the *drives* taken together that constitute his being. Scarcely can he call the cruder ones by name:

their number and strength, their ebb and flow, their play and counterplay, and, above all, the laws of their *alimentation* remain completely unknown to him. This alimentation thus becomes the work of chance: our daily experiences toss willy-nilly to this drive or that drive some prey or other that it seizes greedily, but the whole coming and going of these events exists completely apart from any meaningful connection to the alimentary needs of the sum drives: so that the result will always be twofold: the starving and stunting of some drives and the overstuffing of others. With every moment of our lives some of the polyp-arms of our being grow and others dry up, depending on the nourishment that the moment does or does not supply. As stated earlier, all our experiences are, in this sense, types of nourishment—seeds sown, however, with a blind hand devoid of any knowledge as to who hungers and who already has abundance. And as a consequence of this contingent alimentation of the parts, the whole, fully grown polyp turns out to be a creature no less contingent than is its maturation. Said more clearly: Suppose a drive finds itself at the point where it desires gratification—or the exercise of its energy, or the discharge of it, or the satiation of an emptiness—it's all a matter of speaking in images—: then it observes each of the day's occurrences with a view as to how to make use of them for its own end: whether a person be moving or still or angry or reading or speaking or fighting or rejoicing, the drive, in its thirst, fingers, as it were, every situation the person gets into and, on the average, finds nothing there for itself; it must wait and thirst all the more: a little while longer and it grows faint, a few days or months more of no gratification and then it withers up like a plant without rain. Perhaps this cruelty of chance would spring to mind more vividly if all drives wanted to take matters as seriously as does *hunger*: which refuses to be appeased by *dream food*; most drives, however, especially the so-called moral ones, *do exactly that*: if you will permit my suspicion that our *dreams* have precisely the value and meaning of *compensating* to a certain

degree for that contingent absence of "nourishment" during the
day. Why was yesterday's dream full of tenderness and tears,
the one from the day before playful and high-spirited, an earlier one adventurous and full of constant, melancholy seeking?
Why in one dream do I enjoy the indescribable, variform
beauty of music, why in another, blissful as an eagle, do I fly
and soar up and away to the distant mountain tops?[42] These
sorts of make-believe, which give discharge and free rein to
our drives for tenderness or playfulness or adventure, or to our
desire for music and mountain ranges—and everyone will
have on hand his own set of more striking examples—are
interpretations of our nerve impulses during sleep, *very free*,
very arbitrary interpretations of movements of blood and in-
testines, of the pressure of an arm and of bedclothes, of the
sounds from the bell tower, from weathercocks, moths and
other things of this sort.[43] That this text, which, after all,
generally speaking remains pretty much the same from night
to night, should elicit such divergent commentary, that the
make-believing faculty of reason[44] *imagines* today and yesterday
such divergent *causes* for the same nerve impulses: the explanation for this is that today the prompter of this reason is different from yesterday's—a different *drive* wanted to gratify
itself, activate, exercise, invigorate, discharge itself—this
particular drive was at high tide, and yesterday a different one
was surging.—Waking life doesn't have the same *freedom* of
interpretation as dreaming does, it is less poetic and unbridled—but do I have to explain that when we are awake, our
drives, likewise, do nothing but interpret nerve impulses and
ascribe "causes" to them according to our drives' own needs?
That between waking and dreaming no *essential* difference exists? That in comparing very different stages of culture, the
freedom of waking interpretation in the one in no way even
lags behind the freedom of the other while dreaming? that our
moral judgments and evaluations are, as well, mere images
and fantasies stemming from a physiological process we know
nothing of, a kind of acquired language for denoting various

nerve impulses? That all our so-called consciousness is a more or less fantastical commentary on an unknown, perhaps unknowable, yet felt text?—Take a quotidian experience. Suppose one day at the marketplace we notice someone laughing at us as we pass by: depending on whether this or that drive happens to be surging in us at the moment, the event will assume for us this or that meaning—and depending on the type of person we are, it will be a completely different event. One person takes it in like a drop of rain, another shakes it off like an insect, one tries to pick a fight, another checks his clothes to see if there's a reason to laugh, yet another is moved to reflect on the nature of laughter *per se*, and someone else takes pleasure in having added a ray, unintentionally no less, to the sunshine and cheeriness in the world—and in every case it is a drive that is being gratified, be it the drive for anger or truculence or reflection or benevolence. The drive seized the incident as its prey: why this particular drive? Because, thirsty and starving, it was lurking in wait.—One morning recently at eleven o'clock a man suddenly collapsed directly in front of me as if struck by lightning, all the women in the vicinity cried aloud; for my part, I set him on his feet and attended to him until he regained his speech—during this time not a muscle of my face moved nor did there stir in me any emotion whatsoever, either of fright or of compassion; I did what was obvious and sensible and went dispassionately on my way. Suppose I had been informed the day before that tomorrow at eleven o'clock someone would crash to the ground in front of me like that—I would have suffered all manner of torments ahead of time, would not have slept the whole night through, and at the moment of truth, instead of helping the man, would perhaps have acted as he had done. For during the interval every existing drive would have *had time* to imagine the experience and to render its commentary on it.—What then are our experiences? Much *more* what we put in them than what is in them already! Or must we go so far as to claim: In and of themselves, there is nothing in them! To experience is to make believe?—

120

To reassure the skeptic. — "I have no idea what I'm *doing*! I have no idea what I *should do*!" You're right, but make no mistake about it: *you are being done*! moment by every moment! Humanity has, through all ages, confused the active and the passive, it is its everlasting grammatical blunder.[45]

121 [46]

"Cause and effect!" — Something transpires on this mirror — and our intellect is a mirror — that evinces regularity, one particular thing follows each and every time upon another particular thing — we *label* that, if we perceive it and want to give it a name, cause and effect, we fools! As though we had understood or could understand something or other here! We have indeed seen nothing other than *images* of cause and effect! And precisely this *imagery* renders impossible any insight into a connection more essential than that of plain succession!

122 [47]

Purposes in nature. — Any impartial researcher who pursues the history of the eye along with the forms it takes among the lower creatures, and who demonstrates the entire, step-by-step evolution of the eye, inevitably reaches the grand conclusion: that sight was *not* the intention behind the origin of the eye; on the contrary, it turned up once *chance* had brought the apparatus together. One single such example: and "purposes" fall away like scales from our eyes!

123

Reason. — How did reason come into the world? As is only fitting, in an unreasonable way, by a coincidence. We will just have to figure it out like a riddle.[48,49]

124[50]

What does it mean to want! — We laugh at anyone who steps out of his chamber the moment the sun exits its own and says, "*I want* the sun to rise"; and at anyone who cannot stop a wheel from rolling and says: "*I want* it to roll"; and at anyone who is thrown down in a wrestling match and says: "Here I lie, but *I want* to lie here!" Yet, despite all the laughter! Are we, after all, ever acting any differently from one of these three whenever we use the phrase: "*I want*"?

125[51]

Concerning the "realm of freedom." — We are able to think many, many more things than we can do or experience — that is to say, our thinking is superficial and satisfied with the surface, indeed, it doesn't even notice it's the surface. Had our intellect *evolved* strictly according to the measure of our strength and the measure of its employment, then the uppermost principle of our thinking would be that we can comprehend only what we can *do* — *if* such a thing as comprehension exists at all. A person is thirsty and without water, but his thoughts constantly create an image of water before his mind's eye as if nothing could be easier to procure — the superficial and easily satisfied type of intellect cannot grasp the suffering agony of real need and feels superior on this account: it is proud of being able to do more, to run faster, to reach its goal almost instantaneously — and thus in comparison with the realm of doing, wanting, and experiencing, the realm of thoughts appears to be a *realm of freedom*: whereas, as stated, it is only a realm of surface and complacency.

126

Forgetting. — It has yet to be proven that there is such a thing as forgetting; all we know is that the act of remembering is not within our power. For the time being we have placed the word "forgetting" into this gap in our power: as if it were but one more faculty to add to our collection. But what, in the end, does lie within our power!—If that word plugs a gap in our power, shouldn't there be other words to plug the gap in our *knowledge about our power*?

127

For a purpose.—Of all actions, the ones least understood are those undertaken for a purpose, no doubt because they have always passed for the most intelligible and are to our way of thinking the most commonplace. The great problems are right before one's very eyes.

128

Dream and responsibility.—You wish to take responsibility for everything! Only not for your dreams! What miserable frailty, what poverty in the courage of your convictions! Nothing is *more* your own than your dreams! Nothing more *your* work! Content, form, duration, actor, spectator—in these comedies you yourselves are everything! And this is just the place in yourselves you shun and are ashamed of, and even Oedipus, the wise Oedipus, knew how to derive consolation from the idea that we cannot do anything about what it is we dream![52] I conclude from this: that the vast majority of human beings must be aware that they have abhorrent dreams. Were it otherwise: how greatly this nocturnal poeticizing would have been plundered to bolster human arrogance!—Do I have to add that wise Oedipus was right, that we really aren't responsible for our dreams, but no more so for our waking hours either, and that the doctrine of free will has as its mother and father human pride and the human feeling of power? Perhaps I say this too often: but at least that doesn't turn it into an error.

129[53]

The supposed clash of motives.—One speaks of a "clash of motives," but designates with the term a clash that is *not* the clash of motives. Namely: before we perform an action, the *consequences* of all the different actions we believe ourselves capable of undertaking march across our reflective consciousness one after the other, and we compare these consequences. We believe we have decided on a particular action once we have determined that its consequences will be the predominantly more advantageous ones; before we come to this conclusion in our deliberation, we often honestly torture ourselves on account of the great difficulties involved in divining the consequences, seeing them in their full force, and in fact seeing all of them without committing the mistake of omission: whereby, moreover, chance still has to be factored into the equation. Indeed, to come to the most difficult point: all the consequences that, even on their own, are so difficult to determine must now be weighed side by side on a *single* scale against one another; and due to the difference in the *quality* of all these possible consequences, we all too frequently lack the proper scale and weights for this casuistry of advantage. Let's assume, however, that we were able to work all this out and that contingency placed onto the scales consequences that balanced each other out: then we do in fact now possess in our *image of the consequences* of *one* particular action a *motive* for performing just this action — Yes, *one* motive! But at the moment we finally act, we are often enough driven by a category of motives different from those discussed here as the category "image of consequences." At this point there comes into play the way we customarily expend our energy, or a slight provocation from a person whom we fear or honor or love, or indolence, which prefers to do what's closest at hand, or the excitation of our imagination brought on by whatever trivial occurrence comes our way at the decisive moment; completely incalculable somatic factors come into play, caprice and mood come into play, the surge of some distress or other, which, coincidentally, at that precise instant, happens to be at the bursting point, comes into play: in short, there come into play motives that we in part do not recognize at all and in part recognize only very dimly, motives that we can *never* compare with one another and take account of *in advance. In all likelihood*, a clash takes place among them as well, a pressing to and fro, a balancing and counterbalancing of the various parts—and this would be the actual "clash of motives": something completely invisible to us of which we are equally unconscious. I have calculated the consequences and outcomes[54] and have thus set one very essential motive into the battle line of motives—but as for the battle line itself, I in no way set it up, nor can I even see it: the clash itself, and likewise the victory, as victory are hidden from me: for even though I do indeed learn what it is I end up *doing*—I do not learn which motive actually was thus crowned victorious. *But we are certainly accustomed not* to take all these unconscious processes into account and to think about preparing for an action only to the extent that it is conscious: and thus we confuse the clash of motives with our comparison of the possible consequences of different actions—a confusion itself extraordinarily rife with consequences, and one most disastrous for the development of morality!

130[55]

Purposes? Will?—We have grown accustomed to believing in two realms, the realm of *purposes* and *will* and the realm of *chance events*;[56] in the latter everything is senseless, things in it come and go, stand and fall without anyone's being able to say why? or to what end?—We are afraid of this powerful realm of great cosmic stupidity, for we most often come to know it when it falls like a slate tile from the rooftop into the other world, the one of purposes and intentions, and strikes dead some precious purpose of ours. This belief in the two realms is an age-old romance and fable: we clever dwarfs with our will and our purposes are harassed, overrun, and often trampled to death by those stupid, arch-stupid giants, the Chance Events—but in spite of all this, we would not wish to be without the terrifying poesy of their proximity, for often, when life within the *spiderweb* of purposes has grown too boring or too frightening, these monsters come along and provide us with a sublime diversion in that their hand suddenly *destroys* the whole web—not that they intended to, these irrational brutes! Not that they even noticed! But their crude bony hands break through our web as if it were air.—The Greeks called this realm of the incalculable and of sublime everlasting philistinism Moira[57] and placed it around their gods as the horizon beyond which they could neither see nor exert any control: herein they display that secret defiance of the gods met with among many peoples in the following form: they worship the gods, to be sure, all the while holding up their sleeve a final trump card against them,[58] as, for example, when the Indians or Persians believe their gods to be dependent upon human *sacrifice* so that in the worst case, the mortals could let the gods go hungry until they starved to death; or when the austere melancholy Scandinavian,[59] in his conception of an impending twilight of the gods,[60] creates for himself the pleasure of silent revenge as recompense for the fear that his spiteful gods constantly evoke in him. Christianity is different; neither Indian nor Persian nor Greek nor Scandinavian,[61] its quintessential emotion would have us bow down in dust to worship *the spirit of power* and kiss even the dust itself: this made it clear that the almighty "realm of stupidity" is not as stupid as it looked, that instead *we* are the stupid ones who didn't notice that standing behind it was—dear old God, who does indeed love to work in dark, twisted, and mysterious ways,[62] but who certainly always makes things "turn out gloriously" in the end. This new fable about dear old God, who up until then had been mistaken for a race of giants or for Moira and who alone weaves the purposes and the web, finer even than those of our understanding—so that they appear, and indeed *would have* to appear incomprehensible to it—this fable offered such a bold inversion and such a daring paradox that the ancient world, having grown too subtle,[63] could not resist it no matter how mad and *contradictory* the thing sounded—for, spoken in confidence, there was a contradiction in it: if our understanding cannot make out the understanding and purposes of God, how could it come to make out this aspect of its understanding? And this aspect of God's understanding? — In fact, as of late, skepticism has been mounting rapidly as to whether the slate tile that falls from the rooftop is thrown down by "divine love" after all — and people are beginning once again to pick up the trace of the old romance of giants and dwarfs. Let us *learn* therefore, because it is high time we did: in our supposedly favored realm of purposes and reason, the giants rule as well! And our purposes and our reason are not dwarfs, but giants! And our own webs are destroyed just as often and just as coarsely *by our own doing* as by slate tiles! And not everything that is so labeled is a purpose, even less so is everything that passes for will truly will! And should you wish to conclude from this: "there is therefore only *one* realm, that of chance events and stupidity?" — then one must add: Yes, perhaps there is only *one* realm, perhaps there is no such thing as will and purposes and we just imagined them. Those iron hands of necessity, which shake the dice-cup of chance, play their never-ending game so long that rolls of the dice, which completely resemble purposiveness and rationality of every degree, *must* turn up. *Perhaps* our acts of will, our purposes, are nothing other than just such rolls of the dice — and we are merely too limited and too vain to comprehend our utmost limitation: namely, that we ourselves shake the dice-cup with iron hands, that even in our intentional actions we ourselves do nothing more than play the game of necessity. Perhaps! — In order to get beyond this *perhaps* one would have to have been already a guest in the underworld and beyond all surfaces and to have sat at Persephone's table, rolling dice and betting with the goddess herself.[64]

131[65]

Moral fashions. — What a shift there has been in the whole panoply of moral judgments! Those greatest marvels of antique morality, Epictetus, for example, had no concept of the now common glorification of thinking about others or of living for others; according to our moral fashion, we would have to brand them downright immoral, for they fought with all their might *for* their ego and *against* empathy with others (particularly with the suffering and moral frailties of others). Perhaps they would reply to us: "If to your own selves you are such boring or loathsome objects, go right ahead and think of others more than yourselves. You're doing the right thing by it."

132[66]

The last gasp[67] *of Christianness in morality.* — "*On n'est bon que par la pitié: il faut donc qu'il y ait quelque pitié dans tous nos sentiments*"[68] — that is the sound of morality these days. And where does it come from? That the person whose actions are congenial, disinterested, generally useful, and affable is now felt to be prototypically *moral*— that is perhaps the most pervasive effect and change of heart wrought on Europe by Christianity: although it was neither its intention nor its teaching. But it was the residuum, what was left of Christian sentiments once the extremely antithetical, strictly egotistical foundational belief in the "one thing needful,"[69] in the supreme importance of eternal, *personal* salvation, along with the dogmas upon which it rested, gradually receded and into the foreground was shoved the ancillary belief in "love," in "love thy neighbor,"[70] harmonizing with the prodigious practical consequences of ecclesiastical charity. The more one disassociated oneself from these dogmas, the more one sought, as it were, the *justification* for this disassociation in a cult of love for humanity: not to lag behind the Christian ideal in this matter, but *to surpass it* wherever possible was a secret spur of all French freethinkers from Voltaire through to Auguste Comte: and with his famous moral formula, "*vivre pour autrui*,"[71] the latter did in fact outchristian Christianity. On German soil, it was Schopenhauer, on English John Stuart Mill who made most famous the teaching of sympathetic affects and of compassion, or the benefit of others, as the principle of action:[72]

but they themselves were only an echo—with powerful ger-
minating force, those teachings were sprouting up everywhere
in both the finest and the crudest forms from about the time
of the French Revolution onward, and all socialist systems
have, as if involuntarily, rooted themselves in the common
ground of these teachings. There is today perhaps no more
firmly held prejudice[73] than this: that one *knows* what actually
constitutes morality. It seems *to do* every single person *good*
these days to hear that society is on the road to *adapting* the
individual to fit the needs of the throng and that the *individual's happiness as well as his sacrifice* consist in feeling himself to be a useful member and tool of the whole: only, at the
present time it is still very much up in the air as to where this
whole might be found, whether in an existing nation or in one
that must be founded, in a nation state or in a brotherhood
of peoples or in small new economic communities. On this
matter there is currently a great deal of reflection, doubt, argument, a great deal of agitation and passion, but marvelous and
pleasing to the ear is the harmony that reigns in the demand
that the ego must deny itself to the point where, in the guise
of adapting to the whole, it regains its solid circle of rights
and duties— to the point where it has become something
completely new and different. What is wanted—whether
one admits it or not—is nothing short of a thoroughgoing
transformation, indeed a debilitation and cancellation of the
individual: one never tires of enumerating and excoriating everything evil and malicious, prodigal, costly, and extravagant
in the prior form of individual existence; one hopes to manage
more cheaply, more safely, more uniformly, more centrally if
there remain only *large bodies and their limbs*. Everything that
in some way supports both this drive to form bodies and limbs
and its abetting drives is felt to be *good*, this is *the basic moral
current* of our age; individual empathy and social sentiment[74]
here go hand in hand. (Kant remains outside this movement:
he teaches emphatically that we must be insensitive to the
suffering of others if our benevolence is to have any moral

value[75] — which Schopenhauer, highly outraged as one can well imagine, calls *Kantian tastelessness*.[76])

133

"No more thinking about yourself." — One ought indeed to ponder the question seriously: why do we jump in after someone who has fallen into water right in front of us even though we are not at all drawn to that person? Out of compassion: at that moment we are thinking only about the other person — so says lack of thought. Why do we feel pain and queasiness in common with a person who is spitting blood, whereas normally we are ill-disposed and even hostile toward him? Out of compassion: at that point we are no longer thinking of ourselves — says the same lack of thought. The truth is: not out of, but inside compassion — I mean what customarily and misleadingly passes for compassion — we are thinking about ourselves, no longer consciously, to be sure, but *very powerfully so unconsciously*, just as, when our foot slips out from under us, we initiate, without any immediate consciousness of the action, the most purposive countermovements and in the process plainly make use of our entire faculty of understanding. The other person's accident insults us, it threatens to deliver us into the hands of our own impotence, perhaps even our cowardice were we not to offer our help. Or the accident *per se* involves a depletion of our honor in the eyes of others or of ourselves. Or lurking in the accident and suffering of another person is the indication of some danger for us; and simply as the mark of human imperilment and fragility in general it can have a painful effect on us. We reject this type of pain and insult and requite it through an act of compassion in which there may exist a subtle self-defense or even revenge. That at bottom we are thinking very strongly about ourselves can be ascertained from the decision we make in all cases where we *are able* to avoid the sight of someone who is suffering, starving, lamenting: we decide *not* to do so if we can present ourselves as someone more powerful, a bearer of aid, if we are certain of approval, if we

wish to feel how fortunate we are by contrast, or even if we hope the sight will wrest us from our boredom. It is misleading to call the suffering inflicted on us by such a sight, which can be of many different sorts, com-passion,[77] for under all circumstances, it is a suffering of which the sufferer in front of us is *free*: it is our own just as his suffering is his own. It is *only this suffering of our own*, however, that we eliminate when we perform acts of compassion. Yet we never do anything of this sort from one motive; as surely as we wish to free ourselves of suffering through such an act, we are, with the same act, just as surely surrendering to *an impulse for pleasure* — pleasure arises in viewing a contrast to our situation, in the very idea of being able to help if only we so desired, in the thought of praise and gratitude were we to help, in the very activity of helping insofar as the act is successful and succeeds step by step, thus allowing the performer to delight in himself, but especially in the sensation that our action has put an end to an injustice that arouses our indignation (already the release of indignation in itself is invigorating).[78] All these things, all of them and a host of finer subtleties as well, make up "compassion": how crudely with its single word does language assault so polyphonic an essence! — That compassion, by contrast, should be *of the same ilk* as the suffering in view of which it arises or that compassion possesses an especially keen and penetrating understanding of that suffering, both these claims are contradicted by *experience*, and anyone who has glorified compassion based on just these two aspects *lacked* sufficient experience in precisely this domain of the moral. Such is my doubt in the face of all the incredible things Schopenhauer was capable of saying about compassion: he, who would have us believe in his great new discovery that compassion — the very compassion he observed so inadequately and described so miserably — is the supposed source of each and every, once and future moral action — and all because of the selfsame capabilities he *invented* for it in the first place. — What, in the end, differentiates people without compassion from the compassionate? Above all — to sketch only a rough outline here — they lack fear's easily stimulated imagination, the subtle capacity to sniff out danger; nor is their vanity so quickly offended when something happens that they could prevent (their pride's caution bids them not to meddle needlessly in the affairs of others, indeed, of their own accord they love for everybody to fend for himself and to play his own cards). In addition, they are usually more accustomed than are the compassionate to enduring pain; and because they themselves have suffered, they hardly find it so unfitting that others suffer too. Finally, the condition of being softhearted is as awkward and painful for them as is stoic equanimity for the compassionate; they impose disparaging words on the condition and believe that it threatens their manliness and their icy courage — they conceal their tears from others and wipe them away, exasperated with themselves. They are egotists of a type *different* from the compassionate; — but to call them in an exceptional sense *evil* and the compassionate *good* is nothing more than a moral fashion that is having its day: just as the inverse fashion had its day, and a long day at that!

134[79]

The extent to which one must guard against compassion. — Compassion, insofar as it really creates suffering[80] — and this is our only viewpoint here — is, like every loss of self to an *injurious* affect, a weakness. It *increases* the amount of suffering in the world: even if, here and there in the short run, suffering is lessened or even eliminated as a result of compassion, one may not utilize these occasional and on the whole insignificant results in order to justify compassion's essential nature, which is, as stated, injurious. Suppose it reigned for even a *single* day: humanity would immediately be destroyed by it. In and of itself it has as little good character as any other drive: only when it is required and extolled — and this happens once one fails to apprehend what is injurious about it and discovers in it instead a *source of pleasure* — does a good conscience adhere to it, only then does one surrender to it readily and not shy away from the impulse. Under other conditions where it is apprehended as injurious it is considered a weakness: or, as with the Greeks, a pathological recurring affect, the danger of which one can remove by temporary, voluntary discharges.—Whoever even attempts at some point consciously to pursue for a period of time in his daily life every inducement to compassion will invariably turn sick and melancholic. But whoever wishes to serve as a physician to humanity *in any sense whatsoever* will have to be very cautious with regard to that sentiment—it lames him in all decisive moments and paralyzes his knowledge and his benevolent delicate hand.

135

Being the object of compassion.—Among savages the idea of being the object of compassion excites moral terror: it strips one of all virtue. To grant compassion is tantamount to showing contempt: one doesn't wish to see a contemptible creature suffer, this grants no pleasure. On the other hand, to see an enemy suffer whom one recognizes as one's equal in pride and who does not relinquish his pride under torments and, in general, to see any creature who will not stoop to pleas for compassion, in other words, to the most ignominious and profoundest humiliation—that is the pleasure of pleasures, during which the savage's soul is elevated to *admiration*: in the end, if it's within his power, he kills this valiant creature, conferring upon him, the *unbroken one*, his final *honor*: had he whined or had the look of cold defiance vanished from his face, had he shown himself contemptible—then, then he would have been allowed to live, like a dog—no longer would he have excited the onlooker's pride, and admiration would have given way to compassion.

136

Happiness in feeling compassion.—If, like the people of India, one establishes knowledge of human *misery* as the *goal* of all intellectual activity and remains faithful to such a horrible objective throughout many generations of spirit, then, in the eyes of such people of *inherited* pessimism, *feeling compassion* acquires, in the long run, a new value as a *life-preserving* power that makes existence bearable, even though it seems, for all the disgust and horror it evokes, worth tossing away. As a sensation containing pleasure and meting out superiority in small doses, feeling compassion becomes the antidote to suicide: it diverts from oneself, quickens the heart, chases away fear and torpor, incites speech, protest, and action — it amounts to *a relative happiness* compared to the misery of the knowledge emanating from all sides, driving the individual into a dark corner, robbing him of breath. Happiness, however, no matter what the sort, confers air, light, and freedom of movement.

137

Why double your "ego"! — To view our own experiences with the same eye we tend to use when viewing the experiences of others — this greatly soothes us and is a commendable medicine. By contrast, to view and take in the experiences of others *as if they were our own* — as is the imperative of a philosophy of compassion — this would destroy us, and in very short order: just give it a try and then stop all your fantasizing! Moreover, the former maxim is certainly more *in accord* with reason and with the good will to be reasonable, for we judge more objectively the value and meaning of an event if it happens to others and not to us: the value, for example, of a death, a financial setback, a slur. Compassion, as a principle of action with the imperative suffer ⟨the ills of another *exactly* as he himself⟩ suffers them, would, by contrast, require that the ego's viewpoint, with its exaggeration and excess, would, in addition, still have to become the viewpoint of the other person who feels compassion: so that we would have to suffer from our ego and simultaneously from the ego of the other, and would thereby voluntarily overburden ourselves with a doubled irrationality instead of making the load of our own as light as possible.

138

Growing more tender. — If we love, honor, admire someone and then afterward discover he is *suffering* — always to our great amazement, for we cannot help but imagine that the happiness we feel streaming to us from him comes from *his own* overflowing fountain of happiness — our feeling of love, honor, and admiration thus changes in an *essential respect*: it grows *more tender*, that is to say: the gulf between him and us appears to find a bridge, a move toward equality seems to take place.[81] Only now do we think it might be possible *to repay* him, whereas previously he dwelt in our imagination sublimely above our gratitude. This ability to repay him gives us a good deal of joy and exaltation. We seek to divine what would allay his pain and to give this to him; if he wishes comforting words, reassuring looks, attentive acts, little favors, gifts — we give them; above all, however: if he wishes us *to suffer* from his suffering, then we pretend to suffer, yet, in the midst of it all, we have the *pleasure of active gratitude*: which is, in short, none other than *charitable revenge*. If he neither wants nor accepts anything at all from us, then we walk away chilled and saddened, almost offended: it is as if our gratitude had been repulsed — and on this point of honor even the most charitable of persons remains ticklish. — It follows from all this that even in the very best of circumstances there lies in suffering something that degrades, in compassion something that elevates and bestows superiority; which separates the two sensations from each other for all eternity.

139

Allegedly higher! — You say that the morality of being compassionate is a higher morality than that of Stoicism?[82] Prove it! But remember that what is "higher" and "lower" in morality is not, in turn, to be measured by a moral yardstick: for there is no absolute morality. So take your rule from somewhere else and — now beware!

140

Praise and blame. — If a war concludes unhappily, one searches for the person who is "guilty" of starting it; if it ends in victory, one praises its instigator. Guilt is always in demand wherever there is failure; for failure brings with it a type of discord against which one involuntarily applies the lone remedy: a new excitation of *the feeling of power* — and this is found in the *condemnation* of the "guilty party." This guilty party is hardly something akin to a scapegoat for the guilt of others: he is a sacrifice to the weak, the humbled, the dejected, who wish to prove on something or other that they still have strength. Self condemnation can also be a means of helping oneself attain this feeling of strength after a defeat. — By contrast, glorification of the *instigator* is often the equally blind result of a different drive that wants its sacrifice, and this time the sacrifice smells sweet and inviting to the sacrificial lamb: when, namely, the feeling of power in a people or a society has reached an excess through magnificent and bewitching success and a *weariness with victory* sets in, one surrenders some of one's pride; the feeling of *adoration* arises and seeks its object. — Be we *blamed* or *praised*, what we normally create in the process is nothing more than opportunities, and all too often arbitrary opportunities seized out of the blue, for those around us to open up the floodgates for the swollen drive in them to blame or to praise: either way, we render them a service for which we deserve no credit, and they reserve no thanks.

141[83]

More beautiful, but less valuable. — Picturesque morality: that is the morality of precipitously exploding emotions, of abrupt transitions, of solemn, importunate, fearsome, ceremonious gesture and sound. It is the *half-savage* stage of morality: one mustn't let its aesthetic appeal tempt one into according it a higher rank.

142[84]

Empathy.[85] — In order to understand another person, in other words, *to reproduce his feeling in ourselves*, we do indeed from time to time return to the *reason* for his feeling one way or another and ask, for instance: Why is this person depressed? — In order, then, for the same reason, to experience the same depression ourselves; but it is much more common to dispense with this and to produce the feeling in ourselves according to the *effects* it exerts and displays on the other person in that we reproduce with our body (at least we approach a faint similarity in the play of muscle and in innervation) the expression of his eyes, his voice, his gait, his bearing (or even their reflection in word, painting, music). Then there arises in us a similar feeling, as a result of an age-old association between movement and sensation, which have been thoroughly conditioned to move back and forth from one to the other. We have come a long way in developing this skill for understanding other people's feelings, and in the presence of another person we are, almost automatically, always employing it: observe in particular the play of lineaments on the faces of women, how they quiver and glitter from ceaseless reproduction and mirroring of everything that is being sensed around them. It is music, however, that demonstrates most clearly what masters we are in the rapid and subtle deciphering of feelings and in the art of empathy: music is, namely, an imitation of an imitation of feelings and yet, despite this remoteness and indefiniteness, it often enough still makes us partake of these emotions to the degree that, like complete fools, we grow mournful without the slightest cause for mourning merely because we hear tones and rhythms that somehow remind us of the voice or movement of mourners or even of their customary practices. The story is told of a Danish king who was transported into such bellicose frenzy by a minstrel's music that he leaped up and killed five members of his assembled court: there was no war, no enemy, quite the opposite, in fact, but the force that *from a feeling infers a posteriori a cause* was strong enough to overwhelm blatant reality and reason. Yet, this is almost always music's effect (provided it does indeed generate an effect—) and one doesn't need such paradoxical cases to realize this: the state of feeling into which music moves us is almost always in contradiction to the blatant reality of our actual situation and to reason, which recognizes this actual situation and its causes.—If we ask ourselves how the reproduction of other people's feelings has become such second nature for us, there can be no doubt about the answer: as the most timorous of all creatures, the human being, by virtue of his subtle and fragile nature, has had in his *timidity* the instructress of that empathy, of that rapid understanding for the feelings of others (and of animals as well). For millennia upon millennia he saw in everything alien and alive a danger: with each such appearance he immediately reproduced the expression of features and bearing and formed his conclusion about the type of malevolent intent behind these features and this bearing. Humans have even applied this interpretation of all movements and lineaments *as emanating from intentions* to the nature of inanimate things—in the delusion that nothing inanimate exists: I believe that this is the origin of everything we call, when viewing sky, field, cliff, forest, storm, stars, sea, landscape, springtime, a *feeling for nature*—without the age-old operation of fear that views all these things in reference to a second, ulterior meaning, we would now take no joy in nature, just as we would take no joy in people and animals without that instructress of understanding, fear. Joy and agreeable amazement, and finally a feeling for the ridiculous, are, namely, empathy's later-born children and fear's much younger siblings.—The capacity for rapid understanding—which in turn rests on the capacity *to dissimulate rapidly*—diminishes among proud, tyrannical individuals and peoples because they have less fear: by contrast, all forms of understanding and of dissimulation are at home among fearful peoples: this is also the true homeland of the mimetic arts and of higher intelligence.—When I proceed from a theory of empathy such as I have presented here and then consider the contemporary favorite and downright sacred theory of a mystical process, by virtue of which *compassion* transforms two essential beings into one and to such an extent that each is vouchsafed unmediated understanding of the other: when I recall that such a clear-headed thinker as Schopenhauer took pleasure in such rapturous[86] and worthless poppycock and in turn transplanted this pleasure into the minds of other clear and not-so-clear thinkers: then my astonishment and sense of pity[87] know no end. How great must be our desire for, our pleasure in, incomprehensible nonsense! How close to the madman the sane man still stands when he attends to his *secret* intellectual desires!—(*For what*, actually, did Schopenhauer feel so gratefully disposed, so profoundly indebted, toward Kant? He once let slip the answer most unambiguously: someone had remarked how the *qualitas occulta*[88] had been stripped from Kant's categorical imperative and that it could be made *comprehensible*. At that Schopenhauer bursts out with the following words: "Comprehensibility of the categorical imperative! What a fundamentally wrongheaded thought! Egyptian obscurity! Heaven forbid that it should ever become comprehensible! Precisely that such a thing as incomprehensibility exists, that *this misery of the understanding* and its concepts are limited, conditional, finite, deceptive; this certainty is Kant's greatest gift."[89]—One ought to consider whether someone who, from the outset, is perfectly happy to believe in the *incomprehensibility* of things moral can be sincerely interested in acquiring knowledge of such things. Someone who still honestly believes in illuminations from above, in magic and spiritual apparitions and in the metaphysical ugliness of the toad!)

143[90]

Woe to us if this drive ever rages!—Supposing the drive for attachment and for the care of others (the "sympathetic affection") were twice as strong as it is; then life on earth would be *unbearable*. Merely consider all the foolishness each of us commits out of attachment and care *for ourselves*, daily and hourly, and how insufferable we are in the process: what would it be like if *we* became *for others* the object of the same foolishness and importunities with which up until now they had only plagued themselves! Wouldn't we take blind flight the moment the next person drew near? And heap the same imprecations on sympathetic affection that we currently heap on egotism?

144

Turning a deaf ear to lamentation. — If we allow the lamentation and suffering of other mortals to make us gloomy and to send dark clouds across our own heaven, who then has to bear the consequences of this gloominess? Precisely those other mortals, and on top of all their other burdens to boot! We cannot be of any *assistance* or *invigoration* to them if we wish to be the echo of their lamentation, or indeed even if we are only always keeping an ear out for it — unless, of course, we mastered the Olympians' art and were henceforward *edified* by human misfortune instead of ourselves being rendered unhappy by it. That is, however, a little too Olympian for us: although with our pleasure in tragedy we have already taken a step toward this ideal divine cannibalism.[91]

145[92]

"Unegotistical!" — One person is empty and wants to be full, the next is overfull and wants to be drained — this drives each to search for an individual who can service his need. And in each case this process, considered in its most ultimate sense, goes by a *single* word: love — What was that? Love is supposed to be something unegoistical?

146[93]

Even ignoring your neighbor.[94] — What was that? The essence of what is genuinely moral is supposed to lie in our keeping our eye attuned to the most immediate and direct consequences our actions have for others and in our making decisions accordingly? This may even be a morality, but only a narrow and petty bourgeois morality: it seems to me, however, to be a higher and freer manner of thought that *looks beyond* these most immediate consequences for others and to further more distant aims, under some circumstances *even at the expense of the suffering of others*—for example, to further knowledge despite the insight that our freethinking will at first plunge others directly into doubt, dire distress, and even worse. Are we not permitted at least to treat our neighbor as we treat ourselves? And if, with regard to ourselves, we do not heed, in narrow, petty bourgeois fashion, immediate consequences and sufferings: why should we *have* to do so with our neighbor? Supposing we went in for self-sacrifice: what would prohibit us from sacrificing our neighbor as well?—just as state and prince have forever done when they sacrificed one citizen to the other "in the universal public interest," as they put it. But we too have universal, perhaps more universal interests: why shouldn't some individuals from the current generation be sacrificed for future generations? Such that those individuals' grief, their restlessness, their despair, their blunderings and fearful footsteps be deemed necessary because a new plowshare[95] is to cleave the ground, rendering it fruitful for all?—Finally: we simultaneously communicate to our neighbor a frame of mind in which he can *see himself as a sacrifice*, we talk him into the task for which we wish to use him. In this case do we lack compassion? But if we wish also *to get beyond our compassion* and to gain a victory over ourselves, does this not constitute a higher and freer bearing and attitude than when one feels safe once one has ascertained whether an action *benefits or hurts* one's neighbor? We, on the other hand, would, through sacrifice—in which we *and our neighbors* are included—strengthen and elevate the general feeling of human *power*, even though we might achieve nothing further. But even this would be a positive increase in *happiness*. In the long run, even if this——but not a word more here! One look suffices, you have understood me.

147[96]

Cause of "altruism."—People have spoken so emphatically and with such idolatry about love, on the whole, *because they have had so little of it* and were never able to take their fill of this ambrosia: accordingly, it became for them the "food of the gods." In the image of a utopia a poet might perhaps be able to depict *universal love* as something real: of course he will have an agonizing and ludicrous situation to describe, something the likes of which the earth has never seen[97]—each person flocked around, pestered, longed for not by *one* lover, as happens nowadays, but by thousands, indeed by each and everyone, thanks to an uncontrollable drive, which one will curse and condemn with the same vehemence that prior humanity reserved for selfishness; and the poets of this new state, provided they are left in peace long enough to write, will dream of nothing other than the blessed loveless past, of divine selfishness and how it once was possible on earth to experience solitude, quietude, being unpopular, hated, despised, and whatever else passes for baseness in the charming animal world in which *we* live.

148

Distant prospect.—If, as one definition puts it, only those actions are moral that are undertaken on behalf of, and only on behalf of, someone else, then there is no such thing as moral actions! If—as another definition has it—only those actions are moral that are undertaken of one's own free will, then there is likewise no such thing as moral actions!—And so what, then, are these things one *calls* moral actions and that at any rate exist and need to be explained? They are the effects of several intellectual slipups.—And supposing one were able to free oneself of these errors, what would happen to "moral actions"?—Owing to these errors we have heretofore ascribed to certain actions a higher value than they possess: we severed them from "egoistical" and "unfree" actions. If, as we are constrained to do, we now reclassify them with the latter, we no doubt *lower* their value (value-feeling, the value we feel they have), and indeed by more than is fair, because, owing to their alleged, profound, and intrinsic difference, the "egoistical" and "unfree" actions in this case were heretofore appraised too low.—Accordingly, will these very actions be performed less frequently from this day forward because from now on they will be less appreciated?—Inescapably! For a good long while, at least as long as the balance of value-feelings remains under the reaction of prior mistakes! But our countercalculation is the following: We return to humanity the healthy courage for, and the good cheer of, those actions decried as egoistical and restore to them their *value—we deprive them of their evil conscience*! And because till now these actions have been by far the most frequent sort and will continue to be so for all time to come, we thus relieve the entire tableau of actions and existence of its *evil appearance*! This is a very great outcome! If humanity no longer considers itself evil, it will cease to be so!

Book Three

149

The need for tiny deviant actions!— Sometimes in matters of *custom* to act contrary to your better judgment, to give in now and then outwardly, in praxis, and yet retain one's inner integrity, to do as everyone else does and thus to render everyone else a courteous good turn as compensation, as it were, for the deviance of our opinions — many tolerably liberal-minded people consider this stance not merely unproblematic but "honest," "humane," "tolerant," "unpedantic," and whatever other lovely words may be found to lull the intellectual conscience to sleep: and so it happens that one person takes his child to a Christian church to be baptized and is himself all the while an atheist, and another does his military service "like everybody else" no matter how vociferously he also condemns hatred among nations, and a third heads straight to church with his little woman and, with no sense of shame, takes marriage vows before a priest, merely because she has pious relatives. "It's of no *essential* importance if people like us also do just as everybody else always does and always has done" — so chimes the crude *presumption*! The *crude* error! For there is nothing *more essential* than when an already powerful, ultratraditional,[1] and irrationally accepted convention is confirmed by the actions of a person accepted as rational: the convention thus acquires in the eyes of everyone who learns of it the sanction of reason itself! All due respect to your opinions! But *tiny deviant actions* carry more weight!

150[2]

The chanciness[3] of marriages. — Were I a god, and a benevolent god at that, then human *marriages* would make me more impatient than anything else. A lone individual can go a long, long way forward in his seventy-odd, indeed, in his thirty years — it is astounding, even for the gods! But when you then see how he takes the inheritance and legacy of this struggle and victory, the laurel wreath of his humanity, and hangs it up on the next best spot that comes along where his little woman can pick it to pieces: when you see how well he knows how to gain and how poorly then to maintain, how indeed it doesn't even occur to him that he could, through the process of procreation, pave the way for an even more victorious life: you grow, as mentioned earlier, impatient and you say to yourself "in the long run nothing can come of these humans, the individuals are all squandered, the chanciness of marriages renders a grand advance of reason and of humanity impossible; let us cease to be the enthusiastic spectators and fools of this spectacle without a goal!" It was in this frame of mind that Epicurus's gods once withdrew to their divine quietude and beatitude: they were tired of human beings and their trafficking in love.[4]

151

Here is where we need to invent new ideals. — One ought not to be allowed to reach a decision affecting one's life while in the state of being in love, and hence to establish once and for all the character of the company we keep on the basis of a heated whim: lovers' vows ought to be publicly declared invalid and marriage denied the pair: and indeed precisely because one ought to take marriage unspeakably more seriously! such that in those very cases where marriage up to now has come about, it would usually not come about! Aren't most marriages of a sort that one desires no third party as a witness?

And such a third party almost always turns up—the child—and is more than a witness, he is the scapegoat!

152

Form of oath.—"If I am now about to lie, then I am no longer a decent, respectable human being, and everyone has the right to tell me so to my face."—Instead of the judicial oath along with the customary appeal to God, I recommend this form: it is *stronger.* The pious person also has no reason to resist it: for the moment the customary oath begins to be uttered *vainly,* the pious person must obey his catechism, which lays down that "thou shalt not take the name of the Lord thy God *in vain!*"[5]

153

A malcontent.—That is one of those old valiant troopers: he is angry and irritated with civilization because he believes its goal is to make all the good things in life accessible: honors, riches, beautiful women—even to the cowardly.

154

Consolation for the endangered.—In a life perched precariously close to great dangers and cataclysms, the Greeks sought a type of emotional security and ultimate *refugium*[6] in contemplating and knowing. In an incomparably more secure condition, we have transferred danger into the act of contemplating and knowing, and recover from them and reassure ourselves by *living.*

155

Expiring skepticism.—Bold and daring exploits are rarer in the modern age than in antiquity and the Middle Ages—in all likelihood because the modern age no longer possesses belief in omens, oracles, planets and fortune-tellers. That is to say: we have become incapable of *believing in a future* determined for *us,* as could the ancients, who—unlike ourselves—were much less skeptical with regard to what *will come* than to what *is here.*

156

Evil through high spirits. — "Only we mustn't let ourselves feel too good!" — that was the Greeks' secret, deep-seated anxiety when times were good. *For this reason* they preached measure to themselves. How about us!

157[7]

Cult of "natural sounds."—What does it indicate that our culture is not merely tolerant toward expressions of pain, toward tears, complaints, reproaches, gesticulations of rage and humiliation, but that it approves of them and considers them to be among life's more noble inevitabilities?—whereas the spirit of ancient philosophy viewed these things with contempt and granted them no necessity whatsoever. One need only recall how Plato—in other words, by no means the least humane of philosophers—speaks of the Philoctetes[8] of classical tragedy.[9] Could it be that our modern culture perhaps lacks "philosophy"? Could it be that in the estimation of those ancient philosophers we, one and all, belong to the "rabble"?

158

The flatterer's climate. — One need no longer look for servile flatterers in the proximity of princes—the latter have all acquired a military taste to which the flatterer runs counter. In the proximity of bankers and artists, however, this flower still continues to bloom.

159[10]

Resurrectors of the dead. — From the moment vain people feel able to empathize with a piece of the past (especially when this is difficult), they value it more highly, indeed, they then wish, wherever possible, to resurrect it from the dead. And because there are always innumerable vain people around, historical studies acquire, once an entire age is devoted to them, a danger that is in fact not insignificant: too much energy is wasted on every possible resurrection from the dead. Perhaps the entire Romantic movement is best understood from this vantage point.[11]

160

Vain, greedy, and little wise. — Your appetites are greater than your understanding and your vanity is even greater than your appetites — for people such as you, I recommend, from top to bottom, a *great deal* of Christian praxis with a little Schopenhauerian theory on the side.

161[12]

Beauty in keeping with the age. — If our sculptors, painters, and musicians wish to capture the sense of the times, they have to picture beauty as bloated, gigantic, and nervous: just as the Greeks, under the sway of their morality of measure, viewed and pictured beauty as the Apollo Belvedere.[13] We ought actually to call him *ugly*! But the foolish "Classicists"[14] have robbed us of all honesty!

162

Contemporary irony. — It is the European's way at the present moment to treat all great interests with irony, because one makes such a business of being busily in their service that no one has time to take them seriously.

163[15]

Against Rousseau. — If it is true that our civilization has something inescapably wretched about it: then you have the choice of concluding, along with Rousseau, that "this wretched civilization is to blame for our *bad* morality," or of inferring, against Rousseau, that "our *good* morality is to blame for this wretchedness in civilization. Our weak, unmanly, societal notions of good and evil and their prodigious hyperdominance over body and soul have, in the end, made all bodies and all souls weak and have shattered self-reliant, independent, and unfettered individuals, the pillars of a *strong* civilization: wherever one still encounters *bad* morality these days, you will find the last ruins of these pillars." Thus paradox would stand against paradox! The truth cannot possibly be on both sides: and is it on either side at all? Examine them and see!

164

Perhaps premature. — At present it seems that under all sorts of false misleading names, and mostly amid great uncertainty even among themselves, those who don't consider themselves bound by existing mores and laws are making the first attempts[16] to organize and thereby to create for themselves a *right*: whereas up until now they lived their lives under the proscription of outlaw and in the jurisdiction of a bad conscience, decried as criminals, freethinkers, immoralists, villains, as depraved and depraving. By and large, one ought to find this development *fitting and good*, even though it will make the coming century a precarious one and will hang a rifle on each and every shoulder: to ensure at least the presence of an oppositional power that constantly admonishes that there is no such thing as a one-and-only-moral-making morality[17] and that every code of ethics that affirms itself exclusively destroys too much valuable energy and costs humanity much too dearly. The deviant, so often the inventive and fructifying person shall no longer be sacrificed; it shall no longer even be considered in the least shameful to deviate from morality, in deed or in thought; numerous new attempts at living life and creating community shall be undertaken; an enormous load of bad conscience shall be purged from the world — these most basic goals shall be recognized and furthered by all honest people in search of truth.

165

Morality that does not bore. — The principal moral commandments that a people is willing to be taught and have preached to it over and over again stand in relation to the people's principal flaws, and for this reason they do not ever become boring. The Greeks, who all too often lost their moderation, cold courage, fair-mindedness, and their understanding altogether, had an open ear for the four Socratic virtues — for they were in such need of, and yet had so little talent for, precisely these virtues!

166

At the crossroads. — Pfooey! You want to become part of a system in which you must either be a cog in the wheel, totally and completely, or else be steamrollered by it! A system in which it goes without saying that every person *is* what he is *made* to be from above! In which the search for "connections" figures among one's natural duties! In which nobody feels offended when, with a wink and a nod toward a man, one is told "he can be of use to you some day;" in which one is not ashamed to go calling just to curry a person's good favor! In which one hasn't even the faintest idea how, through deliberate conformity to such mores, one[18] has stamped oneself once and for all as an inferior piece of nature's pottery that others use up and shatter to pieces without feeling any responsibility whatsoever; just as if one said: "There will never be a dearth of the likes of me: take me, I'm yours! Without further ado!" —

167[19]

Unconditional homages. — When I think of the most read German philosopher, the most listened-to German composer, and the most respected German statesman, then I have to confess to myself: the Germans, this people of *unconditional* feelings, are much put upon these days, and indeed by their own great men. What a magnificent three-ringed spectacle on display: each is a current in his own self-carved riverbed, and so mightily agitated that it might seem, more often than not, as if each wished to flow uphill. And yet, however far one pushes one's veneration: who wouldn't, on the whole, prefer to be of a

different opinion than Schopenhauer!—And who could, on
the whole or in the parts, be of one opinion with Richard
Wagner? However true it may be, as somebody[20] has said, that
wherever he takes or gives offense a problem lies *buried*—no
matter, he himself does not bring it to light.—And finally,
how many would want to be wholeheartedly of one opinion
with Bismarck, were he, that is, of one opinion with himself or
at least making a show of being so in the future! To be sure:
without principles, but with principal drives, a nimble mind in
the service of strong principal drives, and precisely on that account without principles—this shouldn't be anything too unusual in a statesman; on the contrary, it counts as something
right and natural; but up until now it was, alas, so thoroughly
not German! As little so as a din about music and dissonance
and discontent about a composer, as little as the novel and extraordinary position chosen by Schopenhauer: namely, neither
above things nor on his knees before things—both could
have still been called German—but *against* things! Unbelievable! And disagreeable! To set oneself on a par with things
and yet as their enemy, and ultimately even as the enemy of
oneself!—What is the unconditional admirer to do with a
paragon like that! And what in the world with three such para-
gons who don't even desire to keep peace among themselves!
Schopenhauer is an enemy of Wagner's music, and Wagner
an enemy of Bismarck's politics, and Bismarck an enemy of
all Wagneriana and Schopenhaueriana! What's left to be
done! Where to turn to satisfy our thirst for wholesale homages!
Could we perhaps sort out from the composer's music a few
hundred bars of good music that touch the heart, that we take
to heart because they have a heart—could we step aside with
this little theft and—forget all that remains? And then conclude just such a treaty with regard to the philosopher and the
statesman—sort out, take to heart, and especially *forget what
remains*? Yes, if only forgetting weren't so difficult! There once
was a very proud man, who wanted to accept something, good
or bad, only if it came entirely from himself: but when he

needed *to forget*, he wasn't able to supply such a gift himself
and had to invoke the spirits three times; they came, they listened to his demand, and ultimately they said: "This and this
alone does not lie within our power!" Shouldn't the Germans
make use of *Manfred's* experience?[21] Why even invoke the
spirits in the first place! It's useless, we don't forget when we
want to forget. And with these three colossi of the age how
colossal would be "the remains" we would have to forget in
order to be able to go on being their wholesale admirer! It is
certainly more advisable, then, to take advantage of the golden
opportunity to attempt something novel: namely, to increase
one's *honesty toward oneself* and to transform a people of credulous parroting and furious, blind hostility into a people of
conditional consent and charitable opposition; to learn first of
all, however, that unconditional homages to people are rather
ridiculous, that to learn to think differently in this matter is
not ignominious, even for the Germans, and that there exists
a profound adage worth taking to heart: "*Ce qui importe, ce ne
sont point les personnes: mais les choses.*"[22] This adage is, like the
man who uttered it, great, upright, simple and laconic—entirely like Carnot, the soldier and Republican.—But may one
nowadays speak to Germans this way about a Frenchman, and
about a Republican to boot?[23] Perhaps not; perhaps one may
not even recall what Niebuhr was able to say to the Germans
in his day: that no one had given him such a powerful impression of *true greatness* as Carnot.[24]

168[25]

A model. — What do I love about Thucydides, why do I
honor him more highly than Plato? He takes the most extensive and impartial pleasure in all that is typical in humans and
in events and he holds that a quantity of *good sense* adheres to
every type: *this* is what he seeks to discover. He displays greater
practical justice than Plato; he is no maligner or belittler of
persons he doesn't like or who have caused him to suffer in life.
On the contrary: his eye sees through to and adds something

great to all things and persons in that it sees only types; what interest would the whole of posterity, to whom he dedicates his work, have in something that *were not* typical! Thus, in him, the man as thinker and thinker as man, that *culture of the most impartial knowledge of the world*, attains a last magnificent flowering,[26] that culture[27] that had in Sophocles its writer, in Pericles its statesman, in Hippocrates its physician, in Democritus its natural philosopher: that culture that deserves to be baptized with its teachers' name, the *Sophists*,[28] and, from this moment of baptism, at once begins, unfortunately, to turn pale and incomprehensible to us—for now we suspect it would have had to have been a very immoral culture against which Plato, along with all the Socratic schools, fought! The truth here is so convoluted and entangled that to unravel it incites antipathy: so let the age-old error (*error veritate simplicior*[29]) run its age-old course!

169[30]

The Hellenic quite unknown to us. — Oriental or modern, Asiatic or European: for all of these, in relation to the Hellenic, massiveness and pleasure in great quantity are inherent in the language of the sublime, whereas in Paestum, Pompey, and Athens,[31] as with the entirety of Greek architecture, what utterly astounds is *with what small proportions* the Greeks understand how to express and *love* to express the sublime. — Likewise: how simple were the people of Greece *in their own conception of themselves*! How far and away we surpass them in understanding human nature! And how labyrinthian as well do our souls and our conceptions of souls appear in comparison to theirs! If we desired and dared an architecture corresponding to *our own* make of soul (we are too cowardly for it!) — then the labyrinth would have to be our model! You can divine this from the music that is ours,[32] that truly speaks to us and of us! (In music, namely, people let themselves go for they fancy no one can see them concealed *amid* their music.)

170[33]

Feeling's different perspective. — What does all our prattle about the Greeks amount to! What do we, after all, understand of their art, the soul of which — is their passion for naked *male* beauty! — It was only *from that vantage point* that they gained a feeling for female beauty. Accordingly, they had a completely different perspective on female beauty than we do. And similarly with their love of women: they venerated differently, they showed contempt differently.

171

The modern human's diet. — He is capable of digesting a lot, indeed almost everything — it is his sort of ambition: but he would be of a higher order were he *in*capable of this very thing; *homo pamphagus*[34] is not the finest of species. We live between a past that had a crazier and more obstinate taste than ours and a future that will perhaps have a more refined one — we live too much in the middle.

172[35]

Tragedy and music. — Men who are in a fundamentally bellicose state of mind, as for example the Greeks of Aeschylus's[36] day,[37] are *difficult to move*, and when compassion does for once win out over their toughness, it seizes hold of them like a frenzy, like a "demonic power" — they then feel under constraint and aroused by a shiver of religious awe. Afterward, they have their reservations about this condition; as long as they are in it, they enjoy the thrill of the miraculous and of being outside themselves, mixed with the bitterest wormwood of suffering: it is just the right draft for warriors, something rare, dangerous, and bittersweet that doesn't come one's way easily. — Tragedy addresses itself to souls that feel compassion in this way, to tough and bellicose souls that are difficult to vanquish, whether with fear or with compassion,[38] but that find it useful from time to time to be *softened*: but what good is tragedy to those who stand as open to "sympathetic affections"[39] as sails to the winds! Once the Athenians had grown softer and more sensitive, in Plato's time—ah, how far removed they still were from the gushing sentimentality of our own urban dwellers large and small!—And yet the philosophers were already bemoaning the deleteriousness of tragedy.[40] An age, such as the one beginning now, full of dangers, in which courage and manliness are[41] rising in value, will perhaps gradually toughen souls again to the point where they are in need of tragic poets: in the meantime, however, the latter have been a bit *superfluous*—to put it as mildly as possible.—Thus, for music too perhaps, a better age (it will certainly be the *more evil*!) will return, at the point when artists have to address their music to strictly individualist selves tough in themselves and ruled by the tenebrous seriousness of their own passion: but what good is music today to the little souls of this vanishing age, souls too easily moved, undeveloped, half-selves, greedy for anything new and lusting after everything?

173

Eulogizers of work.—In the glorification of "work," in the tireless talk about "the blessing of work," I see the same ulterior motive as in the praise of impersonal actions that serve the public good: the fear of everything individual. At bottom, one feels nowadays at the sight of work—by work one always means that hard industriousness from dawn to dusk—that such work is the best policeman, that it keeps everyone within bounds and manages to hinder vigorously the development of reason, desire, and the craving for independence. For it uses up an extraordinary amount of nervous energy that is thereby taken away from reflection, brooding, dreaming, worrying, loving, hating; it places a tiny little goal always in sight and vouchsafes easy and regular satisfactions. Accordingly, a society in which there is continuous hard work will have more security: and security is currently worshipped as the supreme divinity.—And now! Horror! Precisely the "worker" has turned *dangerous*!

Everywhere it's teeming with "dangerous individuals"! And behind them the danger of dangers—*the* individual.

174[42]

Moral fashion of a commercial society.—Behind the fundamental principle of the contemporary moral fashion: "moral actions are actions generated by sympathy for others," I see the work of a collective drive toward timidity masquerading behind an intellectual front: this drive desires utmost, uppermost, and foremost that life be rid of *all the dangers* it once held and that *each and every person* should help toward this end with all one's might: therefore only actions aimed at the common security and at society's sense of security may be accorded the rating "good"!—How little pleasure people must take in themselves these days, however, when such a tyranny of timidity dictates to them the uppermost moral law,[43] when, without so much as a protest, they let themselves be commanded to ignore and look beyond themselves and yet have eagle eyes for every distress and every suffering existing elsewhere! Are we not, with this prodigious intent to grate off all the rough and sharp edges from life, well on the way to turning humanity into *sand*? Sand! Tiny, soft, round, endless grains of sand! Is this your ideal, you heralds of the sympathetic affections?—In the meantime, the question itself remains open as to whether one is *more useful* to another by immediately and constantly leaping to his side and *helping* him[44]—which can, in any case, only transpire very superficially, provided the help doesn't turn into a tyrannical encroachment and transformation—or by *fashioning* out of oneself something the other will behold with pleasure, a lovely, peaceful, self-enclosed garden, for instance, with high walls to protect against the dangers and dust of the roadway, but with a hospitable gate as well.

175[45]

The fundamental idea of a culture of commercial beings.—One sees repeatedly these days the emergence of a culture within society in which *commerce* is just as much the soul as was individual contest for the ancient Greeks and war, victory, and law for the Romans. Commercial man understands how to assess the value of everything without having made it and, indeed, to assess it not according to his own, most personal need, but *according to consumer need*; "Who and how many will consume this?" is his question of questions. He comes to apply this type of assessment instinctively and at all times: to everything and so also to the fruits of the arts and sciences, of thinkers, scholars, artists, statesmen, nations, and parties, of the entire age: with everything that is created he inquires into supply and demand *in order to affix for himself the value of a thing.* Having made this fundamental idea, thought through unlimitedly and down to the most minute, subtle detail, the character of an entire culture, having imposed it upon every will and every ability: this is what you people of the next century will have to be proud of: provided the prophets of the commercial class are right in delivering it into your possession! But I have little faith in these prophets. *Credat Judaeus Apella*[46] — to speak with Horace.

176[47]

Critique of fathers. — Why is it that we are currently capable of enduring the truth about even the most recent past? Because there is always a new generation in place that feels itself to be *in opposition* to this past and, in this critique, enjoys the first fruits of the feeling of power. Previously, the new generation wanted, inversely, to *found* itself on the older and it began to acquire a *sense of self* not merely by adopting the views of the fathers but, whenever possible, by taking them *more strictly.* In those days critique of the fathers was wicked: now the younger idealists *begin* with it.

177

Learning solitude. — Oh, you poor devils in the great cities of world politics, you talented young men tormented by ambition who consider it your duty to remark on everything that happens—and something is always happening! Who, having drummed up noise and dust in this fashion, believe you are the very chariot of history! Who, because you are always listening in, always watching for the moment when you can throw in your two cents' worth, miss out on any genuine productivity. No matter how greedily you long to do great deeds, the profound speechlessness of pregnancy never comes to you! The event of the day propels you here and there like chaff, while you fancy yourselves to be propelling the event—poor devils!—if you want to cut the figure of a hero here on the stage, you mustn't think about being the chorus, indeed, you mustn't even know how to be the chorus.[48]

178

Those who are worn out daily.[49]—These young men are lacking in neither character, talent, nor diligence: but they have never been left enough time to give themselves a direction; on the contrary, from the time they learn to walk, they have been accustomed to receiving a direction. Then at the point when they were mature enough to "be sent off into the desert," something different was done—they were used,[50] they were purloined from themselves, they were trained to *be worn out daily* and this was transformed into a doctrine of duty for them—and now they can no longer bear to be without it and would not have it any other way. Only don't deprive these poor beasts of burden of their "vacation"—as it is called, this leisure ideal of an overworked century: when one is permitted for once to laze about and be idiotic and childish to one's heart's content.

179

As little state as possible!—Political and economic affairs in their entirety do not warrant obliging, or even permitting, the most talented minds to attend to them: such squandering of spirit is at bottom worse than its lack.[51] Such concerns are[52] and remain the working province of inferior heads and no one other than inferior heads ought to be in the employ of this workshop: better to let the machinery go to pieces again! The way things stand nowadays, however, with everybody not only believing he is obliged *to know* what is going on day in and day out, but also longing at every instant to be actively involved in bringing it about to the point of abandoning his own work, we are in a state of colossal and ridiculous lunacy. This is much too high a price to pay for "national security": and the maddest thing of all is, moreover, that this behavior brings about the very opposite of "national security," as our own dear century is trying to prove: as if it hadn't ever been proven before! To render society safe from thieves and fireproof and endlessly amenable to every sort of traffic and trade and to transform the state into Providence in the good and bad sense[53] — these are lower, mediocre, and by no means thoroughly indispensable goals toward which one ought not strive with the *altogether* highest means and instruments *in existence* — means that one ought to *store up and reserve* for precisely the highest and most exceptional of purposes! Our age, no matter how much it talks and talks about economy, is a squanderer: it squanders what is most precious, spirit.

180[54]

Wars. — The great wars of our day[55] are the effects of the study of history.

181

Governing. — Some govern out of pleasure in governing; others in order not to be governed — to the latter, governing is merely the lesser of two evils.

182

Crude consistency. — It is considered a great distinction when people say: "He has character!" — Certainly! If he displays crude consistency, a consistency obvious to even the dullest eye! But as soon as a more subtle and profound spirit operates and is consistent in its more elevated way, spectators deny the presence of character. For this reason cunning states-men usually play out their comedy behind a cloak of crude consistency.

183

The old and the young. — "There is something immoral about parliaments" — some continue to think — "for you can also express views there *against* the government!" — "One must always have the view of things ordained by His Majesty" — this is the eleventh commandment in many an honorable old head, especially in northern Germany. One chuckles over it as over an outdated fashion: yet formerly it was morality! Perhaps one day a time will come when we will also chuckle at what now passes for moral among the latest generation schooled in the ways of parliament: namely, placing party politics above per-sonal wisdom and answering every question regarding the public good in just the right way to create a favorable wind for the party's sails. "One must have the view of things dictated by the party position" — would be the new canon. In the service of such morality there exists today all manner of sacrifice, over-coming of the self, and martyrdom.

184

The state as product of the anarchists. — In lands where peo-ple are restrained and contained there are nevertheless still plenty of backsliding, unrestrained, and uncontained persons: at the moment they are congregating in the socialist camps more than anywhere else. Should it come to pass that they one day hand down the *laws*, then you can bet they will place them-selves in iron chains and exert a frightful discipline — *they know themselves*! And they will endure these laws, conscious that they and they alone have issued them — the feeling of power, and of *this* power, is too new and delightful for them not to suffer ev-erything on its account.

185

Beggars. — One ought to do away with beggars: for you feel annoyed giving to them and annoyed when you don't.

186

Business people. — Your business — that is your greatest prejudice,[56] it ties you to your locale, the company you keep, to your inclinations. Diligent in business — but lazy in spirit, content in your impoverishment, having tied the apron strings of duty to this contentment: so do you live and so do you want your children to live!

187

From a possible future. — Is it unthinkable to have a state of affairs in which a malefactor turns himself in, publicly dictates his own sentence in the proud feeling that he is thus honoring the law he himself has made, that, in punishing himself, he is exercising power, the power of the lawgiver; he may have transgressed at some point but through his voluntary punishment he elevates himself above his transgression; through candor, greatness, and calmness he not only wipes out his transgression: he performs a public service as well. — This would be the criminal of a possible future, who, to be sure, presupposes a future legislation founded on the idea: "In all things great and small I shall submit only to the law that I myself have given." So many attempts still have to be made! Many a future must still come to light![57]

188[58]

Intoxication and nourishment. — Nations are so exceedingly deceived because they are always *seeking* a deceiver, namely a stimulating wine for their senses. If only they can have *that*, they gladly put up with lousy bread. Intoxication is more important to them than food — this is the bait they will always go after! What do they care about men chosen from their midst—though they be the most expert practical persons—compared to glittering conquerors or grandiose old royal houses! The man of the people must at least hold out to them the prospect of conquests and grandeur: then he will perhaps gain their faith. They will always obey and do more than obey, provided they can intoxicate themselves in the process! One can't even offer them peace and enjoyment without including the laurel wreath[59] with its power to drive one mad. This plebeian taste, which *takes intoxication more seriously than nourishment*, has, however, by no means emerged from the depths of the plebs: on the contrary, it has been transported and transplanted into them where now it merely springs up residually and most opulently, whereas its origin stems from the highest intellects among whom it bloomed for millennia. The common folk is the last *virgin soil* in which this gleaming weed can still flourish. — What! And it is precisely to this folk that politics ought to be entrusted? So that it can turn politics into its daily intoxication?

189[60]

On grand politics. — However much profit and vanity, on the part of individuals as well as nations, play a role in *grand politics*: the mightiest tide driving them forward is the *need for the feeling of power*, which from time to time gushes up from inexhaustible wellsprings in the souls not only of princes and potentates, but also, and not least of all, precisely amid the lower ranks of the common people. Over and over again the hour comes when the masses *are ready* to put their life, their fortune, their conscience, their virtue on the line in order to attain for themselves that highest of pleasures and, as a victorious, tyrannical, impetuous nation, to dispose at will (or to think it is so disposing) over other nations. Then such a plethora of squandering, sacrificing, hoping, trusting, over-audacious, fantastical instincts wells up that an ambitious or shrewdly designing prince can start up a war and pawn his wrongdoing off on the people's good conscience. The great conquerors have always mouthed the pathos-ridden language of virtue: they have always been surrounded by the masses in a state of exaltation and eager to hear only the most exalted language. Strange madness of moral judgments! When a human being is possessed with the feeling of power, he will experience and speak of himself as *good*: and that is precisely the moment when those on whom he *vents* his power experience and speak of him as *evil*! — In the fable of the different ages of humanity Hesiod portrayed the same epoch, that of the Homeric heroes, twice in succession, rendering *two periods out of one*:[61] from the point of view of those who suffered under the horrible iron oppression of these adventurous people of brute force or who learned of them from their ancestors, the age seemed *evil*: but the descendants of these chivalrous houses venerated it as the *good*, dearly departed, dearly blessed age of yesteryear. The poet had no recourse other than to do as he did — no doubt he had about him listeners from both camps!

190[62]

German culture[63] *the way it used to be.* — When the Germans began to become interesting to the other nations of Europe — it wasn't so long ago — it came about due to a culture that they now no longer possess, that they indeed shook off with a blind zeal as if it were a disease: and yet they could come up with nothing better to put in its place than political and nationalistic insanity. To be sure, they have in this way managed to become far more interesting to other nations than they had even been earlier by virtue of their culture: and so may they be content! In the meantime there is no denying that this German culture of old has made fools of the Europeans and that it does not merit the interest, indeed, the imitation and vying emulation it has elicited. Have a look around these days at Schiller, Wilhelm von Humboldt, Schleiermacher, Hegel, Schelling, read their correspondence and initiate yourself into the great circle of their followers: what is it that they have in common, that, as we are today, affects us alternately as insufferable and as so moving and worthy of compassion? For one, the craving to

appear, at all cost, morally *aroused*; then the passionate demand for brilliant boneless generalities combined with an intentional "beautifying vision," the determined desire to view
everything (characters, passions, ages, mores) as more beautiful
than it is—"beautiful," according to an, unfortunately, blurry
bad taste that nonetheless boasted of its Greek ancestry. It is a
soft, good-natured, silver-lined idealism that wants, above all,
nobly affected gestures and nobly affected voices, a thing as
presumptuous as it is naive, animated by a most sincere aversion to "cold" or "dry" reality, to anatomy, to undiluted passions, to every type of philosophical temperance and skepticism, particularly, however, to any natural science that does
not lend itself to some religious symbolism.[64] Goethe observed
this battue of German culture in his own way, standing aside,
mildly demurring, silent, ever more resolved in his own better
course. Somewhat later Schopenhauer observed it as well—a
great deal of the real world and of the world's devilry had become apparent to him, and he spoke of it just as crudely as he
was enthusiastic: for this devilry had its own *beauty*!—And
what was it, at bottom, that seduced foreigners away from observing German culture as had Goethe and Schopenhauer or
from simply ignoring it altogether? It was that faint luster, that
enigmatic Milky Way gleam, that radiated around this culture:
upon seeing it, the foreigner said "That is very, very far away
from us and strange; out there our seeing, hearing, understanding, enjoyment, evaluation cease; nonetheless, those could be
stars! Could the Germans have, on the sly, discovered a corner
of heaven and settled down there? One must try to move closer
to the Germans." And they did move closer: whereas hardly
much later these same Germans began to be at pains to strip
themselves of the Milky Way gleam; they knew all too well they
had not been in heaven—but in a cloud!

191

Better people!—Everyone says to me that our art is directed
toward the greedy, insatiable, unrestrained, disgusted, harassed

people of today and opens up for them an image of bliss, lofti-
ness, and otherworldliness next to their own image of a dissolute wasteland: such that they can for once forget and breathe
a sigh of relief, indeed, perhaps they bring back from that forgetting an impulse toward flight and toward turning back.
Poor artists with such a public as this! With ulterior motives of
such a half-priestly, half-psychiatric bent! How much happier
and more fortunate was "our great Corneille,"[65] as Madame de
Sévigné exclaims with the inflection of a woman in the presence of a complete *man*—how much loftier was *his* audience
whom he could benefit with images of valiant virtues, strict
adherence to duty, magnanimous sacrifice, heroic self-restraint!
How differently did he and they love existence, not out of a
blind dissolute "will" that one curses because one is unable to
kill it, but as a place instead where greatness and humanity are
possible side by side and where even the strictest constraint of
forms, subjugation to princely and priestly arbitrariness, is able
to suppress neither pride, nor valor, nor grace, nor the spirit
of each individual; on the contrary, it is experienced much
more as an *antithetical stimulus and spur* toward innate self-
sovereignty and nobility, to an inherited power of the will and
passion!

192[66]

Wishing perfect adversaries for oneself. — There is no arguing
with the French that they have been the *most Christian* nation
on earth:[67] not in the sense that the faith of the masses has
been greater there than elsewhere, but because in France the
most difficult Christian ideals have been converted into persons and have not remained mere idea, embryo, half measure.
There is Pascal, in the unification of ardor, spirit, and honesty
foremost among all Christians—and consider all that needed
to be unified here![68] There is Fénelon, the perfect and enchanting expression of *ecclesiastical culture* in all its powers: a golden
mean that, as a historian, one might tend to view as something
impossible, whereas it was only something unspeakably diffi-

cult and improbable. There is Madame de Guyon among her peers, the French quietists,[69] and everything that the apostle Paul's grandiloquence and fervor[70] sought to divine regarding the Christian condition of most sublime, loving, tranquil, and enraptured quasi-godliness has here become truth and, owing to a genuine, feminine, subtle, refined, Gallic naïveté of word and gesture,[71] has, in the process, shed that Jewish importunity that Paul displayed toward God. There is the founder of the Trappist monasteries,[72] he who took the ascetic ideal of Christianity with utmost seriousness, not as an exception among the French but as genuinely French: for until this day, his gloomy creation has been capable of remaining natural and vigorous only among the French; it followed them into Alsace and to Algeria. Let's not forget the Huguenots:[73] heretofore there has never existed a more beautiful union of militant and industrious disposition, of more refined customs and Christian severity. And in Port-Royal[74] the tradition of great Christian erudition flourished for the last time: and great persons in France understand the flourish better than elsewhere. Far from being superficial, a great Frenchman nevertheless maintains his surface, a natural skin for his content and his profundity—whereas the profundity of a great German is most often kept bottled up in an intricate capsule as an elixir that seeks to protect itself from the light and from frivolous hands through its tough and strange cover. — Now go figure why this nation of consummate types of Christianness also had to produce the consummate countertypes of unchristian freethinking! The French freethinker struggled within himself against great persons and not merely against dogmas and sublime monstrosities as did the freethinkers of other nations.

193[75]

Esprit[76] *and morality.* — The German who understands the secret of managing to make spirit, knowledge, and soul boring and who has accustomed himself to experiencing boredom as moral — is afraid of French *esprit*, afraid it might just poke out the eyes of morality—and yet it is a captivated fear as with a little bird before a rattlesnake. Of the illustrious Germans none perhaps has had more *esprit* than *Hegel*[77]—but he also had, as a corollary, so great a German fear of it that it spawned the bad style characteristic of him.[78] A style, namely, whose essence consists in wrapping round a kernel and wrapping round it again and again until it barely peeks through, abashed and curious—the way "young women glimpse through their veils," as Aeschylus, the age-old misogynist, would say—: that kernel is, however, a witty, often brazen aperçu regarding the most intellectual subjects, a subtle and daring juxtaposition of words, which, as a condiment to learning,[79] belongs in the *society of thinkers*—but cloaked in all that wrapping it presents itself as the very embodiment of abstruse learnedness and utterly as the highest moral boredom! Here the Germans had a form of *esprit* they could *permit* themselves and they enjoyed it with such unrestrained delight that Schopenhauer's astute, very astute understanding came to a standstill—he ranted[80] his whole life long against the spectacle that the Germans presented to him, but he was never able to explain it to himself.

194[81]

Vanity of the teachers of morality. — The explanation for the, on the whole, paltry success of the teachers of morality may be found in the fact that they wanted too much all *at once*, that is to say they were too ambitious: they wanted all too eagerly to lay down precepts *for everyone.* This, however, amounts to flailing about in generalities and to preaching to animals that they turn into humans: what a miracle that the animals find this boring! One should seek out limited circles and seek and promote the morality appropriate for them; accordingly, preach to wolves, for example, that they turn into dogs. Above all, however, great success is reserved for him who wishes to educate neither everyone nor limited circles, but a single individual and who, in so doing, glances neither left nor right. The previous century is superior to ours precisely because it contained so many individually educated persons along with just as many educators who had here discovered their lives' *mission*—and with this mission also *dignity* with regard to themselves and to all others of "good society."[82]

195[83]

The so-called classical education.—To discover that our life is *consecrated* to the pursuit of knowledge; that we would be throwing it away, no! that we would have already thrown it away if this consecration weren't protecting it from our own selves; to recite to ourselves again and again with staggering emotion the following verses:

"Fate, I *follow* you! And were it not my wish
I'd *have to* nonetheless and take along my sighs!"[84]

—And now to look back on the course of our lives and also to discover something that is no longer reparable: the squandering of our youth in which our educators failed to employ those inquisitive, impassioned, thirsty years to lead us toward *knowledge* of things, but used them instead for the so-called "classical education"! The squandering of our youth in which a scanty understanding of the Greeks and Romans and their languages was drilled into us in a manner as inept as it was torturous and that runs counter to the first rule of all education: that one should give a particular dish only to those *who hunger for it*! In which mathematics and physics were forced upon us in a violent manner *instead* of our first being led to feel the despair of ignorance and of having our small quotidian lives, our activities and everything that occurred in the house, in the shop, in the sky, in the countryside, from morning till evening, dissolve into thousands of problems, tormenting, mortifying, irritating problems—in order to demonstrate to our yearning that we *needed* straightaway a scientific knowledge of mathematics and physics and then to impart to us our first *delight* in science through the absolute logicality of such scientific knowledge. If only we had been taught *to revere* these sciences, if only our souls had ever once been shaken by the struggles and defeats and renewed battles of past luminaries, by the martyrdom that comprises the history of *rigorous* scholarship![85] On the contrary, we caught wind of a certain disdain for the actual sciences in favor of history, "formal education," and "the classics"! And we allowed ourselves to be deceived so easily! Formal education! Could we not have pointed to the best teachers at our high schools and laughingly, skeptically inquired: "Where in the world is their formal education? And if they don't have it, how are they supposed to teach it?" And the classics! Did we learn any part of what these same ancients instructed their youth? Did we learn to speak like them, write like them? Did we practice unremittingly the fencing art of conversation, of dialectics? Did we learn to move beautifully and proudly like them, to wrestle, throw, and box like them? Did we learn any part of the asceticism practiced by all Greek philosophers? Were we trained in a single ancient virtue and in the manner in which the ancients exercised it? Wasn't our education altogether lacking in any reflection upon morality whatsoever, let alone in the only possible critique of it, that rigorous and courageous attempt *to live* within some morality or other? Did anyone ever stir in us any feeling at all that the ancients valued more highly than the moderns? Was the arrangement of the day and of life, along with life's goals, presented to us in the spirit of antiquity? Did we even learn the languages of antiquity in the way we learn those of living nations — namely, in order to speak well with ease? Nowhere a real ability, no new capability resulting from years of toil! Only a knowledge of what people once were able and capable of! And what a knowledge! Nothing grows more clear to me from year to year than that the nature of anything Greek or ancient, no matter how transparently and universally accepted it seems to lie before our very eyes, is extraordinarily difficult to make out, indeed, is hardly comprehensible and that the customary carefreeness with which one speaks of the ancients is either itself a case of carelessness or an age-old, inherited arrogance based on the

absence of thought. The similarity of words and concepts deceives us: but behind them there always lies a hidden sensation
that *has to be* foreign, incomprehensible, or painfully shameful
to the modern sensibility. And these are the fields in which
young boys are allowed to romp about! In any case, we did so
when we were boys and in the process we came away with an
almost insurmountable antipathy toward antiquity, an antipathy born seemingly of too great an intimacy. For the proud
delusion of our classics teachers goes so far in imagining themselves, as it were, *in possession of the ancients*, that they allow
this arrogance to spill over onto their students, along with the
suspicion that such a possession, even if it most likely cannot
make us happy,[86] is good enough for upstanding, poor, foolish, old book-dragons: "may these dragons brood over their
hoard! It will surely be worthy of them!" — With this silent,
ulterior thought our classical education reached its culmination.
This is no longer reparable — for us! But let's not think only
of ourselves!

196

Truth's most personal questions. — "What is it that I actually
do? And what is it that precisely *I* wish to accomplish
thereby?" — This is the question of truth that is not taught,
and consequently not asked, by our current type of education;
there is no time for it. On the other hand, to speak with children about all sorts of nonsense and not about truth, to speak
pleasantries with women who are subsequently supposed to
become mothers and not about the truth, to speak with young
people about their future and their amusement and not about
truth — there is always time and desire for that! — But what,
after all, are seventy years! — They run their course and are
soon over; there is so little reason for the wave to know how
and where it is flowing. Indeed, it could be a clever mark of
prudence *not to know.* — "Admittedly: but not even *to inquire*
about it hardly indicates a sense of pride; our education does
not make people proud." — So much the better! "Really?"

197[87]

The Germans' hostility to the Enlightenment. — Consider the intellectual contribution the Germans of the first half of this century have rendered to culture at large, and take first the German philosophers: they retreated to the first and oldest level of speculation, for, like the thinkers of dreamy ages, they found satisfaction in concepts rather than in explanations — they resuscitated a prescientific type of philosophy. Second, the German historians and Romantics:[88] their general concern amounted to bestowing honor upon older, primitive sensibilities, especially Christianity, the folk soul, folklore, folk language, medievalism, Oriental asceticism, the world of India. Third, the natural scientists:[89] they fought against the spirit of Newton and Voltaire and, like Goethe and Schopenhauer, sought to erect once again the idea of a divine or demonic nature suffused with its universal ethical and symbolic significance. The whole tremendous proclivity of the Germans ran contrary to the Enlightenment and contrary to the revolution in society that, through vulgar misunderstanding, passed as the result of Enlightenment: piety toward everything then in existence sought to metamorphose into piety toward everything that once had existed in order that heart and spirit might once again grow *full* and no longer have any room for future, innovative goals. The cult of feeling was erected in place of the cult of reason, and German composers,[90] as artists of the invisible, of raptures, fairy tale, yearning, built on the new temple more successfully than all artists of the word and of thoughts. Even if we take into account that in the particulars a great deal of value has been uncovered and disseminated and that many things are judged more fairly than before: one cannot help but conclude that, with regard to the big picture, the *widespread danger* was *by no means slight* that under the guise of attaining fullest and ultimate knowledge of the past, knowledge itself was being suppressed beneath feeling and — in the words Kant used to define his own project — "once again room for faith was to be made by demonstrating the limits of knowing."[91] We can breathe freely again: the hour of this danger has passed! And strange to say: the very spirits that the Germans had so eloquently invoked became, in the long run, the most injurious for their invokers—history, understanding of origin and evolution, sympathy with the past, the newly aroused passion for feeling and knowledge, after having for a time appeared to be beneficial companions of the spirit of rapturous obscurantism and reaction, assumed one day a different nature and now fly on the widest wings above and beyond their earlier invokers as new and stronger geniuses of *that very Enlightenment* against which they had been invoked. This Enlightenment we now must carry on—unperturbed that there has existed a "great Revolution" and then again a "great reaction" against it, that indeed both still exist: they are, after all, the mere ripple of waves in comparison to the truly great tide in which *we* surge and want to surge!

198[92]

Giving one's nation stature. — To possess many great inner experiences and to gaze upon and beyond them with a spiritually reflective eye—that is what creates people of culture who give *stature* to their nation. In France and Italy it was the aristocracy who accomplished this; in Germany, where the aristocracy on the whole has heretofore counted among the spiritually impoverished (perhaps no longer for long), it was the priests, teachers, and their descendants who accomplished it.

199[93]

We are more noble. — Loyalty, magnanimity, concern for one's good reputation: these three united in a single disposition—we call *noble, refined, dignified,* and herein we surpass the Greeks. Let us not relinquish the disposition owing to the feeling that the ancient objects of these virtues have sunk in esteem (and rightly so), but carefully ensure instead that this exquisite, inherited drive of ours be directed toward new objects. — In order to grasp that, within our own, still

chivalrous and feudalistic nobility, the disposition of the noblest Greeks has to be experienced as lowly and even indecent,
one need only remember those words of comfort Odysseus
was always spouting in ignominious situations: "Bear up, dear
heart! You've already borne worse dog's treatment!"[94] And in
addition take as a practical application of the mythic model the
story of that Athenian officer, who, when threatened by another officer with a stick in front of the entire general staff,
shrugged off this humiliation with the words: "Strike me if
you will! But then listen to me as well!"[95] (This was Themistocles, that highly nimble Odysseus of the Classical age who, in
this ignominious moment, was just the man to send down to
his "dear heart" those needed lines of consolation.) The Greeks
were far from taking life and death as lightly as we do over an
insult, owing to the influence of inherited chivalrous adventur-
ousness and desire for self-sacrifice; or from searching out opportunities for staking life and death in a game of honor the
way we do in duels; or from valuing the preservation of one's
good name (honor) higher than the conquest of a bad name, if
the latter is consonant with fame and the feeling of power; or
from remaining true to class prejudices[96] and articles of faith
should they hinder one from becoming a tyrant. For this is the
ignoble secret of every good Greek aristocrat: owing to a most
profound jealousy, he considers every one of his peers to be on
equal footing with him, but, like a pouncing tiger, he is prepared at any moment to unleash forceful rule upon his prey:
what does a little lying, murder, betrayal, selling out of his
home city along the way matter to him! Justice was extraordinarily difficult for this species of persons; it was considered
something nearly unbelievable; "a just man" — for Greeks that
sounded the way "a saint" does for Christians. When, however,
even a Socrates said: "the virtuous person is the happiest person," they simply didn't believe their ears, they supposed they
had heard something deranged. For, as the image of the happiest person, every man of noble descent thought of the consummate ruthlessness and devilry of the tyrant who sacrifices

everything and everyone to his wantonness and his pleasure. Among people who secretly fantasized wildly about this sort of happiness, a veneration for the state could not, to be sure, be implanted deeply enough—but I opine: people whose craving for power no longer rages as blindly as that of those noble Greeks are, likewise, no longer in need of that idolization of the concept of the nation-state through which the earlier craving was kept under control.

200

Bearing poverty. — The greatest advantage of noble descent is that it allows one to bear poverty better.

201[97]

Future of the aristocracy. — The gestures assumed by members of refined society express the fact that the consciousness of power is constantly executing its charming[98] play in their limbs. Accordingly, the person, man or woman, of aristocratic custom does not like to sink, as if completely exhausted, into an armchair; where all others make themselves comfortable, for example on the train, the aristocrat avoids leaning against his back; he appears not to grow tired when he is on his feet for hours at court; he furnishes his house not with an eye for comfort, but expansively and illustriously, as if it were the domain of grander (and taller) beings; he responds to a verbal provocation with composure and a clear head, and is not horrified, crushed, mortified, breathless in the plebeian fashion. Just as he knows how to preserve the appearance of ever-present, dignified physical strength, he also wishes, through constant serenity and civility even in distressing situations, to maintain the impression that his soul and his spirit are equal to all dangers and vagaries. With regard to the passions, a refined culture can resemble either the rider who experiences the ecstasy of having a passionate, proud animal march to the Spanish step[99]—imagine the age of Louis XIV—or the rider who feels his horse beneath him shoot forth like a force of nature right to

the borderline where horse and rider lose their head, yet from
sheer pleasure in the ecstasy to keep head held high precisely
at that moment: in both cases a refined *culture* is breathing in
power, and even if very frequently its manners demand merely
the semblance of the feeling of power, the very impression that
this performance makes on the nonrefined as well as the the-
atricality[100] of the impression, nonetheless continuously increase
the genuine sense of superiority. — This indisputable happiness
of refined culture, which is based on the feeling of superiority, is
beginning these days to climb to an even higher level, because,
thanks to all the free spirits, it is now permitted and no longer
disgraceful for those born and raised in the aristocracy to enter
into the orders of knowledge and to obtain there a more intellectual ordination, to learn more exalted deeds of chivalry than
heretofore, and to gaze up to that ideal of *victorious wisdom*,
which no previous age has been able to erect for itself with so
good a conscience as the age that is just on the verge of arriving.
And in the end: what is the aristocracy supposed to do with itself when, with each passing day, it appears to grow more and
more *indecent* to engage in politics? —

202[101]

For the cultivation of health. — We have barely begun to reflect on the physiology of the criminal and nevertheless we
have already come to the irrefutable view that there is no essential difference between criminals and the mentally ill: provided we *believe* that the *customary* moral way of thinking is
the way of thinking that promotes *mental health*. But no belief
is still believed as solidly as this latter, and so let's not shy away
from drawing the obvious conclusion and treating the criminal like someone who is mentally ill: above all not with lofty
charity, but with the medical acumen and goodwill of a physician. The criminal is in need of a change of air, different
company, a temporary absence, perhaps solitude and a new
occupation — fine! Perhaps he himself finds it to his advantage
to spend some time in custody in order thereby to find protec-

tion against himself and an irksome *tyrannical drive*—fine!
We must present to him clearly the possibility and the means
of being healed (eradication, transformation, sublimation of
that particular drive) and also, in the worst case, the unlikeli-
hood of a cure. We ought to offer the incurable criminal who
has become a horror to himself the opportunity to commit
suicide. Reserving this as the most extreme means of alleviation: shouldn't we leave no stone unturned in, above all, re-
storing the criminal to his good spirits and peace of mind; we
should wipe from his soul, as a matter of uncleanliness, pangs
of conscience and give him an indication of how he can make
up, and even more than make up, for the injury he perhaps
inflicted on one person by coming to the aid of another, or
indeed perhaps of the whole community! Everything with utmost care and consideration! And especially with anonymity
or under assumed names and frequent changes in location so
that, in the process, the integrity of his reputation and his future life run into as little danger as possible. At present, admittedly, anyone who receives an injury, altogether irrespective of
how this injury might be made good, desires to have his *revenge*, and appeals for it to the courts—and this is what, for
the time being, perpetuates our abominable penal codes along
with their shopkeeper scales and their *desire to counterbalance
guilt with punishment*: but might we not be able to get beyond
this? How much lighter and easier our sense of existence would
be if, together with the belief in guilt, one could free oneself
from the age-old instinct for revenge and could even regard it
as the subtle wisdom of those who are happy to join with
Christianity in blessing one's enemy and in *showing kindness*
to those who have offended us! Let's rid the world of the notion of *sin*—and let's soon send the notion of *punishment* that
follows packing along behind it! In the future may these banished monsters live somewhere other than among people if
they insist on wanting to survive and are not destroyed by their
own self-disgust!—In the meantime we should consider that
the loss society and individuals suffer at the hands of criminals

is very similar to the loss suffered from sick people: sick people spread worry and ill humor, are not productive, exhaust other people's revenues, require caretakers, doctors, upkeep, and live off the time and energy of the healthy. Nevertheless, one would consider inhuman anyone who wanted to take *revenge* on a sick person on account of this. Previously, to be sure, this is just what one did: in primitive states of culture, and even now among many wild tribes, the sick person is indeed treated as a criminal, as a danger to the community and as the dwelling place of some sort of demonic being that has invaded his body due to an incurred guilt—here the word is: every sick person is a guilty person! And we—are we really not yet ready for the opposite view? Are we really not yet able to say: every "guilty" person is a sick person? No, the hour for this is yet to come. As yet we lack above all the physicians for whom what up until this point we have called practical morality will have been transformed into a part of their art and science of healing; as yet we lack in general that consuming interest in these matters, which perhaps one day will seem not dissimilar to the storm and stress of those religious excitements of old; as yet the churches do not possess cultivators of health; as yet instruction about the body and about diet are not among the required courses at all middle and high schools; as yet there exist no quiet organizations of like-minded people who together have vowed to renounce the aid of the courts along with punishment and revenge on those who do them wrong; as yet no thinker has had the courage to measure the health of a society and of the individual according to how many parasites they can support; and as yet no founder of a state has turned up who wielded the plowshare in the spirit of that generous and mildhearted motto: "Wouldst thou cultivate the land, then cultivate it with the plow: for the bird and the wolf who follow behind the plow shall rejoice in thee—*all creatures shall rejoice in thee.*"[102]

203[103]

Against bad diet. — Phooey on the meals people cook these days, in restaurants as well as everywhere society's well-to-do class resides! Even when scholars of the highest reputation come together, they load their table according to the same custom as the banker loads his: following the principle of "much too much" and "ever such variety" — from which it follows that the dishes are prepared with an eye to their effect instead of their efficacy, and stimulating drinks have to assist in driving out the heaviness from both stomach and brain. Phooey, what widespread dissoluteness and overexcitability as the inevitable consequence! Phooey, what dreams these people must have! Phooey, what arts and which books will be the dessert of such dinners! And no matter what they do: pepper or contradiction or world-weariness will rule their actions! (The wealthy class in England needs its Christianity to be able to endure its digestive difficulties and its headaches.) Finally, in order to mention what is humorous and not just disgusting about this situation, these people are by no means gormandizers; our century with its type of hustle and bustle exerts more power over their limbs than does their stomach: what purpose then do these dinners serve? — *They represent!* What, in heaven's name? Class? — No, money: one no longer belongs to a class! One is an "individual"! But money is power, fame, dignity, preeminence, influence; money, depending on how much of it one has, determines these days the extent of one's moral presumption! No one wants to hide it under a bushel and no one would want to place it on the table; accordingly, money must have a representative that one can place on the table: see our dinners.

204

Danaë and god in gold.[104] — Where does this excessive impatience emanate from, an impatience that is currently turning people into criminals under circumstances that are more conducive to the opposite tendency? For if one person employs

false weights, another burns down his house after having in-
sured it to the maximum, a third participates in minting
counterfeit currency, if three-quarters of the upper class gives
itself over to sanctioned fraud and has the stock exchange and
all forms of speculation on its conscience: what is driving
them? Not actual want, they are not doing any too poorly, perhaps they even eat and drink without worrying—but they are
pressed and pressured day and night by a terrible and fearful
impatience at the sluggish rate at which money is accumulating
and by an equally terrible and fearful craving for, and love of,
accumulated money. In this impatience and this love, however,
there appears once again that fanaticism of the *appetite for
power* that formerly was ignited by the conviction of being in
possession of the truth[105] and that went by so many beautiful
names that, as a result, one could, *with a good conscience*, dare
to be inhuman (to burn Jews, heretics, and good books and to
eradicate highly developed cultures like those of Peru and
Mexico).[106] The means of the appetite for power have changed,
but the same volcano still burns, impatience and excessive love
demand their sacrifice; and what one formerly did "for God's
sake" we now do for the sake of money, that is to say, for the
sake of that which *now* imparts to the highest degree the feeling of power and a good conscience.[107]

205[108]

On the people of Israel. — Among the spectacles to which the
coming century invites us belongs the verdict regarding the
fate of the European Jews. That they have cast their die, crossed
their Rubicon,[109] is palpably clear: the only choice left for them
is to become Europe's masters or to lose Europe, just as they
once long ago lost Egypt, where they had placed themselves
before a similar either-or.[110] In Europe, however, they have
gone through eighteen centuries of schooling such as no other
people here can point to, and indeed, in such a manner that it
was precisely not the community but all the more so the individuals who benefited from the experiences of this horrible

period of apprenticeship. As a result, among the Jews of today
the psychological and spiritual resources of support are extraordinary; in times of affliction, in order to escape a profound predicament, they turn least of all people living in Europe to the bottle or to suicide—as is the wont of the less
gifted. In the history of his fathers and grandfathers every Jew
has a storehouse of examples of the coldest self-possession and
steadfastness in terrible situations, of the most subtle outwit-
ting and exploitation of misfortune and chance; their courage
under the cloak of wretched subservience, their heroism in
sperneri se sperni[111] surpassed the virtue of all the saints put together. Throughout two millennia one has attempted to make
them contemptible by treating them contemptibly, by denying them access to all honors and everything honorable, by
shoving them instead ever more deeply into the dirtier businesses—and it is true they have not grown cleaner as a result of
this treatment. But contemptible? They themselves have never
ceased believing that they are called to the highest things, and
the virtues of all who suffer have never ceased to adorn them.
The way they honor their forefathers and their children and the
reasonableness of their marriages and marriage customs distinguish them from all other Europeans. In addition to all this,
they managed to create for themselves a feeling of power and of
eternal vengeance out of the very businesses that had been
handed over to them (or to which one had handed them over);
one must also say in defense even of their usury that without
this occasional, pleasant, and beneficial torturing of those who
had contempt for them, they would hardly have been able to
preserve their self-respect[112] for so long. For our self-respect is
bound to our ability to practice restitution in matters both
good and bad. Yet the Jews do not easily get carried away in
their vengeance: for they all have the openness of mind and
also of spirit that is inculcated into one by frequent changes
in residence and climate, in the mores of neighbors and op-
pressors; they possess by far the greatest experience in all
human intercourse and, even with regard to passion, practice

the circumspection born of this experience. They are so certain of their mental suppleness and shrewdness that they never, not even in the severest of circumstances, find it necessary to earn their bread with physical energy as a rough laborer, a porter, a field slave. One can still tell from their manners that their soul has not known chivalrous, genteel sentiments nor their body beautiful shining armor: something of the importunate vies with an often tender, almost always embarrassing obsequiousness. But now, as they inevitably from year to year marry ever more into Europe's best nobility, they will soon come into a goodly inheritance of both spiritual and bodily manners: so that in a hundred years they will already look genteel enough not to arouse, as masters, *shame* in those who are subservient to them. And that is what matters! This is the reason why a resolution of their affairs is, for the time being, premature. They know best of all themselves that a takeover of Europe or violence of any kind is unthinkable for them; but they know equally well that sometime or other Europe, like a fully ripened fruit, ought to fall right into their hand, which only ever so slightly reaches out to it. For this to transpire they need, in the meantime, to distinguish themselves in all fields of European distinction and to stand among the first rank: until they get to the point where it is they themselves who mandate what it is that constitutes distinction. Then they will be hailed as the inventors and guideposts of the nations of Europe and will no longer offend the general sense of shame. And toward what, moreover, is this abundance of accumulated great impressions, which for every Jewish family constitutes Jewish history, this abundance of passions, virtues, choices, renunciations, battles, victories of all kinds supposed to lead — toward what should it be rushing forward if not, finally, toward mentally and spiritually great people and great works! Then when the Jews can display as their work such jewels and golden vessels as the European nations of shorter and less profound experience are, and were, incapable of producing, when Israel has transformed its eternal vengeance into an eternal blessing for Europe: then there shall arrive here once again that seventh day on which the age-old God of the Jews is allowed to *rejoice* in himself, in his creation, and in his chosen people[113] —and we all, all want to rejoice along with him!

206[114]

The impossible class.[115] —Poor, cheerful, and independent!— these things can exist side by side; poor, cheerful, and a slave!— these things can also exist—and I can think of no better news for the workers in today's factory servitude: provided they don't feel that it's altogether a *disgrace* to be *used* and *used up*, in the way this happens, as a wheel in the machine and, as it were, a stopgap to plug the hole in human inventiveness! Phooey! To believe that higher payment could lift from them the *essence* of their misery, by which I mean their impersonal enslavement! Phooey! To let oneself be talked into believing that through a heightening of this impersonality within the mechanical workings of a new society the disgrace of slavery could be turned into a virtue! Phooey! To set a price for oneself whereby one becomes no longer a person but merely a cog! Are you co-conspirers in the current folly sweeping over nations, which, above all else, want to produce as much as possible and to be as rich as possible? Your concern ought to be to hold out to them a counter-reckoning: what vast sums of genuine *inner* value are being squandered on such a superficial external goal! Where is your inner value, however, when you no longer know what it means to breathe freely? You don't have yourselves even barely under control? You all too often grow tired of yourselves as of a drink that has stood too long? You attend to the newspaper and look askance at your rich neighbor, growing covetous over the rapid rise and fall of power, money, and opinions? When you no longer have any faith in a philosophy that wears rags and in the candor of those who live modestly? When the voluntary, idyllic poverty and freedom from job and marriage that would suit quite well the more spiritual among you has become a laughing stock? When you always have ringing in your ear instead the fife of the socialist pied pipers who want to inflame[116] you with mad hopes, who enjoin you *to be prepared* and nothing more, prepared at any moment such that you are waiting and waiting for something external, but otherwise you continue to live in every way the same as you had otherwise lived before—until this waiting turns to hunger and thirst and fever and madness, and finally the day of the *bestia triumphans*[117] rises in all its glory?—Instead, everyone ought to think to oneself: "Better to emigrate, to seek in wild and fresh parts of the world to become *master*, and above all master of myself; to keep moving from place to place as long as any sign of slavery whatsoever still beckons to me; not to avoid adventure and war and, if worst should come to worst, to be ready for death: only no more of this indecent servitude, only no more of this growing sour and venomous and conspiratorial!" This would be the right conviction: the workers of Europe ought in future to declare themselves *as a class* a human impossibility and not merely, as most often happens, as a somewhat brutal and unsuitable construction; within the European beehive, they ought to precipitate an age of grand swarming-out such as has never been seen before and, through this freedom of domicile in the grand style, to protest against the machine, against capital, and against the choice currently threatening them of *having* to become either slave of the state or slave of a party of insurrection. May Europe be relieved of a quarter of its inhabitants! This will bring relief to it and to them! Only in faraway lands, through the ventures of swarming migrations of colonists, will one come to recognize just how much common sense and fairness, how much healthy distrust mother Europe has incorporated into her sons—these sons who were no longer able to endure being near her, the stupefied old crone, and were in danger of becoming as grumpy, irritable, and addicted to pleasure as she herself is. Outside Europe, Europe's virtues will be journeying along with these workers; and what inside the homeland began to degenerate into dangerous ill humor and criminal tendencies, will outside, take on a wild, beautiful naturalness and will be called heroism. — Then, at long last a pure air would certainly return to the old Europe, which is currently overpopulated and brooding in itself! So what if, after all, its "workforce" is a little diminished! In this event we will perhaps recall that we have grown accustomed to many needs only once it became so *easy* to satisfy them — we will again unlearn some of them! Perhaps we will also bring in the *Chinese* at that point: and they would bring along the ways of thinking and living that are suitable for diligent ants. Indeed, they could in general assist in transfusing into the blood of a restless and worn out Europe a little Asian calm and contemplation — and what is surely needed most — Asian *perseverance*.

207[118]

The German approach to morality. — A German is capable of great things, but it is unlikely that he will accomplish them: for, as befits a basically torpid spirit, he obeys *wherever he can*. If he is forced to stand on his own and throw off his torpor, if it is no longer possible for him to disappear like a numeral within a sum (wherein he is not nearly as valuable as a Frenchman or Englishman) — then he will discover his powers: then he will turn dangerous, evil, profound, daring, and he brings to the light of day the hoard of sleeping energy he carries inside himself in which no one else (not even he himself) believed. When in such cases a German obeys himself — and it is the great exception — it transpires with the same ponderousness, relentlessness, and endurance with which he otherwise obeys his prince and his official duties: so that he, as previously stated, is then equal to great things that are no way in keeping with the "weak character" that he presupposes for himself. Usually, however, he is afraid to rely *upon himself alone*, to *improvise*; this is why Germany uses up so many officials and so much ink. — Rashness is alien to him, it is too unnerving for him; but in completely new situations that wrench him out of his drowsiness he is *almost* rash; he enjoys the rarity of the new situation like an intoxication, and he knows a thing or two about intoxication! So it happens that the German these days is almost rash with regard to politics: even though the presumption of thoroughness and seriousness adheres to him in this area as well, a presumption of which he makes abundant use in interaction with other political powers, he is nonetheless secretly full of high spirits at being permitted for a change to wax enthusiastic and be temperamental and eagerly innovative and to exchange persons, parties, and prospects as if they were masks. — German scholars, who heretofore have enjoyed the reputation of being the most German of Germans, were, and perhaps still are, on a par with German soldiers in their profound, almost childlike tendency to obey in all outward matters and in being required by scholarship to stand on their own a great deal and to take responsibility for a great deal; if they understand how to maintain their proud, straightforward,[119] and patient manner and their freedom from political folly in times where the winds are blowing in another direction, then great things are still to be expected of them: such as they now are (or were), they are the embryonic state of something *higher.* — The advantage and disadvantage of the Germans, even of German scholars, was heretofore that they have been more inclined to superstition and to the desire to believe[120] than other nations; their vices are, now as ever, drunkenness and the tendency toward suicide (the latter being an indication of the ponderousness of their spirit that is easily led to toss away the reins); their danger lies in anything that binds the powers of understanding and unleashes the affects (as, for example, excessive use of music or spirituous drinks): for, in a German, affect goes against his own advantage and is self-destructive like the affect of a drunkard. Enthusiasm itself is of less value in Germany than elsewhere, for it is fruitless. Whenever a German has done something great, it took place in a moment of urgency, a state of courage, of clenched teeth, of the most strained self-possession, and often of magnanimity. — Contact with them is certainly to be recommended — for virtually every German has something to *give*, if one understands how to lead him to the point where he *discovers* and *rediscovers* it (the German is disorderly inside).— —Now, if a people of this sort occupies itself with morality: which morality will it be that especially satisfies it? It is sure to insist first of all that its heartfelt tendency toward obedience appear idealized in this morality. "A human being must have something that he can *obey categorically*"—this is a German sentiment, German logicality: one runs into it at the foundation of all German moral teachings. What a different impression one has when confronting the entire morality of antiquity! All these Greek thinkers, however heterogeneous their image appears to us, seem to resemble as moralists a gym teacher[121] who enjoins a young pupil: "Come! Follow me! Surrender yourself to my discipline! And then maybe, just maybe you might succeed in carrying away the prize before all the Hellenes." Personal distinction—that is virtue for antiquity. To subordinate oneself, to follow publicly or in secret—that is virtue for the Germans. Long before Kant and his categorical imperative, Luther had spoken out of the same sensibility: there must be a being whom we as humans can trust unconditionally—it was his *proof of the existence of God*; he desired, more crudely and more in tune with the people than Kant, that one obey unconditionally not a concept but a person, and, in the end, Kant too took his detour through morality only for the purpose of arriving at *obedience toward a person*: precisely that is the cult of the Germans, to an ever greater degree the less they have remaining of a religious cult. Greeks and Romans had a different sensibility and would have made fun of such a conviction as "there *must* be a being": it is part of their Mediterranean freedom of feeling to guard against "unconditional trust" and to hold back under lock and key, in the last recess of their heart, a little bit of skepticism for each and every thing, be it god, human, or concept. Especially the ancient philosopher! *Nil admirari*[122]—in this proposition, he sees the whole of philosophy. And a German, namely Schopenhauer, goes so far to the opposite extreme as to say: *admirari id est philosophari*.[123] — But now, what if for a change the German, as sometimes happens, ended up in a position where he is capable *of great things*? When the hour of *exception*, the hour of disobedience comes? — I don't believe Schopenhauer was correct in saying that the only merit the Germans possessed before other peoples was that among them there were more atheists than elsewhere — but one thing I do know: when a German ends up in a position where he is capable of great things, *each and every time he will raise himself above morality*! And how could he not? Now he has to do something new, namely command — himself or others! His German morality, however, did not teach him to command! Commanding is something it has simply forgotten!

Book Four

208

Question of conscience. — "And *in summa*:[1] what is it you want that is actually new?" — We no longer want to turn the causes into sinners and the consequences into executioners.

209[2]

The usefulness of the strictest theories. — One overlooks many moral weaknesses in a person, wielding in the process a crude sieve, *provided* that person always professes allegiance to the strictest *theory of morality*! One has, by contrast, always placed the life of the free-spirited moralist under the microscope: with the ulterior motive that a false step in life is the surest argument against an unwelcome insight.

210

The "in itself." — Formerly one used to ask: What is it that is laughable? As if there existed outside ourselves things to which the laughable could adhere as a quality, and one exhausted oneself in coming up with possibilities (a theologian[3] even opined that it is the "naïveté of sin"). Nowadays one asks: What is laughter? How does laughter come about? One thought about it and finally determined that nothing good, nothing beautiful, nothing sublime, nothing evil exists in itself, that there no doubt are, however, states of the soul in which we impose such words on things outside and inside of us. We have *taken back* the predicates of things or at least reminded ourselves that we have *lent* them to things: — let us see to it that with this insight we do not lose the *ability* to lend and that we have not simultaneously grown *richer* and *greedier*.[4]

211[5]

To the dreamers of immortality. — So you wish this lovely consciousness of yourselves *to last forever*? Isn't that shameless? Have you then no consideration for all the other things that would have to *put up with* you for all eternity, just as they have put up with you this far with more than Christian patience? Or are you of the opinion that you can arouse in them an everlasting sense of well-being in your presence? One single immortal human being on the face of the earth would, in fact, be enough to drive singlehandedly everyone else on earth into a universal rampage of death and suicide out of being *sick and tired* of him! And you earth inhabitants with your mini-notions of a few thousand mini-minutes of time want to be an eternal nuisance to eternal, universal existence! Is there anything more impertinent! — Finally, let us be indulgent toward a creature of seventy years! — he hasn't been able to imagine the "eternal ennui"[6] that he *himself* would go through — he lacked the time!

212[7]

How one knows oneself. — As soon as one animal sees another, it measures itself against it in its own mind; and people in primitive ages do likewise. From which it follows that every person here gets to know himself almost exclusively with regard to his powers of defense and attack.

213

People with misspent lives. — Some are of such *material* that society may *fashion* this or that of them: do with them what one will, they will consider themselves content and find no reason to bemoan a misspent life. Others are made of too ex-

ceptional a material—it needn't be, for all that, exceptionally
fine, but merely uncommon—not to consider they are sure to
fare ill unless, as the sole exception, they are able to live in
keeping with their sole purpose in life:—in all other cases society will suffer the subsequent damages. For everything that
appears to the individual as part of a misspent, failed life, his
whole load of despondence, paralysis, malaise, irritability, cov-
etousness, he hurls back onto society—and thus there forms
around society a bad, stifling atmosphere and, in the most favorable case, a storm cloud.

214

What sort of indulgence![8]—You suffer and then demand that
we be indulgent toward you, if, in your suffering, you treat
things and people unfairly! But what good is our indulgence!
You, on the other hand, ought to be *more cautious* for your own
sake! What a fine way of compensating for your suffering, that
on top of it you *mar your own judgment*! Your own revenge
comes back to haunt you when you denigrate something; for in
so doing, you cloud *your* eye, not someone else's: you get used
to *seeing askew*!

215

Morality of sacrificial animals.—"Enthusiastic devotion,"
"self-sacrifice"—these are the buzzwords of your morality,
and I readily believe that, as you say, you "mean them honestly
and truly": only I know you better than you know yourself
when it comes to your "honesty" with its ability to walk arm
in arm with such a morality. From the heights of this morality
you look down at that other more sober morality that demands
self-control, rigor, obedience; you are apt to call it even egotistical and by all means!—You *are* being honest with yourselves
if it displeases you—it *must* displease you! For by devoting
yourselves enthusiastically and sacrificing yourselves, you enjoy
that intoxication stemming from the thought that you are now
at one with the powerful being, whether god or human, to

whom you have consecrated yourself: you feast on the feeling of his power, which has once again just been confirmed by a sacrifice. In truth you only *seem* to sacrifice yourselves; instead, in your thoughts you transform yourselves to gods and take pleasure in yourselves as such. Considered from within this feeling of pleasure—how weak and poor that "egotistical" morality of obedience, duty and reasonableness appears to you; it displeases you because in it sacrifice and devotion really do take place *without* the one who sacrifices fancying himself transformed into a god, as all of you fancy. In short, *you* want the intoxication and the excess, and that morality you despise raises a warning finger *against* intoxication and excess—I do certainly believe you when you say this causes you great distress!

216

Evil people and music.—Could the full bliss of love, which lies in *unconditional trust*, ever have been granted to anyone who was not profoundly mistrustful, evil, and caustic? For they, namely, relish in it the tremendous, never believed and never believable *exception* within their soul! One day they are overcome by that limitless, dreamlike sensation, which stands in contrast to the entire rest of their life, both hidden and visible: like a precious mystery and miracle, full of golden radiance, transcending all description. Unconditional trust renders one speechless; indeed, there is even a suffering and heaviness in this blessed speechlessness, which is also why souls thus pressed by happiness tend to be more grateful to *music* than all other and better people: for through music, as through a colorful smoke, they see and hear their love having become, as it were, *more distant*, more moving, and less heavy; music is for them the only means of *viewing* their extraordinary condition and only with a sort of alienation and relief do they gain access to this view. Upon listening to music, every lover thinks: "It is speaking about me, it speaks for me, *it knows everything*!" —

217

The artist. — Germans want to achieve, through the artist, a kind of imaginary, longed-for passion; Italians want through him to take a rest from their real passions; the French want from him the chance to display their judgment and occasions to speak. Let us therefore be fair!

218[9]

Maneuvering one's weaknesses like an artist. — If we are absolutely bound to have weaknesses and end up having to acknowledge as well that they exercise control over us, then I wish for everyone at least sufficient artistic energy to understand how to turn his weaknesses into a foil for his virtues and how, through his weaknesses, to make us desirous of his virtues: something the great composers have understood to such an exceptional degree. How often do we find in Beethoven's music a coarse, obstinate, impatient tone, in Mozart a joviality of trusty fellows at which heart and spirit have to wince a bit, in Richard Wagner an impulsive and importunate agitation from which the good mood of *even* the most patient listener wants to take its leave: at *that* point, however, he returns to his strength as do the others; with their weaknesses they have given us a craving for their virtues and a palate ten times more sensitive for every drop of musical spirit, musical beauty, and musical goodness.

219

Deception in humiliation. — Through your irrationality you have inflicted profound suffering on your neighbor and have destroyed an irretrievable happiness—and now you overcome your vanity sufficiently to go to him; you humble yourself before him, expose your irrationality to his contempt, and believe that after this difficult, and for you extremely burdensome scene, everything has basically been put to rights—your voluntary loss of honor evens out the other's involuntary loss of happiness: in this feeling you walk away uplifted and restored to your virtue. But the other has his profound suffering just the same; for him there is nothing at all comforting in the fact that you are irrational and have admitted it; even the mortifying sight you presented to him as you expressed to his face your contempt for yourself he experiences as a fresh injury for which he has you to thank—but he does not contemplate revenge nor does he grasp how anything between you and him could be *evened out*. Basically you performed that scene before, and for yourself: you had invited a witness to it, once again for your own sake and not for his—don't deceive yourself!

220

Dignity and fearfulness.—The ceremonies, the uniforms of office and rank, the earnest expressions, the solemn stare, the deliberate gait, the roundabout speech, and in general everything that goes under the name of dignity: these are the forms of dissimulation for those who are at bottom fearful—they long in this way to make others afraid (of themselves or what they represent). The fearless, which meant originally the constantly and unquestionably fearsome, have no need for dignity and ceremonies; they bring honesty and directness in word and gesture into repute, and even more into disrepute, as an indication of self-assured fearsomeness.

221

Morality of sacrifice.—A morality that measures itself according to the amount of sacrifice is a morality still in the half-savage stage. Here reason gains only a difficult and bloody victory within the soul—powerful counterdrives must still be overthrown; and without a type of cruelty such as the sacrifices demanded by the cannibalistic gods, this victory will not happen.

222

Where fanaticism is desirable.—One can make phlegmatic natures enthusiastic only by turning them into fanatics.

223

The feared eye. — Artists, poets, and writers fear nothing more than the eye that discerns their *little deception*, that perceives after the fact how often they have stood at the crossroads where it led either to naive pleasure in themselves or to the production of effects; that checks the figures when they wanted to sell a little for a lot, when they sought to adorn and elevate without themselves being elevated; that sees straight through all their art's deception to the thought as it first appeared to them, perhaps as an enchanting figure of light, but perhaps also as a theft on the world at large, as a quotidian thought that they had to stretch, shorten, dye, develop, spice up, in order to make something out of it instead of the thought making something out of them — oh this eye that notes in your work all your restless anxiety, your greedy spying about, your imitation and outdoing (the latter is merely envious imitation), that knows your blush of shame just as well as your art — of concealing this blush and reinterpreting it for yourself!

224

What is "elevating" in our neighbor's misfortune. — He is in a state of misfortune and now along come the "compassionate ones" and paint for him his misfortune in detail — finally they walk away feeling satisfied and elevated: they have gloated over the terror of the misfortunate man as if it were their own terror and have had for themselves one fine afternoon.

225

Surefire means of being despised. — A person who speaks quickly and a lot sinks extraordinarily low in our estimation, after the briefest of associations and even if he speaks intelligently — not merely to the degree that he is irritating, but to a much more profound degree. For we discern how many people he has already irritated and, to the displeasure he does cause, we throw in for good measure the disdain for him that we presuppose in others.

226

On associating with celebrities. — A: But why are you avoiding this great man? — B: I wouldn't want to come to misjudge him! Our failings are incompatible with one another: I am nearsighted and mistrustful and he wears his fake diamonds as happily as his genuine ones.[10]

227

Chain bearers. — Beware of all spirits lying in chains! Of shrewd women, for example, whose fate has confined them to a stale environment and who grow old there. To be sure, they lie there seemingly torpid and half blind in the sunlight; but at every unfamiliar step, at everything unexpected, they flare up to bite, they take revenge on everything that has escaped their doghouse.

228

Revenge in praise. — Here is a written page full of praise and you call it shallow: but when you discern that revenge lies hidden in this praise, you then find it almost too subtle and amuse yourself greatly over the richness of bold little strokes and figures. Not the person but his revenge is so subtle, rich, and resourceful; he himself is hardly aware of it.

229

Pride. — Ah, none of you knows the feeling that the tortured man has after the torture when he is taken back to his cell along with his secret! — He still holds on tightly to it with his teeth. What do you know about the jubilation of human pride!

230

"Utilitarian." — These days sensibilities for things moral are running in so many directions[11] that for this person morality

is proven by its usefulness, for that person its usefulness is precisely what refutes it.

231[12]

On German virtue. — How degenerate in its taste, how slavish before titles, ranks, uniforms, pomp, and pageantry a people must have been when it esteemed the *simple* as the *bad*,[13] the simple man as the bad man! One need counter the moral arrogance of the Germans with nothing more than this little word "bad"!

232[14]

From a disputation. — A: Friend, you've talked yourself hoarse. B: Then I'm refuted. Let's not discuss it any further.

233

The "conscientious." — Have you ever paid attention to what type of person places the most value on strictest conscientiousness? Those who are aware of many wretched sentiments in themselves, who think anxiously in general and particularly about themselves and are afraid of others, who want to hide their inner world as fully as possible — they are seeking *to impress themselves* through this strict conscientiousness and severity of duty and by means of the strict and severe impression this inevitably makes on others (especially subordinates).

234

Shyness in the face of fame. — A: That a person avoids fame, deliberately insults the very individual who sings his praises, shies away from hearing judgments about himself — *you run into that sort of thing, it happens* — believe it or not! — B: You run into that sort of thing, it happens! Only a little patience, Junker Arrogance![15] —

235[16]

Refusing gratitude. — One may certainly refuse a request, but one must never refuse gratitude (or, what amounts to the same thing, accept it coldly and conventionally). This offends profoundly — and why?

236

Punishment. — A strange thing, our punishment! It does not cleanse the criminal, it is not *ex*piation: quite the opposite, it sullies more than the crime itself.[17]

237

Party difficulty. — A ludicrous, but hardly innocuous malaise turns up in almost every political party: all those who for years were the loyal and worthy champions of the party platform and one day suddenly notice that someone much more powerful has taken over the reins suffer from it. How are they supposed to endure being silenced! And so they grow loud — even, from time to time, to the beat of a new tune.

238[18]

The striving for grace. — If a strong nature lacks a tendency toward cruelty and is not always occupied with itself, then it strives instinctively for *grace* — this is its true stamp. Weak characters, by contrast, prefer harsh judgments — they join with the heroes of misanthropy, the religious or philosophical blackeners of existence or else they withdraw behind strict morals and agonizing "lifelong callings":[19] in this way they seek to create for themselves a personality and a type of strength. And this they likewise do instinctively.

239

Tip for moralists. — Our composers have made a great discovery: *interesting ugliness* is also possible in their art! And so like drunkards they cast themselves into this disclosed ocean of ugliness, and never before has it been so easy to make music! Not until now did composers come by this generally dark-colored background against which even a small flash of good music attains the brilliance of gold and emerald; not until now did one dare to drag the listener, robbed of breath, into storm and outrage in order afterward to give him, in a moment of collapse into peace, a feeling of bliss, which has an altogether favorable effect on his appreciation of music. Composers have discovered contrast: only now are the strongest effects possible — and so *cheaply*: no one any longer asks for good music. But you must hurry! There is only a short time span left for every one of the arts once it has arrived at this discovery. — Oh, if our thinkers only had ears to listen in on the souls of our composers by way of their music! How long must one wait before there appears another such opportunity for catching a person's inner world in an evil act and in the innocence of this act! For our composers haven't the slightest scent of the fact that they are setting their own history, the history of the uglification of the soul, to music. Formerly, a good composer was obliged to become, almost for the sake of his art, a good person — . And now![20]

240

On the morality of the stage.[21] — Anyone who comes along and claims that Shakespeare's theater has a moral effect and that the sight of Macbeth[22] irresistibly detracts from the evils of ambition is in error: and he errs again if he believes Shakespeare felt as he does. Anyone who is really possessed by insane ambition views this image of himself with *joy*; and if the hero is destroyed by his passion, this is simply the sharpest spice in the hot drink of his *joy*. Can the poet have felt any differently? From the moment of the great crime on, how regally and not in the least like a villain does his ambitious hero pursue his course! Only from that moment on does he exert "demonic" attraction and excite similar natures to emulation — demonic means here: in defiance *against* advantage and life in favor of an idea and a drive. Do you suppose Tristan and Isolde[23] to be offering a lesson *against* adultery because they both are destroyed by it? This would amount to turning upside down those authors who, like Shakespeare in particular, are enamored of the passions as such and not least of all of their moods that *embrace death*: — those in which the heart clings to life no more firmly than a drop of water to a glass. It is not guilt and its grim denouement they take to heart, Shakespeare as little as Sophocles (in Ajax, Philoctetes, Oedipus):[24] as easy as it would have been in the aforementioned instances to make guilt the focal point of the drama, just as certainly has this been avoided. Just as little does the tragic poet wish, with his images of life, to turn us *against* life! On the contrary, he shouts: "It is the stimulus of all stimuli, this exhilarating, vacillating, dangerous, tenebrous and often sun-drenched existence! It is an *adventure* to live — take whatever stand you want in it, it will always retain this character!" — He speaks this way out of a restless and powerful epoch that is half drunken and dazed by its surfeit of blood and energy — out of a more malevolent epoch than ours is: which is why we need first to *adjust* and *justify* the point of a Shakespearean play, which is to say, not to understand it.

241

Fear and intelligence. — If it is true, as people are claiming with utmost certainty, that the cause of black skin pigment is *not* to be found in the amount of light: could it perhaps be the last effect of frequent attacks of rage (and undercurrents of blood under the skin) accumulated over millennia? Whereas with other *more intelligent* races the just as frequent trepidation and turning pale in the end resulted in white skin color? For the degree of fearfulness is a barometer of intelligence: and giving oneself over to rage is often the indication that animality is still very close by and eager to assert itself. — The human being's original color would, then, most likely be brown-grey — something ape- and bear-like, as is only fitting.

242[25]

Independence. — Independence (known in its weakest dosage as "freedom of thought") is the form of renunciation that a person craving to rule finally adopts — the person who has long been looking for what he could rule over and has found nothing but himself.

243[26]

The two directions. — If we attempt to examine the mirror in itself, we uncover, finally, nothing but the things upon it. If we want to seize hold of the things, we come up, in the end, with nothing but the mirror. — This is, in the most general terms, the history of knowledge.

244

Pleasure in what is real. — Our current tendency to take pleasure in what is real — almost all of us have it — is comprehensible only by virtue of the fact that for so long and to the point of bored disgust, we took pleasure in what is unreal. In itself, as it now appears involuntarily and without refinement, it is not exactly an innocuous tendency: the least of its dangers is bad taste.

245

Subtlety[27] of the feeling of power. — Napoleon was exasperated that he spoke poorly, and he did not try to deceive himself on that account: but his lust for power, which passed up no opportunity and was more subtle than his subtle intellect, led him to speak more poorly *than he was capable of.* So he took revenge on his exasperation (he was jealous of all his emotions because they held *power*) and delighted in exercising his autocratic *pleasure.* Then, with regard to the ears and the judgment of his listeners, he delighted in this pleasure once again: as if speaking to them thus were, after all, good enough. Indeed, he gloated in secret over the thought of having, through the thunder and lightning of the highest authority—which consists in the allegiance of power and genius—stilled their judgment and deceived their taste; whereas both held in him coldly and proudly steadfast to the truth that he spoke *poorly.*—As the personification of a single drive that has been completely developed and thought through to the end, Napoleon belongs to the humanity of antiquity: whose distinguishing features—the simple construction and the resourceful cultivation and elaboration of a single motive or a very few motives—are recognized easily enough.

246

Aristotle and marriage.—Among the children of people of great genius, madness breaks out; among the children of people of great virtue, dull stupidity—remarked Aristotle.[28] Did he mean by this to encourage exceptional people to get married?

247

Origin of intemperateness.—What is unjust and erratic in the disposition of many people, their disorder and excessiveness, are the last consequences of countless logical imprecisions, superficialities, and overhasty conclusions that their ancestors were guilty of committing. Temperate people, on the other hand, descend from circumspect and thorough lineages that set greater store in reason—whether to praiseworthy or to evil ends is not so much the issue.

248

Dissimulation as duty.—For the most part, goodness has been developed by extended dissimulation that sought to appear as goodness: wherever great power has taken hold one has recognized the necessity of precisely this type of dissimulation—it exudes certainty and confidence and increases hundredfold the sum of real physical power. The lie is, if not the mother, then the wet nurse of goodness. Honesty too has, for the most part, been reared to maturity on the requirement that one seem honest and upright: within the hereditary aristocracies. The long-standing practice of dissimulation turns into, at last, *nature*: in the end dissimulation cancels itself out, and organs and instincts are the hardly anticipated fruits in the garden of hypocrisy.[29]

249

Who is, after all, ever alone!—The fearful person doesn't know what it means to be alone: an enemy is always standing behind his chair.—Oh, for the person who could tell the history of that subtle feeling called solitude!

250

Night and music.—The ear, the organ of fear, was only able to develop as richly as it has at night and in the half night of dark woods and caves, in keeping with the fearful, that is to say, the very longest period to have existed in human history: in the light of day the ear is less necessary. Hence the character of music as an art of the night and half night.

251[30]

Stoical.—There is a serenity the Stoic possesses whenever he feels constricted by the duties he has prescribed for his way of life; he takes pleasure in himself as the ruler.

252

Consider!—The one who is punished is no longer the one who did the deed. He is always the scapegoat.

253

What lies before one's very eyes.—Terrible! Terrible! What has to be proven most clearly and most persistently is what lies before one's very eyes. For all too many lack the eyes to see it. But it is so boring!

254

Anticipators. — The distinguishing but also dangerous feature of poetic natures is their *exhaustive* fantasy: which anticipates, sees in advance, enjoys in advance, suffers in advance what will occur and what might occur and finally in the actual moment, is *tired* of the occurrence and the deed. Lord Byron, who knew about this all too well, wrote in his diary: "If I have a son, he should become something entirely prosaic — a lawyer or a pirate."[31]

255

Conversation about music. — A: What do you say to this music? — B: It overwhelmed me, I don't have anything at all to say. Listen! It's beginning all over again! — A: So much the better! Let's see to it that *we* overwhelm it this time. May I accompany this music with a few words? And show you a drama as well that you perhaps did not want to see upon first hearing? — B: Be my guest! I have two ears and more if necessary. Pull up close to me! — A: — This is not yet what *he* wants to say to us, he has only promised up until now that he's going to say something, something unheard-of, as his gestures indicate. For they are gestures. How he signals with his hand! Pulls himself upright! Waves his arms! And now it seems to him that the supreme moment of tension has come: two more fanfares, and he presents[32] his theme, magnificent and adorned, as if clattering with precious stones. Is it a beautiful woman? Or a beautiful horse? Whatever, he looks around him, enraptured, for his job is to collect enraptured looks — only at this point is he totally pleased with his theme, now he grows inventive, ventures new and bold strokes. How he amplifies his theme! Ah, pay attention — he understands not only how to adorn it, but how to apply *makeup*[33] to it too! Indeed, he knows what the color of health looks like; he understands the knack of making it appear — his self-awareness is more subtle than I thought. And now he's convinced that he's convinced his listeners, he pre-

sents his ideas as if they were the most important things under
the sun, he points shamelessly at his theme, as if it were too
good for this world. — Ha, how mistrustful he is! What if we
should become tired! So he douses his melodies in confection-
er's sugar — now he even appeals to our cruder senses in order
to excite us and thereby to bring us back into his power! Listen
how he invokes the elemental forces of stormy and thundering
rhythms! And now that he sees that they are taking hold of us,
strangling, almost crushing us, he ventures once again to fuse
his theme into the play of these elements and to *convince* us
half-stupefied[34] and shattered listeners that our stupefaction
and shattered state result from the effect of his miracle-theme.
And from that point on his listeners believe him: as soon as it
sounds, there arises in them a recollection of that shattering
elemental effect — this recollection strengthens the theme —
it has now become "demonic"! What a connoisseur of the
soul he is! He holds sway over us with the tricks of a soapbox
orator. — But the music has stopped! — B: And a good thing
that it has! For I cannot bear to listen to *you*! I'd certainly prefer to *let myself be deceived* ten times over than to know a single
truth after your fashion! — A: That's what I wanted to hear
from you. The best people now are just like you: you are satisfied with letting yourselves be deceived! You arrive with crude
and lecherous ears, you fail to bring the conscience of art with
you to listen, you have thrown away the *finest part of your honesty* along the way! And you are thus ruining art and the artists!
Whenever you clap and shout you hold the artists' conscience
in your hands — and woe to you if they notice you cannot
distinguish between innocent and guilty music! I truly do not
mean "good" and "bad" music — there is good and bad music
of both sorts! But I call an *innocent music* that type that con-
templates completely and solely itself, believes in itself, and in
its self-absorption has forgotten the world — the self-enacted
resounding of deepest solitude that speaks of itself to itself, no
longer realizing that outside there exist listeners and eavesdrop-
pers and effects and misunderstandings and failures. — Finally:

the music that we just heard *is* precisely of this noble and rare species, and everything I said about it was made up—forgive me my malice, if you care to! B: Oh, then you love *this* music as well? Then you are forgiven many sins!

256

Happiness of the wicked.—These quiet, somber, evil people have something you cannot deny them, a rare and strange pleasure in the *dolce far niente*,[35] an evening and sunset calmness, as only a heart can know it that has been all too often consumed, torn to pieces, poisoned by passions.

257[36]

Words present in us.—We always express our thoughts with the words that lie ready to hand. Or to express my entire suspicion: we have at every moment only that very thought for which we have ready to hand the words that are roughly capable of expressing it.

258

Petting the dog!—You need only stroke this dog's fur once: immediately he lights up with a crackle and shoots off sparks, like every other flatterer—and is witty after his own fashion. Why shouldn't we put up with him that way!

259

The former panegyrist.—"He has fallen silent about me, although he now knows the truth and could tell it. But it would sound like revenge—and he, so worthy of respect, respects the truth so highly!"

260

Amulet of the dependent.—Anyone who is unavoidably dependent upon a patron should have something with which he imbues fear and keeps the patron within boundaries, for example, uprightness or honesty or a wicked tongue.

261

Why so exalted!—Oh, I know these beasts. Of course they please themselves more when they come striding in on two legs "like a god"—but when they fall back down on all fours they please me more: this posture is so incomparably more natural for them!

262

The demon of power.—Not the bare necessities, not de-sire—no, the love of power is humanity's demon. You can give people everything—health, room, board, amusement—they are and remain unhappy and low-spirited: for the demon is waiting and waiting and wants to be satisfied. You take away everything from people and satisfy this demon: then they are almost happy—as happy as precisely humans and demons can be. But why am I still saying this? Luther already said it, and better than I, in the verses: "Take they our life, goods, fame, child, and wife; let these all be gone—the Kingdom ours re-maineth!"[37] Yes, yes, the "Kingdom"!

263

Embodied and animated contradiction.—In the so-called genius there is a physiological contradiction: on the one hand, he possesses much wild, disorderly, involuntary motion and then, on the other hand, much of the highest purposiveness of motion—in the process he appears to himself as a mirror that displays both motions side by side and entwined with one another, but also often enough against one another. As a result of this spectacle he is often unhappy, and when he feels his best, in creating, then it is because he forgets that at that very moment he is doing (and must do) something fantastical and irrational (such is all art) with the highest purposiveness.

264[38]

Wanting to err. — Envious people with a keen sense of smell try not to get to know their rival too precisely so as to be able to feel superior to him.

265[39]

The theater has its age. — When a people's imagination wanes, there arises in it the tendency to have its sagas presented on stage, now it can *endure* the crude substitutes for imagination — but for that epoch to which the epic rhapsodist[40] belonged, the theater and the actor dressed up as hero were a brake upon the imagination and not its wings: too near, too definite, too heavy, too little dream and flight of bird.

266

Without grace. — He lacks grace and knows it: oh, how he understands the knack of masking it! Through strict virtue, through somberness of gaze, through an assumed mistrust of people and existence, through crude farces, through contempt for the finer style of life, through pathos and demands, through cynical philosophy — indeed, in the constant awareness of his lack, he has turned into a character.

267[41]

Why so proud? — A noble character differentiates itself from a base one in that it *does not have ready to hand* a number of habits and points of view like the latter: for him they are random, not inherited and not instilled.

268

The orator's Scylla and Charybdis.[42] — How difficult it was in Athens to speak in such a way as to win one's listeners *for* an issue without disgusting them *through the form* of speech or diverting them *from* the issue with it. How difficult it still is in France to write in this way!

269

The sick and art. — To fight against every sort of woe and misery of the soul one ought first to attempt: change of diet and hard physical work. But in such cases people are used to resorting to means of intoxication: to art, for example — much to their own detriment and to that of art! Don't you realize that if in sickness you turn to art you will make the artists sick?

270[43]

Seeming toleration. — These are all good, well-intentioned, sensible words for and about scholarship, but! but! I see *through* this toleration of yours for scholarship![44] In your heart of hearts, despite all you say, you think *you have no need of it*, that it's magnanimous of you to put up with it, indeed even to be its advocate, especially as scholarship doesn't exactly exercise the same magnanimity toward your opinions! Do you realize that you have no right whatsoever to this exercise in toleration? That this gracious gesture is a cruder denigration of scholarship than the open derision of it that some supercilious priest or artist allows himself? You lack that strict conscience vis-à-vis what is true and real, it does not torture and torment you to find scholarship at direct odds with your feelings, you don't know what it means to have the insatiable longing for knowledge rule over you as a law; in the desire to have an ever-present, open eye *wherever* anything comes to be known, you feel no duty not to let any part of *whatever* has become known slip away. You *do not know the very thing* that you treat so tolerantly! And only *because* you do not know it can you succeed in assuming such indulgent expressions! You, precisely you would glare with fanatical embitterment if scholarship were ever to shine the light from *its* eyes into your face! — What do we care, therefore, if you exercise tolerance — toward a *phantom*! And not even toward us! And what do we matter!

271

Festive atmosphere.—Precisely for those people who strive most feverishly for power it is pleasant to feel oneself be *overwhelmed*! Suddenly to sink deep down into a feeling! To permit the reins to be torn from one's hands, to watch as one takes off in who knows what direction! Who is it, what is it that is rendering us this service—it is a great service: we are so happy and breathless and sense an exceptional stillness around us as if at the centermost point of the earth. For once completely without power! A ball at play in the hands of primordial forces! There is a type of relaxation in this happiness, a casting-off of the great burden, a rolling downhill without effort like a blind gravitational force! It is the dream of the mountain climber who, though he has his *goal* before him, owing to fatigue, falls asleep along the way and dreams of the *happiness of the opposite*— of precisely the most effortless rolling downhill.—I am describing happiness as I conceive of it for our current, stressed, power-thirsty society in Europe and America. Here and there one wants to tumble back into a state of *powerlessness*[45]—this is the pleasure one receives from wars, the arts, religions, geniuses. If from time to time one abandons oneself to a crushing, all-consuming impression—this is the modern *festive atmosphere*!—then one is once again freer, more rested, colder, stricter, and again resumes one's tireless quest for the opposite: for *power.*—

272

Purification of the race.—There is in all likelihood no such thing as pure races but only races that have become pure and this only with extreme rarity. What is customary are the mixed races in which one inevitably finds, along with disharmony in physical forms (when, for example, eyes and mouth do not go together) disharmonies in customs and value judgments. (Livingstone heard someone remark: "God created white and black people, the devil, however, created half-breeds.") Mixed races are always simultaneously mixed cultures, mixed moralities as well: they are usually more evil, cruel and restless. Purity is the last result of numberless conformities, absorptions and expulsions, and progress toward purity is revealed in the fact that the strength present in a race is *restricted* more and more to particular selected functions, whereas before it had to deal with too many things that often contradicted one another: such a restriction will simultaneously always look like an *impoverishment* as well and needs to be judged carefully and gingerly. In the end, however, if the process of purification is successful, all the strength that was earlier expended on the battle of disharmonious qualities is now at the disposal of the entire organism: which is why races that have become purified have always grown *stronger* and *more beautiful* as well. — The Greeks provide us with the model of a race and a culture that has become pure: and it is to be hoped that one day Europe will also succeed in becoming a pure European race and culture.

273

Praising. — Here is somebody, who, as you notice, wants *to praise* you: you bite your lips together, your heart constricts: let *this* cup pass![46] But it does not pass, it approaches! Let us drink then the panegyrist's sweet impertinence, overcome our disgust and profound contempt for the essence of his praise, spread the wrinkles of grateful joy across our face! — he meant after all to do us good! And now, after it's all over, we realize that he feels very exalted, he gained a victory over us — yes, and over himself as well, the dog! — for it wasn't easy for him to wrest this praise from himself.

274

Human right and privilege. — We humans are the only creatures who, if they turn out unsuccessfully, can cross themselves out like an unsuccessful sentence — whether we do so to honor humanity or out of pity for it or out of revulsion for ourselves.

275[47]

The convert. — Now he grows virtuous only in order to make others suffer from it. Don't pay so much attention to him!

276

How often! How unexpected! — How many married men have experienced the morning when it dawned on them that their young wife was tedious and fancied herself the opposite! Not to speak at all of those women whose flesh is willing and whose spirit is weak!

277

Warm and cold virtues. — Courage as cold bravery and imperturbability and courage as feverish, half-blind bravura — one calls both things by the same name! How different are the *cold virtues* from the *warm ones*! And anyone would be a fool to believe that "being good" occurs only when warmth is added: and no less a fool anyone who wanted to ascribe being good to the cold! The truth is that humanity has found warm and cold courage very useful and, what is more, of sufficient rarity to count it in both colors among the precious stones.

278

Obliging memory. — Anyone of high rank does well to get himself an obliging memory, that is to say, to retain all possible good things about people and to draw the line at anything else: one thus keeps people in a pleasant sort of dependence. A person can also deal with himself in similar fashion: whether one has an obliging memory or not decides, in the end, one's attitude toward oneself, the refinement, kindness, or the mistrust one feels upon observing one's own inclinations and intentions as well as, in the end again, the type of inclinations and intentions themselves.

279

Wherein we become artists. — Whoever makes someone his idol is attempting to justify himself to himself by elevating this person to an ideal; he becomes its artist in order to have a good conscience. When he suffers, he doesn't suffer from *not knowing* but from self-deception, from the pretense of not knowing. — The boatload of such a person's inner needs and desires — and all passionate lovers are to be numbered here — cannot be bailed out with normal-sized buckets.

280[48]

Childlike. — Anyone who lives like children — in other words, does not struggle for his daily bread and does not believe that a final meaning attaches to his actions — remains childlike.

281

The ego wants to have it all. — It seems that the sole reason for human action is *in order* to possess: at least this idea is suggested by the various languages that view all past action as if we possessed something ("I *have* spoken, struggled, conquered": that is to say, I am now in possession of my saying, struggle, victory). How greedy[49] humans appear here! Not to permit even the past to be wrest from them, to want *to continue to have* it and especially it as well!

282

Danger in beauty. — This woman is beautiful and clever: ah, but how much cleverer would she have become if she weren't beautiful!

283

Domestic tranquility and tranquility of soul. — Our customary mood depends upon the mood in which we manage to maintain our surroundings.

284

Putting forward the new as old. — Many appear piqued when they are told something new, they sense the advantage that the newness of a thing confers on the one who knows it first.

285

Where does the ego end? — Most people take a thing they *know* under their protection, as if knowing it turned it into their possession. The ego's pleasure in and desire for appropriation knows no bounds: the great men speak as if all of history stood behind them and they were the head for this long body, and the good women take full credit for the beauty of their children, their clothing, their dog, their doctor, their city, and merely do not dare to say "all that is me." *Chi non ha, non è,*[50] as they say in Italy.

286[51]

House pets, lap dogs, and similar such things. — Is there anything more nauseating than the sentimentality lavished on plants and animals by a creature who, since the beginning of time, has dwelt[52] among them like the most raging of foes and in the end lays claim to tender feelings from its weakened and mutilated victims! In the face of this type of "nature," what is appropriate to a human being, if he is otherwise a thinking person, is gravity.

287

Two friends. — There once were friends who have ceased to be so, and from both sides they severed their friendship at the same time, the one, because he believed himself way too misunderstood, the other because he believed himself way too well understood — and both were deceiving themselves! — for neither of them knew himself well enough.[53]

288

The nobles' comedy. — Those who are incapable of noble, sincere intimacy attempt, through reserve and sternness and a certain disdain of intimacy, to let others detect their noble nature: as if their feeling of intimate trust were so strong it was ashamed to show itself.

289

Where one may not say anything against a virtue. — Among cowards it is considered bad form to say anything against bravery and it arouses contempt; and ruthless people act incensed any time something is said against being compassionate.

290

A squandering. — The first words and deeds of excitable and impulsive people are usually *atypical* of their actual character (they are prompted by the prevailing circumstances and are, as it were, imitations of the spirit of these circumstances), but once they have been spoken and performed, the words and deeds that follow later and that are actually indicative of their character are often *frittered away* in making up for the previous words and deeds or in offsetting them or ensuring that they be forgotten.

291[54]

Presumption. — Presumption is an affected and feigned pride; it is, however, precisely characteristic of pride that it is incapable of and dislikes affectation, dissimulation, and hypocrisy — in this regard the presumption consists in the hypocrisy of being incapable of hypocrisy, something very difficult and almost always unsuccessful. But assuming things transpire as usual and the hypocrisy is exposed, a threefold unpleasantness now awaits the presumptuous one: we are angry at him because he wanted to deceive us, angry at him because he wanted to show he was above us, and finally, in addition, we laugh at him because he failed at both. How very inadvisable it is, then, to engage in presumption!

292[55]

A kind of misprision. — When we hear someone speaking, the sound of a single consonant (an "r" for instance) is often enough to infuse us with a doubt as to the honesty of his feeling: *we* aren't used to this sound and would have to *affect* it consciously — it sounds "affected" to us. Here is an area of crudest misprision: and the same goes for the style of a writer who has mannerisms that aren't everybody's mannerisms. His "naturalness" is experienced as such only by him alone, and it is precisely by means of those elements, which he feels are "affected" because for once he gave in to the prevailing fashion and to so-called "good taste," that he pleases and inspires confidence.

293

Grateful. — One grain of grateful sentiment and piety too much: — and you suffer from it like a vice, and, despite all your integrity and honesty, you fall prey to an evil conscience.

294

Saints. — It is the *most sensual* men who *have* to flee from women and torment their flesh.

295

Delicacy in serving. — Within the great art of serving one of the subtlest tasks is to serve an ambitious master who is, to be sure, the strongest egotist in all matters but by no means desires to be taken for such (this precisely is part of his ambition), who requires that everything transpire according to his wishes and whim, but always such that it has the appearance that he is sacrificing himself and rarely ever desires anything for himself.

296

The duel. — I consider it an advantage, someone said, to be able to have a duel if I absolutely need one; for there are always good comrades around me. The duel is the last remaining, completely honorable way to commit suicide, alas a circuitous way and not even a completely sure one.

297

Ruinous. — The surest way to ruin a youth is by teaching him to respect those who think like him more highly than those who think differently.

298[56]

The hero cult and its fanatics. — The fanatic of an ideal that has flesh and blood is usually right as long as he *denies*, and therein he is dreadful: he knows what it is he's denying as well as he knows himself, for the most simple reason that he comes from there, is at home there, and in secret always fears having to go back there — he wants to make the return impossible through the manner in which he denies. As soon as he affirms, however, he half closes his eyes and begins to idealize (often merely in order to hurt those who stayed at home —); to be sure, one labels this something artistic — fine, but there is something dishonest in it as well. Someone who idealizes a person places this person at such a distance that he can no longer see him sharply — now his reinterpretation of what he still sees transposes it into "the beautiful," that is to say, into the symmetrical, soft-lined, undetermined. Because from now on he wants to worship his ideal hovering in the distance and the heights, he needs, as protection against the *profanum vulgus*,[57] to build a temple for his worship. To this temple he brings all the venerable and consecrated objects otherwise in his possession in order that their magic may rub off onto the ideal and so that through this *nourishment* the ideal will grow and become ever more godlike. At last he really has completed[58] his god—but alas! There is one who knows how this came about, his intellectual conscience[59]—and there is also one who, completely unconsciously, protests against it, namely, the deified one himself, who, as a result of the cult, hymns of praise, and incense, grows insufferable from now on and betrays himself blatantly and in repulsive fashion as not the god and all-too-much the human. At this point there is only one way out for such a fanatic: he patiently submits himself and his kind to mistreatment and continues to interpret the whole misery *ad majorem dei gloriam*[60] through a new form of self-deception and noble lie: he takes sides against himself and, as one mishandled and as interpreter, experiences something akin to martyrdom— he thus climbs to the pinnacle of his arrogance.—People of this sort lived, for example, around *Napoleon*: indeed, perhaps it was precisely he who introduced into the soul of this century the Romantic prostration before the "genius" and the "hero," a prostration so alien to the spirit of Enlightenment—he of whom a Byron was not ashamed to say, he was a "worm compared to such a being."[61] (The formulas for such prostration were founded by that presumptuous old muddle- and surly-head, Thomas Carlyle, who spent a long life trying to make reason romantic for his fellow Englishmen: to no avail!)

299[62]

Appearance of heroism. — To rush into the midst of the enemy can be a sign of cowardice.

300

Gracious toward the flatterer. — The ultimate wisdom exercised by people of insatiable ambition is not to reveal the contempt for humanity induced in them at the sight of flatterers: but instead, to appear gracious toward them, like a god who can be nothing but gracious.

301

"Full of character."—"Once I've said I'll do something, I'll do it"—a person with this way of thinking is considered full of character. How many actions are performed, not because they have been chosen as the most reasonable but because, as they occurred to us, they somehow piqued our ambition or our vanity such that we stuck with them and blindly carried them out! In this manner they increase our belief in our own character and in our good conscience and accordingly, on the whole, in our *strength*: whereas choosing the most reasonable action possible fuels skepticism toward us and, to that extent, a feeling of weakness.

302

Once, twice, and three times true!—People lie unspeakably often, but they don't think about it afterward and in general don't believe it.

303

Pastime of the keen observer of humanity.—He thinks he knows me and feels subtle and important when he acts this way or that toward me: I take care not to disabuse or disappoint him. For I would have to answer for it, whereas now he *wishes* me *well*, because I provide him with a feeling of knowing superiority.—Along comes another: he's afraid I fancy I've got his number and he feels humiliated by it. So he behaves hideously and vaguely and seeks to lead me astray where he's concerned—in order to feel superior to me again.

304[63]

The world-destroyer.—This man keeps failing at something; finally he cries out indignantly: "Then let the whole world go up in smoke!" This disgraceful sentiment is the height of envy, which concludes: because there's *something* I cannot have, the whole world shall have *nothing*, shall *be* nothing!

305

Greed. — Our greed when buying increases the cheaper the articles become — why? Is it that the little differences in price are precisely what *create* greed's little eye?

306

Greek ideal. — What did the Greeks admire in Odysseus? Above all his talent for lying and for cunning and dreadful retaliation; being equal to the situation at hand; appearing, when it matters, more noble than the noblest; being able to be *what one wants*; heroic stick-to-it-iveness; having all means at his command; having intellect — his intellect is the admiration of all the gods, they smile just thinking about it —: all this is the Greek *ideal*! The strangest thing about it is that the conflict between being and appearing is not felt at all and therefore not taken into account morally either. Have there ever been such consummate actors!

307

Facta! Yes, facta ficta![64] — The writer of history deals not with what really happened but merely with supposed[65] events: for only the latter have *had an effect*.[66] Likewise with supposed heroes as well. His theme, so-called world history, is suppositions about supposed actions and their supposed motives, which in turn give rise to further suppositions and actions whose reality, however, immediately vaporizes again and only as vapor does it have an *effect* — a constant procreation of and becoming pregnant with phantoms above the thick fog of inscrutable reality. All historians speak of things that have never existed except in imagination.

308[67]

Not knowing anything about commerce is noble. — To sell one's virtue only at the highest price, let alone to practice usury with it as teacher, civil servant, artist — turns genius and talent into a shopkeeper's affair.[68] One ought not to use one's *wisdom* to become *clever*!

309[69]

Fear and love. — Fear has furthered the universal knowledge of humanity more than love, for fear wants to discern who the other person is, what he can do and what he wants: to deceive oneself here would mean danger and disadvantage. Inversely, love has a secret impulse to see in the other as much of the beautiful as possible or to elevate the other as high as possible: for love to deceive itself here would mean pleasure and advantage — and so it does.

310[70]

The good-natured. — Good-natured people have acquired their character through the constant fear, which their ancestors had, of foreign attack — they mollified, pacified, wheedled up, bowed down, diverted, flattered, cowered, hid the pain, the annoyance, smoothed back their features right away — and finally they bequeathed this whole delicate, tried and true[71] mechanism to their children and grandchildren. A more propitious fate gave them no cause for that constant fear: nevertheless they keep on constantly whistling the same old tune.

311

The so-called soul. — The sum of inner movements that *are easy* for a person and that he consequently performs happily and with grace is called his soul; — if inner movements obviously cause him difficulty and effort, he is considered soulless.

312[72]

The forgetful. — In outbursts of passion and in the fantasizing of dreams and madness a person rediscovers his own prehistory and that of humanity: *animality*, with its wild grimaces; for a change, his memory extends far enough back, whereas his civilized condition evolves from a forgetting of the primordial experiences and thus from a waning of that memory. Anyone who, as a forgetter of the highest breed, always maintains a great distance from all this *does not understand human beings*—but it is an advantage for everyone if there are here and there such individuals who "do not understand us" and are, as it were, begotten by divine seed and born of reason.

313

The friend no longer desired.—The friend, whose hopes we cannot fulfill, we would prefer to have as an enemy.

314

From the company of thinkers.—In the middle of the ocean of becoming we awaken on a tiny island no larger than a skiff, we adventurers and birds of passage, and for a little while we take a look around: as quickly and curiously as possible, for how fast might a wind scatter us or a wave wash across our tiny island so that nothing more is left of us! But here, in this small space we find other birds of passage and hear of earlier ones still—and we thus experience a precious minute of knowing and divining amid the merry beating of wings and chirping with one another and in spirit we adventure out over the ocean, no less proud than the ocean itself!

315

To divest oneself.—To let go of some of one's property, to relinquish one's rights—gives pleasure, provided it is an indication of great wealth. Here is where magnanimity takes root.

316 [73]

Weak sects. [74]—Those sects that sense they will remain weak go out hunting for particular, intelligent followers and strive to replace with quality what they lack in quantity. This presents no small danger for people of intelligence.

317

Evening judgment. — Anyone who reflects upon his daily and life's work at the end of the day, when he is fatigued, usually comes to a state of melancholy contemplation: this has nothing to do with the day or his life, but with the fatigue. — In the midst of work we usually do not take the time to make judgments about life and existence, nor do we do so in the midst of enjoyment; but should we ever happen to do so, we would no longer agree with him who waited for the seventh day and its rest in order to find that everything here was very beautiful — for he had let the *better* moment slip by.

318

Beware the systematizers! — There is playacting going on among systematizers: inasmuch as they want to make the system whole and round off the horizon around it, they must attempt to have their weaker qualities appear in the same style as their stronger ones — they want to act out complete and uniformly strong natures.

319

Hospitality. — The meaning inside the rites of hospitality is: to disable the hostility in the stranger. Where one no longer senses a stranger first and foremost as enemy, hospitality wanes; it blossoms as long as its evil assumption blossoms.

320

About the weather. — A very unusual and unpredictable weather makes people mistrustful, even of others; under such conditions they become addicted to novelty, for they are obliged to depart from their usual habits. For this reason despots love all climactic zones where the weather is moral.

321

Danger in innocence. — The innocent will be the victims in every respect, because their lack of knowledge prevents them from differentiating between moderation and immoderation and from bringing themselves in check soon enough. Accordingly, innocent, that is to say unknowing young wives grow accustomed to frequent enjoyment of the pleasures of sex and miss them later greatly if their husbands have become ill or prematurely debilitated; precisely the harmless and trusting view that this frequency of intercourse was a right and the rule generated in them a need that later exposed them to the most violent temptations and worse. But speaking quite generally and in the best possible light: anyone who loves a person or a thing without knowing him or it becomes the prey of something he would not love if he could see it. In all those areas where experience, caution, and measured steps are required, it is precisely the innocent person who will be ruined most thoroughly, for he must blindly drink the dregs and the basest poison from every single thing. Think about the practice of all princes, churches, sects, parties, corporations: is not the innocent person always used as the sweetest bait in the most dangerous and atrocious cases? — just as Odysseus uses the innocent Neoptolemus to swindle the sick old hermit and fiend from Lemnos out of his bow and arrows.[75] — With its contempt for the world, Christianity has turned ignorance into a *virtue*, namely Christian innocence, perhaps because the most frequent result of this innocence is precisely, as hinted at already, guilt, the feeling of guilt and despair and thus a virtue that, by way of a detour through hell, leads to heaven: for only then can the somber propylaea[76] of Christian salvation swing open, only then will there be great resonance for the promise of a posthumous *second innocence*: — it is one of the loveliest of Christianity's inventions!

322

If possible live without a physician. — It seems to me that an invalid acts more rashly if he has a physician than if he tends to his health himself. In the first instance it suffices for him to behave strictly in accordance with all prescribed measures; in the other instance, we ponder with considerably more conscience the aim of those prescriptions, namely our health, and we notice much more, adjure and abjure ourselves much more than would occur upon doctor's orders. — All rules have the following effect: to drive one away from the purpose behind the rule and to make one more rash. And to what heights of unrestraint and destruction would humanity have climbed if it had ever, with complete honesty, turned everything over to the divinity as their physician according to the motto "God's will be done!" —

323[77]

Darkening of the sky. — Are you familiar with the revenge of timid people who behave in society as if they had stolen their limbs? The revenge of the meek, Christian-like souls who do no more than skulk through the world? The revenge of those who always judge quickly and are always quickly proved wrong? The revenge of drunkards of all stripes for whom the morning is the most dreadful time of the day. Of the invalids of all stripes, the sickly and oppressed who no longer have the courage to get healthy? The number of these little revenge-addicts, not to mention that of their little revenge-acts, is immense; the whole air is constantly buzzing from the arrows and darts launched by their malice such that the sun and sky of life are darkened by it — not just for them but even more so for us, the others, the remaining ones: which is worse than the all too frequent barbs that pierce our hide and heart. Don't we end up *denying* from time to time sun and sky simply because we haven't seen them for so long? — Therefore: solitude! Solitude for this reason as well!

324

Actors' philosophy.[78] — It is the gratifying delusion on the part of great actors that the historical personages they portray really felt the same as they do during their portrayal — but they are mightily mistaken in this: their power of imitation and divination, which they would gladly have us believe is a clairvoyant faculty, penetrates just barely enough to capture gestures, voice tones and looks, and what is altogether external; that is to say, they snatch the shadow of the soul of a great hero, statesman, warrior, of a person of ambition, jealousy, despair; they push in close to the soul but never into the spirit of their subject. It would certainly be quite a discovery if, instead of the many thinkers, experts, professionals, all that was needed to illuminate the *essence* of this or that state of affairs was clairvoyant actors! Let us by no means ever forget that the moment presumptuousness of this stripe becomes audible the actor is nothing more than an ideal ape, and so much the ape that he's not in the least capable of believing in "essence" or the "essential": for him, everything turns into play, tone, gesture, stage, setting, and audience.[79]

325[80]

Living and believing apart. — The means of becoming the prophet and miracle man of one's age are the same as in days gone by: one lives apart, with little learning, a few thoughts, and a great deal of arrogance — eventually the belief takes hold in us that humanity cannot get on without us, *because we, namely, as is plainly apparent,* can get along without humanity. As soon as this belief turns up, one also finds believers. Lastly, a piece of advice for anyone who may be in need of it (it was given to Wesley by Böhler, his spiritual mentor): "Preach belief until you have it, and then you will preach it because you have it!"[81]

326

Knowing one's circumstances. — We can appraise our powers but not our *power*. Circumstances not only conceal and reveal it—no! They increase and diminish it. One ought to think of oneself as a variable quantity whose capacity for accomplishment can perhaps under favorable circumstances match the highest ever: one ought then to reflect on the circumstances and to spare no diligence in the contemplation of them.

327[82]

A fable.—The Don Juan of knowledge: he has yet to be discovered by any philosopher or poet. He is lacking in love for the things he comes to know, but he has intellect, titillation, and pleasure in the hunt and intrigues involved in coming to know—all the way up to the highest and most distant planets of knowledge!—until finally nothing remains for him to hunt down other than what is absolutely *painful* in knowledge, like the drunkard who ends up drinking absinthe and *acqua fortis*.[83] Thus he ends up lusting for hell—it is the last knowledge that *seduces* him. Perhaps, like everything he has come to know, it will disillusion him as well! And then he would have to stand still for all of eternity, nailed on the spot to disillusionment, and himself having become the stone guest[84] longing for an evening meal of knowledge that he never again will receive!—For the entire world of things no longer has a single morsel to offer this hungry man.

328

What idealistic theories lead us to surmise.—One is most certain to encounter idealistic theories among unreflective practical persons; for they need the radiant brilliance of such theories for their reputation. They reach for them instinctively and have in so doing no feeling of hypocrisy whatsoever: as little as an English person feels a hypocrite with his Christianness and his sanctified Sunday.[85] Conversely, contemplative natures who keep a tight check on all types of fantasizing and shy away from the reputation of being dreamers are satisfied only with rigorous, realistic theories: they reach for them with the same instinctive urge and without, in so doing, losing their honesty.

329[86]

The slanderers of cheerfulness. — People who have been deeply wounded by life are suspicious of all cheerfulness, as if it were childlike and childish and betrayed a sort of irrationality at the sight of which one could only feel moved to pity[87] as for a child on its deathbed who still caresses his toys. Such people see hidden and concealed graves beneath all roses; festivities, boisterous crowds, joyful music appear to them like the resolute self-delusion of someone who is gravely ill and wants to gulp down one last minute of life's intoxication. But this judgment on the cheerfulness of life is nothing other than its refraction through the somber terrain of fatigue and disease: it is itself something moving, irrational, urging compassion, indeed even something childlike and childish, but from that *second childhood* that succeeds old age and precedes death.

330

Not yet enough! — It is not yet enough to prove a thing, one must seduce people to accept it or raise them up to it. That is why a knowledgeable person ought to learn to *speak* his wisdom: and often in such a way that it *sounds* like foolishness.

331

Rights and limits. — Asceticism is the right way of thinking for such people as must wipe out their sensual drives because they are raging beasts of prey. But only for such people![88]

332

Inflated style. — An artist who doesn't wish to relieve himself by unloading his high-swelled feeling through his work and prefers instead to communicate precisely that feeling of swelling is bombastic and his style is the inflated style.

333[89]

"Humanity."—We don't consider animals to be moral creatures. But do you think animals consider us moral creatures?—An animal that could talk said: "Humanity is a presumption from which we animals, at least, do not suffer."

334

The good Samaritan.—When the good Samaritan does a good deed, he satisfies a need that is part of his disposition. The stronger the need, the less he puts himself in the place of the other who serves to still his need; he turns indelicate and upon occasion he insults. (This is often said of Jewish beneficence and charity: which, as is known, is somewhat more heated than that of other peoples.)

335[90]

For love to be felt as love.—We need to be honest with ourselves and to know ourselves very well in order to be able to practice toward others that philanthropic dissimulation that goes by the name of love and kindness.

336

What are we capable of?—A man was so tortured the whole day long by his wayward and malicious son that in the evening he beat him to death, and turning to the rest of the family he said with a sigh of relief: "So! Now we can go and sleep in peace!"—Who knows what circumstances *could* drive us to?

337

"Natural."—That in his faults, at least, he is natural—is perhaps the ultimate praise for a mannered, and, in every other way, theatrical and half-genuine artist. This is why such a creature will jauntily parade precisely his faults.

338

Substitute-conscience. — One person is another person's conscience: and this is particularly important if the other has
none otherwise.

339[91]

Transformation of duties. — When duty ceases to be difficult,
when, after years of practice, it has been transformed into a
pleasurable inclination and a need, then the rights of others — to
whom our duties, now our inclinations, relate — turn into
something different, namely occasions for pleasant feelings for
us. From that point on, the other, owing to his rights, becomes
lovable (instead of revered and feared, as before). We are now
seeking our *pleasure* when we recognize and support the domain of his power. Once the Quietists[92] no longer experienced
their Christianity as a burden, they adopted as their motto
"Everything for the glory of God!": and no matter what they
did in this spirit, it was not a sacrifice; their motto amounted
to the same thing as saying, "Everything for our enjoyment!"
To require that duty *always* be somewhat burdensome — as
does Kant — amounts to requiring that it never become habit
and custom: in this requirement there lingers a tiny remnant of
ascetic cruelty.

340

What meets the eye is against the historian. — It is a well-proven
matter that human beings issue from their mother's bodies:
nevertheless, grown-up children standing next to their mother
make the hypothesis appear very illogical: it has against it what
meets the eye.

341

Advantage in misprision. — Someone said that as a child he
had such contempt for the coquettish caprices[93] of the melancholic temperament that until the middle of his life he failed

to grasp what temperament he had: namely, precisely the melancholic. He declared this to be the best of all possible types of ignorance.

342

Not to be confused!—He views the thing from all sides and you opine that he was a true man of knowledge. But he just wants to knock down the price—he wants to buy it!

343[94]

Supposedly moral.—You insist on never being dissatisfied with yourselves, never suffering from yourselves—and call this your moral proclivity! Fine and dandy, but another might call it your cowardice. But one thing is certain: you will never make the journey around the world (that you yourselves are!), but will remain trapped within yourselves like a knot on the log you were born to, a mere happenstance. Do you believe that those of us who think differently subject ourselves to the journey through our inner wastelands, quagmires,[95] and icy glaciers from sheer foolishness and voluntarily choose pain and weariness, like the stylites?[96]

344[97]

Finesse[98] in fumbling.—If, as one claims, Homer occasionally nodded off on the job,[99] then he was wiser than all artists whose ambition never sleeps. One must allow one's admirers to catch their breath by turning them from time to time into critics; for no one can endure uninterruptedly brilliant and wakeful excellence; and instead of giving pleasure, a master of this sort becomes a taskmaster whom one hates as he marches on ahead of us.

345

Our happiness is no argument for or against.—Many people are capable only of moderate happiness: that it cannot confer greater happiness on them is no more a mark against their wisdom[100] than it is a mark against medicine that many people cannot be cured and that others are always sickly. May each individual have the good fortune to find precisely the view of life that allows him to realize *his* highest portion of happiness: even so, his life can still be pathetic and hardly enviable.

346

Misogynists. — "Woman is our enemy" — whoever talks this way, as a man to other men, out of his mouth there speaks the unharnessed drive[101] that hates not only itself but also its means of satisfaction.

347[102]

An orator's school. — If one remains silent for a year, one unlearns how to chatter and learns how to speak. The Pythagoreans[103] were the best statesmen of their age.

348

Feeling of power. — Be sure to distinguish clearly: he who still wants to gain the feeling of power resorts to any means and eschews nothing that will nourish it. He who has it, however, has grown very particular and refined in his taste; rarely does something satisfy him.

349[104]

Not all that important. — When one witnesses a death, a thought regularly arises, which one, out of a false sense of decency, immediately represses in oneself: that the act of dying is not as significant as the universal awe of it would have us believe, and that the dying person has probably lost more important things in life than he is now about to lose. Here is the end, certainly not the goal. —

350[105]

How best to promise. — When a promise is made, it is not the word that promises but instead what lies unspoken behind the word. Indeed, words make a promise less forceful in that they discharge and use up a part of the very force that promises. Therefore give one another your hand and place your finger on your lips—that's the way to make the surest vows.

351

Commonly misunderstood. — In a conversation you observe that one speaker is busy setting a snare into which the other is ensnared, not out of malice, as one would think, but out of pleasure in his own cleverness: then again others who set up a joke so that someone else can make it and who tie a bow so that someone else can unravel the knot: not out of good will, as one would think, but out of malice and contempt for crude intellects.

352

Center. — That feeling: "I am the middle point of the world!" arises very powerfully when one is suddenly overcome by shame; one stands there as if stunned among crashing breakers and feels blinded and bedazzled as though by one great eye staring at us and through us from all sides.

353

Freedom of speech. — "The truth must be told though the world fall to pieces!"—so cries with his great big mouth the great big Fichte![106]—Indeed! Indeed! But one has to have it first!—But he feels everybody ought to voice his opinion even if everything turns topsy-turvy. One could argue with him on that score.

354

Courage to suffer. — Such as we are now, we can endure a fair amount of distress and our stomach is prepared for this hard diet. Perhaps without it we would find life's meal insipid: and without a positive attitude toward pain we would have to abandon too many pleasures![107]

355

Admirers. — Anyone who admires in such a way as to crucify someone who does not admire is among the executioners of his party. You guard against giving him your hand, even if you belong to his party.

356

Effect of happiness. — The first effect of happiness is the *feeling of power*: this wants to *express itself*, whether it be vis-à-vis ourselves or vis-à-vis other people or vis-à-vis ideas or vis-à-vis imaginary beings. The most typical ways of expressing oneself are: gift giving, ridiculing, destroying — all three with a common basic drive.

357[108]

Moral horseflies. — Those moralists who lack the love of knowledge and whose only enjoyment is causing pain have the mind and the tedium of provincials; their favorite pastime, which is just as cruel as it is pathetic, is to keep a sharp eye on their neighbor and surreptitiously to lay a needle in such a way that he cannot help but prick himself on it. They have not outgrown the naughtiness of little boys who cannot be happy unless they are hunting down and mistreating the living and the dead.

358[109]

Grounds and their groundlessness. — You have an aversion to him and voice ample grounds for this aversion as well — I, however, believe only your aversion and not your grounds! It is self-posturing to represent to yourself and to me as a syllogism something that happens instinctively.

359

Approving. — One approves of marriage first because one does not yet know it; secondly, because one has grown used to it; thirdly, because one has entered into it—so it is approved in almost all cases. And yet none of this proves anything whatsoever about the goodness of marriage as such.

360[110]

No utilitarians. — "Power that is assaulted and defamed is worth more than impotence that receives only loving-kindness"—thus felt the Greeks. That means: they valued the feeling of power more highly than any sort of utility or good reputation.

361[111]

Seeming ugly. — Moderation looks beautiful to itself; it is innocent of the fact that in the eye of immoderation it appears harsh and austere, consequently ugly.

362[112]

Different in hate. — Some hate only once they feel weak and tired: otherwise they are fair and forgiving. Others hate only once they see the possibility of revenge: otherwise they guard against all secret and open anger, and when an occasion for it comes up, they think about something else.

363

People of chance. — What is essential in every invention is the work of chance, but most people do not encounter this chance.

364[113]

Choice of environment. — One ought to guard against living in an environment in which one can neither maintain a dignified silence nor communicate what we find most exalting, so that only our complaining and our needs and the whole history of our distress are left to communicate. Under such circumstances we grow dissatisfied with ourselves and with our environment, indeed, tack on top of the distress that makes us whine the displeasure we feel at always being the whiner. One ought instead to live where one *is ashamed* to talk of oneself and is in no need of it. — But who thinks of such things, of a *choice* in such matters! You speak of your "cursed fate,"[114] lower your shoulder and sigh, "What a poor unfortunate Atlas I am!"[115]

365

Vanity. — Vanity is the fear of appearing original, thus a lack of pride, but not necessarily a lack of originality.

366[116]

Criminal woes.[117] — As a convicted criminal one suffers not from the crime but from shame or from displeasure over a stupid blunder one committed or from deprivation of one's customary milieu, and it takes a person of rare subtlety to make this distinction. Anyone who has frequented prisons and penitentiaries is astonished how seldom one encounters there unambiguous "pangs of conscience": much more often, however, one finds homesickness for the old, wicked, beloved crime.

367[118]

Seeming always happy. — When philosophy was a matter of public competition, in Greece of the third century, there were a few philosophers who were happy with the secret idea that others, who lived according to other principles by which they were tormented, were bound to be annoyed over their own happiness: they believed that their happiness was the best means of refuting the others and to do so it was sufficient for them to seem always to be happy; but as time went on they were bound in the process *to become* happy. This was for example the lot of the Cynics.[119]

368

Reason for a great deal of misprision. — The morality associated with increasing nervous energy is joyful and restless; the morality associated with decreasing nervous energy, in the evening or with sick and older people, is suffering, calming, forbearing, nostalgic, indeed, not infrequently somber. Based on which of these moralities we possess, we will not understand the one we lack, and we often interpret it in someone else as immorality and weakness.

369

Raising oneself above one's wretchedness. — To me there are awfully proud fellows who, in order to establish their own feeling of dignity and importance, always first need others whom they can hector and treat with violence: such people, namely, whose impotence and cowardice allow someone to be able with impunity to direct a haughty and angry display at them! — so that they require the wretchedness of their environment in order to be able to raise themselves for a moment above their own wretchedness! — This is why one person requires a dog, a second a friend, a third a wife, a fourth a political party, and a very rare soul an entire age.

370[120]

To what extent a thinker loves his enemy. — Never hold back or conceal from yourself anything that can be thought against your thoughts! Vow this to yourself! It is the first requirement for honesty of thought. Each and every day you must also conduct your campaign against yourself. A victory and a conquered bulwark are no longer your matter, what matters is the matter of truth — but your defeat is no longer your matter either!

371[121]

The evil of strength. — Acts of violence resulting from passion, for example anger, are to be understood physiologically as the attempt to avert an impending attack of suffocation. Countless acts of wantonness discharged upon other people are diversions of a sudden rush of blood into strong muscle actions: and perhaps the entire issue of the "evil of strength" should be viewed from this perspective. (The evil of strength does harm to others without thinking about it—it *must* discharge itself; the evil of weakness *wants* to do harm and see the signs of suffering it has caused.)

372

In honor of the connoisseur. — As soon as someone who is not a connoisseur begins to play the arbiter of judgment, one ought to protest straightaway: whether the creature be a little man or a little woman. Enthusiasm for and delight over a thing or a person are not arguments: nor are disgust and hatred for them either.

373[122]

Telltale reproof. — "He doesn't know human beings"—in the mouth of one person this means: "he doesn't know what is common[123] to, and in, humans"; in the mouth of another: "he doesn't know what is exceptional and knows the common far too well."

374

Value of sacrifice. — The more one denies states and princes the right to sacrifice individuals (as in the administration of justice or compulsory military service) the higher will rise the value of self-sacrifice.

375

Speaking too clearly. — One can for different reasons articulate oneself too clearly when speaking: first out of mistrust of ourselves in a new, unpracticed language, but also, however, out of mistrust of others owing to their stupidity or slowness of understanding. And so it is in matters of the spirit as well: from time to time we communicate too clearly, too painstakingly because those with whom we are communicating would not understand us otherwise. Accordingly, the perfect and buoyant style is only *permissible* in the presence of the perfect audience.

376

Sleep a lot!—What's to be done to stimulate ourselves when we are tired and fed up with ourselves? One person recommends the casino, the other Christianity, a third electricity. The best thing, however, my dear melancholic, is and remains: *sleep a lot*, literally and figuratively! That way one will also awaken again upon a new morning! The artistry of life's wisdom is knowing how to fit in both types of sleep at the right time.

377

What fantastic ideals lead us to surmise. — There where our deficiencies lie we revel in rapturous enthusiasm. The enraptured dictum, "love your enemy!"[124] had to have been invented by the Jews, the best haters who have ever lived, and the loveliest glorification of chastity was composed by the likes of those who, in their youth, lived a foul and disgraceful life.

378

Clean hands and clean wall. — Thou shalt paint neither God nor the devil on the wall.[125] In so doing, you ruin your wall and your neighborhood.

379

Plausible and implausible. — A woman secretly loved a man and elevated him high above herself and said a hundred times in her most secret soul: "If such a man loved the likes of me, it would be a favor I so little deserve that I would have to bow down before him in the dust!" — And the man felt entirely the same way and in relation to this very woman, and he said to himself in his most secret soul the very same thought as well. When one day at last they loosened their tongues and told one another all that was repressed and most suppressed in their hearts, there ultimately arose a silence and some moments of reflection. After which the woman began in a cold voice: "But it's all clear! Neither of us is what we have loved! If you are who you say you are and no more, I have debased myself and loved you for nothing; the daimon[126] seduced me as well as you." — This highly plausible story never happens — why not?

380

Tried and true advice. — For people in need of solace, no means of receiving it is more comforting than the assertion that for their situation there is no solace. It carries with it such a mark of distinction that they hold up their head again.

381[127]

Knowing one's "particularity." — We too easily forget that in the eyes of strangers who are seeing us for the first time, we are something completely different from what we consider ourselves to be: usually nothing more than an eye-catching particularity determines the impression. Accordingly, the most gentle and fair-minded person on earth can, if he merely happens to have a large mustache, sit, as it were, in its shade, and sit calmly — ordinary eyes will see in him the *accessory* to a large mustache, in other words, a militaristic, quick-tempered, under certain circumstances violent character — and they act toward him accordingly.

382

Gardener and garden. — Out of damp dreary days, solitude, and heartless words directed at us, *conclusions* spring up like mushrooms: one morning they are there, we know not where they came from, and stare at us, peevish and grey. Woe to the thinker who is not the gardener but only the earth for the plants that grow in him!

383

The comedy of compassion. — No matter how much we want to sympathize with a misfortunate person: in his presence we always enact something of a comedy; we don't say a lot about what we think and how we think it; we exercise the cautious discretion of the physician at the bedside of the gravely ill.

384

Strange saints. — There are fainthearted people who don't think much of their best work and its best fruits and are bad at communicating them or presenting them publicly: but out of a type of revenge, neither do they think much of the sympathy of others nor even believe in sympathy at all; they are ashamed to seem carried away by themselves and experience a defiant sense of well-being in becoming ridiculous. — These are states that are present in the soul of melancholy artists.

385

The vain. — We are like storefront windows in which we ourselves constantly arrange, cover up, or light up the supposed qualities that others ascribe to us — in order to deceive *ourselves.*

386

The pathetic and the naive. — To let no possible opportunity for exhibiting one's lofty solemnity slip by can be a very ignoble habit: and simply for the pleasure of imagining a spectator who beats his breast and feels himself to be petty and pathetic. To make fun of lofty and solemn occasions and to behave in them in an undignified manner can, consequently, also be a sign of a noble disposition. The old bellicose aristocracy of France possessed this type of superiority and refinement.

387

Rehearsal of a consideration before marriage. — Assuming she loved me, how irritating to me would she become in the long run! And assuming she doesn't love me, at that point how really irritating would she become! — It is merely a matter of two different kinds of irritation: well then, let's get married!

388[128]

Villainy with a good conscience. — To be cheated in a small transaction — in some regions, Tyrol for example, this is so unpleasant because on top of the bad bargain we also get the nasty face and the vulgar lust for gain, along with the bad conscience and the blatant antagonism the deceitful salesman conceives for us. In Venice, on the other hand, the swindler is heartily delighted by his successful bamboozlement and not at all antagonistic toward the one swindled, indeed, he's inclined to pay him a compliment and particularly to have a good laugh with him if he should feel like it. — In short, even for villainy one must have spirit and a clean conscience: this just about reconciles the duped to the dupe.

389

A little too weighty. — Very good people who are, however, a little too weighty to be polite and charming, seek immediately to answer a courtesy with an earnest act of service or with a contribution from their resources. It is touching to see how they shyly proffer their pieces of gold when another has offered them gilded pennies.

390

Concealing spirit. — If we catch someone in the process of concealing their spirit from us, we call him evil: and indeed, all the more so when we suspect that courtesy and philanthropy have driven him to it.

391

The evil instant. — Lively natures lie for only an instant: immediately thereafter they lie to themselves and are convinced and upright.

392

Condition for politeness. — Politeness is a very good thing and really one of the four cardinal virtues (if admittedly the last): in order not to annoy ourselves and each other with it, however, the person with whom I am currently dealing must be one degree more or less polite than I — otherwise we shall get nowhere, and the salve not only salves but glues us firmly in place.

393

Dangerous virtues. — "He forgets nothing, but he forgives everything." — In that case he will be hated twofold, for he shames twofold, with his memory and his magnanimity.

394

Without vanity. — Passionate people think little about what other people think about; their state elevates them above vanity.[129]

395

Contemplation. — With the one thinker the contemplative state particular to the thinker always follows upon a state of fear, with the other always upon a state of desire. Accordingly, for the first contemplation seems to be bound up with a feeling of *security*, for the other with a feeling of *saturation* — that is to say: the former is courageously disposed, the latter sick and tired and neutral.

396

On the hunt. — The one is on the hunt to nab pleasant truths, the other — unpleasant ones. But even the former has more pleasure in the hunt than in the prey.[130]

397

Education. — Education is a continuation of procreation and often a type of beautification of it after the fact.

398

Whereby we recognize who is more hot-tempered. — Of two people who fight with one another, love one another, or admire one another, the one who is more fervent always assumes the more uncomfortable position. The same is true of two nations.

399

Defending oneself. — Many people have the greatest right to act in such and such a manner; but once they start defending that right, we no longer believe in it — and are mistaken.

400

Moral mollycoddling. — There are tender moral natures, who experience shame at every success and pangs of conscience at every failure.

401[131]

Most dangerous unlearning. — One begins by unlearning how to love others and ends by finding nothing more worth loving in oneself.

402

A kind of tolerance as well. — "To have lain one minute too long on glowing coals and to have gotten a little *burnt* — there's no harm in that, for people and chestnuts! This little bitterness and hardness are what allow us to taste how sweet and mild the kernel is." — Yes, this is how you judge, you hedonists! You sublime cannibals!

403

Different kinds of pride. — Women are the ones who turn pale at the thought that their lover may not be worthy of them; men are the ones who turn pale at the thought that they may not be worthy of their lover. I am speaking here of complete women, complete men. Such men who are *customarily* people of confidence with a feeling of power, have, in a state of passion, a sense of shame as well as self-doubts; such women, however, normally feel themselves to be weak and prepared for any sacrifice, but in the lofty *exception* of passion they have their pride and feeling of power—which asks: who is worthy *of me?*[132]

404

To whom one seldom does justice.—Many people cannot warm to something good and grand without committing serious wrong in some other quarter: this is *their* type of morality.

405[133]

Luxury.—The proclivity to luxury goes to the depths of a person: it reveals that superfluity and immoderation are the water in which his soul most likes to swim.

406

Making immortal.—Anyone who wants to kill his enemy should consider whether this very act will immortalize his enemy for him.

407

Contrary to our own character.—If the truth that we have to utter runs contrary to our character—as is often the case—we behave as if we were lying badly and arouse mistrust.

408

Where much charity is needed.—Many natures only have the choice of being either open criminals or secret mourners.

409

Sickness.—Sickness is to be understood as: a premature approach of old age, ugliness, and pessimistic judgments: which all belong together.

410

The timorous. — It is precisely the inept, timorous natures who easily become murderers: they do not understand minor defense or revenge appropriate to the situation; from lack of intellect and presence of mind, their hate knows no way out other than destruction.

411[134]

Without hatred. — You want to take leave of your passion? Do so, but *without hatred* for it! Otherwise you have a second passion. — The Christian soul that has freed itself from sin is usually ruined afterward by hatred of sin. Have a look at the faces of great Christians. They are the faces of great haters.

412

Brilliant and limited. — He doesn't know how to appreciate anything other than himself; and when he wants to appreciate others, he must always first transform them into himself. But in this he is brilliant.

413

Private and public prosecutors. — Have a good look at anyone who prosecutes and investigates — in the process he reveals his character: and indeed, not infrequently a worse character than that of the victim whose crime he's pursuing. The prosecutor believes in all innocence that the enemy of a crime and of a criminal must as such necessarily be, or be considered to be, of good character — and so he lets himself go, that is to say: he *exposes* himself.

414[135]

The voluntarily blind. — There is a kind of rapturous, extreme devotion to a person or party which betrays that in secret we feel superior to him or it and are carrying on a thundering grudge against ourselves on this account. We blind ourselves voluntarily, as it were, as punishment for our eyes having seen too much.

415

Remedium amoris.[136]—In most cases the best cure for love is still that age-old radical medicament: requited love.

416

Where is the worst enemy?—The person who can advance his cause well and is conscious of that fact is most often disposed to be conciliatory toward his adversaries. But to believe that one is in possession of the good cause and to know that one is *not* adept at defending it—this makes for a furious and irreconcilable hatred directed against the enemies of one's own cause. Let everyone calculate from this where his worst enemies are to be found!

417

Limit of all humility.—Many people have certainly already achieved the humility that says: *credo quia absurdum est*[137] and have sacrificed their reason to it: but no one, as far as I know, has ever achieved that humility, which after all is only one small step further, that says: *credo quia absurdus sum.*[138]

418

Playacting at truth.—Many people are truthful—not because they detest dissimulating feelings but because they would have a hard time getting people to believe their dissimulations. In short, they don't trust their talent as play-actors and favor honesty over "playing at truth."

419

Courage within the party.—The poor sheep say to their shepherd: "You go on ahead at all times, and we will never lack the courage to follow you." The poor leader, however, thinks to himself: "Keep on following me at all times, and I will never lack the courage to lead you."

420

The sacrificial animal's cunning. — It is a sad show of cunning when we want to deceive ourselves about someone to whom we have sacrificed ourselves and we present him with an occasion where he has to appear as we wish he were.

421

Through others. — There are people who do not wish to be seen in any way whatsoever other than as shimmering through others. And in this there is a great deal of cleverness.

422[139]

Bringing joy to others. — Why is bringing joy the greatest of all joys? — Because we thereby bring joy to our separate fifty drives at one fell swoop. Individually they may each be very small joys: but if we put them all in one hand, then our hand is fuller than at any other time — and our heart as well! —

Book Five

423

In the great silence. — Here is the sea, here we can forget the city. To be sure, you can still hear the bells sounding the Angelus[1] just now — it is that somber and foolish, yet sweet sound at the crossroads of day and night — but only for one moment more! Now all is silent! The sea lies before one pale and shimmering; it cannot speak. The sky plays its eternal mute evening game of red, yellow, and green colors; it cannot speak. The small crags and ribbons of rock descending into the sea as if to find the most solitary spot, none of them can speak. This prodigious muteness that suddenly overcomes us is beautiful and terrifying, it swells the heart. — Oh, the hypocrisy of this mute beauty! How much good it could speak, and how much evil too, if it so wanted! Its bound tongue and expression of long-suffering happiness are a ruse used to ridicule your sympathy! — So be it! I'm not ashamed to be the ridicule of such powers. But I have compassion for you, Nature, because you must remain silent, even if it is only your malice that binds your tongue: indeed, I have compassion for you on account of your malice! — Ah, it's growing stiller yet, and my heart swells again: it is startled by a new truth; *it too cannot speak*, it joins in the ridicule whenever a mouth cries out into this beauty; it enjoys its own sweet malice of silence. I come to hate speech, even thought: don't I hear behind every word the laughter of error, wishful thinking, delusion? Mustn't I ridicule my own compassion? Ridicule my ridicule?—Oh sea! Oh evening! You are terrible mentors! You teach the human being to *cease* being human! Ought he to sacrifice himself to you? Ought he to become as you are now, pale, shimmering, mute, prodigious, reposing above oneself? Sublimely above oneself?

424[2]

For whom truth exists. — Up till now it has been mistakes that were the powers *capable of consoling* humanity: nowadays we expectantly await the same result from recognized truths and have already been waiting a bit long. What if this—namely, consolation—were the very thing that truths were incapable of rendering? — Would this then constitute an objection to truths? What do the latter have in common with the conditions of suffering, atrophied, sick human beings that they must necessarily be useful to such people in particular? It is certainly no proof against the *truth* of a plant, if one establishes that it does not contribute anything to the recovery of sick people. Formerly, however, the conviction that humans were the purpose of nature was ingrained to such a degree that it was assumed without further ado that knowledge could uncover nothing that was not useful and salutary for them, that any such things simply *could* not, *ought* not *be* at all. — Perhaps there follows from all this the proposition that truth *as a whole* and something wholly coherent exists only for souls that are at once powerful and harmless, full of joy and peace (as was Aristotle's), just as it is no doubt only such souls as these who will be in a position *to seek truth*: for the others, no matter how proud they may be of their intellect and its freedom, seek *remedies*[3] for themselves—they do *not* seek the truth. This is why these others have so little genuine joy in scholarship and reproach it for its coldness, dryness, and inhumanity: this is the judgment of the infirm about the games of the healthy. The Greek gods knew nothing about how to console either; when the Greeks, one and all, finally grew infirm, this was a reason for the downfall of such gods.

425

We gods in exile!—Through *mistakes* about its origin,[4] its uniqueness, its destiny, and through *claims* that were made based on these mistakes, humanity has elevated itself on high and has time and time again "surpassed itself": but through these same mistakes unspeakably much suffering, mutual persecution, suspicion, misprision, and even greater misery for the individual, within and as himself, have entered into the world. Human beings have become *suffering* creatures as a consequence of their moralities: what they have bought with them in return is, all in all, a feeling that they are too good and too significant for this earth and that they are only paying it a passing visit. In the meantime "the proud sufferer" is still the highest type of human being.

426

Color-blindness of thinkers.—How differently the Greeks viewed their nature[5] if, as one must admit, they had a blind eye for blue and green and saw the former as deep brown, the latter as yellow (if, therefore, they used the same word to describe, for example, the color of dark hair, the cornflower, and the Mediterranean, and again the same word for the color of the greenest plants and human skin, honey, and yellow resin: so that, as is well-known, their best painters reproduced their world in black, white, red, and yellow)—how differently and how much closer to humankind nature must have appeared to them because in their view the color of human beings also predominated in nature, and the latter, as it were, swam in the atmospheric palette of humanity! (Blue and green dehumanize nature more than anything else.) It was upon this *deficiency* that the playful ease, so characteristic of the Greeks, with which they view natural processes as gods and demigods, that is to say as humanlike figures, grew to grand fruition. — But let this be merely the metaphor for a further supposition. Every thinker paints his world and every individual thing in it

with fewer colors *than actually exist* and is blind to certain particular colors. This is not merely a deficiency. Owing to this
approximation and simplification he reads *into the things themselves* color harmonies that have great appeal and that can
amount to an enrichment of nature. Perhaps this is even the
path on which humanity first learned to take *pleasure* in viewing existence: in that this existence was initially presented in
one or two shades of color and thereby harmonized; humanity
practiced, as it were, on these few shades before it was able to
move on to many others. And even now many an individual
works from a partial color-blindness out into a richer form
of seeing and differentiating: whereby he not only finds new
pleasures but also *must give up and lose* several of the earlier
ones.

427[6]

The beautification of scholarship.[7] — Just as the art of rococo
gardening[8] arose from the feeling that "nature is ugly, wild,
boring — come, let's beautify it! (*embellir la nature*)!"[9] — so
from the feeling that "scholarship is ugly, dry, dreary, difficult,
tedious — come, let's beautify it!" there arose time and time
again something that calls itself *philosophy*. It wants what all
art and poetry want — above all *to entertain*: in keeping with
its inherited pride, however, it wants to do this in a more sublime and elevated manner among a group of select spirits. To
create for these a garden art whose main charm, as with the
"more common" variety, is visual deception (by means of, to
stay within the metaphor, temples, vistas, grottos, mazes, waterfalls), to display scholarship in a procession[10] with all sorts
of wondrous, sudden lighting and with so much vagueness, irrationality, and reverie mixed in that one could wander in it as
"in the wilds of nature" and yet without toil or boredom — that
is no small ambition: anyone possessed of it even dreams of, in
this fashion, rendering religion, which among earlier humanity supplied the highest genre of the art of entertainment, dis-
pensable. — This runs its course and one day reaches its high

tide: already these days voices are being raised against philosophy and they cry "back to scholarship! To the true nature and naturalness of scholarship!" — with which *begins* perhaps a new age that discovers the most powerful beauty in the "wild, ugly" parts of scholarship, just as it was only since Rousseau that one first discovered a feeling for the beauty of the Alps and the desert.

428

Two types of moralists. — To see for the first time a law of nature and to see it completely, *to demonstrate it*, in other words (for example, the law of gravity, of light and sound reflection), is something different from and a matter for a different type of mind than *to explain* such a law. In the same manner, those moralists who see and expound human laws and customs — the fine-eared, fine-nosed, fine-eyed moralists — differ thoroughly from those who explain what they observe. The latter must be above all *resourceful* and have a fantasy that is *unbridled* by discernment and knowledge.

429[11]

The new passion. — Why do we fear and hate the possible return to barbarism? Because it would make people unhappier than they are? Ah, no! In all ages barbarians were *happier*: let's not deceive ourselves! — Instead, our *drive for knowledge* is too strong for us to be able still to value happiness without knowledge or the happiness provided by a strong, deeply rooted delusion; we find it painful even to imagine such a state! The restlessness of discovery and ascertainment has become just as appealing and indispensable to us as an unrequited love is to the lover, a love he would never trade at any price for a state of apathy; indeed, perhaps we too are *unhappy* lovers! Knowledge has been transformed into a passion in us that does not shrink from any sacrifice and, at bottom, fears nothing but its own extinction; we honestly believe that under the pressure and suffering of *this* passion the whole of humanity must believe itself to be more sublime and more consoled than previously, when it had not yet overcome its envy of the cruder pleasure and contentment that result from barbarism. Perhaps humanity will even be destroyed by this passion for knowledge! — Even this thought holds no sway over us! After all, has Christianity ever shied away from a similar thought? Are love and death not siblings?[12] Yes, we hate barbarism — we all prefer the destruction of humanity to a decline in knowledge! And ultimately: if humanity is not destroyed by a *passion* it will be destroyed by a *weakness*: which does one prefer? This is the main question. Do we desire for humanity an end in fire and light or in sand?

430

Also heroic. — To do absolutely the most noisome of things of which one hardly dares to speak but that are useful and necessary — is also heroic. The Greeks were not ashamed to include among Heracles' great labors the cleaning of a stable.[13]

431

Adversaries' opinions. — In order to measure how naturally subtle or feebleminded even the cleverest of heads are, pay attention to the way they apprehend and recount the opinions of their adversaries: this process betrays the natural measure of every intellect. — The perfect sage, without intending to do so, elevates his adversary into the realm of the ideal and cleanses the latter's opposition of all blemishes and contingency: only once his adversary has become in this way a god with shining weapons does he do battle against him.

432[14]

Researchers and experimenters.[15] — There is no one and only scientific method that leads to knowledge![16] We must proceed experimentally with things, be sometimes angry, sometimes affectionate toward them and allow justice, passion, and coldness toward them to follow one upon the other. One person converses with things like a policeman, another as father confessor, a third as a wanderer and curiosity seeker. Sometimes one wrings something from them through sympathy, sometimes through violent force; reverence for their mysteries leads one person forward and eventually to insight, whereas another employs indiscretion and roguery in the explanation of secrets. Like all conquerors, discoverers, navigators, adventurers, we researchers are of a daring morality and have to put up with being considered, on the whole, evil.

433[17]

Seeing with new eyes. — Assuming that by beauty in art one always understands *imitation of happiness* — and I hold this to be the truth — depending on how an age, a people, a great person who makes his own internal laws imagines happiness: what then does the so-called *realism* of contemporary artists give us to understand about the happiness of our age? *Its* type of beauty is undoubtedly the one we currently know how to grasp and to enjoy most easily. Accordingly, aren't we definitely obliged to believe that *our* own particular happiness now lies in what is realistic, in having the most acute senses possible, and in faithful apprehension of actuality — not therefore *in* reality but *in knowing about reality*? Science has gained such a profound and widespread effect that artists of this century, without intending to do so, have already become the true glorifiers of scientific "ecstasies"!

434

Putting in a good word. — Unprepossessing terrain exists for the great landscape painters, striking and rare terrain for the minor ones. Namely: great things in nature and humanity have to put in a good word for all the minor, mediocre, and ambitious among their admirers, but those who are *great* put in a good word for *simple* things.

435

Do not be unwittingly destroyed. — Our greatness and ability crumble away not all at once but constantly; the little vegetation that grows in between everything and understands how to cling to everywhere, this is what ruins what is great in us — the quotidian, hourly pitifulness of our environment that goes overlooked, the thousand tiny tendrils of this or that small and small-minded feeling growing out of our neighborhood, our job, the company we keep, the division of our day. If we allow these small weeds to grow unwittingly, then unwittingly they will destroy us! — And if you positively want to be destroyed, be so *all at once* and suddenly: then perhaps you will leave *sublime ruins*! And not, as one now has reason to fear, molehills! And grass and weeds on them, these small victors, unassuming as before and too pitiful even to celebrate their triumph!

436

Casuistical. — There is a terribly wicked dilemma to which not everyone's courage and character are equal: to discover as a passenger on board a ship that the captain and helmsman are making dangerous mistakes and that one's own nautical skills are superior to theirs — and now to ask oneself: What if you were to incite a mutiny against them and have both of them arrested? Does your superiority not oblige you to do so? And then again, don't they have the right to lock you up for insubordination? — This is a metaphor for higher and trickier situations: whereby, in the end, the question always remaining is what vouchsafes our superiority, our belief in ourselves in such situations. Success? But in that case one must indeed already *have done* the thing, which holds along with it all the dangers — and not only dangers for us, but for the ship as well.

437[18]

Privileges. — Whoever is really in possession of himself, that is, whoever *has conquered* himself once and for all, from that point on views it as his own privilege to punish himself, pardon himself, be compassionate toward himself: he doesn't need to concede this to anyone else, but he can, by the same token, freely yield it into the hands of another, a friend for example— but he knows that in so doing he conveys a *right* and that one can only convey rights from a position of *power*.

438[19]

People and things.—Why don't people see things? They themselves are standing in the way: they cover up things.

439

Marks of happiness.—All sensations of happiness have two things in common: *abundance* of feeling and *high-spiritedness* within it, such that one feels like a fish in water and leaps about in it. Good Christians will understand what Christian exuberance is.

440

Do not renounce!—To relinquish the world without knowing it, like a *nun*—that leads to an infertile, perhaps melancholic solitude. This has nothing in common with the solitude of the thinker's *vita contemplativa*:[20] when he elects *it*, he in no way wishes to renounce; on the contrary, it would amount to renunciation, melancholy, downfall of his self for him to have to endure the *vita practica*:[21] he relinquishes the latter because he knows it, knows himself. Thus he leaps into *his* water, thus he attains *his* serenity.

441[22]

Why what is closest becomes ever more distant.—The more we think about everything that we were and will be, the paler what we are right now becomes. When we live with the dead and, in their dying, die along with them, what do our "neighbors" matter at that point? We grow more solitary—and indeed *because* the whole flood of humanity resounds around us. The fire within us that burns for everything human glows ever brighter, ever hotter—and *for this reason* we gaze upon what surrounds us as if it had become more indifferent and shadowy.—But our cold gaze *offends*!

442[23]

The rule.—"The rule is always more interesting to me than the exception"—anyone who feels this way is far advanced in scholarship and belongs to the initiated.

443

On education.—Light on the most widespread deficiency in our type of education and upbringing has gradually dawned on me: no one learns, no one strives toward, no one teaches—*to learn to endure solitude.*

444[24]

Astonishment at resistance.—Because something has become transparent to us, we believe it can no longer offer us any resistance—and are then astounded that we can see through it and yet not get through it! This is the same foolishness and the same amazement that overtakes a fly before every pane of glass.

445

Wherein the noblest misreckon.—You finally give someone your very best, your jewel—now love has nothing more to give: but the person who receives it certainly does not have in it *his* best and consequently he lacks that full and ultimate gratitude with which the giver had reckoned.

446

Hierarchy.—There are, first of all, superficial thinkers, secondly, deep thinkers—those that go to the depths of a matter—thirdly, thorough thinkers who get to the foundation of a matter—which is a great deal more valuable than just descending into its depths!—Finally, there are those who stick their heads in the morass: which shouldn't be taken as either a sign of depth or of thoroughness! They are the dear old shallow and fallow ones.

447[25]

Master and pupil. — It is part of a master's humanity to warn his pupil about himself.

448

Honoring reality. — How can one watch this jubilant crowd of people without being moved to tears and agreeing with them! Previously we thought very little of the object of their jubilation and would still continue to think little of it *if* we had not experienced it! To where in the world then might our experiences not carry us off? What really are our opinions? One must, in order not to lose one's self, not to lose one's *reason*, flee from experiences! Thus Plato fled from reality and wanted to intuit things only in the pallid images of ideas; he was full of sensibility and knew how easily the waves of sensibility had engulfed his reason.[26] — Would the wise man accordingly have to say to himself: "I want to honor *reality*, but to turn my back on it in so doing, *because* I know and fear it"? — Would he have to act like the African tribes vis-à-vis their princes: approach them only backward and know how to show simultaneously their veneration and their fear?

449[27]

Where are the spiritually needy? — Ah! How it nauseates me *to impose* my thoughts on another! How I take pleasure in every mood and secret conversion within myself by which the thoughts *of others* prevail over my own! From time to time there occurs an even higher celebration, when for a change one is *allowed* to give *away* one's spiritual house and possessions like the father confessor who sits in the corner, eager for *one in need* to come and recount the travail of his thoughts[28] in order that he, the father confessor, might once again fill his hand and heart and *lighten* his burdened soul! Not only does he eschew all praise for what he does: he also would like to avoid any gratitude, for gratitude is invasive and has no respect for solitude and silence. He seeks to live nameless or lightly ridiculed, too humble to awaken envy or enmity, armed with a head free of fever, a handful of knowledge, and a bag full of experiences, to be, as it were, a doctor of the spirit to the indigent and to aid people here and there whose head *is disturbed by opinions* without their really noticing who has helped him! Not to be right vis-à-vis this person and to celebrate a victory, but to speak with him in such a way that, after a tiny unobserved hint or objection, he himself says what is right and, proud of the fact, walks away! Like a modest hostel that turns away no one in need, that is, however, forgotten about afterward or laughed at! To have no advantage, neither better food, nor purer air, nor a more joyful spirit—but to share, to give back, to communicate, to grow poorer! To be able to be humble so as to be accessible to many and humiliating to none! To have experienced much injustice and have crawled through the worm tunnels of every kind of error in order to be able to reach many hidden souls along their secret paths! Always in a type of love and a type of self-interest and self-enjoyment! To be in possession of a dominion and at the same time inconspicuous and renouncing! To lie constantly in the sun and the kindness of grace and yet to know that the paths rising to the sublime are right at hand!—That would be a life! That would be a reason to live, to live a long time.

450[29]

Knowledge's lure. —A look through the portal of science affects passionate spirits like the magic of all magic; and in the process such spirits presumably become fantasists or, under propitious circumstances, poets: so vehement is their craving for the happiness of the knowledgeable. Doesn't it course through all your senses—this tone of sweet allure with which science proclaimed its glad tidings, in a hundred phrases and in the hundred and first and fairest: "Let delusion disappear! Then 'woe is me!' will also have disappeared; and with the 'woe is me!' the woe will also go." (Marcus Aurelius)[30]

451

For whom a court jester is necessary. — People who are very beautiful, people who are very good, people who are very powerful almost[31] never learn the complete and base truth about anything at all — for in their presence one involuntarily lies a little, because one always feels their influence and in keeping with this influence presents the truth one could communicate in the form of an *adaptation* (by falsifying shades and degrees of the factual, by omitting or appending details, and by suppressing behind one's lips anything that cannot be adapted). If, despite everything, people of this sort absolutely insist on hearing the truth, then they must maintain their *court jester* — a creature with the madman's privilege of not being able to adapt himself.

452[32]

Impatience. — There is a degree of impatience in people of action and of reflection that, in the event of failure, immediately compels them to switch over to the opposite domain where they grow impassioned and enter into endeavors — until a delay in attaining success drives them away from here again as well: and so they err, adventurously and vehemently, through the practices of many domains and temperaments, and in the end, through the immense knowledge of people and things that they have acquired through prodigious travel and constant exercise of their endeavors and through some moderation of their impatient drive, they are able to become — powerful practitioners. Thus does a character flaw turn into a school for genius.

453[33]

Moral interregnum. — Who would already, at this very moment, be capable of describing what will one day *do away with*[34] moral feelings and judgments!—no matter how certainly one is able to realize that all the foundations for these have been laid out incorrectly and that their edifice is beyond repair: their binding force must constantly decline from day to day to the extent that the binding force of reason does not decline! To build anew the laws of life and of behavior—for this task our sciences of physiology, medicine, sociology and solitude are not yet sure enough of themselves: and only from them can we take the foundation stones for new ideals (if not the new ideals themselves). Thus we are living either a *preliminary* or *posterior* existence, depending on taste and talent, and it is best in this interregnum to be to every possible extent our own *reges*[35] and to found little *experimental nations*. We are experiments:[36] let us also want to be such!

454[37]

Interpolation. —A book such as this is not for reading straight through or reading aloud, but for cracking open, especially during a walk or on a journey; you must be able to stick your head into it and out again over and over and find about you nothing you are used to.

455

First nature. — The way we are being brought up these days we first receive a *second nature*: and we have it when the world labels us mature, of age, usable. A select few are snakes enough to shed this skin one day: at that point when under its cover their *first nature* has matured. With most people its embryo dries up.

456

A virtue in the making. —Assertions and promises such as those made by ancient philosophy as to the unity of virtue and happiness or the Christian "Seek ye first the kingdom of God: and all these things shall be added unto you!"[38]—have never been made with complete honesty and yet always without a bad conscience: one set up such propositions, the truth of which one greatly desired, audaciously against all evidence, as the truth, and experienced in the process not one religious or moral pang of conscience—for one had transcended reality *in honorem majorem*[39] of virtue or God and not with any self-serving intentions! Many decent people still stand on this *rung of truthfulness*: when they *feel* themselves selfless, it seems to them permissible *to take* truth *less seriously*. Take note, however, that among neither the Socratic nor the Christian virtues does *honesty* appear: it is one of the youngest virtues, still quite immature, still frequently mistaken and misconstrued, still barely aware of itself—something in the making, which we can advance or retard, as we see fit.

457

Ultimate discretion.[40] — Some individuals are like treasure hunters: they accidentally uncover things in the soul of another that had been kept hidden and this knowledge is often a heavy load to bear! There are circumstances under which one can get to know the living and the dead so well and to such a degree that inwardly one catches oneself finding it embarrassing to speak of them to other people: with every word one is afraid of being indiscreet. — I can imagine on the part of the wisest historian a sudden falling silent.

458

The jackpot. — It is something very rare, but a thing in which to delight: the person, namely, with a beautifully formed intellect who has the character, the inclinations, and *also the experiences* in keeping with such an intellect.[41]

459[42]

The thinker's magnanimity. — Rousseau and Schopenhauer— both were proud enough to inscribe upon their existence the motto: *vitam impendere vero.*[43] And again—how they both must have suffered in their pride in that they could not succeed in making *verum impendere vitae!*[44] — *verum*, as each of them understood it — in that their lives tagged along beside their knowledge like a temperamental bass that refuses to stay in tune with the melody! But knowledge would be in a sorry state if it were meted out to every thinker only as it suited his person! And thinkers would be in a sorry state if their vanity were so great that they could endure only this! The great thinker's most beautiful virtue radiates precisely from: the magnanimity with which he, as a person of knowledge, undauntedly, often ashamed, often with sublime mockery and smiling — offers himself and his life in sacrifice.

460[45]

Taking advantage of one's dangerous hours. — One gets to know persons and states of affairs completely differently when each of their movements represents for us and our loved ones a danger to our belongings, honor, life, and death: Tiberius,[46] for instance, must have reflected more profoundly and known more about the inner workings of Emperor Augustus[47] and his regiment than is even possible for the wisest historian. Nowadays we all live, comparatively speaking, in much too great a safety to be able to become real knowers of humanity: one person pursues knowledge as a hobby, another out of boredom, the third out of habit; never does it come down to: "Know or be destroyed!" As long as truths do not slice themselves into our flesh with knives, we retain within us a secret residue of disdain for them: they still seem to us too similar to "winged dreams," as if we were free to have them and also not to have them — as if something about them were up to us, as if from these truths of ours we could also *awaken*!

461

Hic Rhodus, hic salta.[48] — Our music, which[49] can metamorphose into everything and must metamorphose because, like the demon of the sea,[50] it has no character of its own: in bygone days this music chased after the *Christian scholar* and was able to translate his ideal into sounds: why, at long last, shouldn't it be able to find as well that brighter, more joyful, and widespread sound that corresponds to *the ideal thinker*? — A music that only is able to be *at home* swaying up and down in the broad floating vaults of *his* soul? — Our music was up until now so great, so good: nothing has been impossible for it! So let it show then that it is possible to experience these three things at once: sublimity, deep and warm illumination, and the bliss of the highest logical consistency.

462

Slow cures. — Chronic diseases of the soul, like those of the body, very rarely emerge merely through onetime gross offenses against the rationality of body and soul, but usually instead through countless unnoticed little acts of negligence. — For example, anyone who day in and day out, and even to an as yet insignificant degree, breathes too weakly and takes too little air into his lungs so that on the whole they are not sufficiently exerted and exercised, eventually ends up with a chronic lung infection as a result: in such a case the cure cannot come about by any means other than to resolve, once again, on countless little offsetting exercises and to cultivate unwittingly different habits; for example, to make it a rule for oneself once, every quarter of an hour, to breathe deeply and strongly (if possible lying out flat on the ground; a watch that chimes on the quarter hour must be chosen as one's life companion). All these cures are *slow* and persnickety; also, anyone who wants to heal his soul should reflect on changing the smallest of his habits. Many a person has a cold, malicious word to say for his environment ten times a day and doesn't think anything of it, especially because, after a few years, he has created for himself a *law* of habit that from now on *compels* him ten times every day to sour his environment. But he can also accustom himself to doing it a kindness ten times! —

463

On the seventh day.[51] — "You praise that as my *creation*? I have only cast off from me what I found irksome! My soul is elevated above the vanity of creators. — You praise this as my *resignation*? I have only cast off from me what I found irksome! My soul is elevated above the vanity of the resigned."

464

The gift giver's shame. — It is so ungenerous to always play the giver and the presenter and to show one's face in the process. But to give and to present and to conceal one's name and one's favor! Or to have no name, like nature in which what refreshes most of all is precisely that, finally and for once, we no longer encounter there a giver or presenter, no longer a "gracious countenance"! — To be sure, you foolishly forfeit this refreshment as well, for you have stuck a God into this nature — and now everything is once more unfree and uneasy! What? Never permitted to be alone with oneself? Nevermore unobserved, unguarded, free of leading reins and gift giving? Whenever another is around us, then the best of courage and goodness in the world is rendered impossible. Isn't this intrusiveness on heaven's part, on the part of this unavoidable supernatural neighbor, enough to drive us to the devil! — But it needn't be, it was indeed only a dream! Let's wake up!

465[52]

At an encounter. — A: What are you staring at? You've been standing here silently for so long. — B: Always the same old and the same new thing! The neediness of a matter pulls me so far and so deeply into it that I finally get to the bottom of it and realize that it is not really worth as much as all that. At the end of all such experiences there comes a type of mourning and paralysis. I live through this on a small scale three times a day.

466

In fame a loss. — What a privilege and advantage to be allowed to address people as an unknown! The gods rob us of "half our virtue" when they take away our incognito and make us famous.

467[53]

Forbearance twice. — "You will cause a lot of people pain that way." — I know it; and know as well that I will suffer doubly for it, once from compassion with their suffering and then from the revenge they will take on me. Nevertheless, it is no less necessary to act as I am acting.

468[54]

The realm of beauty is bigger. — In the way we go around in nature with cunning and glee in order to discover and, as it were, to catch in the act the beauty that is particular to all things; in the way we, be it in sunshine, under stormy sky, in the palest twilight, make the attempt to see how every piece of coastline with its cliffs, inlets, olive trees, and pines achieves its perfection and mastery: so too ought we to go around among people, as their discoverers and scouts, demonstrating to them what is good and bad so that their own particular beauty can reveal itself, a beauty that for one person unfolds in sunshine, for another in the storm, and for a third only halfway into the night when the sky is pouring rain. Is it forbidden to *enjoy* an *evil* person like a wild landscape full of its own bold lineaments and play of light if the same person, as long as he pretends to be good and law-abiding, appears to our eye as an inept sketch and caricature and, as a blot on nature, causes us *mortification*? — Yes, it is forbidden: up until now it was only permitted to search for beauty in the *morally good* — reason enough that one found so little and had to look around for so many imaginary things of beauty without bones! — Just as surely as evil people have a hundred types of happiness about which the virtuous have no clue, they also have a hundred types of beauty: and many have not yet been discovered.

469

The sage's inhumanity. — Given that the heavy march of the sage, who as the Buddhist hymn intones "walks alone like the rhinoceros,"[55] crushes everything in its path, there is, from time to time, a need for signs of a conciliatory and tempered humanity: and indeed, not merely a faster pace or courteous and amiable expressions of spirit, not merely wit and a certain self-mockery, but instead contradictions and even an occasional relapse into the inanities currently in vogue. In order to resemble a steamroller that comes rolling down like some disaster, the sage who wants to instruct must use his *faults* to extenuate himself, and when he says "despise me!", he is pleading for the favor of being the advocate for a presumptuous truth. He wants to lead you into the mountains, he will perhaps endanger your lives: in return he is willing, before and afterward, to let you take your revenge on such a leader — it is the price he pays for giving himself the pleasure of *going on ahead*. — Do you recall what went through your mind when he once led you on slippery paths through a dark cavern? How your heart, pounding and sullen, said to itself: "that leader there could be doing something better than crawling around in this place! He belongs to a curious breed of idlers: — doesn't it already do him too much honor that we seem to grant him some sort of value at all by *following* him?"

470

At the banquet of many. — How happy one is when one is provided for like the birds,[56] out of the hand of one who broadcasts grain for the birds without looking too closely at them and evaluating their worthiness. To live like a bird that comes and flies away and carries no name in its beak! Thus it is my pleasure to eat my fill at the banquet of the many.

471[57]

A different love-thy-neighbor. — The excited, noisy, inconsistent, nervous being constitutes the antithesis of *great passion*: the latter, like a silent, dark fire dwelling within and storing up everything there that is hot and inflamed, makes the person look outwardly cold and indifferent and impresses on his features a certain impassivity. Such people are certainly capable upon occasion of *loving their neighbor*[58] — but it is of a different ilk from that of the gregarious and eager to please: it is a tempered, contemplative, composed friendliness; they gaze, as it were, out the windows of their castle, which is their fortress, and, owing precisely to this, their prison: — to gaze into what is foreign, free, and *different* does them so much good.

472[59]

Not justifying oneself. — A: But why don't you want to justify yourself? — B: I could do so in this and in a hundred things, but I disdain the pleasure that lies in justification: for these things aren't large enough for me and I prefer to bear some blemishes than to assist those petty sorts toward their malicious satisfaction in being able to say: "He certainly takes these things very seriously!" This is simply not true! Perhaps I ought to care more about myself in order to make it a duty to correct fallacious ideas about me; — I am too indifferent and lethargic toward myself and consequently toward the effects I produce.

473[60]

Where one should build one's house. — If in solitude you feel great and fruitful, then the company of others will diminish you and make you barren: and *vice versa*. Powerful kindness, like that of a father: — where this disposition seizes you, found your house there, be it in the milling crowd or in a place of quietude. *Ubi pater sum, ibi patria.*[61]

474[62]

The only ways. — "Dialectics is the only way to reach the divine being and get behind the veil of appearance" — this was asserted by Plato just as solemnly and passionately as Schopenhauer asserted it for the opposite of dialectics — and both were wrong. For the thing to which they want to show us the way does not *exist* at all. — And up until now haven't all of humanity's great passions been just such passions for nothing? And all their solemnities — solemnities about nothing?

475[63]

Growing heavy. — You do not know him: he can hang many weights on himself, yet he takes them all with him into the heights. And based on the tiny beating of your wings, you conclude he wanted to remain *below because* he hung these weights on himself.

476

At the harvest feast of the spirit. — They accumulate from day to day and well up, experiences, events, thoughts about them and dreams about these thoughts — an immeasurable, delightful wealth! The sight of it makes one dizzy; I can no longer comprehend how one can call the poor in spirit *blessed*![64] But I envy them from time to time at those moments when I am tired: for the *administration* of such wealth is a heavy job, and its heaviness not infrequently overwhelms all happiness. — Indeed, if it were only enough to look and admire the sight of it! If only one were the skinflint of one's knowledge!

477

Redeemed from skepticism. — A: "Others emerge from a general moral skepticism ill-humored and weak, chewed up, worm-infested, indeed, half eaten away — I, however, emerge more courageous and healthier than ever, once more in possession of my instincts. Where a sharp wind blows, the sea rises high, and no small danger exists, that is where I feel good. I did not turn into a worm even though I often had to work and dig like a worm." B: You have simply *ceased* to be a skeptic! For you *deny*!—A: "And that's how I've learned once again *to say yes*."

478

Let's pass on!—Spare him! Leave him to his solitude! Do we want to break him completely? He received a crack, as happens with a glass into which one suddenly poured something too hot—and it was such a precious glass!

479

Love and truthfulness.—Love turns us into inveterate felons against truth and into people who habitually thieve and habitually receive stolen goods, who permit more to be true than seems true to us—the thinker must therefore constantly from time to time chase away the people he loves (it will not necessarily be those who love him) so that they may reveal their sting and their malice and stop *seducing* him. Accordingly, the thinker's kindness will have its waxing and waning moon.

480

Unavoidable.—No matter what you experience: anyone who does not wish you well will see in that experience an occasion to diminish you! Undergo the most profound existential and epistemological upheavals and at long last emerge, like a convalescent with a pained smile into freedom and luminous quietude: someone will then surely say "That fellow there considers his illness to be an argument, his impotence to be proof that everyone is impotent; he is vain enough to get sick in order to feel the superiority of the sufferer."—And supposing that someone explodes his own fetters and wounds himself deeply in the process: then another will point to him with ridicule. "How great his ineptitude certainly is!" he will say: "That's the way it's bound to go for a person who is used to his fetters and is fool enough to rip them off!"

481[65]

Two Germans. — If one compares Kant and Schopenhauer with Plato, Spinoza, Pascal, Rousseau, Goethe with regard to their soul and not their mind: then the former are at a disadvantage: their thoughts do not comprise a passionate history of the soul, here there is no novel,[66] no crises, catastrophes, final hours to discern; their thinking is not at one and the same time an involuntary biography of a soul, but in Kant's case, of the *head*, in Schopenhauer's case, the description and mirroring of a *character* ("the immutable") and the pleasure in the "mirror" itself, that is to say in a first-rate intellect. Kant appears, when he does appear through his thought, as upright and honorable in the best sense, but as insignificant: he lacked breadth and power; he did not experience very much and his way of working[67] deprived him of the *time* to experience anything — I have in mind, of course, not those crude "events" that come from without, but the destinies and throes that befall the most solitary and quiet life that has leisure and that burns with the passion of thinking. Schopenhauer has an edge on Kant: at least he possesses a certain *vehement ugliness* of nature; in hatred, cravings, vanity, distrust, he is by disposition more savage and had time and leisure for this savagery. But he lacked "development": just as it is lacking in the sphere of his thoughts; he had no "history."[68]

482[69]

Searching for one's company. — Are we then searching for too much when we search for the company of men who have grown mild, savory, and nutritious, like chestnuts that have been placed in the fire and removed at the right time? Who expect less from life and would rather take this less as a gift than as something earned, as if the birds and the bees had brought it to them? Who are too proud to be able to feel they could ever be paid what they've earned? And too earnest in their passion for knowledge and honesty as to still have the time and obsequiousness requisite for fame? — We would call such men philosophers, but they themselves will still find a more modest name.

483[70]

Sick and tired of people. — A: Know! Yes, but always as a human being! What? Always to sit before the same comedy, to act in the same comedy? Never to be able to see things with any eyes other than *these* eyes? And how many countless types of beings might there be, whose organs are better suited to knowledge! What will humanity have known at the end of all its knowledge? — its organs! And that might well mean: the impossibility of knowledge! Misery and disgust! — B: That is a wicked attack — *reason* is attacking you! But tomorrow you'll be right back in the midst of knowing again and so also in the midst of unreason, by which I mean: in the *pleasure* of being human. Let's go down to the sea!

484

One's own way. — When we take the decisive step and set out on the way one calls one's "own way": a secret suddenly reveals itself to us: even all those with whom we were friendly and intimate — all have imagined themselves superior to us and are offended. The best among them are lenient with us and wait patiently for us to rediscover the "right way" — they know it, of course! Others make fun and act as if one had gone temporarily batty or else point spitefully to a seducer. The more malicious declare us to be vain fools and attempt to blacken our motives. The worst ones see in us their worst enemy, one who[71] thirsts for revenge after a long period of dependence — and is afraid of us. What's to be done? I advise: we initiate our sovereignty by assuring all our acquaintances a year's amnesty in advance for their sins of every kind.

485[72]

Distant perspectives. — A: But why this solitude? — B: I'm not angry with anyone. But on my own I seem to see my friends more clearly and more appealingly than when together with them; and at the time when I loved music most and was most sensitive to it, I lived at a distance from it. It seems I need distant perspectives to think well of things.

486

Gold and hunger. — Here and there you find a person who turns everything he touches into gold.[73] One good, evil day he will discover that he must starve to death in the process. Everything around him is gleaming, magnificent, ideally unapproachable, and now he longs for things that are *altogether impossible for him* to turn into gold — and *how* he longs! As someone starving longs for food! What will he reach for?

487[74]

Shame. — There stands the beautiful steed and paws the ground; it snorts, it yearns for a ride and loves the one who usually rides it — but oh shame! The rider cannot swing himself up into the saddle today, he is tired. — Such is the shame of the exhausted thinker before his own philosophy.

488[75]

Against squandering love. — Don't we blush when we catch ourselves in the middle of a violent aversion? But we ought to do so with violent attractions as well, owing to the injustice that lies in them too! Indeed, all the more so: there are people who feel hemmed in and whose heart constricts whenever someone gives them the benefit of his affection only by *withdrawing* something of his affection from others. If we discern from his voice that *we* are being selected, preferred! Ah, I'm not grateful for this selection, I notice that I hold it against him for wanting to distinguish me in this way: he ought not to love me at the *expense* of others! I'll just have to manage to endure myself on my own! And often my heart is full and I have grounds for high spirits—to such a one with such as this, one ought to bring nothing that *others* need, need desperately!

489

Friends in need.—From time to time we notice that one of our friends belongs to another more than to us, that his sense of delicacy is tortured by, his selfishness inadequate to, the decision: then we have to make things easier for him by *estranging* him from us *through insults.*—This is also necessary in those cases where we are moving on to a way of thinking that would be calamitous for him: our love for him must drive us, through an injustice that we take on ourselves, to create for him a good conscience for his break with us.

490

These petty truths!—"You're familiar with all this, but you've never experienced it—I don't accept your evidence. These 'petty truths'!—you fancy them petty because you've never paid for them with your blood!"—But are they then grand simply because you paid *too much* for them? And blood is always too much!—"You think so? How stingy you are with blood!"

491

Another reason for solitude.[76]—A: So you want to go back to your desert again?—B: I'm not quick, I have to wait for myself—it always gets late, each time before the water from the well of my self comes to light and often I have to suffer thirst beyond my patience. For this reason I enter into solitude—so as not to drink out of everyone's cisterns. Amid the many I live like the many and don't think as I; after some time I always feel then as if they wanted to ban me from myself and rob my soul—and I turn angry toward everyone and fear everyone. Then I need the desert to turn good again.[77]

492

Under south winds. — A: I no longer understand myself! Yesterday I still felt so turbulent inside and yet so warm, so sunny—and bright in the extreme. And today! Everything is now motionless, remote, mournful, somber, like the lagoon of Venice:[78] I want nothing and draw a deep breath of release thereby, and yet secretly I am indignant with myself over this wanting nothing: thus do the waves lap back and forth in the lake of my melancholy. B: You're describing here a pleasant little illness. The next northeaster will sweep it right out of you!—A: Why should it?

493[79]

On one's own tree. — A: "I don't have as much pleasure in the thoughts of any other thinker as I do in my own: to be sure, that says nothing about their value, but I would have to be a fool to denigrate the fruits I find most delicious because they happen to grow on *my* tree!—And I once was this fool."—B: "With others it is just the reverse: and this too says nothing about the worth of their thoughts and especially nothing as of yet against their value."

494

Last argument of the brave. — "There are snakes in these bushes." — Good, I'll go into the bushes and kill them. — "But perhaps you'll be their victim and they won't even be yours!" — What a burden I must bear![80]

495[81]

Our teachers. — In our youth we take our teachers and guides from the present and from the circles we run in: we trust mindlessly that the present must have teachers suited to us and to everyone else and that we will inevitably find them without too much searching. For this childishness we later have to pay a high ransom: *we must atone for our teachers in ourselves.* Then, to be sure, we go out into the entire world, including the world of the past, in search of the right guides—but it is perhaps too late. And in the worst case we discover that they lived when we were young—and we overlooked them at the time.

496[82]

The evil principle. —Plato described splendidly how, in the midst of every existing society, the philosophical thinker has to be considered the paragon of all infamy: for as critic of all morals he is the antithesis of the moral person, and if he doesn't manage to become the legislator of new morals, he remains in the memory of the people as "the evil principle." From this perspective we may gather why the rather liberal and reform-minded city of Athens played rough with Plato's reputation during his lifetime: is it any wonder that he—who as he himself says, had the "political drive" in his blood,[83] made three attempts to settle in Sicily[84] at precisely the time when a Panhellenic Mediterranean city[85] appeared to be in the offing? In this city and with its help Plato hoped to do for the Greeks what Mohammed later did for his Arabs: to lay down the large and small customs and especially the daily way of life for everyone. His ideas were *possible*, just as surely as Mohammed's were possible: after all, much more unbelievable ideas, those of Christianity, have been proven possible! A couple of accidents fewer, a couple of different accidents more—and the world would have lived through the Platonization of the European south; and supposing this state were still in place, then we would presumably revere Plato as the "good principle." But success eluded him: and he was left with the reputation of being a fantasist and utopian—the more severe names were destroyed along with ancient Athens.

497[86]

The purifying eye. —We can talk of "genius" most readily with regard to such people as Plato, Spinoza, and Goethe, whose spirit seems only *loosely bound* to their character and temperament, like a winged essence that can separate itself from the latter and soar high above them. On the contrary, precisely such people who have spoken most animatedly of their "genius" are those who *never escaped* from their temperament and who managed to lend it the most spiritual, grand, widespread, indeed, under certain conditions, cosmic expression (Schopenhauer, for example). These geniuses were unable to fly away, above and beyond themselves; instead they fancied they met up with *themselves* no matter where they flew—that is *their* "greatness," and *can* be greatness!—The others, for whom the name is actually more appropriate, have the *pure, purifying eye* that does not seem to grow out of their temperament and character, but is instead free of and usually in mild contradiction to them and that gazes at the world as if it were a god, a god it loves. Even they, however, did not receive this eye all at once as a present: seeing requires practice and apprenticeship, and whoever is properly fortunate finds at the proper time a teacher of pure seeing.

498[87]

Do not demand!—You do not know him! Yes, he *submits* easily and freely to people and things, and is kind to both: his only request is to be left in peace—but only *so long as* people and things do not *demand* submission. All demands make him proud, withdrawn, and bellicose.

499

The evil one. — "Only the solitary man is evil,"[88] cried Diderot and immediately Rousseau felt mortally wounded. Consequently, he admitted to himself that Diderot was right. It is a fact that, in the midst of society and sociability, every evil proclivity has to undergo so much restraint, take up so many masks, lay itself so often in the Procrustean bed[89] of virtue that one could quite properly speak of a martyrdom of evil. In soli-

tude this all falls by the wayside. Whoever is evil is at his most
evil in solitude: also at his best—and consequently, to the eye
of anyone who everywhere sees only playacting, also at his
most beautiful.

500

Against the grain.—A thinker can force himself year after
year to think against the grain: I mean, to pursue not the
thoughts that present themselves to him from within, but those
to which an office, a prescribed schedule, an arbitrary type of
diligence seem to commit him. In the long run, however, he
will grow ill: for this apparently moral overcoming ruins the
vitality of his nerves just as fundamentally as could any habitually indulged, extreme intemperance.

501

Mortal souls!—With regard to knowledge the most useful
accomplishment is perhaps: that the belief in the immortality
of the soul has been abandoned. Now humanity is allowed to
wait; now it no longer needs to rush headlong into things and
choke down half-examined ideas as formerly it was forced to
do. For in those days the salvation of poor "eternal souls" depended on the extent of their knowledge during a short lifetime; they had to *make a decision* overnight—"knowledge"
took on a dreadful importance! We have seized once again
the good courage to make mistakes, attempts to take things
provisionally—everything is less important!—and precisely
for this reason individuals and generations can set their sights
on undertakings of a grandeur that would have appeared to
earlier ages as insanity and a toying with heaven and hell. We
may experiment with ourselves! Indeed, humanity can do so
with itself! The greatest sacrifices to knowledge have not yet
been made—indeed, previously it would have meant blas-
phemy and the surrender of one's eternal salvation even to
have a presentiment of the thoughts that precede our actions.

502

One word for three different states. — With one person passion brings out the wild, dreadful, insufferable beast; it elevates another into a height and greatness and splendor of bearing compared to which his customary state of being appears paltry. A third, ennobled through and through, has as well the noblest storm and stress;[90] in this state he is *nature in its wild beauty* and only one degree *more profound* than nature in its serene beauty, which he usually presents: but people understand him more when he is passionate and they revere him more owing precisely to these moments — he is a step closer to them and more related. They feel delight and dread before such a sight and call him *on the spot*: divine.

503

Friendship. — The objection to the philosophical life that claims that through it one becomes *worthless* to one's friends would never occur to a modern: it belongs to antiquity. Antiquity profoundly and intensively lived out and thought through friendship to the limit and almost took friendship along with itself to the grave. This is its advantage over us: by comparison we offer idealized sexual love. All great abilities possessed by the people of antiquity took their purchase from the fact that *man stood beside man*, and that no woman was permitted to lay claim to being the nearest, highest, let alone exclusive object of his love — as sexual passion teaches us to feel. Perhaps our trees fail to grow as high owing to the ivy and grape vines that cling to them.

504

Reconcile! — Is it supposed to be the task of philosophy to *reconcile* what the *child* learned with what the *man* has come to know? Is philosophy supposed to be the special task of youths because they stand in the middle between child and man and possess the mean of both sets of needs? It almost

seems so when one considers at what period in life philosophers nowadays are in the habit of coming up with their grand
design: at an age when it's too late for belief and too soon for
knowledge.

505

The practical. — We thinkers are the ones who first have to
determine the *savoriness* of all things and, if need be, to decree
it. Practical people eventually pounce upon this asset; their
dependence on us is unbelievable and the most ludicrous spectacle in the world, no matter how little they know of it and
how haughtily they love dismissively to discourse about us
impractical ones: indeed, they would scorn their practical life
should we choose to scorn it: — something to which a little
desire for revenge might spur us now and then.

506

The necessary curing of everything good. — What? We have to
interpret a work exactly as the period that produced it? But we
have more pleasure, more amazement, and also more to learn
from it precisely if we do not interpret it that way! Haven't you
noticed that as long as it lies in the damp air of its time, every
good work possesses its least value — precisely because it still
bears so strongly the smell of the market and of squabbles and
of the latest opinions and of everything transitory between
today and tomorrow? Later it dries out, cures, its "timeliness"
withers away — and only then does it acquire its deep luster
and delectable fragrance, indeed, if this is what it's after, its
quiet eye of eternity.

507

Against the tyranny of the true. — Even if we were crazy
enough to believe all our opinions were true, we still would not
want them alone to exist —: I have no idea why the dictator-
ship and omnipotence of truth would be desirable; it's sufficient for me that it has *great power*. But it has to be in a position

to *fight* and have an adversary, and one has to be, from time to time, in a position to *recover* from it in untruth — otherwise it will become boring, powerless, and tasteless for us, and will make us just the same as well.

508[91]

Not with pathos. — Whatever we do for our own *benefit* ought not garner for us any moral encomium, either from others or from ourselves; the same is true for whatever we do to take *pleasure* in ourselves. In such cases to eschew lofty pathos and to refrain, oneself, from all putting-on of airs are *good form* among all superior human beings: and anyone who makes a habit of it is granted a second *naïveté*.

509

The third eye. — What? You still need the theater! Are you still so young? Wise up and look for tragedy and comedy where they are better acted! Where what transpires is more interesting and more interested! It's true, then it's not so easy to remain a mere spectator — but learn to! And in almost all situations that are difficult and painful for you, you will then have a little gateway to pleasure and a refuge, even when you are overcome by your own passions. Open your theater-eye, the great third eye that, through the other two, looks into the world!

510

Running away from one's virtues. — What good is a thinker if he doesn't know how to run away from his own virtues on occasion![92] He ought indeed to be "not only a moral being"!

511

The temptress. — Honesty is the great temptress of all fanatics. What appeared to approach Luther in the form of the devil or a beautiful woman and what he defended himself against in such an uncouth way[93] was no doubt honesty and perhaps, in rarer cases, even the truth.[94]

512

Courageous when it comes to causes. — Anyone who is by nature considerate or wary of people, yet has courage when it comes to causes,[95] eschews new and closer acquaintanceships and limits his old ones: so that his incognito and his ruthlessness with regard to truth grow together.

513

Limit and beauty. — Are you searching for people of *beautiful* culture? Then you must, just as with beautiful landscapes, be satisfied with *limited* prospects and views. — Certainly there are panoramic people, and certainly they are, like panoramic landscapes, instructive and astounding: but not beautiful.

514[96]

To the stronger. — You stronger and arrogant spirits, I ask of you only one thing: do not lay upon the rest of us any new burden, but instead take some of our burden upon yourself because you are, after all, the stronger! But you relish so much doing just the opposite: for *you* want to fly and therefore we're supposed to carry your burden on top of ours: which is to say, *we* are supposed to crawl!

515

Increase in beauty. — Why does beauty increase with civilization? Because with civilized people the three occasions for ugliness occur seldom and ever more seldom: first, the emotions in their wildest explosions; second, physical exertions of the most extreme degree; third, the need to inspire fear through one's presence, which in the lower and endangered rungs of culture is so great and ubiquitous that it even determines gestures and ceremonies and turns ugliness into a *duty*.

516

Do not drive your demon into your neighbors![97] — For the time being, at least, let's stick to the idea that benevolence and beneficence are what constitute a good person; only let's add: "provided that he is benevolently and beneficently disposed *toward himself.*" For *without this* — if he runs from himself, hates himself, causes injury to himself — he is certainly not a good person. Because he is rescuing himself from himself *in others*: the others had better see to it that they don't end up badly no matter how well-meaning toward them he appears! — But here's the point: to run from the ego and to hate it and to live in others, for others — has, heretofore, been called, just as unreflectedly as assuredly, *"unegotistical" and consequently "good"*!

517

Seducing into love. — Whoever hates himself is a person to fear, for we will be the victim of his rancor and his revenge. Let's see therefore how we can seduce him into loving himself!

518

Resignation. — What is resignation? It is[98] the most comfortable position of someone ill, who has for ages tossed and turned in torment in an effort *to find* it and has thereby *grown tired* — whereupon he also found it!

519

Being swindled. — The moment you want to act you must close the door to doubt — said a man of action. — And you are not afraid of thus being *swindled*? — replied a man of contemplation.

520[99]

Everlasting funeral rites. — Someone could imagine hearing beyond the realm of history a continual funeral oration: one has buried and always buries what one loves most, one's thoughts and hopes, and has received and receives pride in return—*gloria mundi*,[100] that amounts to the pomp of a funeral oration. It is supposed to make everything all right! And the funeral orator is still the greatest public benefactor!

521[101]

Exceptional vanity.—This person has one superior quality as his solace: what remains of his being—and it is almost all that remains!—his gaze passes over contemptuously. But he finds relief from himself whenever he returns to it as if to his shrine; already the pathway there seems to him like an ascent up a wide, gentle stairway:—and on this account you vicious ones call him vain!

522

Wisdom without ears.—To hear what is being said about us day after day or even to rack our brains trying to guess what is being thought about us—that destroys the strongest man. Indeed, others allow us to live in order, day after day, to have the last word on us! They wouldn't be able to endure us if we had or even *wanted to have* the last word on them! In short, for the sake of general compatibility let us make the sacrifice of not listening when we are spoken of, praised, blamed, when someone desires or hopes something from us, let's not even think about it at all!

523

Ulterior questions.[102]—With everything that a person allows to become visible one can ask: What is it supposed to hide? From what is it supposed to divert our gaze? What presumption is it supposed to excite? And then finally: Just how far does the subtlety of this dissembling extend? And where in the performance does he play the wrong note?

524

The solitaries' jealousy.—Between gregarious and solitary natures exists this difference (provided both have spirit!): the former become satisfied or almost satisfied with a situation, no matter what it is, from the instant they have, in their spirit, discovered for it a communicable, felicitous turn of phrase—this would reconcile them to the devil himself! The solitary, however, have their secret silent transports, their secret silent torments over a situation; they hate the witty glittering exhibition of their inmost problems the way they hate the all-too-carefully chosen attire on their lover: they look toward her with melancholy and watch, as if in them the suspicion were arising that she wanted to appeal to others! This is the jealousy all solitary thinkers and passionate dreamers have of *esprit*.[103]

525

Effect of praise.—Some become, from grandiose praise, shamefully modest, others shamelessly bold.

526

Unwilling to be a symbol.—I feel for princes: they are not allowed to lose themselves among society from time to time and thus they get to know people only from an uncomfortable position and through dissembling; the constant compulsion to signify something ends up actually turning them into mere solemn ciphers.—And this is what happens to everyone who sees it as his duty to be a symbol.

527

The hidden.—Have you never yet run into those people who hold on fast to their hearts, even when overjoyed, and who would rather be struck dumb than lose the modesty of moderation?—And you never ran into those awkward and often so mild-mannered people either, who don't wish to be recognized and who over and over wipe out their footprints in the sand, who are indeed deceivers of others and of themselves, in order to remain concealed?

528

Rare abstemiousness. — It is often no minor sign of humanity not to want to judge another and to refrain from thinking
about him.

529

How people and nations receive their shine. — How many genuine *individual* acts are left undone, because, before doing them,
one realizes or suspects that they will be misunderstood! —
and these are precisely the actions that altogether *have value*,
good or bad. Thus the higher an age or a nation regards individuals and the more rights and the more predominance one
grants them, the greater the number of acts of this kind that
will dare to make it to the light of day — and finally a shimmer
of honesty, of genuineness in the good and the bad, spreads out
across entire ages and nations so that they, like many stars,
shine on for millennia after their destruction, as for example do
the Greeks.

530

Thinker's digressions. — With many thinkers the course of
their thought as a whole is rigorous and unrelentingly bold,
indeed from time to time cruel to itself, but in the details they
are mild and pliant; they circle around a subject ten times with
benevolent hesitation, but in the end they resume their rigorous course. They are streams with many bends and turns and
secluded hermitages; there are places along their route where a
stream plays hide-and-seek with itself and makes for itself a
brief idyll with islands, trees, grottos and waterfalls: and then
it moves on again past cliffs, forcing itself through the hardest
stone.

531[104]

Feeling art differently. — From the time in life when one
lives secludedly-sociably, consuming and consumed, with

profound fructifying ideas and only with them, one no longer
demands anything at all from art or demands something completely different from before — that is to say, one's taste changes.
For before one wanted, through the doorway of art, to dive for
a moment into the very element in which one now lives constantly; formerly through art one dreamed of the delight of possession, and now one does possess. Yes, to throw off for a while
what one now has, and to imagine oneself poor, as child, beg-
gar, and fool — can from now on occasionally give us delight.

532[105]

"Love makes the same." — Love wants to spare the other to
whom it consecrates itself every feeling of *being different*; consequently, it is full of dissembling and a show of similarity; it
deceives continually and playacts a sameness that in truth
does not exist. And this happens so instinctively that women
in love deny this dissembling and constant, tenderest deception, boldly asserting that love *makes the same* (that is to say, it
performs a miracle!). — This process is simple if one person *lets
himself be loved* and doesn't find it necessary to dissemble, but
on the contrary leaves that up to the other lover: but there exists no more complicated and impenetrable spectacle than
when both are in the full throes of passion for one another and
consequently both relinquish themselves, feign sameness of
the other and want to imitate that other and that other alone:
and in the end neither knows any longer what one's imitating,
why one's dissembling, who one's pretending to be. The beautiful madness of this spectacle is too good for this world and
too subtle for human eyes.

533

We beginners! — What all an actor discerns and sees when
he sees someone else act! He knows when, in producing a gesture, a muscle fails in its duty; he sorts out those little invented
things that are practiced one by one and cold-bloodedly in
front of the mirror and cannot seem to be integrated back into

the whole; he senses it when the actor is surprised in a scene by his own inventiveness and through that inventiveness *ruins* the scene. — How differently as well a painter observes a person moving before him! In particular, he immediately envisions a great deal *in addition* in order to complete what is present and to bring it to its fullest effect; in his mind he tries out various types of lighting for the same object; he divides the whole of the effect by a contrast that he adds. — If we only had the eye of this actor and this painter for the realm of human souls!

534

Small doses. — If you want to effect the most profound transformation possible, then administer the means in the smallest doses, but unremittingly and over long periods of time! What great things can be accomplished at one fell swoop! Thus we want to guard against exchanging head over heels and with acts of violence the moral condition we are used to for a new evaluation of things — no, we want to keep on living in that condition for a long, long time — until we, very late, presumably, become fully aware that *the new evaluation* has become the predominant force and that the small doses of it, *to which we will have to grow accustomed from now on,* have laid down in us a new nature. — Indeed, we are beginning to realize as well that the last attempt at a great transformation of evaluations, and specifically with regard to things political — the "Great Revolution"[106] — was nothing *more* than a pathetic and bloody *quackery,* which understood how, through sudden crises, to supply a trusting Europe with the hope of a *sudden* recovery — and in so doing has rendered, right up to the present moment, all the politically sick impatient *and dangerous.*

535

Truth needs power. — In itself truth is no power whatsoever — no matter what the affected Enlightenment poseur was in the habit of saying to the contrary! Truth must, on the

contrary, pull power over to its side or else join sides with
power, otherwise it will be destroyed over and over! This has
by now been proven often enough and more than enough!

536[107]

The thumbscrew. — In the end it causes outrage to see over
and over again how cruelly every person reckons his few private
virtues against others who happen not to have them and how
he jabs and plagues others with them. And so let us also act
humanely with that "sense of honesty," even though we certainly possess in it a thumbscrew with which we could hurt,
down to their very core, all these grandiose narcissists who still,
even these days, want to impose their belief on the whole
world: we have tested the thumbscrew on ourselves!

537

Mastery. — Mastery has been attained at the point when, in
the performance, one neither errs *nor hesitates.*

538

The genius's moral madness. — Among a certain category of
great minds one can observe a painful, in part terrible spectacle:
their most fruitful moments, their flights upward to distant
heights, appear not to be in keeping with their constitution as
a whole and somehow to exceed their power, so that each time
a defect, and in the long run the *defectiveness in the machinery,*
is left behind, which in turn, however, in the case of such highly
intellectual natures as are here intended, manifests itself much
more regularly in all sorts of moral and mental symptoms
rather than in physical emergencies. Thus the incomprehensible
sense of fearfulness, vanity, spitefulness, enviousness, of being
constricted and constricting that suddenly leaps out from them,
that altogether all-too-personal quality and sense of unfree-
dom in natures like Rousseau's and Schopenhauer's, could
well be the consequence of periodic heart disorder: something
else, however, the consequence of nervous disorder and yet

another thing, in the end, the consequence of——. As long as genius dwells within us we are brave-hearted, indeed, insanely so, and pay no attention to life, health, and honor; we fly through the day freer than an eagle and are more sure in the dark than an owl. But then suddenly genius departs and just as suddenly a profound fearfulness overcomes us: we no longer understand ourselves, we suffer from everything we experience and from everything we do not experience; we are as if among bare rocks before a storm and at the same time like pathetic childish souls who fear a rustling and a shadow.—Three quarters of all the evil done in the world happens out of fearfulness: and this is above all a physiological phenomenon!—

539

Do you even know what you want?—Have you never been plagued by the fear that you might be completely unsuited for knowing what is true? The fear that your mind is too dull and even your subtlety of vision still much too crude? What if you noticed for once *what sort of* will was governing your vision? How yesterday, for example, you wanted to see *more* than the other, today want to see *differently* than the other, or how from the outset you long to find either agreement with or opposition to what others heretofore have imagined they found! Oh, the shameful craving! How often you are on the lookout for something that affects you strongly, then something calming— because you are at the moment tired! Always full of secret predeterminations as to *how* the truth would have to be constituted if you, precisely you, were able to accept it! Or are you of the opinion that today, because you are frozen and dry like a bright day in winter and have nothing pressing on your heart, you would have better eyes? Aren't warmth and enthusiasm required if a thing of thought is to receive *justice—and that is precisely what is called vision*! As if you *could* interact with things of thought altogether differently than with people! In this interaction too there is the same morality, the same sense of honor, the same ulterior motive, the same slackness,

the same fearfulness—your entire lovable and hateful ego!
Your physical lassitudes will imbue things with a listless hue,
your fever will turn them into monsters! Doesn't your morning shine differently on things than your evening? In the cavern of every type of knowledge, are you not afraid once more
of running into your own ghost, the ghost that is the cloak in
which truth has disguised itself from you? Is it not a ghastly
comedy in which you wish, so thoughtlessly, to play a role?[108]—

540

Learning.—Michelangelo saw in Raphael study, in himself
nature: there *learning,* here *talent.* However, this is pedantry,
with all reverence for the great pedant. What is talent other
than a name for an *older* piece of learning, experience, practice, appropriation, absorption, be it on the level of our fathers
or even earlier! And in turn: the person who learns *imparts
talent to himself*—only it is not so easy to *learn* and not merely
a matter of will; one must *be able* to learn. With an artist it is
often envy that blocks learning, or that pride that, upon sens-
ing something strange, immediately raises its hackles and involuntarily shifts to a defensive stance rather than into that of
the learner. Raphael, like Goethe, lacked this envy and pride,
and therefore they were both *great learners* and not just the
exploiters of those lodes of ore that had been separated out of
the deposits and the history of their ancestors. Raphael disappears as a learner before our very eyes in the midst of appropri-
ating what his great rival referred to as *his* "nature"; every day
he carried off a piece of it, this noblest of thieves; but before he
had transported the entire Michelangelo into himself he
died—and the last series of his works, as the *beginning* of a
new course of study, is less perfect and quintessentially good,
precisely because, in his most difficult curriculum, the great
learner was interrupted by death, and he took with him the
ultimate justifying goal for which he was on the lookout.

541

How one should turn to stone. — Slowly, slowly become hard like a precious stone—and finally lie there still and silent, to the joy of all eternity.

542[109]

The philosopher and old age. — It is not wise to let evening judge the day: for all too often weariness then becomes the judge of energy, success, and good will. And likewise great care ought to be exercised with regard to *old age* and its judgment of life, especially because old age, like the evening, loves to dress itself up in a new and charming morality and understands how, through sunset, twilight, peaceful or longing quietude, to shame the day. The piety that we show toward an old man, especially if he is an old thinker or sage, makes us blind to the *aging of his spirit*, and it is always necessary to draw out the *features* of such an aging and weariness from their hiding place, that is to say: to draw out the *physiological* phenomenon behind positive moral judgments and moral presumptions, so as not to become the fools of piety and the damagers of knowledge. For it occurs not infrequently that an old man enters into the illusion of undergoing a great moral regeneration and rebirth and from out of this feeling pronounces judgments on his work and the course of his life as if he had only now grown clairvoyant: and yet standing behind as the trumpeters of this feeling of well-being and these confident judgments is not wisdom, but *fatigue*. *Belief in one's own genius* may well be described as its most dangerous indication, which tends to overtake these great and semigreat men only on this life's borderline: belief in an exceptional position and exceptional rights. The thinker, stricken with such a belief, considers it permitted from now on *to make it easier on himself* and, as genius, to decree more than to prove: in all likelihood, however, the drive for *relief* that spiritual fatigue feels is the strongest source of that belief, no matter how different things might seem. Then:

in keeping with desire on the part of the weary and the old to enjoy, one wants at this time to *enjoy* the results of one's thought instead of testing them again and disseminating them, and, to this end, it is necessary to make them palatable and enjoyable and to get rid of their dryness, coldness, and lack of spice; and so it happens that the old thinker seems to elevate himself above his life's work; in truth, however, he ruins it by infusing it with rhapsodies, confections, spices, poetic fog, and mystic lights. In the end this is what happened to Plato, what happened in the end to that great, upright Frenchman, next to whom, as an embracer and tamer of the strict sciences, the Germans and English of this century can place no rival, Auguste Comte. A third feature of weariness: that ambition that took storm in the breast of the thinker when he was still young and in those days was satisfied with nothing, has now also grown old; he grasps, like one who has no time left to lose, after cruder and more ready-made means of satisfaction, that is to say, after those of active, dominating, powerful, conquering natures: from now on, he wants to found institutions that will bear his name and no longer edifices of thought; what does he care any more about the ethereal victories and honors in the domain of proofs and refutations! What does he care about being immortalized in books, about a trembling moment of elation in the reader's soul! The institution, on the other hand, is a temple — he knows this full well, and a temple of stone and duration keeps its god alive more surely than the sacrificial offerings of tender and rare souls. Perhaps at this time he also encounters for the first time that love intended more for a god than for a person, and, like a fruit in autumn, his whole being becomes milder and sweeter under the rays of such a sun. Indeed, he grows more divine and beautiful, the great old man — and nevertheless it is old age and fatigue that *allow* him to ripen in this way, to become still and to take repose in the resplendent idolatry of a woman. His earlier, defiant, self-surpassing desire for genuine pupils, namely for genuine continuers of his thought, that is to say, for genuine adversaries, is now completely a thing of the past: that desire came from undiminished power, from conscious pride in still being able at every moment to become one's own adversary and the archenemy of one's own teaching—now he wants confirmed party supporters, unproblematic and safe comrades, reserve units, heralds, a procession full of pomp and circumstance. Now he altogether cannot endure the terrible isolation in which every forward and forward-flying spirit lives; he surrounds himself from now on with objects of veneration, of communality, of touching emotion and love; at long last he too wants to have it as good as all the religious and to celebrate in the *community* what he values highly; indeed, he will invent a religion merely in order to have that community. Thus lives the wise old man and, in the process, slips imperceptibly into such wretched proximity to priestly and poetic excesses that one can hardly remember his wise and rigorous youth, his taut intellectual morality back then, his truly manly aversion to half-baked ideas and bouts of enthusiasm. Whenever he used to compare himself with other, older thinkers, he did so in order to measure in all seriousness his weakness against their strength and to grow colder and freer toward himself: now he does so only, by means of the comparison, to intoxicate himself with his own delusion. Formerly, he thought with assurance about thinkers to come, indeed, with ecstasy did he see himself eclipsed by their more intense light; now it tortures him not to be able to be the last; with the legacy he will bestow upon humanity, he reflects over ways to enjoin them to limit independent thinking; he fears and denigrates the pride and the thirst for freedom displayed by individual spirits—: after him, no one else ought to give their intellect totally free rein; he wants himself to remain standing forever as the sole bulwark against which the breakers of thought might break—those are his secret, perhaps not even always secret wishes! The hard fact behind such desires is, however, that he *has come to a halt* before his own teaching and has erected in it his boundary marker, his "To this point and no further."[110] By *canonizing* himself, he has also posted above him his own death certificate: from now on his spirit *may* not develop any further, its time is up, the clock hand falls.[111] When a great thinker wants to turn himself into a binding institution for the future of humankind, one may with certainty assume that he has gone beyond the peak of his power and is very tired, very near his sunset.

543[112]

Do not turn passion into an argument for truth!—Oh you good-natured and even noble enthusiasts, I know you! You want to have the last word with us, but also with yourself, above all with yourself! And an irritating and subtle evil conscience pricks and prods and incites you so often precisely *against* your very enthusiasm! How deft you then become in the duping and benumbing of this conscience! How you hate people who are honest, simple, pure, how you avoid[113] their innocent eyes! That *knowing better* whose representative *they* are and whose voice you hear in yourself only too plainly, how it casts doubts on your belief—how you seek to cast suspicion on it, as bad habits, as sickness of the times, as neglect and contagion of your own spiritual health. You push it all the way to the point of hating criticism, science, reason! You have to falsify history in order for it to bear witness on your behalf; you have to deny virtues in order not to overshadow your idols and ideals! Colored pictures where rational grounds are needed! Ardor and power of expression! Silvery mists! Ambrosial nights![114] You know how to illuminate and to darken, and to darken *with light*! And really, when your passion moves into a frenzy, there comes a moment when you say to yourself: Now I have *conquered and won* my gut conscience, now I am magnanimous, courageous, self-denying, magnificent, now I am honest! How you thirst for these moments where in your own mind your passion bestows upon you categorical right and as it were innocence, where in battle, intoxication, anger, hope you are beside yourselves and beyond all doubt, where you decree "anyone who is not beside himself as we are cannot possibly know what and where truth lies!" How you thirst to find people of your belief in this state—it is the state of *depravity of the intellect*— and to ignite your flames[115] at their fires! Oh your despicable martyrdom! Your despicable victory of the sanctified lie! Must you cause yourselves *so much* suffering? — Must you? —

544

How one pursues philosophy today. — I have taken careful note: our philosophizing youths, women, and artists of today are now demanding from philosophy just *the opposite* of what the Greeks derived from it! Anyone who doesn't hear that constant cry of joy running through every give and take of a Platonic dialogue, the cry of joy over a new discovery of *rational* thought, what does such a person understand about Plato, about ancient philosophy? In those days souls swelled with drunkenness when the rigorous and sober play of concepts,[116] of generalization, refutation, limitation was practiced— with that drunkenness with which perhaps the old great rigorous and sober contrapuntal composers[117] were familiar. In the Greece of those days there still clung to the palate the other older and previously omnipotent taste: and the new stood so magically in contrast to it that one sang and stammered, as if delirious in love, of dialectics, the "divine art." That other older taste amounted to thinking under the spell of convention, for which there existed nothing but preestablished judgments, preestablished causes,[118] and no reasons other than those of authority: so that thinking was a matter of *repeated speech* and all pleasure in speaking and in conversation had to reside in the *form*. (Anytime meaning is thought of as eternal and universally valid, there exists only one great magic, that of alternating form, which is to say, of fashion. In their poets as well, from the days of Homer on, and later in their sculptors, the Greeks took pleasure not in originality but in its opposite.) It was Socrates who discovered antithetical magic, that of cause and effect, ground and consequence: and we moderns are so accustomed to and brought up on the necessity of logic that it lies on our palate like the normal taste and, as such, must be repellent to the lascivious and conceited. The latter delight in anything that stands in contrast to the normal taste: their subtler ambition would like all too happily to convince itself that their souls are exceptions, not dialectical and reasonable beings, but instead—well, for example, "intuitive beings," gifted with "inner sense" or "intellectual intuition." Above all, however, they want to be "artistic natures" with a genius in their head and a demon in their body, and consequently also with special rights and privileges for both worlds, especially with the privilege of the gods to be incomprehensible. — *That* is what's driving philosophy today too![119] I'm afraid they'll notice one day that they have made a mistake—what they wanted was religion!

545

But we don't believe you!—You might well like to pass yourself off as someone with a savvy understanding of people, but we're not going to let you slip by with it! Are we not supposed to notice that you represent yourselves as more experienced, profound, involved, complete than you are? Just as we feel with a certain painter that there is presumptuousness merely in his wielding a brush. Just as with a certain composer we hear in the way he introduces his theme that he wants it to appear more elevated than it is. Do you have within yourselves a *history* that you have experienced, upheavals, earthquakes, long deep depressions, lightning-like delights? Have you been foolish along with great and little fools? Have you really borne the delusion and suffering of those who are good?[120] And on top of it the suffering and the kind of happiness of those who are worst? If so, you can talk to me about morality; otherwise don't!

546[121]

Slave and idealist. — The Epictetean person would truly not be to the taste of those who are now striving for the ideal. The constant tautness of his being, the tireless, inwardly turned gaze, the reserve, circumspection, incommunicativeness of his eye should he for a change turn to the outside world; not to mention his silence or taciturnity: all signs of the most rigorous valor—what use would that be to our idealists, who above all are greedy for *expansion*! On top of everything else, he is not fanatical, he hates the showcasing and vainglory of our idealists: his pride, great as it is, does not wish, however, to trouble others, he admits a certain mild rapprochement and does not wish to spoil anyone's good mood—Yes, he can smile! There is a great deal of ancient humanity in this ideal! The most beautiful thing, however, is that a fear of God is totally alien to him, that he believes rigorously in reason, that he is not a preacher of penitence. Epictetus was a slave: his ideal person is classless and possible in all classes, above all, however, he is to be sought in the lower depths of the masses, as the quiet, self-sufficient one among a general enslavement, one who defends himself against the outside world and constantly lives in a state of highest valor. He differs from the *Christian* above all in that the Christian lives in hope, in the consolation of "unspeakable glories"[122] to come, in that he allows himself to be given gifts and expects and accepts the best of life to come from divine love and grace and not from himself: whereas Epictetus does not hope and does allow his best to be given him—he possesses it, he holds it valiantly in his hand, and he would take on the whole world if it tries to rob him of it. Christianity was invented for another type of ancient slave, for those weak of will and mind, thus for the great mass of slaves.

547[123]

Tyrants of the spirit.—Now the course of science is no longer being crossed, as was the case for all too long, by the accidental fact that people live to be approximately seventy years old. Formerly one wanted during this time period to arrive at the end of knowledge, and one evaluated the methods of knowing according to this widespread craving. The small individual questions and experiments were regarded with contempt; one wanted the shortest way, one believed, because everything in the world seemed to be arranged *to accommodate human beings*, that the knowableness of things was also arranged to suit a human time span. To solve everything at one fell swoop, with one single word—that was the secret wish: this was the task one imagined in the image of the Gordian knot[124] or of Columbus's egg;[125] one did not doubt that in the realm of knowledge as well it was possible to reach one's goal after the manner of an Alexander or a Columbus and to solve all questions with *one* answer. "There is a *riddle* to solve"; this is how life's goal appeared before the philosopher's eye. First one had to find the riddle and compress the problem of the world into the simplest riddle-form. The boundless ambition and jubilation of being the "unriddler of the world" were the stuff of the thinker's dreams. Nothing seemed worth troubling about if it was not the means of bringing everything to a conclusion *for him*! Philosophy was thus a sort of supreme struggle for the tyrannical rulership of the spirit—that such a rule was intended and reserved for some such very fortunate, subtle, ingenious, bold powerful person—a single individual!—this no one doubted, and several, most recently Schopenhauer, have fancied themselves this very individual.—From which it follows that the quest for knowledge, by and large, has been held back by the *moral narrow-mindedness* of its disciples and that in the future it must be pursued with a higher and *more magnanimous* basic feeling. "What do I matter!" stands over the door of the future thinker.

548

Victory over energy. — If one considers everything that has heretofore been honored as "suprahuman mind," as "genius," one comes to the sad conclusion that, on the whole, humanity's intellectuality must truly have been something most abject and impoverished: so little mind has heretofore been necessary in order to feel oneself considerably superior to it! Ah, the cheap fame of the "genius"! How quickly his throne is erected, his worship turned into a ritual! We still remain down on our knees before *energy*—in keeping with the age-old slave habit—and yet if we wish to determine the degree to which something is *worthy of being honored*, only *the degree of reason in the energy* is decisive: we have to measure to what extent precisely this energy has been overcome by something higher and is at its service as tool and means! But for such a measuring there are far too few eyes, indeed measuring a genius at all is still usually considered a sacrilege. And so perhaps what is most beautiful walks along in darkness and sinks, barely born, into eternal night—namely the spectacle of that energy that[126] a genius expends *not on works*, but *on himself as a work*, that is, on his own mastery, on the purification of his fantasy, on the ordering and selection of the onrushing stream of tasks and sudden insights. Even[127] now a great person is still, precisely in the greatest thing that commands honor, invisible like a too distant star: his *victory over energy* remains without eyes to see it and consequently without song and singers. Even now the ranking of greatness for all past humanity has not yet been determined.

549[128]

"Flight from oneself."—Those people who are intellectually convulsive, who are impatient with themselves and gloomy, like Byron or Alfred de Musset, and in everything they do resemble stampeding horses, who glean from their own creative work only a short-lived joy and ardor that virtually explodes their veins before falling into so wintery a desolation and woebegoneness,[129] how are they supposed to endure *within themselves*! They thirst to dissolve in a *"beside themselves"*; if, with such a thirst,[130] one is a Christian, one aims at dissolving into God, at "becoming completely one with him"; if one is Shakespeare, one is only satisfied with dissolving into images of the most passionate life; if one is Byron,[131] one thirsts for *deeds*, because these divert us from ourselves even more than

thoughts, feelings, and works. And thus the entire drive toward deeds and action is perhaps after all, at bottom, flight from oneself? — Pascal would ask us.[132] And indeed! In the most extreme examples of the drive for action the proposition would seem to hold: we should, as is appropriate, ponder the knowledge and experience of the psychiatrist — that four of the most deed-thirsty men of all time were epileptics (namely, Alexander, Caesar, Mohammed, and Napoleon): just as Byron was also subject to this malady.

<h2 style="text-align:center">550[133]</h2>

Knowledge and beauty. — If, as they still are wont to do, people as it were save up their veneration and their feeling of happiness for works of imagination and dissemblance, then it should come as no surprise if the opposite of imagination and dissemblance leaves them cold and listless. The delight sparked by even the tiniest certain, conclusive step, step forward in insight, which today's brand of science is pouring forth so abundantly and already to so many people — this delight, in the meantime, is not *credited* by all those who are used to always being delighted only by taking leave of reality, by plunging into the depths of appearance.[134] These people are of the opinion that reality is ugly: but it does not occur to them that knowledge even of the ugliest reality is itself beautiful, nor as well that whoever spends a lot of time inquiring into knowledge ends up being far-removed from finding the great whole of reality, the discovery of which has always given him so much pleasure, ugly. Is there after all anything "beautiful in itself"? The happiness of those who seek knowledge increases the amount of beauty in the world and makes everything that is here sunnier; knowledge places its beauty not merely around things but, in the long run, into things — may future humanity bear witness to this proposition! In the interim let us remember an old experience: two such fundamentally different people as Plato and Aristotle were in agreement as to what constitutes the *highest happiness*, not only for them personally or for humans, but in itself, even for the most blissful of gods: they found it *in knowledge*, in the activity of a well-trained, inquisitive, and inventive *understanding* (*not* somehow in "intuition," as do German theologians and semitheologians, *not* in vision, as do the mystics, and likewise *not* in productivity, as do all practical people). Descartes and Spinoza came to a similar judgment: how they all must have *enjoyed* knowledge! What a danger for their honesty of becoming, through this enjoyment, a panegyrist of things! —

551

Of future virtues. — How does it happen that the more comprehensible the world has become the more solemnity of all kinds has decreased? Is it that fear was so much a fundamental element of that reverence[135] that overcame us in the face of everything unknown and mysterious and that taught us to sink down before the incomprehensible and plead for mercy? And hasn't the world, now that we have grown less fearful, lost for us some of its appeal? And hasn't along with our fearfulness some of our own dignity and solemnity, *our own fearsomeness*, grown slighter? Perhaps we view ourselves and the world more slightly because we started thinking more courageously about it and ourselves? Perhaps there will be a future in which this courage of thought has swelled so large that, as the absolute height of arrogance, it feels itself to be *above* people and things — in which the wise person, as the most courageous of persons, views himself and existence as the farthest beneath him? — This species of courage, which is not far from being an excessive magnanimity,[136] has been heretofore *lacking* in humanity. — Oh, if only the poets longed to become what they once were supposed to have been: — *seers*, who recounted to us something of the *possible*! Now that reality and the past are, and must be, taken more and more out of their hands — for the age of harmless counterfeiting is at an end! If only they wanted to let us experience in advance something of the *future virtues*! Or of virtues that will never exist on

earth, although they could exist somewhere in the world—
of purple-glowing galaxies and whole Milky Ways of the beautiful! Where are you, you astronomers of the ideal?

552

Ideal selfishness.—Is there a more consecrated condition
than that of pregnancy? To do everything one does in the unspoken belief that it must be for the good of the one who is
coming to be in us! This has to *enhance* its mysterious value
upon which we think with delight! One thus avoids a great
deal without having to force oneself too hard. One thus sup-
presses a violent word, one offers a conciliatory hand: the child
must emerge from the mildest and best of conditions. We
shudder at the thought of our sharpness and abruptness: what
if it poured a drop of calamity into our dearest unknown's cup
of life! Everything is veiled, full of presentiment, one has no
idea how it will go, one waits it out and seeks to be *ready*. In
which time there reigns in us a pure and purifying feeling of
profound irresponsibility, rather like a spectator has before the
closed curtain—*it* is growing, *it* is coming to the light of day:
we have in our hands nothing to determine, either its value or
its hour. We are thrown back solely on that mediate influence
of protecting. "It is something greater than we are that is
growing here" is our innermost hope: we are preparing everything for it so that it will come into the world thriving: not
only everything beneficial but also the affections and laurel
wreaths of our soul.—One ought to live *in this state of consecration*! One can live in it! And if what is expected is a thought,
a deed—toward all that we bring forth we have essentially no
other relationship than that of pregnancy and ought to let
blow in the wind all presumptuous talk of "willing" and "creating"! This is the proper *ideal selfishness*: always to care for the
soul, to guard over it and keep it in repose, so that our fructi-
fication *comes to a beautiful conclusion*! Thus, in this mediate
way, we care for and guard over the *benefit of all*; and the
mood in which we live, this proud and tempered mood, is a

balsam that extends far and wide around us even onto restless souls. — But the pregnant are *strange*! Let us therefore be strange as well and not be annoyed with others if they need to be so! And even if this turns out to be bad and dangerous, let us not, in our reverence for what is coming to be, lag behind worldly[137] justice,[138] which allows neither judge nor executioner to lay a hand on one who is pregnant!

553[139]

Via detours. — Where is this whole philosophy headed with all its detours? Does it do more than translate, as it were, into reason a constant concentrated drive, a drive for mild sunshine, clearer and fresher air, southerly vegetation, sea air, quick repasts of meat, eggs, and fruit, hot water to drink, daylong silent wanderings, little speaking, infrequent and careful reading, solitary living, pure, simple, and almost soldierly habits,[140] in short for everything that tastes best to me and me alone, to me and me alone is the most beneficial? A philosophy that at bottom is the instinct for a personal diet? An instinct that is searching for my own air, my own heights, my own weather, my own type of health, through the detour of my head? There are many other and certainly many loftier sublimities of philosophy and not just those that are more gloomy and more ambitious than mine — perhaps they too are, each and every one, nothing other than intellectual detours for these kinds of personal drives? — In the meantime I observe with a new eye the secret and solitary swarming of a butterfly high on the rocky seashore where many good plants are growing; it flies about, untroubled that it only has one day yet to live and that the night will be too cold for its winged fragility. One could certainly come up with a philosophy for it as well: although it is not likely to be mine.[141] —

554

Stepping on ahead. — When one praises *progress*,[142] one is praising only the movement and those who do not allow us to

stay in the same place—and certainly under some circumstances this accomplishes a great deal, especially if one lives
among Egyptians. In movable Europe, however, where movement, as they say, "goes without saying"—ah, if only *we* knew
what to say about it!—I, for my part, praise *stepping on ahead*
and those who do so, that is to say those who time and time
again leave themselves behind and who do not think for a moment whether or not someone else is following them. "Wherever I come to a stop, I find myself alone: why should I come
to a stop! The desert is still vast!"—this is how such a person
feels who steps on ahead this way.

555[143]

The most trifling are already enough.—We should avoid
events if we know that the most trifling of them already leave
a strong enough mark on us—and we certainly cannot escape these latter ones.—The thinker must have within himself a rough canon of all the things in general he still *wants to
experience.*

556

The good four.—*Honest* toward ourselves and whatever *else*
is our friend; *courageous* toward the enemy; *magnanimous* toward the defeated; *polite*—always: this is how the four cardinal virtues want us to be.

557

Off after an enemy.—How good bad music and bad reasons
sound when one marches off after an enemy.

558

But don't conceal your virtues too!—I love those people who
are transparent water and who also, to speak with Pope, "do
not hide from view the turbid bottom of their stream." Even
for them, however, there remains one vanity—to be sure, of a
rare and sublimated ilk: some of them want us to see only just

the turbidity and ignore the water's transparency, which makes seeing the former possible. No less a person than Gautama Buddha came up with this vanity of the few in the formula: "let your sins be seen before people and hide your virtues!"[144] But this amounts to presenting to the world a lousy spectacle—it is a sin against good taste.

559

"Not too much!"—How often is the individual advised to set for himself a goal that he cannot attain and that exceeds his powers, in order at least to obtain whatever he can accomplish through *utmost exertion*! But is this really so desirable? Don't the best people who live according to this doctrine, along with their best actions, acquire necessarily something exaggerated and contorted, precisely because there is too much tension in them? And doesn't a gray veil of *failure* spread over the world when one sees nothing but struggling athletes, terrible gestures, and nowhere a laurel-crowned and triumphant victor?[145]

560

What we are free to do.—One can handle one's drives like a gardener and, though few know it, cultivate the shoots of one's anger, pity, musing, vanity as fruitfully and advantageously as beautiful fruit on espaliers; one can do so with a gardener's good or bad taste and, as it were, in the French or English or Dutch or Chinese style; one can also let nature have her sway and only tend to a little decoration and cleaning up here and there; finally, one can, without giving them any thought whatsoever, let the plants, in keeping with the natural advantages and disadvantages of their habitat, grow up and fight it out among themselves—indeed, one can take pleasure in such wildness and want to enjoy just this pleasure, even if one has one's difficulties with it. We are free to do all this: but how many actually know that they are free to do this? Don't most people *believe* in *themselves* as completed, *fully grown facts*? Haven't great philosophers, with their doctrine of the immutability of character, pressed their seal of approval on this presumption?[146,147]

561

Let your happiness also radiate. — Just as painters who in no way can attain the deep, radiant hue of the real sky find it necessary to modulate down all the colors that they use in a landscape by a few hues deeper than they appear in nature; just as through this artifice they attain once again a similarity in luster and a harmony of hues that corresponds to that of nature: so must the poet and philosopher for whom the radiant luster of happiness is unattainable know how to assist themselves as well; in that they color all things a few degrees darker than they are, their use of light, in which they are well versed, makes that light appear almost sunny and similar to the light of complete happiness. — The pessimist, who gives all things the blackest and gloomiest colors, makes use of only flames and bolts of lightning, celestial effulgence, and everything that has glaring brilliance and confuses the eye; brightness is only there for him to increase the horror and to make us sense that things are more terrifying than they really are.

562

The settled and the free. — Only in the underworld are we shown something of that gloomy backdrop to all those adventurer's joys that engulfed Odysseus and his kind like an eternal marine phosphorescence — that gloomy background that one then never again forgets: Odysseus's mother died of grief and longing for her child! One is driven from place to place and the other, the *settled* and tender one receives a broken heart as a result: it is always so! Sorrow breaks the heart of those who live to see the very person they love most turn their back on their opinion, their faith — this belongs to the tragedy that free spirits *create* — of which they sometimes are also *aware*! Then, like Odysseus, they too at some point have to descend to the dead to alleviate their grief and soothe their tenderness.

563

The delusion of a moral world order. — There is no eternal *necessity whatsoever* that demands that every guilt be atoned and paid for — that such a thing exists was a dreadful delusion, useful only to the tiniest extent —: just as it is also a delusion that everything is guilt that is felt as such. Not *things*, but opinions *about things that do not even exist* have confused and upset people so.

564[148]

Just to the other side of experience! — Even great spirits have only their five-finger breadth of *experience* — just to the other side of it their contemplation ceases: and there begins their infinite empty space and their stupidity.

565

Dignity and ignorance in league. — When we understand, we become courteous, happy, inventive, and whenever we have learned enough and have *made* eyes and ears for ourselves, our soul displays more suppleness and grace. But we understand so little and are poorly instructed, and so it is rare that we fully embrace a thing and thereby make ourselves lovable: on the contrary, we tend to walk stiffly and insensitively through city, nature, and history, and we come rather to fancy this posture and this coldness, as if they were the effect of superiority. Indeed, our ignorance and our minimal thirst for knowledge are most adroit at strutting about as dignity and as character.

566[149]

Living cheaply. — The cheapest and most harmless way to live is that of the thinker: for, in order to say the most important thing right away, he is most in need of just those things others think little of and pass over —. And moreover: he is easily pleased and is unfamiliar with expensive pleasures; his work is not hard, but, as it were, Mediterranean; his day and his night are not ruined by pangs of conscience; he moves about, eats, drinks, and sleeps to the degree that his spirit grows ever calmer, stronger and brighter; he takes pleasure in his body and has no reason to fear it; he has no need of society, unless from time to time to embrace all the more tenderly afterward his solitude; the dead are his substitute for the living and even for friends: these dead being the best who ever lived. — Consider whether it is not the opposite cravings and habits that make people's lives costly, and consequently laborious, and often unendurable. In a different sense, to be sure, the thinker's life is the most costly — nothing is too good for him; and to be deprived of precisely the *best* would be here an *unbearable* deprivation.

567

In the field. — "We must take things more joyfully than they deserve; especially because for a long time we have taken them more seriously than they deserve." — So speak good soldiers of knowledge.

568

Poet and bird. — The bird Phoenix showed the poet a flaming scroll turning to ashes. "Do not be terrified!" it said, "it is your work! It does not possess the spirit of the times and still less the spirit of those who are against the times: consequently, it has to be burned. But this is a good sign. There are many types of dawn."

569

To the solitary. — If in our private conversations with ourselves we do not treat the honor of others with the same consideration as we do in public, then we are indecent people.

570

Losses. — There are losses that impart a grandeur to the soul under whose influence it refrains from lamentation and seems to walk about in silence among tall black cypresses.

571[150]

Field-dispensary of the soul. — What is the strongest medicine for a cure? — Victory.

572

Life should calm us. — If, like the thinker, one usually lives in the great stream of thought and feeling and even our dreams at night follow this stream:[151] then one desires from *life* calm and quietude — whereas others, when they give themselves over to meditation, positively want to take a rest from life.

573

Shedding one's skin. — The snake that does not shed its skin perishes. So too with spirits who are prevented from changing their opinions; they cease to be spirit.

574

Don't forget! — The higher we soar, the smaller we appear to those who cannot fly.

575

We aeronauts of the spirit! — All these bold birds who fly out into the wide, wide, widest open — it is true! At some point they will not be able to fly any farther and will squat down on some pylon or sparse crag — and very grateful for this miserable accommodation to boot! But who would want to conclude from this that there was *no longer* a vast and prodigious trajectory ahead of them, that they had flown as far and wide as one *could* fly! All our great mentors and precursors have finally come to a stop, and it is hardly the noblest and most graceful of gestures with which fatigue comes to a stop: it will also happen to you and me! Of what concern, however, is that to you and me! *Other birds will fly farther!* This our insight and assurance vies with them in flying up and away; it rises straightaway above our head and beyond its own inadequacy into the heights and looks out from there into the distance, sees the flocks of birds much more powerful than we are, who are striving to get to where we were striving toward and where everything is still sea, sea, sea! — And where, then, do we want to go? Do we want to go *across* the sea? Where is it tearing us toward, this powerful craving that means more to us than any other pleasure? Why precisely in this direction, toward precisely where heretofore all of humanity's suns have *set*? Will it perhaps be said of us one day that we too, *steering toward the west, hoped to reach an India* — that it was, however, our lot to shipwreck upon infinity?[152] Or else, my brothers? Or else? —

Notes

Dawn: Thoughts on the Presumptions of Morality appears from Ernst Schmeitzner in Chemnitz at the end of June 1881, eighteen months after *The Wanderer and His Shadow*. It is the result of N's meditations at the various locations of his travels in the year 1880: Venice, Marienbad, Naumberg, Stresa, Genoa. In Venice (spring 1880), N dictated to his "disciple" Peter Gast a collection of 262 aphorisms under the title *L'Ombra di Venezia* {"The Shadow of Venice"}, the result of notes that he had written in two small volumes {*Hefte*} from the beginning of the year. In summer and autumn 1880 as in winter 1880/81, N used five further notebooks, from which both an extensive posthumous material (*CW* 13, 4[1]–8[120]) and the second draft to *Dawn* have been created. On 25 January 1881, he sent this second draft from Genoa to Peter Gast for transcription; the title of the new book on the first page of the second draft was "The Plowshare: Thoughts on the Presumptions of Morality." On the first page of his copy Peter Gast placed the words: "There are so many dawns that have not yet broken. Rig Veda." Nietzsche liked this quote so much that he changed the title of his book to "A Dawn: Thoughts on the Presumptions of Morality" (see N's letter to Gast 9 February 1881 {*KGB* III:1, 61}). The article ("A") then was dropped. Immediately after, N sent another addendum to the transcription to Peter Gast, in which he had recorded about 90 aphorisms from *L'Ombra di Venezia* (with more or less significant changes). These were cut into strips and with N's aphorism numbers ordered, copy was then pasted by Peter Gast for the creation of a printer's manuscript {clean final copy of handwritten manuscript} and sent in mid-March to Schmeitzner in Chemnitz. From mid-April to mid-June, N and Peter Gast read the corrections. These as well as the printer's manuscript have not survived. In 1887 stocks of *Dawn* appeared from E. W. Fritzsch in Leipzig, provided with a preface, as *Dawn: Thoughts on the Presumptions of Morality. New Edition with an Introductory Preface.*

Unless otherwise indicated, all fragment numbers refer to *Nachlass* fragments that appear in *CW* 13.

The following symbols are used throughout the text and notes:

[ ]	Deletion by Nietzsche
| |	Addition by Nietzsche
[?]	Uncertain reading
⟨ ⟩	Addition by the editors (Colli and Montinari)
{ }	Addition or annotation by the translator
— — —	Unfinished or incomplete sentence or thought
Italics	Underlined once by Nietzsche
Bold	Underlined twice or more by Nietzsche
NL	Books in Nietzsche's personal library
P	Preface

Variants and editions of Nietzsche's works are referred to by the following abbreviations:

CW	*The Complete Works of Friedrich Nietzsche*
KGB	*Briefwechsel: Kritische Gesamtausgabe*
KGW	*Kritische Gesamtausgabe*
KSA	*Kritische Studienausgabe*
Fe	First edition
Le	Twenty-volume 1894 Leipzig edition of Nietzsche's works (*Großoktav-Ausgabe*)

Pd	Preliminary draft
Sd	Second draft
Se	Subsequent emendations

Titles of Nietzsche's works are referred to by the following abbreviations:

AC	*The Anti-Christian*
BGE	*Beyond Good and Evil*
BT	*The Birth of Tragedy*
D	*Dawn*
DD	*Dionysus Dithyrambs*
DS	*David Strauss the Confessor and the Writer*
EH	*Ecce Homo*
GM	*On the Genealogy of Morality*
HAH	*Human, All Too Human*
HL	*On the Utility and Liability of History for Life*
JS	*The Joyful Science*
MM	*Mixed Opinions and Maxims*
NCW	*Nietzsche Contra Wagner*
SE	*Schopenhauer as Educator*
TI	*Twilight of the Idols*
UO	*Unfashionable Observations*
WA	*The Case of Wagner*
WB	*Richard Wagner in Bayreuth*
WP	*The Will to Power*
WS	*The Wanderer and His Shadow*
Z	*Thus Spoke Zarathustra*

A Note on the Subtitle

Presumptions] Vorurtheile. *Vor*= "before" or "pre." *Urtheile*= "judgments." *Vorurtheile*, literally "prejudgments," is often rendered as "prejudices" and also means "presuppositions." All these variants are implied in the subtitle. When the singular or plural of *Vorurtheile* is translated other than as "presumption(s)," it will be noted.

Preface

1. *faith]* *Glaube*. German uses the word *Glaube* to denote what is meant in English by both "faith" and "belief." As with its English counterparts, *Glaube* can mean either faith (or belief) in something specific or religious faith (or belief).

2. *Trophonius]* {Son of King Erginus, who, with his brother Agamedes, built the temple of Apollo at Delphi. According to one legend, he and his brother built a treasure chamber for King Hyprieus of Boeotia, and using a secret entrance, they stole the king's fortune. Following the discovery of the crime, Trophonius fled into the cavern at Lebadaea and disappeared forever. In later times, Trophonius's cave itself became a popular oracular site.}

3. *belated Preface]* {N wrote the Preface to *Dawn* in the autumn of 1886. It was added to the unsold inventory of the first edition of 1881, which was then published as a "New Edition with an Introductory Preface" in 1887 by E. W. Fritzsch. On "belated," cf. note 1 to Aphorism 1 in Book One.}

4. *tunneled . . . foundation;]* N utilizes the many connotations of the German word *Grund*, translated here as "foundation." Additionally, *Grund* denotes ground both in the material sense (earth, soil) and in the abstract sense (basis, first principles). Furthermore, *Grund* is the common German word for "reason" in the instrumental meaning of "motive" (as in the phrase "The reason I'm calling . . .").

5. *dig away]* *angraben*. A Nietzschean coinage that allows him to play with the same root as in the key word for "undermine" (*untergraben*): *Grab* = "grave"; *begraben* = "to bury."

6. *trust]* *Vertrauen*. Also implies in this context confidence, faith, reliance.

7. *good and evil:]* {N began work on this Preface to the second edition of *Dawn* in October 1886; *BGE* was published in August of the same year.}

8. *"inspire."]* *begeistern*, "to inspire," "to enthuse," "to breathe spirit (*Geist*) into."

9. *evince . . . convince!]* Pun on the customary German words for "to speak" (*reden*) and "to convince" (*überreden*), literally "to speak over."

10. *Circe]* {Daughter of Helios, the sun god, and a very powerful sorceress, Circe is famous for enticing passersby to her island of Aeaea, where she transforms men into beasts. Circe is also a "subterranean," as she shows Odysseus the pathway into Hades. Cf. Homer's *Odyssey*, bk. 10, Ovid's *Metamorphoses*, bk. 14, Virgil's *Aeneid*, bk. 7.}

11. *aere perennius]* "more lasting than bronze."

12. *entirety"]* {Apparently quoting from memory, N summarizes a point that Kant makes in several places throughout the beginning of *The Critique of Pure Reason*. In keeping with the standard page numbering of the second edition (1787), cf. A xi (footnote) and B xxxv.}

13. *ground!] Boden* = "soil," "ground," "floor," "base," "basis." Similar to *Grund*, translated as "foundation" (cf. note 4 above), *Boden* has connotations both material (soil, ground, floor) and abstract (basis, first principles).

14. *Critique . . . 257]* N cites from Rosenkranz's 1883 edition of *The Critique of Pure Reason*. Cf. B 375–76.

15. *rapturous enthusiasm;] Schwärmerei*

16. *sensualism]* {Aligned with empiricism, sensualism is the doctrine that all our knowledge derives from sense perceptions.}

17. *1794)]* "to found on earth the empire of wisdom, justice, and virtue." N quotes from Edmond Scherer, *Études sur la littérature contemporaine* (*Studies on contemporary literature*) (Paris{: Calmann Lévy,} 1885), 8:79. *NL*.

18. *"moral realm,"] "moralisches Reich."* Kant's term is usually translated as "moral realm," but *Reich* also means "empire."

19. *Critique . . . Reason!]* {N has in mind the famous passage from the preface to the second edition of Kant's *Critique of Pure Reason*: "I therefore had to abolish *knowledge* in order to make room for *faith*." B xxx. All quotations from the *Critique of Pure Reason* are from the translation by Norman Kemp Smith (New York: St. Martin's Press, 1929).}

20. *credo* quia *absurdum est]* "I believe *because* it is absurd."

21. *themselves"]* {Only the second clause, "all things contradict themselves," is a direct quote from the German philosopher G.F.W. Hegel. See the *Wissenschaft der Logik II* (*Science of Logic*

II) in Hegel, *Werke in zwanzig Bänden* (Frankfurt: Suhrkamp, 1969), 6:74. With the first clause, "Contradiction moves the world," N paraphrases the conclusion to the next paragraph of the *Science of Logic*: "only insofar as something has a contradiction within itself does it move, does it have force and activity" (ibid., 75).}

22. *upward"*] {Allusion to the last lines of *Faust,* pt. II, by Germany's most celebrated writer, Johann Wolfgang von Goethe: "The Eternal-Feminine / Draws us upward." Lines 12110–11.}

23. *the self-sublation of morality.]* die Selbstaufhebung der Moral.

24. *lento.]* "slowly."

25. *Ruta near Genoa]* {A coastal town southeast of Genoa where, coincidentally, N had spent the winter months of 1880 and 1881 while working on *Dawn*.}

Book One

1. *Retroactive]* Nachträgliche, which also could be translated by "belated" or "deferred," is related to the word for "supplement," "addendum," and "postscript."

2. *lineage]* Abkunft = also "descent from," "origin in," "blood lineage." *Ab* = "down from"; *Kunft* = Old and Middle High German derivation from *kommen* = "to come" and signals "arrival." First usage in *D* of N's language of genealogy, which he will deploy throughout the work. Cf. *Herkunft* (*Her* = "motion toward the present"); *Ursprung* ("origin" or "source"), which is related to *entspringen* = "to arise" and "to originate"; and *Entstehung* (in this instance, the prefix *ent-* = "the beginning of action or activity"; *stehung* = the noun form of the verb *stehen* = "to stand," "to be upright," "to rise," "to become"). Unless otherwise indicated, the following translations will be used: *Abkunft* = "lineage"; *Entstehung* = "emergence"; *Herkunft* = "descent"; *Ursprung* = "origin."

3. *emergence]* Entstehung. Cf. note 2 above.

4. *judgment]* The parallelism between judgment (*Urtheil*) and presumption or prejudice (*Vorurtheil*) is even more exact in German than in English.

5. *gender]* German attributes a gender (masculine, feminine, neuter) to all nouns.

6. *sun]* The word for "sun" is feminine in German; neuter in Russian; and masculine in Greek, Latin, and the Romance languages.

7. Cf. 3[80].

8. *conjurer . . . contrary.]* Pun on the German words *Taschenspieler* (literally, "one who plays from out of the pockets") and *Widerspiel* (literally, "counterplay").

9. *Transfiguration.]* {At the time of his death in 1520, the Italian Renaissance painter Raphael was working on a painting of the transfiguration in which, according to tradition, Jesus, accompanied by Moses and Elias, appears opposite the disciples Peter, James, and John, who are overwhelmed by the light from Christ's transfiguration. N mentions this painting in *BT* 4.}

10. Cf. 3[93], 4[13].

11. *mores.]* plural of *mos* = "custom."

12. *morality of mores.]* *Sittlichkeit der Sitte.* Highly polyvalent, *Sitte* can mean "custom," "habit," "practice," "etiquette," "propriety." This translation almost always renders *Sitte* as "custom" (rarely, as in the title to this aphorism, as "mores" or, very rarely, as "propriety"). N's use of *Sitte* consistently puts the nuances listed above into play, and the reader should keep them in mind upon encountering the word *custom*. The plural, *Sitten*, is usually rendered as "mores," occasionally as "customs" when N emphasizes the relationship between the singular *Sitte* (custom) and the plural *Sitten*. *Sittlichkeit* is consistently translated as "morality."

13. *unaccustomed, immoral]* *unsittlich.* Cf. the previous note.

14. *fundamental insights]* *Grundeinsichten.* Throughout *D* N employs the same foundational metaphors (oriented around the root *Grund*) as in the Preface. Cf. P2, note 4. Future instances will not be noted, but such renderings as "basic(ally)," "thorough(ly)," "at bottom," and "fundamental(ly)" are almost always related to *Grund*.

15. *traditional]* *herkömmlich*, literally "coming hither." The noun *Herkommen* (used in the next sentence and throughout the aphorism) means "origin," "extraction," "descent," as well as "tra-

dition," "custom." It is in the same genealogical linguistic field as *Herkunft*. Cf. note 2 to Aphorism 1.

16. *Brahman,]* From Sanskrit: "having to do with prayer." A member of the highest Hindu caste, traditionally assigned to the priesthood.

17. *evil conscience;]* *böses Gewissen*, as distinct from "bad conscience" (*schlechtes Gewissen*), which N employs later in *D* and which is a central concept in *GM*. *Böses Gewissen* is rendered throughout as "evil conscience."

18. *(post hoc),]* "after this," "afterward."

19. *subject to control.]* Crossed out at the conclusion to the *Sd*: We are living in a period of morality in which exists not the slightest physical effect that could prove a moral precept: and morality has taken refuge in the "Ideal."

20. Cf. 3[71].

21. *outcome . . . consequence.]* N puns in order to insist forcefully that the outcome (*Erfolg*) of an action is a consequence (*Folge*) of the action itself and not a divine supplement to the action.

22. *Reeducation . . . Race.]* {Allusion to the short but highly influential deist tract *The Education of the Human Race* (1777/1780) by the German dramatist, critic, and theologian G. E. Lessing (1729–81). Lessing draws an analogy between the history of religion and the education or development of the human race, which, as it becomes more mature, learns to perceive, in the truths of revealed religion, an indication of the necessity of a religion based on reason. In the purportedly imminent age of completion, humanity will act virtuously for virtue's sake, regardless of any fear of punishment or desire for reward. Cf. esp. sec. 85.}

23. *venerated]* *Sd*: baroque.

24. *grain of salt,]* {The connection between genius and salt may be of biblical origin (cf. Mark 9:50 and Colossians 4:6), or N may be drawing on the connection in Italian culture between intelligence and salt. The Tuscan *avere sale per la zucca*, which means "to have salt in the head," is frequently said of a person of wit and keen intelligence.}

25. *madness herb]* *Wahnwurz*, a Nietzschean neologism. *Wurz* is the Old German word for "spice" or "medicinal herb"; *Wahn* means "delusion" or "madness."

26. *madness,"]* Cf. Plato's *Phaedrus* 244a{: "that would be right if it were an invariable truth that madness is an evil, but in reality, the greatest blessings come by way of madness, indeed of madness that is heaven-sent." *The Collected Dialogues*, ed. Edith Hamilton and Huntington Cairns (Princeton: Princeton University Press, 1961), 491. All translations from Plato's works are from this edition.}

27. *the . . . through madness.]* Cf. Plato's *Ion* 533d–534e{, where Socrates attributes poetry to madness and divine possession}.

28. *Solon . . . Salamis.)]* Cf. Plutarch, *Solon* 8. {Solon was instrumental in urging the Athenians (ca. 600 BCE) to renewed battle against Megara, a city-state on the isthmus of Corinth, for possession of Salamis, an island in the Saronic Gulf off the southwest coast of Attica.}

29. *an angekok,]* Eskimo priest and sorcerer, renowned for driving away evil spirits through ecstatic rites and incantations.

30. *a pajee]* Medicine man among the Indian tribes of South America.

31. *going to the wilderness]* {Reference to both Old and New Testaments. In their flight from Egypt, the Jews enter the desert on their way to the promised land (Exodus). John the Baptist also announces the coming of the messiah from the wilderness (Matthew 3; Mark 1:3–51; Luke 3:3–5; John 1:23), and Jesus is tempted in the wilderness by the devil (Matthew 4:1; Mark 1:13; Luke 4:2).}

32. *pillar]* {Reference to the Christian stylites, ascetics who lived standing upon a pillar (Greek: *stylos*). The stylites were highly revered, and through their fervent preaching converted large numbers to Christianity.}

33. *the . . . trance.]* Cf. John Lubbock, *Die Entstehung der Civilisation und der Urzustand des Menschengeschlechtes, erläutert durch das innere und äußere Leben der Wilden . . .* {*The Origin of Civilization and the Primitive Condition of Man: Mental and Social*

Condition of Savages, 1870}, German trans. A. Passow, foreword by
R. Virchow (Jena{: Hermann Costenoble,} 1875), 211f. *NL.*

34. *proposition*] *Satz*, equally common word for "sentence."
There is similar usage of *Satz* near the end of this aphorism and
in Aphorism 9.

35. *customs . . . custom itself:*] "*Sitten . . . Sitte überhaupt:*" Cf.
Aphorism 9 and note 12 above.

36. *painstaking*] *peinlich.* The root, *Pein,* signifies "pain," "agony," "torture"; *peinlich* connotes primarily "embarrassing," "painful," as well as "minute," "painstaking." In legal parlance, *peinlich* indicates an offense that is capital.

37. *Kamchadals*] {A tribe inhabiting the 750-meter-long Kam-
chatka Peninsula on the Pacific coast of Siberia between the Ber-
ing Sea and the Sea of Okhotsk.}

38. *the ultimate?*] *der höchste,* literally "the highest."

39. *It is . . . valuable*] *Pd*: Our suffering pleases the ill-tempered
div⟨inities⟩ and appeases them for us. There⟨fore⟩ volun⟨tary⟩
suffering and torments belong to the mores of the community.
Thus, suffering attains worth. By the same token, one grows
suspicious of well-being. "The virtuous person is in constant
suffering"—an extreme.

40. *compassion!*] *Mitleid.* N's transition to "compassion" is fa-
cilitated by the relationship in standard German between "suffering" (*Leid*) and "compassion" (*Mitleid*= "suffering with"), a relationship that has become archaic in English usage (*passion,* from
Latin: *passio*= "suffering," "submission"). According to the 23rd
expanded edition of Friedrich Kluge's *Etymologisches Wörterbuch
der deutschen Sprache (Etymological dictionary of the German language)* (Berlin: Walter de Gruyter, 1995), 563, *Mitleid* is a "borrowed translation of the mystics from the Latin *compassio.*" Unless otherwise noted, *Mitleid* is rendered as "compassion"; in this
translation "pity" indicates a related concept, but rarely *Mitleid.*

41. *Thus . . . penance*] *Pd*: Dissimulation as a virtue—fear as a
virtue, suffering as a virtue, requital as a virtue. Denial of reason
as a virtue (constancy), compassion as a vice, knowledge as a
vice—laziness, on the aver⟨age⟩, as a consequence of virtue, war

as a time of picturesque morality, peace as danger⟨ous⟩, when seen by the wise, because it unchains the individual. Courage as a cardinal virtue.

42. *inspire . . . belief]* *Glauben finden* = "to find faith." The German allows for the important dual meaning of discovering faith *per se* (i.e., for oneself) and inspiring, in others, faith or belief in themselves.

43. *Every . . . tortures:]* Deleted from *Sd*: we are the heirs of emotional habits that go back for millennia and we can rid ourselves of this legacy only extremely slowly.

44. *stepping forward,]* *Vorwäts-Schreiten.* *Sd:* progress {*der Fortschritt*}.

45. *thirst for knowledge]* *Wißbegier.* *Sd*: knowledge {*Erkenntnis*}.

46. *danger,]* *Sd*: vice.

47. *pity . . . insult,]* *das Mitleiden als Gefahr, das Bimitleidetwerden als Schimpf.* Here, *Mitleid* is translated as "pity" instead of "compassion" in order to accommodate the ensuing term *Bemitleidetwerden* = "to be pitied," which cannot be rendered using "compassion."

48. *Freedoers and freethinkers.]* *Freithäter und Freidenker.* N coins "freedoers" to accompany the more common "freethinkers." Cf. 4[109], where N lists Napoleon and Christ as prototypes for, respectively, the freedoer and the freethinker.

49. *Works and faith.]* {Reference to the advocacy of the principle of *sola fides* ("only through faith") on the part of Martin Luther, leader of the Reformation. Cf. Romans 3:28.}

50. *Pd*: Among primitive peoples, the feeling of power over things, property, etc., is not secure, because they believed things capable of animation and the power to injure. One must secure oneself against them, just as one must with p⟨eople⟩. Flattery and coercion *vis-à-vis* things: basis of most rituals, na⟨tural⟩ causality appeared as magical power. — Powerlessness was infinitely vast and frequent, therefore power's predominant sensation, its subtlety.

51. *the subtlest.]* *am feinsten*, also implying (here, ironically) "the most cultivated, refined, sensitive."

52. *rituals,]* *Gebräuche* denotes "daily habits and customs," but also "religious rites and rituals." Here the single word *Gebräuche* conveys the connection between the day-to-day and the sacred, which N elsewhere evokes in the move from *Sitte* (custom) to *Sittlichkeit* (morality = "the feeling for custom").

53. Cf. 3[71].

54. *precept.]* *Vorschrift*, also "prescription," "regulation," "recipe," "formula." The related passage from the notebooks uses *Gebote* = "commandments."

55. *goodness or badness]* *Güte oder Schlechtigkeit*, employed by N instead of the customary "validity or invalidity" (*Gültigkeit oder Ungültigkeit*).

56. *Russian America]* {Alaska was purchased from the Russians by the United States in 1867, although it did not become a territory until 1912.} On the ensuing commandment not to cast stones, cf. Lubbock, *Die Entstehung der Civilisation*, 376.

57. Cf. 4[280], 10[B17].

58. *Animals and morality.]* *Die Tiere und die Moral.* *Tier*, the common word for "animal," may also mean "beast" in the pejorative sense of the term.

59. *in this depth]* *in dieser Tiefe.* *Tiefe* denotes both spatial depth and conceptual profundity. N deploys a pun that can only be forced here in English: *in dieser Tiefe* also means "at this level of profundity."

60. *mimicry).]* {In English in the original.}

61. *ways]* *Arten* denotes "ways (of doing something)," "manners," and "species."

62. *likeness]* *Gleichnis* (*Gleich* = "same," "like") can mean "comparison," "allegory," "parable," "poetic image."

63. *accord.]* *Vertrag*, common word for "contract" or "treaty."

64. *superhuman]* *übermenschlich.* Early adjectival use of what will later become N's central notion of the "superhuman" or "*Übermensch.*"

65. *pia fraus,]* "pious deception."

66. *prejudice]* *Vorurtheil.*

67. *Pd:* I fear that the m⟨en⟩ most famous for their virtue number among the actors who act to themselves: for this reason they

make me sick. Christianity forbade this sort of playacting—it created the disgusting spectacle of the grandstanding sinner and of fabricated sinfulness (still as "good form" today among Christians).

68. *Actors] Schauspieler*, literally "players of display." *Schau* = "display," "show," "sight," "view"; *Spieler* = "player." Moreover, throughout the aphorism N puns on the fact that the word *Schau* is frequently used in phrases that mean to "display" or "exhibit" (*zur Schau stellen*), often only "for show" (*zur Schau*).

69. *to put on a (dis)play of virtue] Seine Tugend zur Schau zu bringen.* Cf. previous note.

70. *fabricated sinfulness]* {Cf. Romans 5:12.}

71. *pity] Erbarmen.*

72. *Pd*: If one originally presumed that spirit was not merely a human quality but something found everywhere (along with all other drives, evils, sympathies, etc.) and thus did not see in spirit the thing that set humans (or a particular human or a people) apart, then it follows—that in those days there was no such thing as human *pride*{;} one was not ashamed to acknowledge being descended from animals {and} trees.

73. *descent] Abstammung.*

74. *prejudice] Vorurtheil* throughout this section.

75. *Pd*: 4[13]. Cf. 4[143].

76. Cf. 4[144]. *Pd*, at the outset: Is there such a thing as inherited moral feelings? To begin with, one tries to deny the theory of inheritance for as long as possible.—

77. *retroactively,]* Cf. note 1 to Aphorism 1.

78. *justifying foundation] Begründung* = "grounds," "motivation," "justification," "rationale." On *Grund*, cf. note 4 to P2.

79. *origin] Herkunft.* Cf. note 2 to Aphorism 1.

80. *reasons . . . acceptable.] angebbare und annehmbare Gründe.* Complex pun, suggesting that the reasons are also alleged and cozy, a matter of complicit give and take (*geben* = "to give"; *nehmen* = "take"; *-bar* = "-able"). *Angeben*, however, also means "to pretend," and *angeblich* means "alleged," "supposed," "pretended." Similarly, *annehmbar* has close association with *angenehm,* the German word for "comfortable" and "pleasant."

81. Cf. 4[144].

82. *Pd*: What! The inventors of the first rowboat, the first astrologers are supposed to be incomparably greater than our inventors? Just the opposite! In those days chance wrought much more than it does today!

83. *prejudice,]* *Vorurtheil*.

84. *for their emergence?]* {Reference to the widespread belief, based upon the Platonic notion of the transmigration of souls (cf. *Phaedo* 70cff. and *Phaedrus* 248cff.), that the planets were inhabited. Cf. the appendix to Kant's *General History of Nature and Theory of the Heavens* (1755) entitled "Concerning the Inhabitants of the Planets": "So we can infer with more than probable presumption that . . . for the entire range of {inhabitants'} perfection falls under a particular rule according to which the inhabitants become ever more excellent and perfect depending on the distance of their habitat from the sun" (A 187).}

85. Cf. 6[204], 7[55], 7[239], 8[101].

86. *Eris,]* {According to Hesiod, Eris was the personification of strife. In the beginning of the *Works and Days* (20–24), Hesiod recognizes a type of strife, born of envy and competition, that serves as a healthy stimulus to human productivity. Cf. "Homer's Contest" in *CW* 1.}

87. *fable,]* {Allusion to the story of Pandora's box (actually a jar or *pithos*), related in Hesiod's *Works and Days* (94–99). As punishment for the mortal Prometheus's theft of fire, the god Zeus bids his smithy Hephaestus to give Pandora the *pithos* containing all the evils of the world along with the injunction never to open the *pithos*. Out of curiosity, Pandora nonetheless unseals the *pithos*, thereby releasing pain and evil into the human world.}

88. *among the Europeans are,]* *Sd*: Europeans [from the Greeks to the present day] are.

89. *extirpate it!]* N puns on the word *heben*, which means both "to extirpate" and "to elevate." Cf. Aphorisms 33 and 45.

90. *lot]* *das Los*.

91. *Ruminating over rituals.]* *Grübeln über Gebräuche*. The phrase gains a great deal of force by virtue of the highly com-

pressed consonance (*G–G; b–b–b*) and assonance (*ü–ü; e–e– e–e*). *Grübeln* = ruminating in a brooding, obsessive manner. On rituals, cf. Aphorism 23, note 52.

92. Cf. 4[58].

93. *vita contemplativa.]* "contemplative life." Opposed to the *vita activa* (active life).

94. Cf. 3[77], 3[87], 4[43].

95. *Origin] Herkunft.*

96. ⟨*his mind's*⟩*] Le*: added on the basis of the *Pd* and *Sd*.

97. *pudenda origo!]* "shameful origin." Added to the end of *Sd*: For a long time the entire worth of such beings existed solely in the fact that they accustomed other people to their presence and drummed into the sluggish brain of the person of actions the idea of the contemplative life. For contemplative beings, their feeling of contentment in life increases along with an increase in their power; at least they become practical optimists.

98. *science. Hence]* Stricken from *Sd*: science[, the finger exercises, as it were, of scientific thought, in the belief that that is all there is, that the vestibule is the sanctuary]. Hence

99. *Pd*: This seems to me to be my most valuable insight: whereas earlier the closer one came to the origin of things, the stronger one believed one was finding more and more of inestimable significance for human actions and judgments, allowing even eternal salvation to depend on it, now it is the opposite; the further we go back, the less engaged is our interest: the high regard with which we have invested these things loses its meaning the more we return to the things themselves.

100. *and beyond.]* Added to the end in *Sd*: and misery and cage and bars and gap and bliss, everything, everything was a bad dream?

101. Cf. 6[281].

102. *exalted and elevated] erhoben und gehoben.* Not only does the phrase create an effect through rhyme, but N puns once again (cf. Aphorism 39 and note 89).

103. *drive for knowledge] Erkenntnistrieb.* N frequently associates the "drive for knowledge" with philosophy in his notebooks of 1872–74.

104. *high tide.] Flut-Höhe* = "the height" (*Höhe*) "of high tide" (*Flut*). German, however, uses the same word for both "high tide" and "flood." In this aphorism about destruction, N makes a veiled allusion to the flood (*Sintflut* = "deluge") of Genesis.

105. *well-formed head!"]* N's quotation is actually a truncated paraphrase. Cf. Montaigne, *Essais* 3,13: "Oh! que c'est un doux et mol chevet et sain que l'ignorance et l'incuriosité à reposer une teste bien faicte!" {"Oh, what a sweet and soft and healthy pillow is ignorance and incuriosity, to rest a well-made head." *The Complete Essays of Montaigne* (Stanford: Stanford University Press, 1958), 822.} N possessed two editions of Montaigne's work: *Essais avec des notes de tous les commentateurs* {*Essays with the notes of all the annotators*} (Paris{: Chez Firmin Didot Frères, Fils et Cie.,} 1864); *Versuche, nebst des Verfassers Leben, nach der neuesten Ausgabe des Herrn Peter Coste, ins Deutsche übers* {*Essays, together with a biography of the author, based on the edition by Mr. Peter Coste, trans. into German*}, 3 vols. (Leipzig{: Friedrich Lankischens Erben,} 1753–54). N owned a German rendering of Pascal's works, in which Pascal also cites the Montaigne passage quoted above. Cf. Pascal, *Gedanken, Fragmente und Briefe . . . nach der Ausgabe P. Faugère's* {*Thoughts, fragments and letters . . . based on the P. Faugère edition*}, German trans. by Dr. C. F. Schwartz (Leipzig{: Otto Wigand,} 1865), 1:316: "that ignorance and incuriosity are two sweet pillows for a well-organized head." In the German translation of Pascal, which shows many signs of having been read often, N underlined the following relevant passage (2:19, translated here from N's German edition): "It is therefore a misery to doubt; but in the midst of doubt, it is an inescapable duty to seek. Consequently, anyone who doubts and does not seek is both miserable and iniquitous. If, in such a situation, a person remains unruffled and presumptuous, then I lack the words to describe such an extravagant creature." At this juncture, N noted "Montaigne" in the margin. Evidently N was also familiar with Pascal in the original French edition, *Pensées fragments et lettres . . . , publiés pour la première fois conformément aux manuscrits originaux en grande partie inédits . . . {Thoughts fragments and letters . . . published for the first time based on the original*

manuscripts and for the most part previously unpublished . . . }, edited by Prosper Faugère (Paris{: Andrieux,} 1844), for at one juncture (Schwartz, 2:81) he notes "incorrectly translated." References
to Pascal's works are to N's German edition (Schwartz) and to
the French edition (Faugère). *NL.*

106. *no one . . . pillow.] Sd*: he believed himself in possession of
just such a head and felt a similar longing for a lovely pillow.

107. *thyself"]* {Greek inscription at the temple to Apollo at Delphi. Ascribed by Diogenes Laërtius to Thales of Miletus, the only
philosopher among the Seven Sages, philosophy as the pursuit of
self-knowledge is most closely associated with Socrates.}

108. *puto").]* "Any human interest is my concern." {A quotation
from *Heauton Timorumenos* (*The self-tormentor*), one of the
comedies by the Roman playwright Terence (ca. 190–159 BCE):
"CHREMES: 'I am human, so any human interest is my concern.'" *Phormio and Other Plays* (Harmondsworth: Penguin,
1967), 76.}

109. *self";] außer sich*, meaning also, to be "beside oneself"
(with joy, anger, intoxication, etc.).

110. *for . . . world-weariness.] Pd*: because they teach dissatisfaction and disdain for the world along with the obfuscation of
the genius cult. Who will, then, have to suffer from these im-
moderates? Their entire surroundings into the farthest future,
especially the children.

111. Cf. 3[82], 4[318]. *Pd*: The means of solace are what make
life so full of suffering for so many: people get used to combating their pains through intoxication, and suffer afterward from
the repercussions of the intoxication, from the want of it, from the
lasting uncertainty and shakiness of their attitude. Intoxication:
feeling of power. From this it follows that the main suffering is
the feeling of weakness and fear. — For a long time now nothing has contributed so much to the worsening of the health
of humanity as the medicines against the diseases. In the best
of cases, one attended to momentary alleviations, and general
worsening was the result. Whoever advanced to a certain stage
of disease no longer recovered: the physicians made sure of
that. — One says of Schopenhauer that he took human suffering

seriously: now I for a change wish to take the antidotes to suffering seriously.

112. *Pd*: I have no antipathy whatsoever for the pious, rather a quiet respect along with regret that these excellent people do not share my feelings: but from where arises this deep contempt for someone who has had full freedom of spirit and in the long run nonetheless falls prey to faith? It is as if something ignominious had happened, so that everyone who merely heard of it must blush. From where?—Sch⟨openhauer⟩ felt the same way. I would turn my back on the most venerated person if he roused my suspicion in this connection.

113. *spernere . . . ipsum:] Spernere se sperne*: "spurn being spurned oneself." *Spernere se ipsum*: "spurn yourself." Quotations from the *Carmina Miscellanea* (*Miscellaneous poetry*), CXXIV, of Hildebert von Lavardins (1056–1133), archbishop of Tours and master of Latin versification. Goethe alludes to the passage in the *Second Roman Sojourn (1829)* of his *Italian Journey*: "Spurn the world, / Spurn no one, / Spurn yourself, / Spurn being spurned oneself." Goethe, *Werke* (Munich{: Beck,} 1981), 11:466.

114. *apostate] Pd*: renegade

115. *security.] Sicherheit*, the common word for "safety" and for "certainty," as well as for "security." Throughout the aphorism, all forms of the word *security* bear the three meanings of "security," "safety," "certainty." On security, cf. Aphorism 173.

116. *love . . . faith . . . hope]* {Cardinal virtues of Christianity. Cf. 1 Corinthians 13:13.}

117. Cf. 4[151].

118. *spirited] geistreich*, literally "rich in spirit," but, as N no doubt intends here, also "ingenious," "clever."

119. *priesthood,] Geistlichkeit*, meaning "spirituality" as well ("spirit" = *Geist*).

120. *priesthood]* {Referring to priests as "princes of Hell," Martin Luther catalogues their oppressive actions in his open letter *An den christlichen Adel deutscher Nation* (*An appeal to the ruling class of German nationality*) (1520) and *De captivitate babylonica ecclesiae praeludium* (*On the Babylonian captivity of the first church*) (1520).}

121. *"in the wilderness"*] A reference to the devil's temptation of Jesus in the wilderness—cf. note 31 to Aphorism 14. The allusion is strengthened by the fact that, in the same sentence, the word for "experimentally" (*versuchsweise*) has the same root as the word for "temptation" (*Versuchung*).

122. *Pd*: How can a person experience his own opinion about things as a revelation? This is the problem of the origin of all religions: it presumes that one already believes in "revelations." For the blessed rapture of a new hypothesis is so great for its creator that he ascribes it to God: this presumes that one does not believe in humans as founders of great happiness (pessimism). Thus one confirms an opinion by calling it a revelation, one withdraws it from critique: one makes it holy. Thus one does, it is true, degrade oneself to an *organon* {"tool," "instrument"} but our thought triumphs as the thought of God: a prodigious satisfaction of the feeling of po⟨wer⟩. One thereby withdraws it from one's own critique: one places oneself above oneself. This violation of ourselves in favor of our creation is an extreme form of paternal love and pride.

123. *cause . . . cause*] In all three instances, "cause" renders the German *Ursache*, which shares the same prefix as *Ursprung* (cf. note 2 to Aphorism 1). *Ur-* connotes "primary," "original."

124. *organon,*] "tool," "instrument."

125. *Pd*: Supposing we felt toward another as he feels (according to Schopenhauer, compassion; more accurately "a single passion")—then we would hate him if he, as an I, finds himself hateful, as did Pascal. And that is indeed how Pascal felt toward humanity as a whole: and the Christian too for that matter, whom, under Nero, one convicted of *odium generis humani* {"hatred of the human race"}.

126. *onepassion*] Pun that is also forced in German. Transformation of the common word for compassion or sympathy, *Mitleid* (*Mit*="with"; *Leid*="suffering"), into the neologism *Einleidlichkeit* (*Ein*="one"; *Leid*="suffering"; *-keit*="-ness"). This passage refers to the work of Arthur Schopenhauer, particularly *The Basis of Morality* (1840), in which Schopenhauer makes compassion the cornerstone of his ethics. N alludes to Schopenhauer's

concept of individuation, i.e., the will to become an individual, as a process characterized by enormous suffering. Suffering is always a suffering of the lone individual, hence N's word *Einleidlichkeit* = "onepassion."

127. *if . . . hateful.]* Cf. the following underlined passages in N's German edition of Pascal's *Gedanken*: "No other religion has taught that one should hate oneself. Thus, no other religion can satisfy those people who hate themselves and are in search of a being who is truly worthy of love" (Schwartz, 2:118; Faugère, 2:142). "One has only to love God and only to hate oneself" (Schwartz, 2:273; Faugère, 2:380). On Christianity and self-hatred, cf. Aphorism 79.

128. *Nero]* {Nero demonstrated hatred of his neighbor by killing his mother, his first and second wives, and many leading citizens he thought were plotting against him.}

129. *odium generis humani.]* "hatred of humankind." In his *Annals* (15, 44, 4), the Roman historian Cornelius Tacitus writes, "First, then, the confessed members of the sect were arrested; next, on their disclosures, vast numbers were convicted, not so much on the count of arson as for hatred of humankind." *The Annals of Tacitus 13–16* (Cambridge, Mass.: Harvard University Press, 1991), 282–85.

130. Cf. 7[129].

131. Cf. 4[166].

132. *religiosi)]* "moved, touched by God," i.e., mystics.

133. Cf. 6[179].

134. *robber . . . cross]* {During his crucifixion, Christ promises a confessed robber who is being crucified next to him that he and the robber will meet that day in Paradise. Cf. Luke 23:43.}

135. Cf. 4[164, 167, 170, 171, 219, 220, 231, 252, 254, 255, 258]. This aphorism results from N's close reading of Hermann Lüdermann's *Die Anthropologie des Apostels Paulus und ihre Stellung innerhalb seiner Heilslehre: Nach den vier Hauptbriefen dargestellt (The Apostle Paul's anthropology and its position within his doctrine of salvation: Presented according to the four main epistles)* (Kiel{: Universitätsbuchhandlung,} 1872). In particular, cf. 106–48.

136. *pitiable,]* bemitleidenswerth.

137. *of ethical sublimeness]* der sittlichen Erhabenheit.

138. *lust for domination]* Herrschsucht. The root *herrsch-* is the same as in the word for "control."

139. *carnality of "flesh"]* {Cf. 2 Corinthians 12:7.}

140. *Luther . . . ideal:]* {Cf. Aphorism 88.}

141. *outside the law."]* {Cf. Romans 6:14.}

142. *law is dead,]* {Cf. Galatians 2:19.}

143. *one with Christ,]* {Cf. Romans 12:5; 1 Corinthians 10:17; 2 Corinthians 13:1; Galatians 3:28; Ephesians 4:3, 13.}

144. *the Greek, in]* Pd: the Greek (Achilles) in

145. *Christian.]* Added to the end in *Sd*: There's no aping any of that!

146. *boundaries]* Absonderungen, literally that which is "separated," "secluded."

147. *prejudices.]* Vorurtheile.

148. *"aere perennius"]* "more lasting than bronze."

149. *praetors]* "praetor," related to *prae-ire* = "to lead," "to precede." Particularly since 227 BCE the Roman praetors held supreme military and judicial authority in provinces ruled by Rome.

150. *Epicurus]* {Epicurus held that both the body and the soul were composed of atoms and that the latter died with the former, thus ridding his followers of the belief in, and fear of, an afterlife.}

151. *resounds]* ausklingt = literally, "to sound out." N is, however, drawing on the verb's other meaning, namely, "to cease to sound," "to fade away."

152. *Lucretius,]* {In his only work, *De Rerum Natura* (*On the nature of things*), Lucretius expounds the atomistic philosophy of Epicurus in an attempt to free humans from superstition, from belief in the intervention of the gods and in an afterlife.}

153. *Mithras and Isis cults!]* {Originally an Indo-Iranian god of light, truth, and war, Mithras gained a widespread following in Rome during the first half of the first century BCE. In this exclusively male cult that was a serious rival to early Christianity, successfully completing the seventh and final stage of initiation was believed to lead to immortality. Isis figures originally in Egyptian religion as the wife of Osiris, god of death and the underworld,

and mother of Horus. Her cult, associated with magic and with rebirth from the underworld, was firmly established in Greece by the fourth century BCE.}

154. *Maccabees,]* {The Maccabees make up the last two books of the Apocrypha (Greek: "The Hidden Ones"), i.e., the fourteen books included in the Greek, but not the Hebrew, Old Testament (cf. Aphorism 84, note 187).} Cf. 2 Maccabees 7:10–11. Cf. 4[161].

155. *transubstantiation]* *Verwandlung*, a highly polyvalent word that may also mean "conversion," "metamorphosis," "commutation."

156. *theme]* *Vorwurf*, which also means "reproach."

157. *for everyone]* {Cf. the first chapter of Romans, especially 1:6–17, and Romans 10:12.}

158. *resurrection . . . unredeemed;]* {Cf. the final note to this aphorism.}

159. *wages of sin,]* {Cf. Romans 6:23.}

160. *eternally damned,]* {The belief in eternal damnation in hell became official church doctrine in 543 CE in the *Canones adversus Originem* (*Laws contrary to Origines*). Origines (185–253? CE), one of the most influential early Christian theologians, had claimed that, after death, all sinners enter a fire of purification from which they gradually emerge redeemed.}

161. Cf. 5[28].

162. Cf. 3[106].

163. *chasteneth"]* Cf. Hebrews 12:6.

164. *kobolds]* {In German folklore, spirits or goblins that haunt houses or live in mines and other underground places.}

165. *sonnets.]* {Cf. the opening to Sonnet 151: "Love is too young to know what conscience is, / Yet who knows not conscience is born of love?" See also Sonnets 121 and especially 129 and 142.}

166. *revile]* *verlästern*, literally "to turn into a vice" (from *Laster* = "vice").

167. Cf. 6[66].

168. *pity]* *Erbarmen*.

169. *new . . . pity]* Cf. 3[106].

170. *hell,"]* {Cf. the final note to Aphorism 72.}

171. *stone . . . Juan]* {Reference to what is usually the final scene in any number of treatments of the myth of the insatiable seducer Don Juan (most famous are Molière's *Don Juan or the Stone Guest*, 1665, and Mozart's opera *Don Giovanni*, 1787). The "stone guest" is the commander whom Don Juan has slain at the outset and who returns at the end in petrified form to exhort Don Juan to mend his ways. When the latter refuses, the commander's touch commands the impenitent seducer to hell.}

172. *Whitefield]* {George Whitefield was leader of the Calvinist Methodists, missionary to the American colonies, founder of the revival movement, and renowned for his tremendous oratorical powers in the fire-and-brimstone manner.}

173. *when . . . fashion]* Cf. William Edward Hartpole Lecky, *Entstehungsgeschichte und Charakteristik des Methodismus: Aus dem Englischen von Ferdinand Löwe* (*History of the origin and nature of Methodism: From the English by Ferdinand Löwe*) (special printing of the ninth chapter of volume 2 of Lecky's *Geschichte Englands im achtzehnten Jahrhundert* {*History of England in the eighteenth century*}, bearing the heading "The religious revival" (Leipzig and Heidelberg{: C. F. Winter,} 1880), 2:53f. *NL*.

174. *calamity"!] Sd*: what all kept climbing to the light of day out of the [inner] hell into which Christianity had transformed that poor "little soul," the *anima vagula blandula* of the ancients {N refers here to the Roman emperor Hadrian (76–138; emperor, 117–38), whose best-known literary work is a short poem reported to have been composed on his deathbed that begins with the line "*Animula vagula blandula*" (Little soul, wandering and pale). *Animula* is the diminutive of *anima*, which N might have mistakenly misquoted from memory or might have changed intentionally. Cf. *Scriptores Historiae Augustae* (*The Augustan History*), *Life of Hadrian* 25.9.}

175. *"field of calamity"!]* Cf. *WS* 6. The citation is from Empedocles {see *Empedocles: The Extant Fragments*, ed. M. R. Wright (New Haven: Yale University Press, 1981), 278}: ἔργατε ῥευστα Ἄτηςἀν λειμῶνα: {"they wander in darkness over the field of Atë"} (Diehls-Kranz fragment no. 121). {Atë is the daughter

of Eris and sister of Dysnomia (Lawlessness). Cf. *Iliad* 19:90ff., the *Theogony*, line 230, and Aeschylus's *Agamemnon*, lines 1124, 1433.}

176. *One . . . torture.]* N is quoting from Lecky, *Entstehungsgeschichte*, 2:67f.

177. *Let . . . torment]* {Reference to antiquity's tendency to view death as the twin of sleep. The difference between Christian and ancient representations of death is the subject of a famous essay by Lessing, which N undoubtedly knew, entitled "Wie die Alten den Tod gebildet" (How the ancients represented death) (1769).}

178. *"Oh . . . come!"]* Cf. Lecky, *Entstehungsgeschichte*, 2:71ff.

179. *The Greeks . . . misfortune:]* The word is νεμεσσητιχόν. Cf. *CW* 11:17[58]{: The free spirit has the "gods' envy" of humans' dumb contentment. The gods' envy is νεμεσσητιχόν.}

180. *If . . . hateful,]* Cf. Pascal, *Gedanken* (Schwartz, 1:190f.; Faugère, 1:197): "Le moi est haïssable. Vous, Miton, le couvrez; vous ne l'ôtez pas pour cela: vous êtes donc toujours haïssable." {The self is odious. You, Miton, conceal it; but for all that you don't get rid of it: you are therefore still odious.} Cf. *D* 63; *MM* 385.

181. *assume]* annehmen. Also means "to accept."

182. *Pd*: "You have to sort that out yourself: for your life is at stake." Luther. Nothing of the kind! It doesn't matter much.

183. *Spiritual]* Der geistliche. Pun that suggests the attack is by a priest (*Der Geistliche*), which turns out to be the case.

184. *than . . . vulture.]* {Ancient image of extreme suffering. Having deceived Zeus by stealing fire from the gods (or, in some accounts, cheating Zeus out of a sacrifice), Prometheus is chained to a rock, where every day an eagle (N claims a vulture) devours his liver, which then grows back again each night. This suffering is especially significant because the Greeks and Romans thought the liver was the seat of all the passions.}

185. Cf. 4[235], 6[240].

186. *erection . . . snake,]* {Cf. Numbers 21:9.}

187. *Septuagint]* {From *Septuaginta*, "the seventy." Name given to the first translation (supposedly by some seventy scholars) of the Old Testament from Hebrew into Greek.}

188. *Psalm 96:10]* {It is unclear what N has in mind here. A comparison of the psalms in Hebrew, in the Septuagint, the Vulgate, and the Luther and the King James versions does not appear to reveal any emendation.}

189. *Pd:* One (Schopenhauer) mocks the mythology and theology of the Greeks. One ought to admire that they displayed measure precisely at this point and did not apply their acute understanding to these areas. This is a type of tact.

190. Cf. 8[58]. *Pd:* added to the end: And such {are} all pure physicists.

191. Cf. 10[B43]; 4[165].

192. Cf. 4[56], 4[59], 4[261].

193. *locked . . . monastery,]* {Luther broke off his studies in law and entered the monastery in 1505, where his comings and goings were monitored by his Augustinian superiors.}

194. *mines or "mineshafts"]* Tiefen und "Teufen" (pronounced "Teefin" and "Toifin"). *Tiefen* is the normal word for depths, but *Teufen*, from Late Middle High German, would also have been used in Luther's day. The only current usage is as a mineshaft, which is appropriate for Luther, "a trusty miner's son."

195. *self-invented."]* Cf. Luther, *Der große Katechismus (The great catechism)* (1529) in Luther, *Weimarer Ausgabe*, 30:178f.

196. Cf. 4[57], 6[116].

197. *significance"]* Ascribed to Malwida von Meysenbug. Cf. 4[57].

198. *God's honesty.]* Redlichkeit, which also means "sincerity," "integrity," "probity," "fairness."

199. *welfare]* Heil, which also carries the religious implications of "redemption" and "salvation."

200. *intelligence]* Pun on the word Geist = "spirit" as well as "intelligence," "intellect." Accordingly, God lacks spirit.

201. *"hidden God"]* {Cf. Isaiah 45:15. Cf. also Job 23:9; Psalms 10:1 and 13:31.}

202. *"deus absconditus"]* "hidden God."

203. *No one . . . could.]* Cf. the following passage underlined in N's German edition of Pascal's *Gedanken*: "If God constantly revealed Himself to humans then there would be no merit in

having faith in Him; and if He never revealed himself, there would be little faith. But usually He remains hidden and reveals Himself only rarely to those whom He wishes to enlist into His service. This miraculous, and for humans impenetrable, *arcanum* {"mystery, secret"} into which God has retreated leads us urgently into solitude, far away from the gaze of others." (Schwartz, 1:57; Faugère, 1:38. Cf. Schwartz, 2:4, 95, 121f.)

204. *a . . . moralism:] Pd*: a gentle heathenism

205. *"God, . . . immortality"]* {Cf. Kant's *Critique of Pure Reason*, B 7, where Kant identifies these three ideas as the principal concerns of pure reason.}

206. *Who . . . draw:] Pd*: I won't accept a conclusion such as this

207. *remedy.] Heilmittel* = literally, "means of salvation."

208. *In . . . vinces.]* "In this sign you will be the victor." {In the year 312 BCE, on the verge of battle against his rival Maxentius, the Roman emperor Constantine the Great (274–337) is reported to have had a vision in which these words appeared to him along with an image of the cross superimposed against the sun. Constantine defeated Maxentius and converted to Christianity, the first pagan emperor to do so (Constantine had been a worshipper of the Roman sun god, Sol). This is the moment when, symbolically, antiquity yields to Christianity.}

209. *which . . . good.]* Cf. 4[186]. {Cf. J. Wackernagel, *Über den Ursprung des Brahmanismus* (*On the origin of Brahmanism*) (Basel: Schweighauser, 1877), 28f. *NL*.}

Book Two

1. *Pd*: Subjugation to morality can be equally slavish, equally vain, equally egotistical (like France's under Nap⟨oleon⟩{)} or resigned or stupidly rapturous or without thought.

2. *thinking).] Pd*: thought

3. *Awakening . . . dream.]* May also be read as a command: "Awaken from the dream."

4. *music of the spheres:]* {Allusion to the belief of the Greek philosopher Pythagoras (582?–500? BCE) that the planets ex-

isted in ordered distances corresponding to sound intervals, which comprised an imperceptible harmony of the spheres. Cf. Aphorism 4.}

5. *existence.*"] Reference to Schopenhauer.

6. *Problematic . . . accept] Bedenklich . . . annehmen.* These two words set up a contrast between the heading and the body of the aphorism. *Bedenklich* comes from the verb "to consider," "ponder over"; *annehmen* means "to assume" as well as "to accept." Accordingly, one must reflect or else assume blindly.

7. Cf. 8[59]. *Pd*: False generalizations: e.g., one says "an injurious person," others repeat it—but one actually means: besides a great deal that isn't injurious, the person also does something that injures—but one awakens the presumption that the person is always and essentially an injurious being. More precisely: he has injured others once or four times, once intentionally and the rest unintentionally. But based on the one time, one assumes that all acts that injure have been committed intentionally.—These are the false conclusions drawn by fear.

8. *pudenda origo!]* "shameful origin!"

9. *ethical] sittlich.* Whereas the noun, *Sitte*, may be translated as "custom," "habit," "propriety," the adjectival form must be rendered as "ethical" or "moral." Cf. Aphorism 9 and note 12.

10. Cf. 3[24], 5[13].

11. *adopted]* From the verb *annehmen* = "to assume," "accept." Cf. note 6 above.

12. *pretense] Verstellung* in *Se, Sd, Le*; representation (*Vorstellung*) in *Fe*

13. Cf. 4[51].

14. Cf. 1[4], 3[171]. *Pd*: Preserving and advancing humanity are supposed to be the goal of morality! Preserving what? Advancing where? In whatever elevates humans above animals, etc. That means that the essential thing about morality is close-lipped and very difficult to express! The longest possible existence of humanity?—that would be a goal that required completely different means from the most possible distinction from animals. {The} highest advancement of rationality does not guarantee humanity the longest life.

15. *what? . . . where?] worin*? *. . . wohin*? N achieves added effect through the use of rhyme.

16. Cf. 1[4].

17. *Pd*: Aren't precepts as to how we must act altogether limitations on, and even contradictions to, individual happiness?, i.e., happiness that springs from its own impenetrable laws. 1. Provided he wants to be happy, one ought not give the individual any precepts. 2. The so-called moral laws are directed against the individual and do not promote his happiness. 3. Only if humanity had a generally recognized goal could one determine: how should we act? 4. It is not true that happiness is the goal of evolution: either of an art or of human ages, on the contrary there is in all stages an especially incomparable happiness. Change, the need for change is the goal of evolution, viz., evolution wants evolution and nothing more. Habit breeds boredom and this change. 5. It is not true that morality advances reason.

18. Cf. 6[2]. *Pd*: One combats the intensity of a drive 1) in that one avoids opportunities for gratification and through abstinence seeks to weaken it (habit fortifies) 2) by introducing a regiment of gratification; under the yoke of the regimen the drive becomes regimented and leaves periods free in which it doesn't disturb 3) one gives oneself over to the wildest gratification in order to harvest disgust 4) one yokes gratification to some very distressing thought, proximity and derision of the devil and his punishments in hell{,} disdain from those one admires most, etc. 5) one turns proud and does not wish to be ruled.

19. *appetite"]* Lord Byron, *Vermischte Schriften, Briefwechsel und Lebensgeschichte* {*Miscellaneous works, correspondence, and biography*}, ed. Ernst Ortlepp (Stuttgart{: J. Scheible,} no date), 2:31. N is quoting from the German edition in his library.

20. *Pd*: One has to pick up the scent of a new type of pleasure — there thus arises a desire for it{,} and if much of what opposes it is of minor consequence, also minor people — then the goal appears noble, moral, good: now the inherited moral predisposition is transformed into desire, takes desire into itself — I saw this {hi}story {transpire} in me with my own eyes.

21. *goal] Ziel.* Just as in Aphorism 106, *Ziel* is here, for the purposes of consistency, rendered as "goal." Because, however, this aphorism has much in common with Freud's later theory of instincts, the reader should be aware that *Ziel* is the word that the translators of the *Standard Edition* render as the "aim" of an instinct.

22. *practice, ⟨a lot of⟩] Se, Taschen-Ausgabe,* Bd. 5 (1906); *Fe, Le*: Practice

23. *spirit.] Geist=*"mind," "intellect."

24. Cf. 8[99].

25. *every . . . way] der Nächste=*literally, "the next one," whose primary use is as the scripturally inflected word for "neighbor" in expressions like "Love thy neighbor."

26. *King Visvamitra,]* {Indian mythological king who, through years of asceticism, begins to build a new heaven. The god Indra sends a nymph who seduces Visvamitra and thus diminishes his powers.}

27. *Dante]* {In the first part of Dante's *Divine Comedy*, he depicts the sufferings of damned souls in hell.}

28. *Calvin]* {A leading member of the Reformation, Calvin stressed the doctrines of original sin, eternal damnation, and predestination.}

29. Cf. 4[155]. *Pd*: People who are tormented terribly and for a long time without fever and whose mind remains unclouded look out onto things with a terrifying coldness: they know that the encrustation that covers things and people with health and laziness has fallen away: indeed from themselves. Supreme sobering up by means of pain is sometimes the only means to call someone back from a dangerous fantasy world: just as happened to Christ on the cross. The prodigious straining of the intellect that opposes the pain gives a new light to everything one looks at: the attraction of this illumination is a strong stimulant to continuing to live despite all exhortations [?] to suicide. Contempt for the illusionary misty world of cozy warm health, insight into the motives of our being on that occasion when physical pain does not shy away from conjuring up the bitterest pain of the soul only in order to bear the physical agony—clairvoyance! "For once be

your own accuser and executioner, accept [?] your suffering as the punishment you have pronounced! Enjoy your superiority as judge, elevate yourself above your life as above your suffering, look into the depths of meaning!" — Then the appeal of advocating life against all the whisperings of pain, of resisting pessimism lest it appear a consequence. The appeal of exercising justness, of triumphing over oneself in the most agitated of states. The appeal of the most profound solitude and of freedom from all duties: it falls like scales from our eyes. In the meantime the bliss of recovery, alleviation of suffering — we become transformed. In the end, the appeal of not being foolishly proud, as if what we had experienced were something unique: we humble pain's almighty pride after the fact. We long for a powerful self-alienation because the pain made us too powerfully personal for so long. People and nature affect us in a new way: even where the veil has fallen we see about them with rueful joy the subdued lights of life at play, and we smile when we perceive the incrustation — we don't grow angry.

30. *me!"*] {Christ's words on the cross. Cf. Matthew 27:46; Mark 15:34; as well as Psalm 22, which opens with the same words.}

31. *disappointment*] In German the same word is used for "disappointment" and "disillusion": *Enttäuschung* (*Ent*= "un-" or "dis-"; *Täuschung*= "illusion," "fraud," "deception").

32. *Don Quixote.*] {Allusion to the end of *Don Quixote* (1605 pt. 1; 1615 pt. 2), novel of chivalry by the Spanish author Miguel de Cervantes Saavedra. Shortly before his death, Don Quixote, who has supposedly gone benevolently mad from reading too many "profane Stories of Knight-Errantry," renounces "all my pass'd Folies," seems at least to return to his senses, confesses, makes a will, and dies peacefully. *Don Quixote*, trans. Peter Motteux (New York: Modern Library, 1930), 930–34.}

33. *appeal*] *Reiz*. N draws on the polyvalence of this word, which can mean "charm," "attraction," "fascination," "allurement," "enticement," but also "a physical stimulation," "an impulse." N employs the same word two sentences later and also includes its adjectival form (*reizbar*, rendered as "sensitive").

34. *prejudices*] *Vorurtheile*.

35. *prejudices,]* Vorurtheile.

36. *God."]* Quotation from *Aus Schopenhauers handschriftlichem Nachlaß* {*From Schopenhauer's handwritten notebooks published posthumously*} (Leipzig{: F. A. Brockhaus,} 1864), 433f. *NL.*

37. *live and act;]* lebe und webe = literally, "live" and "weave." In addition to the effect of the rhyme, N introduces the motif of weaving that reappears twice near the end of the aphorism.

38. *fate]* Verhängnis = "fate," "destiny," "doom," "curse," "misfortune." Moreover, the related verb *verhängen* = "to cover, veil, conceal" and also "to pronounce judgment or sentence." Accordingly, *Verhängnis* here also implies "sentence."

39. Cf. 6[410], 6[419], 6[418].

40. *neighbor]* der Nächste. Cf. Aphorism 113 and note 25 above.

41. *Experience and make-believe.]* Erleben und Erdichten. These two common words are formed by adding the prefix *er-* to, respectively, the normal verb for "to live" (*leben*) and the customary verb for "to write literature." *Erdichten* means "to make up," "fantasize."

42. *why . . . tops?]* Cf. 7[156].

43. *from . . . sort.]* Sd; Le: from weathercocks, moths, and other things.

44. *make-believing faculty of reason]* die dichtende Vernunft = "poeticizing reason," "reason that is writing literature."

45. *You're . . . blunder.]* Pd: Everything is imagination.

46. *Pd*: 6[433]. Cf. 6[429], 6[431], 6[435], 6[441].

47. Cf. 4[95].

48. *As . . . riddle.]* Pd: Through the roll of the dice of chance. Is that still continuing in humanity? Yes

49. *We . . . riddle.]* Sd: But we haven't figured that out yet.

50. Cf. 5[43], 6[119], 5[47]: { . . . } Wanting is a prejudice.{ . . . }

51. Cf. 4[134].

52. *Oedipus . . . dream!]* Perhaps an allusion to Sophocles' *Oedipus Tyrannos,* lines 981ff.

53. Cf. 6[374].

54. *consequences and outcomes]* "Folgen und Erfolge." Cf. Aphorism 12, note 21.

55. Cf. 4[288], 6[355], 10[B37].

56. *chance events;] Zufälle*, plural of *Zufall* = "chance," "happenstance," "contingency," "accident." This translation usually renders the singular *Zufall* as "chance."

57. *Moira]* "portion," "share," "lot." Greek goddess of fate. Hesiod (*Theogony* 904–6) has three Moirai — Clotho, Lachesis, Atropos—who were the forerunners of the Roman *Parcae*, or fates.

58. *met . . . them,] Sd*: which seems to belong to Indo-Germanic culture (one wants to have a trump card against them up one's sleeve)

59. *austere . . . Scandinavian,] Sd*: Teuton

60. *twilight of the gods,]* {In German and Norse mythology the concept of the destruction of the world. Richard Wagner's *The Twilight of the Gods*, the last opera in *The Ring of the Niebulung*, appeared in 1874, and N's own *Twilight of the Idols* in 1889.}

61. *Persian . . . Scandinavian,] Sd*: Teutonic

62. *God . . . ways,]* {Cf. Romans 11:33.}

63. *ancient . . . subtle,] Sd*: clever and adventurous Europeans

64. *perhaps . . . herself.] Sd*: there is only one realm, but in it there exists neither absolute chance nor absolute stupidity, but instead necessity in everything and everyone and only now and then predictable necessity! of course leaving love and other Christian sentimentalities out of it!

65. Cf. 7[96].

66. Cf. 6[163], 10[D59], 10[D60].

67. *last gasp] ausklingende*, present participle of *ausklingen* = "to sound out," "resound," but also "to fade away." Cf. Aphorism 72.

68. *sentiments"]* "One is only good through compassion: it is therefore necessary that there be some compassion in all our feelings." {From Joseph Joubert, *Pensées, essais, maximes et correspondance de J. Joubert*, ed. Paul Raynal (Paris: Le Normant, 1850), 192.}

69. *needful,"]* {Reference to Christ's response (cf. Luke 10:42) to Martha, when she complains that she is doing all the work, while her sister Mary sits at Christ's feet. Christ's point is that she has chosen faith, which will bring her personal salvation, and that is all that matters. Related to the concept of *sola fides* (cf. Aphorism 22 and note 49).}

70. *neighbor,"*] {Cf. Luke 19:18 and 34; Matthew 19:19 and 22:39; Mark 12:31; Galatians 5:14; James 2:8.}

71. *autrui,"*] "live for others."

72. *or . . . action:*] *Sd*: as the genuine moral feelings

73. *prejudice*] *Vorurtheil*.

74. *individual . . . sentiment*] *"Mitempfindung und sociale Empfindung"*

75. *Kant . . . value*] {On the Kantian position, cf. "The moral disposition must be free from every sensuous condition." *The Critique of Practical Reason*, trans. Lewis White Beck (Chicago: University of Chicago Press, 1949), 183. Cf. the entire first part of the chapter entitled "The Incentives of Pure Practical Reason" (180–95).}

76. *Kant . . . tastelessness.)*] In place of this passage, the *Sd* has: 9[11]. Cf. also Schopenhauer, *Nachlaß* (cf. last note to Aphorism 116), 333.

77. *suffering . . . com-passion,*] Throughout this aphorism N puns on *Mitleid*, translated as "compassion." *Mit* = "with"; *Leid* = "suffering." *Mit-Leid* is uncharacteristically hyphenated here. Cf. note 40 to Aphorism 18.

78. *Yet . . . invigorating).*] *Sd*: Moreover a feeling of pleasure (the opposite of envy) is often activated by the sight of a situation opposed to ours. And then another feeling of pleasure at the idea that we would be able to help if we so chose: and finally, in the act of helping, the pleasure in itself of successful action.

79. *Pd*: 7[285].

80. *Compassion . . . suffering*] *Mitleid . . . Leid*. Cf. note 77 to Aphorism 133 and note 40 to Aphorism 18.

81. *If . . . place.*] *Pd*: To love someone and then to discover that he is suffering! But "to love," in and of itself, is in no way "to pity"! Likewise to admire, honor someone and then to discover that he suffers!

82. *Stoicism?*] {School of philosophy founded by Zeno of Citium around 300 BCE. Major Stoic philosophers included Seneca, Epictetus, and Marcus Aurelius.}

83. Cf. 2[19], 3[50].

84. *Pd*: If music is a reproduction of a reproduction of a feeling and nevertheless, by means of this detour, still allows us to take part in this feeling: — — — In order to reproduce the feeling of an other in ourselves, we either return to the cause of that feeling or to its effects: we ask: Why is he depressed? Or we use the expression of his eyes, voice, gait (or even their imitation in image or tone) and attain the same goal, even more surely through the 2nd as through the 1st way.

85. *Empathy.] Mitempfindung. Mit*= "with"; *Empfindung*= "sensation," "perception," "feeling," "sentiment." Cf. *Mitleid. Mit*= "with"; *Leid*= "suffering," translated as "compassion," but also "pity."

86. *rapturous] schwärmerisch.* Cf. note 15 to P3.

87. *pity] des Erbarmens.* Compared to *Mitleid*, which has been translated throughout as "compassion," *Erbarmen* is more elevated in style and often religiously inflected, as in "*Daß Gott erbarme!*" (God help us!).

88. *qualitas occulta]* "hidden (and hence mysterious) quality, essence."

89. *gift."]* Cf. Schopenhauer, *Nachlaß* (cf. last note to Aphorism 116), 180.

90. Cf. 4[210].

91. *ideal divine cannibalism.]* {Reference to the battle between Zeus and his father, Kronos. Heeding the prophecy that he would be destroyed by one of his children, Kronos devoured them at birth. When Zeus was born, Kronos's wife Rhea deceived her husband by feeding him a stone instead. Later Zeus overtook his father and forced him to regurgitate his children, Zeus's siblings. Cf. Hesiod, *Theogony*, 624ff.}

92. Cf. 3[18].

93. At the outset of *Pd*: It is not true (as Spencer claims) that what is genuinely moral is in the immediate consequences. Cf. H. Spencer, *Die Thatsachen der Ethik* {*Ethical facts*} (Stuttgart{: E. Schweizerbart'sche Verlagshandlung,} 1879, 84). *NL*.

94. *Even . . . neighbor.] Auch über den Nächsten hinweg.* The German phrase can mean both "ignoring" and "getting beyond,"

"transcending" one's neighbor. The same is true for the phrases "looks beyond" and "get beyond" in the body of the aphorism.

95. *plowshare] Pflugschar.* Original title for *Dawn*.

96. *Pd*: 4[210].

97. *likes . . . seen]* The phrase underscores the utopian aspect mentioned earlier in the sentence, for in Greek, "utopia" means "no place."

Book Three

1. *ultratraditional] altherkömmlich.* Cf. Aphorism 9, note 15.

2. Cf. 4[6].

3. *chanciness]* Here and throughout the aphorism, the word rendered as "chanciness" is *Zufall.* Cf. Aphorism 130, note 56.

4. *It . . . love.]* {According to Epicurus, the gods lived an eternal life in intercosmic realms. They were sublimely indifferent to the fate of mortals, as any such consideration would interfere with their own contentment. The gods rendered neither punishment nor reward.}

5. *vain!"]* The second of the ten commandments. Cf. Exodus 20:7. In German the pun on "in vain" (*unnützlich*) emerges much more forcefully; one should not take the lord's name "for nothing," i.e., without getting something for oneself in return.

6. *refugium]* "refuge."

7. Cf. 8[21]. *Pd*: Our culture tolerates expressions of pain whereas the Greek philosophers had profound contempt for them. —Where does this come from?—

8. *Philoctetes]* {In Homer's *Iliad*, Philoctetes is the leader of the seven ships of Methone against the Trojans, but is left behind at Lemnos having suffered a snakebite (*Iliad* 2.718–23). Philoctetes is the subject of an extant play by Sophocles as well as of missing plays by Aeschylus and Euripides.}

9. *One . . . tragedy.]* Cf. Plato's *Republic* 605b–e {*KSA* has c–d}. {As evidence of the mimetic arts' ability to corrupt, Plato shows how we praise the poet for causing us to suffer along with his characters, whereas in life, we think it wise for a man to "remain

calm and endure." In the same passage, Plato consigns the expression of emotion to women.}

10. Cf. 2[64].

11. *Perhaps . . . point.]* Sd: Such was the case for [Friedrich Schlegel] the Romantics with Shakespeare; so too for [Kant's adherents] the Classicists with antiquity.

12. *Pd*: 7[214]. Cf. 7[140].

13. *Apollo Belvedere.]* {Antiquity's most famous statue: a Roman, marble copy of a Greek original bronze, most likely by the fourth-century Athenian sculptor Leochares, and currently in the Vatican. The subject of an influential essay (1764) by the German art historian J. J. Winckelmann (1717–68), who felt it represented the highest ideal of antique art, the Apollo Belvedere has since become, in German culture, shorthand for the art of antiquity as a whole.}

14. *"Classicists"]* Classicisten

15. *Pd*: Who has been upset by these questions before? Rousseau? Just the opposite: he says civilization is to blame for our bad morality. I say: good morality is to blame for our wretched civilization! Preferably in the desert!

16. *attempts]* Versuche. Here as throughout his work, N exploits the nuances of *Versuch*, which means "attempt," "experiment," "proof."

17. *one . . . morality]* allein-moralisch-machende Moral. Nietzschean neologism and a word play on "*{der} alleinseligmachende Glaube*" = "{the} only saving faith," i.e., Catholicism.

18. *mores, one]* Sd: mores [has offered a testimony that cannot be refuted] one

19. Cf. 10[B32], 10[B30].

20. *somebody]* N himself in *WB*.

21. *There . . . experience?]* {Reference to the eponymous hero from Byron's play, *Manfred* (1817). Overcome by the pain of existence and of knowing, Manfred begs the gods for the ability to forget, which they are unable to convey. N also composed a "Manfred" overture.}

22. *"Ce . . . choses."]* "That which is important is not at all the people: but the things." {Carnot; cf. 10[B32].}

23. *But . . . boot?]* {Germany had defeated France in the Franco-Prussian War in 1871 and declared itself a unified nation that same year. Many Germans of this period thus tended to view the French with the condescension of the victor toward the vanquished.}

24. *Niebuhr . . . Carnot.]* Cf. B. G. Niebuhr, *Geschichte des Zeitalters der Revolution* (*History of the age of revolution*) (Hamburg{: Agentur des Rauhen Hauses,} 1845), 1:334–39.

25. *Pd*: 6[383].

26. *flowering,]* *Ausblühen* = both a "blooming" and a "blooming out" or "fading."

27. *culture]* {i.e., Athens in the fifth century BCE}

28. *Sophists,]* From the Greek, meaning "wise person," "person skilled at a particular activity." Around the fifth century BCE, the word became associated with a group of educators (Protagoras, Gorgias, Hippias, to name a few) who offered instruction in oratory and other practical skills. Their skeptical, anthropocentric teachings caused them to be labeled cynics, hair-splitting self-servers, and the corrupters of youth. Hence the attacks on them by the Socratic schools.

29. *error . . . simplicior]* "error is simpler than truth."

30. Cf. 7[1].

31. *Paestum . . . Athens,]* {Three cities in antiquity famous for their architectural treasures.}

32. *music . . . ours,]* {For a characterization of this music, see *HAH* 219 and *MM* 144.}

33. *Pd*: Passion for male nakedness is the soul of art in antiquity. It was only from that vantage point that they gained a feeling for female beauty — this is completely inaccessible to us. What does all our prattle about the Greeks amount to? Cf. 7[150]; also the following underlined passage in N's copy of Stendhal, *Rome, Naples et Florence* (Paris{: Michel Lévy Frères,} 1854), 333: "Le plaisant, c'est que nous prétendons avoir le goût grec dans les arts manquant de la passion principale qui rendait les Grecs sensibles aux arts" {The funny thing is we claim to have Greek taste in the arts while lacking the essential passion that made the Greeks responsive to the arts}.

34. *homo pamphagus]* "all-consuming human."

35. Cf. 7[32].

36. *Aeschylus's]* {Author of the *Oresteia*, a trilogy dealing with the violent history of the house of Atreus, Aeschylus was also a soldier; his epitaph on the monument to him in Gela mentions his deeds in battle and not his poetry.}

37. *Aeschylus's day, are] Sd*: Aeschylus's day [or the English in Shakespeare's day] are

38. *fear . . . compassion,]* Here and throughout the aphorism, N is alluding to the definition of tragedy in Aristotle's *Poetics* as "a dramatic, not . . . narrative form; with incidents arousing pity and fear, wherewith to accomplish its catharsis of such emotions." Quoted from Jonathan Barnes, *The Complete Works of Aristotle* (Princeton: Princeton University Press, 1984), 2320, also cited as 1449b27ff. Cf. *Poetics*, 1452a2, 1452b32–1453a6, 1456a38.

39. *affections" as] Sd*: affections [and to every hint of sentimentality] as

40. *philosophers . . . tragedy.]* Cf. Plato's *Republic* 602bff.

41. *manliness are] Sd*: manliness *and danger* are

42. Cf. 6[163], 8[47], 8[103].

43. *moral law,]* Sittengesetz, in contrast to *das moralische Gesetz*, which one finds in Kant.

44. *by . . . him] Sd*: if one to him — the other we know so poorly!

45. Cf. 7[108].

46. *Credat . . . Apella]* "The Jew Apella believes that." Cf. Horace, *Satires* I, 5, 100. {Apella is a proper name designating here a gullible Jew.}

47. *Pd*: 4[243].

48. *chorus.]* {In Greek tragedy the chorus represented public opinion and often commented on the actions of the hero.}

49. *Those . . . daily.] Die Täglich-Abgenützten.* N continues his assault against utility (*Nützlichkeit*), utilitarianism (*Nützlichkeitslehre*), and efficiency (*Nützeffekt*) by punning on *abnützen* = "to use up," "wear out."

50. *they were used,] man benütze sie.* Cf. the previous note.

51. *lack.]* *Notstand.* Usually means a "state of emergency" (as in a political crisis), but may also denote "a condition of lack" (in this case, lack of spirit).

52. *do . . . are]* *Sd*: are poorly ordered as long as the most talented minds are obliged to attend to them in order that widespread ruin is not unavoidable. Actually they are

53. *transform . . . sense]* {Reference in part to the hotly debated social security legislation (i.e., national accident and health insurance as well as pensions for senior citizens), which Bismarck was designing at the time, in no small measure to thwart the revolutionary aspirations of the socialists, and which he implemented later in the 1880s.}

54. *Pd*: 10[D 88].

55. *great . . . day]* It is clear from the *Pd* (cf. the previous note) that N means, among others, the three wars leading to German unification: The German-Danish War (1864), the Austro-Prussian or Seven Weeks War (1866), and the Franco-Prussian War (1870–71).

56. *prejudice,]* *Vorurtheil.*

57. *So . . . light!]* Variation on the epigraph to *Dawn.*

58. *Pd*: 4[248], 2[249]. Cf. 4[197]; 4[237].

59. *laurel wreath]* {Ancient heroes in battle and conquering generals were crowned with a laurel wreath. It is also the traditional headdress of Dionysus, god of wine, in whose celebration classical tragedy was created.}

60. *Pd*: 4[247]. Cf. 4[244], 4[245], 7[63].

61. *In . . . one:]* Cf. Hesiod, *Works and Days,* 106–201.

62. Cf. 9[7].

63. *culture]* *Bildung*, usually rendered as "education." N is drawing on the extremely important role that the concept of *Bildung* played in the development of German history and culture. Having adopted the Platonic doctrine that to know the good is to do the good and hence to become virtuous, the emerging middle ranks in the eighteenth century relied on the twin pillars of education (*Bildung*) and virtue (*Tugend*) to distinguish themselves from a corrupt aristocracy and to forge their own identity and culture as a distinct, self-empowered class. See especially N's attacks on German culture and education in *UO*.

64. *particularly . . . symbolism.] Sd*: one worshipped nature as symbolism and was religious without faith.

65. *Corneille,"]* {Important in this context is the fact that, in his dramas, Corneille adhered strictly to the three unities of time, place, and plot deemed by Aristotle in his *Poetics* to be the basic requirements of good tragedy.}

66. Cf. 5[37].

67. *most . . . earth:]* {N is referring to the royal style or honorific title *Rex Christianissimus* (Most Christian of Kings), which was reserved for the French monarch. The title is related to France's status as "the eldest daughter of the Church" owing to the spirited Christian advocacy of Clovis I (466?–511). The style had wide currency in the Renaissance.}

68. *consider . . . here!]* {Among other things, Pascal was a leading mathematician, physicist, and inventor, not to mention one of France's preeminent stylists and one of the world's greatest philosophers of religion. He frequently incorporated calculations of probability into his arguments for the existence of God.}

69. *quietists,]* {Adherents of quietism, a type of Christian mysticism that believes that communion with God is possible when the soul is at complete rest, creating a passive receptivity to His spirit.}

70. *fervor] Brunst. Brunst* is most commonly used to denote being "in heat," as in the breeding period for mammals; *Inbrunst* (= inner *Brunst*) is the more customary word for "fervor."

71. *owing . . . gesture,]* Cf. 7[268].

72. *founder . . . monasteries,]* {Armand Jean le Bouthillier de Rancé (1626–1700), commendatory abbot of the abbey Notre Dame de la Trappe, initiated reforms and increased the severity of the observances of the Cistercian order to the degree that his adherents became known as Trappists, subsequently renamed as Cistercians of the Strict Observance. The monks observe absolute silence, are strict vegetarians, and devote their lives to prayer and manual labor.}

73. *Huguenots:]* {French Protestants who held their first synod or council in Paris in 1559. Their rapid increase in numbers and the entry of many well-placed noblemen into their ranks were

viewed as a severe threat to the Roman Catholic Church and to the monarchy and resulted in eight brutal civil wars between 1562 and 1598.}

74. *Port-Royal]* {Port-Royal-des-Champs near Paris, a Cistercian convent. From the 1640s the spiritual center of Jansenism, the Catholic movement that, similar to Calvinism, believed in strict predestination. Blaise Pascal lived in the community of Port-Royal from 1654 until his death in 1662.}

75. Cf. 6[337]. *Pd*: Fear of wit, *esprit* {spirit, wit}, "which pokes out the eyes of the soul," as the German concludes.

76. *Esprit]* Here: "intellectual vitality," "playfulness," "wit."

77. *Hegel]* N here puns on the French translation of *Geist* as *esprit*. Hegel's best-known work, *Phänomenologie des Geistes* (*Phenomenology of Spirit*) was translated into French as *Phénoménologie de l'esprit*.

78. *bad . . . him.]* {Regarding Hegel's style, N was in agreement with Schopenhauer, who refers to "Hegelism" as "senseless gibberish." *The World as Will and Representation II*, trans. E. F. Payne (New York: Dover, 1969), 34 (bk. 1, ch. 4, n. 6).}

79. *learning,]* *Wissenschaft*. Cf. Aphorism 270 and note 44. *Wissenschaft* is rendered as "learnedness" later in this sentence.

80. *ranted]* {Schopenhauer became a lecturer at the University of Berlin in 1820, where Hegel was established as a significant professor and popular lecturer. Schopenhauer scheduled his own lectures at the same time as Hegel's, a challenge he lost insofar as few students showed up for his course, which was canceled, further increasing his animosity toward Hegel and his philosophy.}

81. *Pd*: Philosophical educators want too much: to give precepts for everyone, this is tantamount to flailing about in generalities and preaching to animals. One must choose limited circles and promote the morality appropriate for them, e.g., for human beings thirsty for knowledge.

82. *The previous . . . society."] Sd*: No matter how our century is comprised: one hundred such educators and one hundred of their pupils would suffice to give it a new character.

83. *Pd*: Classical education! And through it you learned nothing of the very things in which the ancients educated their youth,

you didn't learn to speak like them, write like them, to move beautifully and proudly like them, wrestle, throw, box like them! You learned nothing of the asceticism of the ancient pedagogical philosophers! You haven't learned one single antique virtue as the ancients learned them! In general, no feeling that matters more to the ancients than the moderns! Life's goals and the arrangement of the day—nothing is presented to you in the spirit of the ancients! Your festivals and holidays are without a trace of that past! [in all your action and desire] Your friendship, your social interaction conforms to no model! You don't practice unremittingly dialectics or the fencing-art of conversation! You don't even learn to read Greek and Latin the way you read works [in your native language] of living nations! Let alone that you would speak them like your native language—then, namely only then, would the ⟨lang⟩uage teach a little about education! Don't allow yourselves to be deceived! And even if they counter with the phrase "formal education," just laugh and point to [all] the best teachers in our high schools! Do they have "education in form"? And if not, how are they supposed to teach it!—Even so, you managed to experience ever so slightly that the ancients were completely different from us and that they valued completely different things with regard to education: but the detour by which one led you to this experience is, however, simply too strange! Haven't you ever sighed that they squandered your youth by imparting to you a little bit of history in a torturous and presumptuous fashion, along with the arrogance of having thereby partaken of a classical education?—No, you have never sighed! Who, after all, would have taught you to sigh!—

84. *"Fate . . . sighs!"]* {The verses are N's.}

85. *scholarship!] Wissenschaft.*

86. *cannot . . . happy,] selig machen.* The phrase can also have religious connotations meaning cannot "save our soul."

87. *Pd*: 10[D88]. Cf. 4[40], 4[86], 6[428].

88. *German . . . Romantics:]* {F. K. von Savigny (1779–1861), founder of historical jurisprudence, had close ties to the Romantics, who themselves turned to historical studies. The Romantic poet Friedrich von Hardenberg (a.k.a. Novalis—1772–1801) insti-

gated renewed interest in the Christianity of the Middle Ages, and many Romantics had a fascination with the figure of Mary. Both Friedrich Schlegel and the Grimm brothers pursued the history of literature and of language: the latter claimed to have collected their well-known fairy tales from the folk, while Schlegel studied Sanskrit and India as the possible birthplace of poetry.}

89. *natural scientists:]* *Naturforscher*, "nature researchers," but also "seekers in nature." Reference to speculative works such as Schelling's "Ideas Towards a Philosophy of Nature" (1797) and "Views from the Night-Side of Science" (1808) by G. H. Schubert (1780–1860).

90. *German composers,]* {In addition to Wagner, who was for N the Romantic *par excellence*, he might also have in mind C. M. von Weber (1786–1826), F. Schubert (1797–1828), R. Schumann (1810–56), F. Mendelssohn (1809–47) and F. Liszt (1811–86).}

91. *knowing."]* Cf. Kant, Preface to the Second Edition of *The Critique of Pure Reason*, B xxx: "I have therefore found it necessary to deny *knowledge* in order to make room for *faith*."

92. *Pd:* to possess great inner experiences and to look at them with a spiritual eye—in Germany only among the clergy and its successors. In France, England, and Italy the aristocracy lived through and thought through a great deal owing to political and relig{ious} change.

93. Cf. 4[302].

94. *treatment!"]* Cf. *Odyssey* 20:18. {In this particular "ignominious situation" Odysseus is smarting from having, upon his belated return from the Trojan War, found his wife's suitors in his house.}

95. *well!"]* Cf. Plutarch's *Parallel Lives* (Themistocles 11).

96. *prejudices]* *Vorurtheile*.

97. *Pd:* The gestures assumed by members of refined society express that one has the feeling of power, e.g., not fall *[sic]* into an armchair as if exhausted: answer *[sic]* a verbal provocation with composure and a clear head and not horrified and crushed and mortified: in the train not to lean back: not to seem tired even when standing for hours, i.e., one affects constantly dignified physical strength and a psychic feeling of power through constant

serenity and civility.—The priest also represents a feeling of p⟨ower⟩: supposing he and the nobility did not have it but only affected it; then they would acquire a feeling of it as a result of the effect of their role-playing.

98. *charming] reizvoll.* Cf. note 33 to Aphorism 114.

99. *Spanish step]* {The name of an equestrian drill—a type of extremely stylized trot in which the diagonally raised forelegs remain extended for an unusually long period.}

100. *performance . . . theatricality] Spiel . . . Schauspiel. Spiel* = "game" or "play" (as in: a child at play); *Schauspiel* = a "theatrical play" or, more generally, a "spectacle."

101. *Pd*: *Mp* XV 1, 42: (Criminal's) hour not yet come: reflection on the redevelopment of personalities would have to have become as popular as theological problems have been, and the churches would have to be built for this type of teaching. *Mp* XV 1, 79: 1) treat oneself as sick 2) sanatoriums 3) churches 4) voluntary renunciation of justice 5) put up with a good portion of parasites without being destroyed by them 6) we all suffer from the criminal's bad opinion. There are no doctors. *M* II 1: The measures that society metes out to a malefactor create in him a permanent thirst for revenge and for taking a stand against society. The malefactor who acts out of poverty and need becomes, after his punishment, a malefactor out of principle. Protection of society almost seems to require that anyone convicted even once of a crime be viewed as a sworn enemy and kept in permanent custody. By contrast, I recommend creating as much anonymity for the criminal as possible so that, after the punishment, he can regain his reputation for integrity: one ought to treat him as someone who is sick and in need of a change of air and look after him not with lofty charity but with the physician's hand. Should he find it in his own interest to live for a longer period of time under custody—and thus to find protection against himself—then he should remain imprisoned for as long as he himself thinks fit; one must make clear to him the possibility and the means of being healed but also not wish to force him to get well. Society ought to view the Christian principle of forgiving your enemies and blessing them that curse you {Cf. Matthew 5:44} as a piece of wisdom

by virtue of which the sensitivity to life is lightened. In very many cases one can reckon criminality as belonging to spiritual errors in judgment, as the consequences of a bad or deficient intellectual education. Accordingly, criminals would be treated like a less serious species of the mentally ill to whom it would not be impossible to return good spirits and freedom of disposition. Therefore, extreme consideration, anonymity, and frequent change of location. The loss that society suffers from the physically ill is just as great as the one it suffers at the hands of criminals: sick people spread worry and ill humor, are not productive, exhaust other people's revenues, require caretakers, doctors, upkeep, thus the time and energy of those who are healthy. In primitive conditions, the sick person is treated like a criminal; wild horses trample to death every sick horse in their herd, because a sick animal is injurious to the common safety.—Formerly, one viewed a sick person as guilty. The day will come when one will view the guilty person as sick.

102. *thee."]* Cf. *Meier Helmbrecht*, lines 546ff., a didactic and satirical Middle High German poem written ca. 1250–80, by Wernher der Gartenaere. N is quoting from *Alte hoch- und niederdeutsche Volkslieder mit Abhandlung und Anmerkungen* {Old High- and Low-German folk songs with essays and notes}, Bd. 2, ed. Ludwig Uhland (Stuttgart{: Cotta,} 1844), which is vol. 3 of *Uhlands Schriften zur Geschichte der Dichtung und Sage* {Uhland's writings on the history of literature and saga} (Stuttgart{: Cotta,} 1866), 72. Cf. *CW* 10:1[30] and *CW* 11:18[1].

103. *Pd:* Our mealtime (not only in hotels but in all well-to-do classes of society) is barbarism compared to Greek simplicity. What dreams such people must have! What foulness and hypersensitivity must result! Have a look at their arts, the desserts to their meals! See if pepper and contradiction don't rule!

104. *Danaë . . . gold.]* {Danaë, daughter of Eurydice and Acrisius—King of Argos. Having been warned by an oracle that he is to be killed by Danaë's son, Acrisius locks Danaë in a bronze chamber where she is visited by Zeus in the form of a golden shower. As a result of the visit, she gives birth to Perseus, slayer of Medusa as well as Acrisius.}

105. *the conviction . . . truth]* Sd: religions and by wars

106. *with . . . Mexico).]* Sd: commit crimes (break oaths, lay waste to countries, burn heretics, exterminate [nations and people] Jews, lead crusades and so on

107. *that . . . conscience.]* Sd: one just set one's heart on it: this heart that had grown accustomed to, and spoiled by, setting itself on something!

108. Cf. 5[21].

109. *crossed . . . Rubicon,]* {The Rubicon is a river that marked the border between Italy and Cisalpine Gaul (today Rubicone). In 49 BCE Julius Caesar, after some hesitation and purportedly saying that the die was cast, crossed the Rubicon and precipitated civil war.}

110. *just . . . either-or.]* {Reference to the Jews' original prosperity in Egypt. Cf. Exodus 1:7ff.}

111. *sperneri se sperni]* "spurn being spurned yourself." Cf. note 113 to Aphorism 56.

112. *preserve . . . self-respect]* Beginning with the first appearance of "contemptible" above, N has been setting up a forceful pun that operates on the word pair *verachten* (to have contempt for) and *achten* (to have respect for). By using a form of *verachten* four times, N linguistically piles up the weight of "European" contempt for the Jews against which their own "self-respect" (*sich . . . selbst achten*) then stands in powerful contrast.

113. *seventh day . . . people]* {Cf. Genesis 2:2.}

114. Cf. 7[97].

115. *class.]* *Stand*, which may also mean "situation," "condition."

116. *inflame]* *brünstig machen*. The phrase also implies bringing someone to the animal state of "being in heat." Cf. note 70 to Aphorism 192.

117. *bestia triumphans]* "triumphant beast."

118. Cf. 4[68], 6[116], 7[216], 8[45], 10[D74].

119. *straightforward,]* *schlicht*. Cf. Aphorism 231.

120. *superstition . . . believe]* *Aberglauben . . . Glauben*.

121. *gym teacher]* *Turnvater*, literally, "gymnastics father." Reference to Friedrich Ludwig Jahn, a.k.a. "Turnvater Jahn" (1778–1852),

a philologist who came to advocate physical fitness. Jahn was a committed proponent of nationalism.

122. *Nil admirari]* "Marvel at nothing." Cf. Horace, *Epistles* I, 6: "'Marvel at nothing'—that is perhaps the one and only thing that can make a man happy and keep him so."

123. *admirari . . . philosophari.]* "to marvel is to philosophize."

Book Four

1. *in summa:]* "in sum," "in total."

2. Cf. 4[133].

3. *a theologian]* Alexandre R. Vinet {(1797–1847), who was crucial in establishing the Reformation in French-speaking Switzerland}. Cf. 3[67].

4. *greedier.]* Added to the *Sd* at the end: Which state is it in which someone calls a thing beautiful? Perhaps the one that reminds him of what tends to make him happy.

5. Cf. 4[84].

6. *ennui"] Langenweile*, which translates literally as "long while."

7. *Pd*: The animals he runs into most frequently give him the habitual feeling of superiority (pride) or inferiority (humility).

8. *indulgence!] Nachsicht*. N playfully contrasts "indulgence" (*Nachsicht*: *nach*="after," "behind"; *Sicht*="view," "sight") with "more cautious" (*vorsichtiger*: *vor*="before," "ahead"; *Sicht*="view," "sight"). Both words establish a metaphoric of optics upon which the last sentence in the aphorism builds. The view (*Sicht*) ahead (*vor*) or behind (*nach*) returns as "seeing askew."

9. *Pd*: Suspenseful anticipation of the best brought about by: a coarse, imperious tone often in Beethoven's music: in Mozart a joviality of trusty fellows, "let's have a cheery old time," which heart and spirit must put up with a little bit; in Wagner an impulsive and importunate agitation at which the most patient loses his good mood and one comes to cra⟨v⟩e a ["bright view of the beautiful soul"] view of spirit or beauty or soul. (With Wagner silence has something numbing about it, like the smell of morphine.)

Unconscious foil, basis of the effect of many people, from out of this shadow side they step into the light.

10. *he . . . ones.]* Reference to Wagner. Cf. 4[49].

11. *sensibilities . . . directions] Sd*: we are so overrefined in things moral

12. Cf. 3[134] and *GM* I, 4.

13. *the simple as the bad,] das Schlichte als das Schlechte.* The anaphora (*das*, *Schl-*) and the straightforward vowel shift (from *i* to *e*) add to this phrase an arresting exclamation point.

14. *Pd*: "You have grown hoarse, therefore you are refuted." ego

15. *Junker Arrogance!]* {"Junker" is the title for a member of the aristocratic class, particularly in Prussia.} N is alluding to act 2, scene 4, of Wagner's *Meistersinger von Nürnberg*{, where Hans Sachs, the "master singer," says these words to Walter von Stolzing (*Stolz* = "pride"; *Stolzing* = "Prideling")}.

16. Cf. 4[24]. *Pd*: One is on one's guard against rejecting (or treating conventionally) the gratitude of someone who feels truly obliged to us: it offends him profoundly.

17. *Punishment . . . itself.]* {Rousseau makes the same point in his *Confessions*, trans. J. M. Cohen (London: Penguin, 1953), 1:43.}

18. Cf. 7[36].

19. *the . . . callings:] Pd*: philosophers of contempt for the world

20. *And now!]* Crossed out at the end in *Pd*: Where should he take his model of the ocean of ugliness from if not from the affects agitations outrages furies and ecstasies of his own inner sea?

21. *morality . . . stage.]* {Allusion to Friedrich Schiller's address "The Stage Viewed as a Moral Institution" (1784, published 1785) in which Schiller passionately argues that the stage is a powerful instrument of moral education that will advance the aims of a universal humanity.}

22. *Macbeth]* {Title hero in one of Shakespeare's best-known tragedies. Out of ambition to be king, Macbeth, commander to Duncan I, king of Scotland, murders the latter and assumes the throne in 1040.}

23. *Tristan and Isolde]* {Characters in a music drama of the same name (1859) by Richard Wagner, based on the medieval

poem by Gottfried von Straßburg. During her engagement to King Marke, Isolde begins her passionate affair with Tristan, which continues after the marriage.}

24. *Ajax, Philoctetes, Oedipus)]* {Allusion to three (or perhaps five) of the seven complete, extant plays by Sophocles (496?–406 BCE), first of the great Greek tragedians. "*Oedipus*" is probably a reference to *Oedipus Tyrannus*, but may also include *Antigone*, and *Oedipus at Colonus*, the other two plays in the Oedipus trilogy.}

25. *Pd*: 7[13].

26. *Pd*: 6[433]. Cf. also 6[429], 6[431], 6[435], 6[441].

27. *Subtlety] Feinheit*, also "refinement," "sophistication."

28. *Aristotle.]* Cf. *Rhetoric* II, 15, 1390b, 28–31{: "A clever stock will degenerate towards the insane type of character, like the descendants of Alcibiades or of the elder Dionysius; a steady stock towards the fatuous and torpid type, like the descendants of Cimon, Pericles, and Socrates." *The Complete Works of Aristotle*, ed. Jonathan Barnes (Princeton: Princeton University Press, 1984), 2:2215–16}.

29. *The . . . hypocrisy.] Sd*: Through heredity our intentions finally turn into organs and instincts

30. Cf. 6[33], 7[67], 7[284].

31. *pirate."]* N is quoting from Byron, *Vermischte Schriften* II: 108. *NL*.

32. *presents] vorführen*. The verb may be read matter-of-factly as "to present," "bring forward," but it can also connote a certain pomposity (as in "to put on display") as well as a kind of mechanical patness (as in "to trot out").

33. *adorn . . . makeup]* Another example of the poetic effect of N's prose: "*schmücken . . . schminken*." N's depiction of Wagner as a deceiver, an actor (*Schau-Spieler*) climaxes in *WA*, where he is referred to as the Cagliostro of Modernity.

34. *half-stupefied] halb-betäubt*. Pun on *betäubt*, which can also mean "deaf" or "deafened."

35. *dolce far niente,]* "sweet to do nothing."

36. Cf. 2[31].

37. *remaineth!"]* {N quotes, in slightly abbreviated form, the last strophe of Martin Luther's popular hymn "A Mighty Fortress Is Our God."}

38. At the conclusion of *Pd*: so too with women.

39. *Pd*: When fantasy wanes, a people has its sagas presented on stage. For people who feel intensely, this nearness of the illusion is too coarse, compassion too powerfully excited.

40. *epic rhapsodist]* {In ancient Greece a wandering minstrel or court poet who recited poetry from heart or extemporized and stitched together (*rhapsodist*= "stitcher") passages, often from Homer's *Iliad* and *Odyssey*.}

41. *Pd*: 6[201].

42. *Scylla and Charybdis.]* Idiom for a dangerous situation, usually a dilemma, from which it is difficult to escape. Scylla, a six-headed sea monster, lives across from the maelstrom Charybdis, and together they make passage through the narrow Straits of Messina virtually impossible. Cf. Book 12 of Homer's *The Odyssey*.

43. *Pd*: 6[260].

44. *scholarship!]* *Wissenschaft*. Cf. Aphorism 193, note 79.

45. *powerlessness]* *Ohnmacht*, literally "without (*ohne*) power (*Macht*)" and hence a reprise of that phrase earlier in the aphorism. *Ohnmacht* is also the common word for "swoon" or "faint."

46. *let . . . pass!]* {Reference to Christ's plea to his father in the Garden of Gethsemane to be released from the burden of crucifixion. Cf. Matthew 26:39.}

47. *Pd*: The ignoble habit of not letting opportunities to show ourselves in a pathetic light pass by. Many people turn virtuous only in order to make others suffer.

48. *Sd*: With their activity children do not fight for their livelihood; they know that no final significance attaches to their actions. Anyone who lives like children with regard to these two points remains childlike.

49. *greedy]* *habsüchtig*, which means literally: "addicted to having."

50. *Chi . . . è,]* "He who has not is not."

51. *Pd*: How humans have dwelt among animals and plants! As the greatest enemies of both. They live off them and, in the end, grow sentimental toward those they have subjugated and sacrificed.

52. *dwelt] gehaust*, from *hausen* = "to house," "lodge," "reside," "dwell," but also "to wreak havoc," "cause turmoil."

53. *the one . . . enough.] Pd*: the latter because he misunderstood the other way too much, the former because he understood the other too well.

54. Cf. 3[8].

55. *Pd*: The sound of a single consonant (an "r" for instance) is enough to make us doubt the honesty of the expressed feeling. And likewise with style. Here is an area of crudest misprision. E.g., the Germans misapprehend every Jew who expresses himself in German.

56. Cf. 10[E94].

57. *profanum vulgus,]* "profane rabble." {Cf. Horace, *Odes* III, 1, i.}

58. *completed] fertig gemacht*. Humorous pun: the phrase may also mean "exasperated," "drove crazy," or even "lambasted."

59. *intellectual conscience]* Cf. *JS* 2.

60. *ad majorem dei gloriam]* "to the greater glory of God." {Originally a remark by Pope Gregory I (540–604) in his *Dialogues*, it was later adopted as the Jesuit motto. During Gregory's reign the papacy took over the political leadership in Italy and began to consolidate its immense holdings into what was to become, in the next century, the Papal States.}

61. *being."]* N is quoting from Byron, *Vermischte Schriften* II: 146. *NL.*

62. Cf. *JS* 169. *Pd*: The cowardly rush into the midst of the enemy, why?

63. Cf. 4[103].

64. *Facta . . . ficta!]* "Facts! . . . Fictitious facts!"

65. *supposed] vermeintlich*, which means primarily "supposed," "alleged," but can also imply "would-be," "imaginary," "pretended."

66. *had an effect.]* Perfect tense of the verb *wirken*, the stem of the German word *Wirklichkeit* (reality).

67. Cf. 6[10].

68. *To . . . affair.] Sd*: To practice usury with one's self and to sell oneself—as teacher, civil servant, artist—at the highest, indeed at an unfair price, is base.

69. *Pd*: 4[281].

70. *Sd*: Good-natured people have acquired their character through the constant fear of foreign attack. If good-natured people ever get beyond their fear, their outbursts of rage are dreadful. *Pd*: Fear of foreign attack makes good-natured people such that they did not want to appear irritating but instead well-meaning. The rage of good-natured people is then dreadful for they lack all experience and get beyond their fear.

71. *tried and true] wohlgespielt*, which can also mean "well or surely, certainly acted, feigned."

72. Cf. 3[12].

73. At the beginning of *Sd*: The weakest sects are, relatively speaking, the most bearable.

74. *sects.] Pd*: parties.

75. *just . . . arrows.]* {The hermit and fiend is Philoctetes. Having learned from an oracle that Troy will fall only after he retrieves Hercules' bow and arrows, Odysseus travels to the island of Lemnos with Achilles' son Neoptolemus to convince Philoctetes, who is in possession of the bow and arrow and who had been left on the island owing to a severe wound, to sail for Troy (*Iliad* 2:722ff.). In Sophocles' *Philoctetes*, the honest Neoptolemus is an unwilling participant in Odysseus's trickery.}

76. *propylaea]* Plural of *propylaeum*, from the Greek: *propylaion* = "gateway." A vestibule or entrance to a temple. Well known in German culture as the title of an important, programmatic art journal (1798–1800), edited by Goethe and designed to be a gateway into (neo)classicism.

77. *Pd*: Timid people who behave as if they had stolen their limbs take their revenge in solitude through a feeling of power.

78. *philosophy.] Fe*; Psychology in *Le*; faulty manuscript.

79. *audience.]* Added to the end in *Pd*: This is the latest farce concerning German geniuses of originality.

80. *Pd*: Even today a person, if he lives apart, with little learning, a few thoughts, and a great deal of arrogance, easily considers himself a prophet without whom, as he believes with all his heart, humanity cannot get on.

81. *it!"]* Quotation from W.E.H. Lecky, *Methodismus*, 40.

82. Cf. 7[139].

83. *absinthe and acqua fortis.]* {Absinthe is a yellowish-green, distilled liqueur made of wormwood and other spices, which can cause hallucinations and mental deterioration. *Acqua fortis*, another name for nitric acid, was used by the alchemists to separate alloys containing gold and silver. Water-soluble, it is highly caustic and corrosive.}

84. *stone guest]* The dead Commander in any number of treatments of the Don Juan myth. Cf. note 171 to Aphorism 77.

85. *sanctified Sunday.]* {Following from the Old Testament commandment "Remember the Sabbath day, to keep it holy" (Exodus 20:8), proscriptions against activity on Sunday became increasingly severe in Puritan England.}

86. *Pd*: At the sight of cheerful festivities, upon hearing joyful music, people who have been deeply fatigued by life experience an unspeakably moving emotion: a grave veiled with roses and the roses have no idea what they veil. Children who lie on their deathbed amid child's games. This moving emotion is a refraction of cheerfulness through the somber terrain {*Grund*} of fatigue—not a substantiated {*begründetes*} judgment about the cheerful life.

87. *pity]* Erbarmen.

88. *prey . . . people!]* *Pd*: prey: thus are the saints to be judged.

89. *Pd*: We don't consider animals to be moral! And animals wouldn't consider us moral either! Our humanity is perhaps a presumption.

90. Cf. 6[227].

91. Cf. 6[117].

92. *Quietists]* Cf. note 69 to Aphorism 192.

93. *coquettish caprices]* *Sd*: affectation

94. Cf. 6[299], 9[2].

95. *wastelands, quagmires,]* *Sd*: deserts, oceans

96. *stylites?]* {Christian ascetics who lived standing upon a pillar (Greek: *stylos*). Cf. Aphorism 14 and note 32.}

97. *Pd*: If, as one claims, Homer nodded off on the job from time to time, then he was a subtler mind than all those who never slept. From time to time a piece of foolishness: otherwise no one

can endure us, and we turn into taskmasters whom one hates while nevertheless following.

98. *Finesse] Feinheit*, also translated as "refinement," "subtlety."

99. *as . . . job,]* Cf. Horace, *Ars poetica* 357ff: {"and yet I also feel aggrieved, whenever good Homer 'nods.'" In the same passage one finds as well the prototype for an artist "whose ambition never sleeps." It is the epic poet Choerilus, who traveled with Alexander the Great and was paid to sing his praises. According to Horace, his "one or two good lines cause laughter and surprise" (ibid., 357–58).}

100. *their wisdom] Sd*: morality

101. *whoever . . . drive] Pd*: said Sch⟨openhauer⟩ — judgment of an uncontrolled sexual drive

102. Cf. 7[258].

103. *Pythagoreans]* {Members of a philosophical school and religious brotherhood founded by Pythagoras of Samnos (580–500 BCE). According to Diogenes Laërtius, *Lives of the Eminent Philosophers* (7.10), the students of Pythagoras were required to listen to their master in total silence for five years before taking their exams.}

104. At the beginning of *Pd*: Every time I learn of a death, I have [?] the impression that

105. *Pd*: Words don't make promises, but instead what lies unspoken behind them. On the contrary, words discharge a force and make promises less forceful.

106. *"The . . . Fichte!]* {N is summarizing and paraphrasing the sentiments in Fichte's "Demand That the Princes of Europe Return Freedom of Thought" (1793), a powerfully expressed response to the censorship laws that had gone into effect as part of the infamous Prussian Religious Edict instituted by Friedrich Wilhelm II in 1788. Cf. Fichte, *Gesamtausgabe der Bayerischen Akademie der Wissenschaften* ("Collected edition of the Bavarian academy of sciences"), ed. R. Lauth and H. Gliwitzky (Stuttgart/Bad Cannstatt: Frommann-Holzboog, 1964), I, 1:187.}

107. *and . . . pleasures!] Pd*: Many pleasures would be lacking without our courage for pain

108. Cf. 7[42].

109. *Pd*: Most of the time our aversion arises instinctively: the reasons we give are usually something else and don't match the instinct. That we give reasons in the first place is self-cajolery.

110. Cf. 4[301], 4[299].

111. *Pd*: moderation is beautiful, its shortcoming is that it appears rough and austere.

112. Cf. 8[1].

113. Cf. 6[205]. *Pd*: I wish for an environment in which one is ashamed to voice one's weakness and sickness: but the one I have works in the opposite direction, such that one has nothing better to communicate than complaints and needs. Feeling this makes one dissatisfied with and embittered toward this environment.

114. *"cursed fate,"] Verhängnis.* Cf. note 38 to Aphorism 117.

115. *am!"]* Quotation from the opening lines of "Homecoming," no. 24 in the *Book of Songs*, by the German poet Heinrich Heine (1797–1856). {According to Hesiod (*Theogony* 517), Atlas holds up the sky.}

116. Cf. 4[240], 6[390].

117. *Criminal woes.] Verbrecher-Kummer.* N coins a phrase based on the common word for "lovesickness" or "love troubles" (*Liebeskummer*).

118. Cf. 6[301].

119. *Cynics.]* {Group of Greek philosophers following the teachings of Diogenes of Sinope (ca. 400–325 BCE). They believed in simplicity, renunciation of worldly goods combined with self-reliance and independence.}

120. *Pd*: 7[133].

121. Cf. 3[142].

122. *Pd*: "He doesn't know human beings"—that means either: he doesn't understand the individuals—or: he doesn't understand what is common.

123. *what is common] die Gemeinheit.* Here as in the *Pd* (cf. previous note), N is punning off the double meaning that "common" can have in English as well as in German, but the pun is more radical in German. Typically *Gemeinheit* means a "vulgarity," "coarseness," "baseness," "meanness."

124. *"love your enemy!"]* {Cf. Matthew 5:44 and Luke 6:27,35.}

125. *Thou . . . wall.]* In German, the expression "to paint the devil on the wall" means "to accentuate the negative," "to foretell gloom and doom."

126. *daimon]* N's *Dämon,* translated elsewhere as "demon," is here translated "daimon" to note the allusion to the daimon of Socrates.

127. *Pd*: in the shadow of his mustache

128. Cf. 3[169].

129. *little . . . vanity.] Sd*: less about others; that makes them elevated above vanity. Added to the end in *Pd*: Cicero had too little passion, it was Demosthenes who had it.

130. *But . . . prey.] Pd*: Both have pleasure through truth

131. *Pd*: If one unlearns how to love others, one ends up no longer loving oneself. Cf. N's letter to Peter Gast of 18 July 1880 from Marienbad {*KGB* III:1, 30}.

132. *I . . . me?] Pd*: The latter are the men of strength, in passion therefore men of surrender—the former are the weak, in passion therefore the proudest.

133. *Pd*: 4[208]. Cf. *CW* 12:11[6].

134. *Pd*: We ought to take leave of our passions, but without hate. Christians are ruined by their hatred.

135. *Pd*: take note that devotion to ourselves is atonement for inward betrayal and a rebellion!—a sort of intentional blindness.

136. *Remedium amoris.]* "Remedy for love." {Allusion to Ovid's *Remedia amoris*, a mock recantation of his earlier *Ars Amatoria*.}

137. *credo quia absurdum est]* "I believe because it is absurd." Cf. P3.

138. *credo quia absurdus sum.]* "I believe because I am absurd."

139. *Pd*: To create joy is the greatest of all joys: and that has nothing to do with morality.

Book Five

1. *Angelus]* {Since the fourteenth century, Catholic churches sounded a bell at morning, noon, and evening as a reminder to

recite the Ave Maria, a prayer celebrating the annunciation of the birth of Christ to Mary by the angel Gabriel. Cf. Luke 1:26ff.}

2. Cf. 4[7]. *Pd*: If, say, truth didn't console, would this constitute an objection against it? What does it have in common with atrophied invalids {and} pained souls that it must necessarily be useful to such people in particular? — The Greek gods didn't console either.

3. *remedies]* *Heilmittel*, literally "means of salvation, redemption."

4. *origin,]* German: *Herkunft*. Cf. note 2 to Aphorism 1.

5. *How . . . nature]* {In all likelihood, N's ensuing observations on ancient optics are based upon the work of the German linguist Lazarus Geiger (1829–70), who, in a comparative study of ancient languages, discovered that many fewer colors were mentioned there than in modern texts. He developed a theory of the progressive development of the visual faculty in humans, a theory that created quite a sensation in the field of biology during the 1870s. Geiger's hypotheses were developed by Hugo Magnus (1842–1907), professor of ophthalmology at Breslau. On 20/21 August 1881, N requested from his friend Franz Overbeck a copy of the first volume of the journal *Kosmos* in which Magnus summarizes his opinions in "On the Evolution of the Sense of Color" (423–27).}

6. Cf. 4[54]. *Pd*: What the art of rococo gardening wanted, *embellir la nature* {to embellish nature}, and visual deception (by means of temples, etc.) is what philosophers want: beautification of science (Comte). At bottom everything in philosophy up to now has been after entertainment; philosophy had to stand in proportion to the other entertainments: one judged artworks and philosophy and religion and, in addition, natural beauty with one yardstick. Formerly, a "return to science" {was} just as harebrained as Rousseau's "return to nature."

7. *scholarship.]* *Wissenschaft*. Cf. Aphorism 270, note 44.

8. *rococo gardening]* {Originating in France around 1720, rococo is a highly decorative and ornate style in the arts and in decoration developing out of the Baroque. Characterized by artifice, it is conceived of in gardening as an improvement upon nature.}

9. *(embellir la nature)!"]* "to embellish nature."

10. *procession] Abzug*, which also means "exodus."

11. Cf. 7[171]. *Pd*: Fear of barbarism—why? It makes us unhappy?—No, our drive for knowledge is too strong for us to value a happiness without knowledge, it is unpleasant for us. For us the restlessness of knowing is as appealing as love's unhappiness (which one doesn't wish to exchange for an indifferent state). Were we to pursue knowledge as a passion, we would be content if humanity were destroyed because of it: it is not impossible to think something of the sort. Christianity did not shrink from such a thought either. Everyone who loves wants to die. We prefer destruction to decline. But what if! in general, passion for knowledge inescapably led precisely to a decline! a weakness!—[we would thus support an evolution of humanity that would be dualistic: one {aspect of the evolution} would serve barbarism] The moment it wanted to become universal it would grow weak! It is a good thing the other drives likewise wish to assert themselves, each creating its ideal. Ultimately: if humanity is not destroyed by its passions, it will be destroyed by its weakness: which do we prefer!! This is the main question!

12. *us!* . . . *siblings?] Sd*: us: everyone who loves wants to die; Christianity has never shied away from a similar thought either.

13. *Heracles'* . . . *stable.]* {Son of Zeus and Alcmene, Heracles was the most popular of the Greek heroes. While in the service of Eurystheus of Argos, Heracles performed twelve superhuman labors, among them cleaning out the stables of Augeus.}

14. *Pd*: The manner of conversing with things—as policeman or father confessor, or as a wanderer. Sympathy or violent force, reverence before things and their mysteries, indiscretion and roguishness in explanation etc., all this is prevalent among the various researchers. There is no one and only holy method for science: we must experimentally be angry or affectionate toward things, treat them with passion or coldness. As if they were humans? . . . no . . . But there exists as well a torturing of things—and anyone who indulges himself in it—Look out!

15. *experimenters.] Versucher*. Cf. note 16 to Aphorism 164.

16. *one . . . knowledge!] alleinwissendmachende Methode der Wissenschaft!* Nietzschean neologism and a word play on *der alleinseligmachende Glaube*= "the only saving faith," i.e., Catholicism. Cf. note 17 to Aphorism 164.

17. *Pd*: Beauty in art—imitation of happiness or of happiness's environment. These days we believe our happiness must surely lie [in vulgarity!] in the most acute senses possible and in exact apprehension of reality—how is it that artists these days, to everyone's delight, are so realistic?—whereas people are by no means comfortable in their reality. {Cf. Stendhal, *Rome, Naples and Florence*, 34, *NL*: "Beauty is never . . . anything but a promise of happiness," quoted directly by N in *GM* III, 6.}

18. Cf. 8[22].

19. *Pd*: 6[432].

20. *vita contemplativa:]* "contemplative life."

21. *vita practica:]* "practical life."

22. *Pd*: The solitude that arises when one thinks about humanity and feels everyone all around dilute into shadows: our ardor increases as does our indifference to our neighbors. We live with the dead and die along with them.

23. *Pd*: Rules are more interesting than exceptions—a step forward!

24. Cf. 6[430].

25. Cf. 6[315].

26. Cf. *TI* "What I Owe the Ancients" 2.

27. Cf. 5[41]. *Pd*: Always to be thinking how to impose my thoughts onto others is not worthy of me. It nauseates me! To employ every bit of eloquence in order to accommodate the views of others! NB {*nota bene*. "note well"} I only want to be the one to whom others confess their inner world and to speak with them accordingly: I want to make their souls light and to eschew all praise for it. NB There is plain common sense and a handful of knowledge, but perhaps I can help some people whose head is disturbed. I wish to have the advantage over them of my little bit of health and my lack of fever, and I'll gladly laugh when they make their jokes about this pride of mine. NB I don't want to have any advantage at all, the better food I receive oppresses me

as does my better intelligence; I am trying to give back and to distribute and to grow poorer, through giving, the way I was before I was given gifts. I want to be lowly, but accessible to many fellow human beings and for many centuries to bid their heart come unto me: a lowly hostel that turns away no one in need. {Cf. Matthew 11:28.}

28. *time . . . thoughts] Sd*: to be taken under protection! What could I desire more than, at some time or other, perhaps when old age arrives, to resemble the obliging father confessor, who knows all the streets and alleyways of thought and now sits in a corner, eager for a person to come and {communicate} to him some of the old-new travail

29. *Pd*: Cf. 6[10].

30. *"Let . . . Aurelius).]* {Nietzsche is quoting from Marcus Aurelius, *Meditations,* bk. 4, sec. 7.}

31. *almost] Sd*: their whole lives

32. *Pd*: Impatient people who, confronted with failure, immediately make their way over to the opposite field of thought and grow passionate there, learn the practices of many temperaments and can become great practitioners—school for diplomats and students of humanity.

33. *Pd*: I am thoroughly incapable of describing what will one day dissolve moral feelings and judgments. But these are incorrect in all their foundations and must decline in binding force from day to day. The construction of laws of life and of behavior is an enterprise for which our sciences of physiology and medicine, sociology are not yet sure enough. Only then will the basis for new ideals emerge. In the meantime, we must content ourselves with preliminary ideals, e.g., with that of justice despite the very crude paths.

34. *do away with] ablösen*, which may also mean "take the place of."

35. *reges]* "kings."

36. *experimental nations . . . experiments:] Versuchsstaaten, Versuche.* Cf. note 16 to Aphorism 164.

37. Cf. *CW* 12:23[196].

38. *you!"]* Cf. Christ's Sermon on the Mount, Matthew 6:33. {"But seek ye first the kingdom of God, and his righteousness;

and . . ." Consciously or unconsciously, N omits "righteousness" from his quotation.}

39. *in honorem majorem]* "to the greater glory."

40. *Ultimate discretion.]* Letzte Schweigsamkeit, which also means "last silence," an equally appropriate rendering given the aphorism's conclusion.

41. *intellect.]* Added to the end of the *Pd*: e.g., {Paul} Rée.

42. Cf. 5[12].

43. *vitam impendere vero.]* "to dedicate one's life to truth." {Cf. Juvenal, *Satires* I, 4, 91.}

44. *verum impendere vitae]* "to dedicate truth to life."

45. Cf. 10[B20].

46. *Tiberius,]* {Through the marriage of his mother Livia Drusilla, Tiberius became the stepson of the future emperor Caesar Augustus (cf. the next note), whom he succeeded as emperor in 14 CE.}

47. *Emperor Augustus]* {After the defeat of Anthony at the Battle of Actium in 31 BCE, Octavius became the unchallenged ruler of the Roman world. As of 27 BCE, he became Emperor Caesar Augustus (Augustus = "exalted").}

48. *Hic . . . salta.]* "Here is Rhodes, jump here." {In Aesop's fable "The Braggart" a boastful athlete claims to have made a spectacular jump in Rhodes, at which point a bystander speaks the line here quoted.}

49. *Our music, which]* Sd: Music, our new Proteus, which

50. *demon of the sea,]* {Proteus (cf. the previous note). A minor sea-god with the ability to assume any number of shapes. Cf. *Odyssey* 4:385ff. and Vergil, *Georgics* 4:387ff.}

51. *seventh day.]* {Cf. Genesis 2:2.}

52. *Pd*: The neediness of a matter pulls me so far and so deeply into it that I finally get to the bottom of it and realize that it is not really as valuable as all that. Heroism and at the end mourning, my kind of experiences — on a small scale 3 times a day.

53. Cf. 6[379].

54. Cf. 6[450].

55. *rhinoceros,"]* Quotation from the *Sutta Nipata*{, part of the collection of sacred Buddhist texts from the *Pali Canon*, which N

knew in English translation}. Cf. N to Carl von Gersdorff, 13 December 1875 {*KGB* II:5, 127–28}.

56. *How . . . birds,]* {Cf. Christ's words in the Sermon on the Mount: "Behold the fowls of the air: for they sow not, neither do they reap, nor gather into barns; yet your heavenly Father feedeth them. Are ye not much better than they?" Matthew 6:26. Also Luke 12:24.}

57. Cf. 10[19].

58. *certainly . . . neighbor] Sd*: certainly in intercourse of bonhomie

59. *Pd*: I could justify myself in a hundred things, but I disdain the pleasure in justification, and I cannot bear the thought that others might think I do after all take these things so seriously. This is simply not true—I'm not so important and it irritates me to do something that allows someone to conclude that I believe otherwise.

60. Cf. 6[205].

61. *Ubi pater sum, ibi patria.]* "Where I am a father, there is my fatherland." {Cf. *Plutus*, line 1151, by the Greek satirical playwright Aristophanes (448?–385 BCE).}

62. Cf. 4[44]. *Pd*: Dialectics is the only way to reach the divine being: Plato, Mill 67. Schopenhauer makes the same claim for intuition. Cf. John Stuart Mill, *Gesammelte Werke {Collected works}*, ed. Th. Gomperz (Leipzig{: Fues's Verlag,} 1869–80), 67. *NL*.

63. In the *Pd*, N uses first person instead of third.

64. *poor in spirit blessed!]* {Allusion to the Sermon on the Mount: "Blessed *are* the poor in spirit: for theirs is the kingdom of heaven." Matthew 5:3.}

65. *Pd*: Kant {was} an honorable but insignificant human being whose personal needs show through here and there: he did not experience very much and his way of thinking deprived him of the time to experience anything; he lacked breadth and power. Schopenhauer has an advantage, at least he has a certain vehement ugliness, in hatred, cravings, vanity{;} he is more savage by nature and he had time for this savagery. — Neither had a deeper history of themselves, no crises and deadly sins, their thinking is not a biography, but, in Kant's case, a history of the head and in

Schopenhauer's case a description of character and pleasure in the mirror, in the intellect. Schopenhauer's thinking has no experiences, no novel, no catastrophes. Think about Pascal!

66. *novel,] Roman*, which is also slang for a(n often secret) love relationship.

67. *way of working]* {Kant was renowned for the regularity of his schedule and for extreme diligence in his work habits.}

68. *"history."] Geschichte* can mean either "history" or "story."

69. Cf. 9[3].

70. *Pd*: 4[150]. Cf. 6[437].

71. *their . . . who] Sd*: the runaway slave who

72. *Pd*: Why this solitude! I'm not angry with anyone. But on my own I am closer to my friends than when together with them: and at the time when I loved music most, I lived at a distance from it: I listened to what I was working on and averted my face, distorted in disgust.

73. *Here . . . gold.]* {Allusion to the story of King Midas, whose touch transforms everything into gold. Cf. Ovid, *Metamorphoses* 2:85ff.}

74. *Pd*: I am tired: what good does it do me to see the beautiful steed ahead: it paws the ground and snorts, it loves its rider, but, oh shame! The latter cannot swing ⟨himself⟩ up into the saddle!

75. *Pd*: We blush when we catch ourselves in the middle of an aversion. We feel hemmed in whenever someone gives us the benefit of his affection by withdrawing something from others; we hear the beating pulse choosing us and detect the sound in the voice that loves us more—ah, and yet everyone who feels for me thus turns away from me precisely by feeling this way. What a load I must bear! I endure my want and am often full in my heart and high-spirited, one ought to bring me nothing that others need.

76. *Another . . . solitude.]* Cf. the last sentence of Aphorism 323.

77. *after . . . again.] Pd*: and dream as if I were banned and without soul.

78. *lagoon of Venice:]* {From his first arrival in Venice on 14 March 1880 to his departure on 29 June, N's letters reveal a marked improvement in his health and disposition, although he

preferred the open sea to the "narrow lagoons" (27 March 1880 to Franz Overbeck, *KGB* III:1, 14). During May and June N dictated to Peter Gast *L'Ombra di Venezia* (*The Shadow of Venice*), the nucleus of what was to become *Dawn*. Cf. N's Venice poem in *NCW*, Intermezzo.}

79. *Pd*: I don't have as much pleasure in the thoughts of any other thinker as I do in my own: that doesn't constitute their value. But I would have to be a fool to denigrate the fruits I find most delicious because they happen to grow on my tree. I was this fool however. —

80. *What . . . bear!]* This sentiment was a constant refrain in N's notebooks and letters of the time. Cf. 7[45], 7[102], 7[126], 7[158], 7[181] and the variants to Aphorisms 488 and 539, as well as the letters from the period, e.g., to Franz Overbeck from 31 October 1880 {*KGB* III:1, 43}.

81. *Pd*: In your youth you take your teachers from the present and you take them as you find them. Later you must atone for them — — —

82. Cf. 4[286].

83. *who . . . blood,]* Cf. Plato, *Letters* VII, 324b{: "Once upon a time in my youth I cherished like many another the hope of entering upon a political career as soon as I came of age."}

84. *he . . . Sicily]* {Plato first traveled to Sicily in the late 380s BCE, where he formed a lifelong friendship with Dion, an influential statesman at the court in Syracuse. In 367 BCE Plato returned to tutor Dionysius II as a philosopher king but was caught up in rivalries between Dionysius II and Dion. In 361 Plato traveled a third time in an effort to come to Dion's aid, but was deceived by Dionysius II.}

85. *Panhellenic . . . city]* {Syracuse, largest city on the island of Sicily, located on the southeastern coast and founded in 734 BCE.}

86. *Pd*: "Genius!" One can speak most readily of it where spirit seems only loosely bound to character and temperament like a winged essence that can separate itself and soar high above both (whereas Schopenhauer, for example, gave the broadest expression to his temperament and never escaped from himself). To be able to fly above and beyond yourself—that's what makes for

genius. To have eyes that have not developed from one's character and temperament—that takes spite toward us, pride in the face of one's reputation for consistency and inconsistency, loving a hypothesis and proving its contrary with all one's powers (that is a constant, necessary exercise), no enthusiasm for the malice involved in contradicting—

87. *Pd*: My pride awakens as soon as I run into people and things that demand submission—up until that point I submit and am kind, with the single request to be left alone.

88. *evil,"]* {Diderot actually writes the inverse in his play *Le Fils naturel* (*The natural son*) (1757): *"Il n'y a que le méchant qui soit seul"* (Only the evil person is solitary).}

89. *Procrustean bed]* {Generally, any type of severe torture. In Greek mythology Procrustes ("the stretcher") was a robber who tormented his victims by hammering them out to fit the length of his bed or, if they were too tall, by cutting them down to size. He was killed by Theseus, who subjected him to the very punishment he had inflicted on others.}

90. *storm and stress;]* Sturm und Drang. Allusion to the short-lived, pre-Romantic literary movement in Germany during the 1770s. Emphasizing the passions, nature, and creativity over reason, society, and manners, the Storm and Stress movement broke with Enlightenment values and promoted the cult of genius that, through inspiration and expression, aspires to become godlike.

91. *Pd*: An action we perform for our own benefit ought not garner for us any moral encomium: likewise for what we do to take pleasure in us ourselves. Eschewal of taking things loftily in such cases is good form for superior human beings. The opposite is a sign of semibarbarism.

92. *to run . . . occasion!]* *Sd*: to elevate himself above his own virtues!

93. *What . . . way]* {After his papal condemnation in the Edict of Worms (May 1521), Luther was "secretly" granted asylum by Friedrich the Wise, elector of Saxony, at the latter's historic castle, the Wartburg. There, so the legend goes, Luther is supposed to have fought off a seductive and devilish apparition by throwing his inkwell at it.}

94. *truth.]* Crossed out at the end of the *Sd*: For we disguise the best things.

95. *has . . . causes]* *Sd*: preferably wants to speak in general truths

96. *Pd*: 6[376].

97. *Do . . . neighbors!]* {Allusion to Matthew 8:32, which recounts Christ's driving out of the demons into swine.}

98. *It is]* *Pd*: Nothing moral! Rather

99. *Pd*: Pride is supposed to rectify too much, take its place: Napoleonic France wanted to compensate for all its losses in this fashion, indeed, all of humanity wants to do so. To write history as a funeral oration whereby one buries what one loves most, thoughts and hopes: and receives pride in return. *Gloria mundi* {"glory to the world"}.

100. *gloria mundi,]* "glory to the world."

101. *Pd*: Many have one superior quality as their solace; otherwise their gaze passes contemptuously over themselves, but a pathway lined with cypresses leads to a shrine—there they recover from themselves.

102. *Ulterior questions.]* *Hinterfragen* (*Hinter*= "behind"; *Fragen*= "questions"). Nietzschean coinage that plays on the common word *Hintergedanken* (*Hinter*= "behind"; *Gedanken*= "thoughts"), translated throughout *D* as "ulterior motives."

103. *esprit.]* Crossed out at the end of the *Sd*: Truth underneath their hood—that is their taste.

104. *Pd*: When one lives with profound and fructifying thoughts, one demands something completely different from art than before. That is the reason my taste in art has changed. Others demand from art the very element in which I live.

105. Cf. 3[29].

106. *"Great Revolution"]* {The French Revolution of 1789, which resulted in the overthrow of the Bourbon monarchy and the establishment of the First Republic, brought with it the bloody Reign of Terror in 1793–94.}

107. *Pd*: 6[411].

108. *role?]* Crossed out at the end of the *Sd*: And yet! I want to, I must play along—what can I answer? Nothing but the same

thing again and again: What a load I must bear! What a load I must bear!

109. Cf. 4[286], 6[215]. *Sd*: The decline of Auguste Comte—I have in mind that time he himself characterized as the time of his rebirth, which, by comparison with his great and productive past, stood out for him as the "new and the better" period—is perhaps the result of weariness. This shows itself: 1. in the belief in his own genius that bursts forth; his exceptional position now allows him to make it easier on himself, to decree more than to prove. 2. He wants henceforth to enjoy the results and to do so he must rid them of their dryness in order to make them palatable: in this manner poetical chicanery steals its way in. 3. He feels that with institutions his highest ambition will be satisfied more quickly than with proofs and refutations, his walks along the cozier path of ambition. 4. He takes repose in the idolatry of a woman and in the process soothes and sweetens his entire being. 5. He no longer tolerates pupils and thinkers who carry on his thought, only party supporters. The former demand undiminished power. 6. He no longer endured the terrible isolation in which a forward and forward-flying spirit lives; he surrounded himself with objects of veneration, of touching emotion, of love, at long last he too wanted to have it as good as all the rest of the religious do and to celebrate in the community what he valued highly; to this end he invented a religion and deceived himself intentionally by believing its realization to be imminent and a matter of course. 7. He ruminated a great deal on the particulars and details of behavior for people of the future and issued orders like a gardener and fruit grower—an activity for the elderly, idyllic and calming. 8. He ventured into indulgently excessive thoughts, all priestly and poetical: strict abstention from this sort of thing requires taut intellectual morality such as only an indefatigable thinker possesses; indulgent excessiveness in thoughts is the thinker's immorality, disgusting arrogance belongs in this camp as well: the power to compare himself earnestly with other luminaries for the purposes of knowledge had grown tired; in comparing he only wanted to intoxicate himself. 9. He wanted altogether to be the last one able to give completely unhindered rein to his intellect; from now on such sovereignty of

thinking ought altogether not be permitted; he ruminated over a hundred means to destroy freedom of thought forever, he no longer feared anything other than individuals' pride and their thirst for freedom. This all presumes that he has come to a halt before his own contemplation and was the first to canonize himself: to this point and no further! A great spirit, however, can only constrain itself in this way, once it no longer feels itself aspiring ever upward, once, in other words, it has gone beyond the summit of its power and is tired. {Added to the end in *Pd*: } In the end one wouldn't, for the most part, find this decline lamentable, if such a [productive] radical spirit hadn't, again so radically, lived and thought it through to its conclusion, such that it, almost like a— — — [The source for N's reflections on Comte are from J. S. Mill, *Auguste Comte und der Positivismus* {*Auguste Comte and Positivism*}, in Mill, *Gesammelte Werke* {*Collected works*} 9:89–141. *NL*.]

110. *further.*] Cf. Friedrich Schiller, *The Robbers,* act 2, scene 1, from Job 38:11.

111. *its . . . falls.*] Allusion to lines 1705–6 from Goethe's *Faust.* {Faust, who is about to make his wager with Mephistopheles, swears that his time will be up the moment he ceases to strive.}

112. Cf. 5[7].

113. *avoid*] *Sd*; *Le*: envy them

114. *Ambrosial nights!*] {From Greek, meaning immortal. Nectar of the gods (*Odyssey* 9:359) which gave them their immortality. Ambrosial nights = pleasurable revelries.}

115. *flames*] *Sd*; *Le*: flame

116. *concepts*] *Sd*; *Le*: concept,

117. *contrapuntal composers*] {Most notably the sixteenth-century maestros Orlando di Lasso and Giovanni Palestrina, and the eighteenth-century Johann Sebastian Bach. Composers of counterpoint (from the Latin: *punctus contra punctum* = "note against note"), the art of combining two or more melodies such that each has a relatively equal voice and all form a harmonious whole.}

118. *causes,*] *Sd*; *Le*: facts

119. *That . . . too!*] *Das Trieb nun auch Philosophie!* N creates a rather involved wordplay that allows for the alternate translation: "*That* is what philosophy does today too."

120. *Have . . . good?*] Cf. Goethe's *Faust* 464–65{: "I feel the courage to venture into the world / To bear earth's suffering and her happiness." N's readers would have known that Faust utters these lines prior to his departure from a cloistered existence at the university and his entry into a "restlessly active" (line 1759) existence in the world at large.}

121. *Pd*: The Epictetean model person is surely the ideal slave. The tautness of his being, the constant, inwardly turned gaze, the incommunicative, circumspect gaze directed outward would not be to our taste: not to mention his silence and taciturnity. The absence of a troubling pride and a certain mild rapprochement that does not wish to ruin any mood{,} are ancient humanity (as opposed to English Puritans){,} he smiles! Incidentally, the "advancing apprentice" in this discipline would certainly strike us as more unpleasant than the master. — The most beautiful thing about it: he lacks any fear of God and he believes rigorously in reason. He is no penitence preacher. He is the quiet one, the self-sufficient one, disappearing among the mass of the proletariat, the one without want, the satisfied — the isolated individual in all its greatness. He differs from Christians in that they are hopers, consoling themselves with unspeakable glories, accepting ten times more from love and grace, allowing themselves to be given gifts. Epictetus possesses, but does not allow himself to give his best. Christians are weak-willed slaves with weak reason.

122. *"unspeakable glories"*] Cf. 2 Corinthians 12:4.

123. *Pd*: The course of science signals the future course of morality. One underestimated the little questions, one wanted to get to the goal at once, one sought to solve everything at one fell swoop, with *one* word: like a riddle. And the task seemed to be: to compress everything into the simplest riddle-form, such that all questions could be answered with *one* answer, i.e., one exerted the grossest violence on things in order to give oneself the boundless joy of being the unriddler of the world. So with Schopenhauer still. Nothing that doesn't bring everything to an end right away seems worth troubling about. Philosophy was a way of showing power — one wants to be the tyrant of spirit.

124. *Gordian knot]* {According to an ancient oracle, whoever could loosen the Gordian knot would become the ruler of Asia. Alexander the Great (356–52 BCE) is supposed to have cut the knot with one slash of his sword.}

125. *egg;]* {At a banquet honoring his discovery of the "New World," Christopher Columbus reportedly asked those in attendance whether anyone could make an egg stand upon either of its ends. When no one proved able to do so, Columbus smashed one end of the egg and placed it upright on the table.}

126. *Ah . . . that]* Sd: As yet, we don't have a handle on even the crudest of standards when it comes to measuring a genius's greatness: indeed, we are such rank beginners as to consider measuring at all a sacrilege. One has no idea, for instance, that above all one has to take into account the measure of energy that

127. *insights. Even]* Sd: [insights has expended — an amount of energy that suffices, under certain circumstances, to elevate someone to the ranks of the heroes and that, again among others, can be so minuscule as to grow contemptible and base]. Even

128. Cf. 6[436].

129. *glean . . . woebegoneness,]* Sd: have from the fruits of their labor only the evening pleasure of a day's work done and afterward a disgust in facing the morning

130. *thirst,]* Sd: character[o]

131. *Byron,]* N is thinking, for example, of the following passage from Byron: "To withdraw *myself* from *myself* (oh that cursed selfishness!) has ever been my sole, my entire, my sincere motive for scribbling at all; . . ." {*Byron's Letters and Journals, Volume 3: 1813–1814*, ed. Leslie A. Marchand (Cambridge, Mass.: Belknap Press of Harvard University, 1974), 225.}

132. *And . . . us.]* Cf. the chapter entitled "Diversion," which is underlined in several places, from the German translation of Pascal's works (see Aphorism 46, note 105), 2:26–37. Faugère "Divertissement," 2:31–34.

133. Cf. 3[9], 4[44].

134. *appearance.]* Schein.

135. *fear . . . reverence]* N is punning on the etymological relationship in German between "fear" (*Furcht*) and "reverence" (*Ehrfurcht*).

136. *courage . . . magnanimity,]* N's language implies that "courage" (*Muth*), when exaggerated, becomes "magnanimity" (*Grossmuth*).

137. *behind worldly]* Sd: behind the mild thought of worldly

138. *let . . . justice,]* Sd: let's not forget the brake on worldly justice

139. Cf. 7[15].

140. *clearer . . . habits,]* Pd: unadulterated bread, fresh springs to bathe in, ripe fruits, for solitude, order, cleanliness

141. *is . . . mine.]* Sd: is not mine. He has certainly found his philosophy.

142. *Stepping . . . progress,]* Pun on the relationship between "stepping on ahead" (*Vorschritt*) and "progress" (*Fortschritt*).

143. *Pd*: I avoid events. The most trifling of them already leave a strong enough mark on me, and one cannot escape them.

144. *Gautama . . . virtues!"]* Cf. *CW* 12:3[1].

145. *when . . . victor?]* Pd: owing to the otherworldly ideals with which one pulls the wool over our eyes

146. *We . . . presumption?]* Pd: On the whole people know neither what is growing inside them nor how fast and by what means — they believe they are dealing with completed facts, fully grown facts and don't believe that one can also kill some of them.

147. *Haven't . . . presumption?]* The direct reference is to Schopenhauer.

148. At the beginning of the *Pd*: With great spirits we don't consider the extent of stupidity extensively enough —

149. *Pd*: The thinker's independence, he needs less, he doesn't have a hard job, no pangs of conscience, no costly pleasures, the dead are his substitute for the living, the best of the dead his substitute for friends.

150. *Pd*: My strongest medicine is "victory" NB {"Note well"}.

151. *follow . . . stream:]* Sd: spin away on our thoughts

152. *shipwreck . . . infinity?]* Cf. 6[364]. Allusion to the final verse of Giacomo Leopardi's poem "L'infinito" {The Infinity}.

Afterword to *Dawn*[1]

Giorgio Colli

"I examined myself," Heraclitus once said. And what we find in *Dawn* is a rhapsodic variation of this passionate Heraclitean synthesis. By meditating on himself, Nietzsche discovered the world; on all matters he elucidated, he stamped his mark, the mark of the knower.[2] Anyone, however, who reads the book from cover to cover as a successive series of observations — such an assumption would be naïve — will fail to participate in Nietzsche's self-examination. If, with a philologist's recklessness, you rummage through the preliminary writings for this work, you uncover, at first, blazing insights[3] that have no evident connection with one another and then the effort, via an alchemical process, to smelt them into a text. Only after various compilations and architectonic rearrangements of the aphorisms does the entirety appear as a publication. Nietzsche's self-examination is thus disguised, mysteriously hidden

1. This Afterword was the preface written by Giorgio Colli for the Italian paperback edition of *Dawn*, which was translated into German and included in *KSA* 3. All notes and annotations are those of the translator of this volume.

2. *knower.] de{r} Erkennende*{dative ending removed}, from the verb *erkennnen*, which can mean "to know," "detect," "discern," "discover," "perceive," "realize," "recognize." The related noun, *Erkenntnis*, is usually translated in philosophical discourse as "knowledge," but often, as in this instance, carries the connotations of the verbs listed above.

3. *insights] Erkenntisse* — see previous note.

again, manipulated by an artistic instinct, an artistic deception; and the naïve reader, for whom the book appears to have
originated as the very work being read, remains more available
at least, calmer than the savvy reader who has entered the
labyrinth of an interior epistemological process[4] that wants to
reveal itself to the whole world. For as soon as it concerns art,
it is Nietzsche himself who calls on us to be distrustful, moreover in this very book: "Artists fear nothing more than the eye
that discerns their *little deception* . . . that checks the figures
when they wanted to sell a little for a lot" (223).

But the deep delving into the inner well of knowledge,[5] the
upward surge of truths, the quest for a disguise of these truths,
their replacement with a drug, a "little deception"—these are
the things that constitute Nietzsche's fascination: and it is good
for the reader to know all this, as readers must learn to take from
Nietzsche, but to defend themselves against him as well. Incidentally, this is what comprises the education unto knowledge.
If one at least understands that here it's all about a thoroughly
unique way of comprehending and getting a grip on all things
in the world (that is, namely, what it means to search oneself);
if one apprehends how all convictions (and not just moral ones)
are swept away, then that's already enough—for naïve as well
as savvy readers.

In *Human, All Too Human* Nietzsche introduced an intu-
itional science;[6] in *Joyful Science* he will again deliver a science
whose goal is to identify with poetry; here, in *Dawn* he offers a
science whose concerns are more colorful and fluid; they don't
belong to the political or cultural arena and only rarely allude
to philosophers or artists. The soul, the human drive—these
are, in the rule, the concerns—what Nietzsche tends to call
moral speculation or also psychology. And it is appropriate to
provide examples of how the word science operates in this book

4. *epistemological process]* Erkenntnisvorgang{dative ending removed}.
5. *knowledge,]* Erkenntnis.
6. *science;]* Wissenschaft. See Aphorism 193, note 79.

as an extremely noble alibi. In Aphorism 76, which deals with
the Christian profaning of love and reproduction, we read,
"Ultimately, this demonizing of Eros has taken on an ending
straight out of comedy . . . to this very day, the effect has been
that the *love story*[7] became the only real interest that *all* circles
have in common—and to an excess inconceivable in antiquity,
an excess that will, at a later date, elicit laughter" (76). Every
work of our culture, adds Nietzsche, from the loftiest to the
lowest, "has been marked . . . by the excessive importance ascribed to turning the love story into the main story." Thus we
have here an excellent example of "science" that, as a prerequisite, has no need for an extensive collection of material, nor a
spatial-temporal delineation of the object, nor a strictly induc-
tive, nor by extension, deductive method. It is solely a matter of
an intuition based on a normal, immediate or mediate, experience. If we wanted to define it in some way, we could refer to it
as historical intuition in so far as a valuation of the present
(19th-century society) becomes intelligible via an assessment of
the past (Christian world view). But the whole situation is considerably more multilayered, as two further valuations dovetail
with this theme: the valuation of an even more distant past
(antiquity) and of an as yet undetermined future, whereby antiquity lies outside both of the first valuations, indeed doesn't
even know what they mean and the future has a good laugh at
their expense. This is anti-historical "science" about history.
And to recognize its illuminating power, let's take a look at the
aforementioned phenomenon a century after Nietzsche, in our
own era. What was the "love story" back then—isn't that today sexuality and eroticism?

Aphorism 254 provides an example of intuition that one cannot define as historical and even resists being tagged with the
name "science": "The distinguishing but also dangerous feature

7. *love story*] Here and in subsequent quotations in his Afterword, Colli
omits the emphases that appear in *Dawn*. This edition restores Nietzsche's
emphases, which are missing in Colli's Afterword.

of poetic natures is their *exhaustive* fantasy: which anticipates, sees in advance, enjoys in advance, suffers in advance what will occur and what might occur and finally in the actual moment, is *tired* of the occurrence and the deed." To call this sort of writing psychology—wouldn't that be paramount to degradation? What is, after all, the repeated experience, the behavioral rule through which a psychologist could come to such a conclusion? Here, the unique, unparalleled soul is the object of study, perhaps the soul of the one who is writing, as object of his passion.

And if this intuition resists every attempt to be labeled as historical, aesthetic, or psychological, is too intimate for that, what is one supposed to say for starters about the following, which conceals itself behind a nature tableaux that is to be interpreted anthropomorphically? "The sea lies before one pale and shimmering; it cannot speak . . . But I have compassion for you, Nature, because you must remain silent, even if it is only your malice that binds your tongue; indeed, I have compassion for you on account of your malice! . . . and my heart swells again . . . it enjoys its own sweet malice of silence" (423). But Nietzsche's entire life is a "speaking." Thus he perceived his speaking as benevolence and shutting oneself up as malice. He resists this temptation: it is about a moral interpretation of the world whereby the status of action accrues to revealing oneself, to expression, to the word.

If this all applies—and one could cite many additional aphorisms in support—what is one supposed to make of the prevalent opinion that views *Dawn* as an enlightenment, rational and positivistic work? To be sure, in this book you can find many pronouncements against ecstasy, visions, rapture, and trance. But careful, remember what was said about artistic deception. Nietzsche is characterizing as science here the opposite of what one commonly understands by this term, but he persists in good faith upon this word, for he means by it, in addition, to point to the ascetic fervor[8] of self-denial, to objectivity,

---

8. *fervor]* Leidenschaft. See note 70 to Aphorism 192.

understood as identification with reasons and arguments that run counter to his instinct. His model in this instance is Thucydides, who would never let it be known in which direction his sympathies tended. So Nietzsche even takes pains now and then to come up with praise and acknowledgement of Christianity. Once, however, by employing a too casual form of this technique of inversion, he falls into a trap: at the moment when, to our amazement, we hear him intone a paean of praise to the dialectic—his nemesis from the outset: that would be tantamount to hearing Schopenhauer sing the Song of Songs for Hegel. Yet, in Aphorism 544, we read, "I have taken careful note: our philosophizing youths . . . are now demanding from philosophy just *the opposite* of what the Greeks derived from it! Anyone who doesn't hear that constant cry of joy running through every give and take of a Platonic dialogue, the cry of joy over a new discovery of *rational* thought, what does such a person understand about Plato, about ancient philosophy? . . . when the rigorous and sober play of concepts . . . was practiced." You can't believe your own ears, but Nietzsche doesn't relent: "It was Socrates who discovered the . . . magic, that of cause and effect, ground and consequence: and we moderns are so accustomed to and brought up on the necessity of logic that it lies on our palate like the normal taste and, as such, must be repellent to the lascivious and conceited."

If you read the posthumous fragments from this period (see *CW* 13), then you'll find Nietzsche intensively involved with the problems of worldly, particularly political, power. Numerous passages point to his engagement with Napoleon and Paul. But only very little of all this shows up again in *Dawn*, where what dominates is the assertion, *"As little state as possible!"* (179). Here it is knowledge that is elevated to the highest of life's values, and in so doing, Nietzsche forces himself to battle against the opposite value, namely action. For action is judged according to the benchmark of knowledge:[9] "[A]ll actions are

9. *knowledge:] Erkenntnis.*

essentially unknown" (116). But the preeminence of knowledge over action is not merely speculative; it's considered a given: it is thereby a matter of moral preeminence: "And thus the entire drive toward deeds and action is perhaps after all, at bottom, flight from oneself?" (549).

Editor's Afterword

Keith Ansell-Pearson

Nietzsche began research on what was to become *Dawn: Thoughts on the Presumptions of Morality* in January 1880. The manuscript was complete by 13 March 1881 and was published in June of that year. At this point in time Nietzsche had retired on a modest annual pension from his position at Basel University and was travelling in Europe, spending time in Riva, Venice, Marienbad, Stresa, and Genoa, as well as his childhood home of Naumburg, seeking suitable conditions for his health and living on a highly restricted budget.[1] In Genoa, where *Dawn* was completed, Nietzsche found a garret apartment which he had to climb a hundred and sixty-four steps to reach and which was itself located high up on a very steep street. Nietzsche was adjusting to a new lifestyle and the limitations imposed by his pension: the apartment in Genoa was without heating and the winter was extremely cold. His diet was often a simple one of risotto and calf-meat with a frugal supper of porridge. Nietzsche was leading not only a frugal existence but a solitary one too. And yet it was under these harsh conditions that he wrote over the course of a year one of his "sunniest" books. He would later reflect, in a letter to his admirer in Copenhagen, Georg Brandes, that his specialty was to "endure extreme pain, *cru, vert*, with perfect clarity, for

1. See William H. Schaberg, *The Nietzsche Canon: A Publication History and Bibliography* (Chicago: University of Chicago Press, 1995), 77.

two or three consecutive days, accompanied by constant vomiting of bile." Although the report had been disseminated that he was in a madhouse and had died there, he confides that nothing could have been further from the truth: "As a matter of fact my intellect only came to maturity during that terrible time: witness *Dawn*, which I wrote in 1881 during a winter of incredible suffering at Genoa, away from doctors, friends, or relations." For himself, he adds, the book serves "as a sort of dynamometer": "I composed it with a minimum of strength" (10 April 1888; *KGB* III:5, 290). Solitude was for Nietzsche a test of his independence. He wanted, he said, to be his own doctor, to be true to himself and not to listen to anyone else: "I cannot tell you," he wrote on 24 November 1880 to his mother and sister Elisabeth, "how much good *solitude* is doing me" (*KGB* III:1, 51).

After decades of neglect, *Dawn* is a text that has come to be admired in recent years for its ethical naturalism and for its anticipation of phenomenology.[2] In addition, I have sought to interpret the text in terms of its relevance to philosophical therapy and I have drawn on some of this material for this afterword.[3] As Duncan Large has noted, in *Dawn* and the subsequent text *The Joyful Science*—its ideal companion in which the journey continues—Nietzsche consolidates the antimetaphysical stance initiated by *Human, All Too Human* of 1878, completing his metamorphosis from the Schopenhauer- and Wagner-adulating camel to a combative and exploratory lion,

2. See Rüdiger Safranski, *Nietzsche: A Philosophical Biography*, trans. Shelley Frisch (New York: Norton, 2002), 207–19.

3. Keith Ansell-Pearson, "For Mortal Souls: Philosophy and Therapeia in Nietzsche's *Dawn*," in Jonardon Ganeri and Clare Carlisle, *Philosophy and Therapeia* (Royal Institute of Philosophy Supplement 66, Cambridge University Press, 2010), 137–65. See also Ansell-Pearson, "Nietzsche, the Sublime, and the Sublimities of Philosophy: An Interpretation of *Dawn*," *Nietzsche-Studien* 39 (2010): 201–32.

and from the ship of the desert to the ship of high seas.[4] He is charting new land and new seas, unsure of his final destination, and has the confidence needed to take risks and conduct experiments, even to suffer shipwreck in search of new treasure. In this text we encounter the "free spirit" setting off on a new course and away from the old philosophical world of metaphysical and moral presumptions. However, it is no exaggeration to claim that for the greater part of Nietzsche's reception, *Dawn* has been among the most neglected texts in Nietzsche's corpus, and perhaps for understandable reasons: it deploys no master concept, it does not seek an ultimate solution to the riddles of existence (indeed, it warns against such a strategy), its presentation of themes and problems is highly non-linear, and it states his case for the future subtly and delicately. It has also been overshadowed by the more terse and stridently anti-Christian works of the later polemical period. The death of God is presaged and, in fact, announced, but not presented in any dramatic form as we find in the next text, *The Joyful Science* (§ 125). But it is a text that has hidden riches, a text that has to be read between the lines (as Nietzsche disclosed to his sister Elisabeth in the case of *Dawn*'s fifth and final book).[5] And, as Nietzsche notes in *Ecce Homo*, although the book mounts a "campaign" against morality, the reader should not think it has about it "the slightest whiff of gunpowder"; rather, the reader should "make out quite different and more pleasing

4. Duncan Large, "Nietzsche and the Figure of Columbus," *Nietzsche-Studien* 24 (1995): 162–83, 163.

5. See the letter dated mid-July 1881: "So read the book, if you will pardon my saying so, from an angle I would *counsel* other readers *against*, from an entirely personal point of view (sisters also have privileges, after all). Seek out everything that you guess is *what* might be most useful for your brother and what he might need most, *what* he wants and does not want. In particular you should read the fifth book, where much is written between the lines. *Where all* my efforts lead cannot be said in a word—and if I had that word, I would not utter it" (*KGB* III:1, 108).

scents" (*EH* "Why I Write Such Good Books" D1). The claims Nietzsche wishes to make about *his* conception of the tasks of morality — or ethics, if one prefers — are more modest ones in comparison with the *immodest* claims traditionally and typically made on behalf of morality.

Dawn is a pathbreaking work and an exercise in modern emancipation — from fear, superstition, hatred of the self and the body, the short cuts of religion, and the presumptions of morality. But its ends are modest — an ethics of self-cultivation centered on the drives. In *Dawn* Nietzsche is less of the disappointed idealist he was in the *Human, All Too Human* texts, more assertive about the emerging "rights" of new individuals who have hitherto been decried as freethinkers, criminals, and immoralists, more metaphorically exuberant,[6] and with glimpses of new dawns on the horizon about to break. And yet Nietzsche offers his readers wise counsel, outlining in the book a therapy made up of slow cures (*D* 462) and small doses (*D* 534). As Gary Handwerk notes in his afterword to *HAH II,* the texts of Nietzsche's middle period assume more the form of a method of inquiry than a doctrine: Nietzsche has invented "an experiential and experimental philosophy," one that expresses itself in the form of the essayistic aphorism: "In these ground- and spirit-breaking works, Nietzsche invents for himself a form that is non-linear, interruptive, interrogative, recursive, and, above all, remarkably flexible with regard to scope and span."[7]

Dawn grew out of notebooks Nietzsche kept during 1880, including notes for a new book to be entitled *L'Ombra di Venezia* (*CW* 13, 3[1–172]): the title pays homage to the welcome shade he had discovered for himself in the city of four hundred bridges and numerous dark and narrow streets.[8] He had been intrigued by the prospect and promise of a new dawn

6. See Gary Handwerk, afterword to *Human, All Too Human II* (Stanford: Stanford University Press, 2012).

7. Ibid.

8. See Curtis Cate, *Friedrich Nietzsche* (London: Hutchinson, 2002), 298.

since the time of his early reflections on the ancient, pre-Platonic philosophers. In one note from 1872–73, Nietzsche writes that the role of the philosophers was to prepare the way for the Greek reformer and precede him "as the dawn precedes the rising sun." Alas, the sun did not rise in this instance, and the reformer failed with the dawn remaining "a ghostly apparition" (*CW* II, 23[I]).[9] *Dawn* (*Morgenröthe*, literally "morning redness"), the second installment in what was to become the free spirit trilogy, is one of Nietzsche's "yes-saying" books, a work of enlightenment which, he tells his readers, seeks to pour out "its life, its love, its tenderness upon bad things alone," giving back to these things the "supreme right and *prerogative* to exist" (*EH* "Why I Write Such Good Books" D1). The Indian motto from the Rig Veda's "Hymn to Varuna," "there are so many dawns that have not yet broken" lies inscribed on the door to the book (ibid.). Nietzsche's amanuensis Peter Gast (Heinrich Köselitz) had written the motto on the title page while making a fair copy of the manuscript and this, in fact, inspired Nietzsche to adopt the new title and replace its original title of "The Plowshare."[10] In 1888 Nietzsche speaks of the book as amounting to a search for the new morning that ushers in a whole series of new days and he insists that not a single negative word is to be found in it, and no attack or malice either. In this book we encounter a thinker who lies in the sun, "like a sea-creature sunning itself between rocks" (*EH* "Why I Write Such Good Books" D1) — and the book was largely conceived in the rocks near Genoa in solitude and where, so Nietzsche discloses, he

9. See also *HAH* 638 on "the mysteries of the dawning day."

10. See *CW* 13:9: "*Die Pflugschar*: Gedanken über die moralischen Vorurtheile." Nietzsche also had this title for his aborted fifth untimely meditation, and it was also for a time the working title for *Human, All Too Human*. See also *SE* 3, on Schopenhauer's "plowshare" that will "cut into the soul of modern humanity." For further insight into the image of the plowshare and Nietzsche's adoption of it, see Duncan Large, "Nietzsche's 'Helmbrecht,' or: How to Philosophise with a Ploughshare," *Journal of Nietzsche Studies* 13 (Spring 1997): 3–23.

"had secrets to share with the sea."[11] *Dawn* is a book that journeys into the future, and which for Nietzsche constitutes, in fact, its true destination: "Even now," he writes in a letter of 24 March 1881 to his old friend Erwin Rohde, "there are moments when I walk about on the heights above Genoa having glimpses and feelings such as Columbus once, perhaps from the very same place, sent out across the sea and into the future" (*KGB* III:1, 75). Nietzsche's appeal to Columbus is figurative; he is, in fact, critical of the real Columbus (*D* 37). But as a figure of thought Columbus the seafarer serves *Dawn* well; he denotes "the true experimenter, who may have an idea of where he thinks he is heading but is always prepared to be surprised by the outcome of his experiments."[12]

In fact, the book is more complex than Nietzsche admits to in 1888. Some of this complexity is revealed in the letters he wrote to Gast advising him of the title, which he kept changing, sometimes in slight and subtle ways. In a letter to Gast of 9 February 1881, the work is now to carry the title "A Dawn: Thoughts on the Presumptions of Morality." By way of explanation Nietzsche added in his letter, "There are so many bright and indeed red colors in it" (*KGB* III:1, 61). However, a few weeks later Nietzsche wrote to Gast again expressing anxiety over the new title, considering it "too gushing, oriental and of less good taste" (22 February; *KGB* III:1, 63). Nevertheless he persisted with it for the time being and largely on account of the advantage it enjoys over the original title of giving the book a more cheerful tone and placing the reader in a different frame of mind: "it stands the book in good stead, which would be much too *gloomy* without the glimpse of the morning!" This reveals that the book is, in fact, a complex one:

11. Nietzsche first visited Genoa in October 1876 as a stopover on the way to Nice. He resided in Genoa and its environs for three successive winters in 1880–81, 1881–82, and 1882–83. On Nietzsche's fondness for the maritime city that also gave him access to the mountains, see Large, "Nietzsche and the Figure of Columbus."

12. Ibid., 174.

there are sufficient grounds for gloom, but Nietzsche does not wish to be gloomy or promote gloominess; a book needs to emit rays of hope, expectation, and anticipation even if the seriousness cannot be concealed. In a letter to Gast of 30 March, Nietzsche reveals that he is basically writing for himself and for Gast, his closest associate and dearest companion (his fellow free spirit). He writes of gathering "a treasure out of things that are our own, for our old age!" and of the need to "be *vain for ourselves* and as much as possible!" (*KGB* III:1, 77). In the text itself Nietzsche posits the philosopher's existence in terms of an "ideal selfishness" in which one freely gives away one's spiritual house and possessions to ones in need. In this condition of solitude the satiated soul lightens its own burden, eschewing both praise for what it does and avoiding gratitude which is invasive and fails to respect solitude and silence. This is to speak of a new kind of teacher who, armed with a handful of knowledge and a bag full of experiences, becomes "a doctor of the spirit to the indigent and to aid people here and there whose head *is disturbed by opinions* . . ." (*D* 449). The aim is not to prove that one is right before such a person, but rather "to speak with him in such a way that . . . he himself says what is right and, proud of the fact, walks away!" In a letter to Gast of 10 April, Nietzsche discloses that he has modified the title by simplifying it to "Dawn" and not "A Dawn." By way of justification he adds: "A title must, above all, be *quotable* [*citirbar*]" and that there was something too "precious" about the "A" in the title (*KGB* III:1, 83). The title Nietzsche settled on for the book is significant for several reasons that are clear in the meaning of the word "dawn," notably the expectation of a new beginning; the first light of day or daybreak; the incipient appearance of something; a new reality which is beginning to become evident and understood, and so on. As we have seen, the color "red" was important to Nietzsche in his own understanding of the book, and here he was perhaps influenced by Homer's *Odyssey* and the various references to "the rosy-fingered dawn" that, in the tale, provides a sharp contrast to the gruesome battle scenes going on below.[13]

The book concludes on an enigmatic note with Nietzsche asking his readers and fellow travelers whether it will be said of them one day that they too, "*steering toward the west, hoped to reach an India*" but that it was their fate to shipwreck upon infinity (*D* 575). At this point in his writings, "India" denotes for Nietzsche the path to self-enlightenment. Nietzsche holds that Europe remains behind Indian culture in terms of the progress it needs to make with respect to religious matters since it has not yet attained the "freethinking naïveté" of the Brahmins. The priests of India demonstrated "pleasure in thinking" in which observances—prayers, ceremonies, sacrifices, and hymns—are celebrated as the givers of all good things. One step further, he adds, and one also throws aside the gods—"which Europe must also do one day!" (*D* 96). Europe remains distant, he muses, from the level of culture attained in the appearance of the Buddha, the teacher of self-redemption. Nietzsche anticipates an age when all the observances and customs of the old moralities and religions have come to an end. In a reversal of the Christian meaning of the expression "*In hoc signo vinces* [In this sign (cross) you will be the victor]," which heads *Dawn* 96, Nietzsche is suggesting that the conquest will take place under the sign that the redemptive God is dead. Buddha is a significant teacher because his religion is one of self-redemption, and this is a valuable step along the way of ultimate redemption from religion and from God. Instead of speculating on what will then emerge into existence, he calls for a new community of non-believers to make their sign and communicate with one another: "There exist today perhaps ten to twenty million people among the different countries of Europe who no longer 'believe in God'—is it too much to ask that they *give a sign* to one another?" (*D* 96). He imagines these people consti-

13. See references to *The Odyssey* and Odysseus in *D* 306, 562; see also *MM* 408; see Homer, *The Odyssey*, 2:1–2, 12:3–7.

tuting a new power in Europe, between nations, classes, rulers and subjects, and between the un-peaceable and the most peaceable. It is in this section of the book that Nietzsche advances the thesis that "morality" (*die Moral*) in the old sense has died.

The final aphorism of book five and of the text as a whole returns us to the final book's opening aphorism on the silent sea and is not insignificantly entitled "We aeronauts of the spirit [*Wir Luft-Schifffahrer des Geistes*]!"[14] The aphorism begins by noting that although all the brave birds that fly out into the farthest distance are unable to go on at a certain point, this does not mean we can infer from this that an immense open space did not lay out before them. All that can be inferred is that they had flown as far as they could. The same applies, Nietzsche holds, to all our great teachers and predecessors who have come to a stop, often with weariness (see also *D* 487 on the weary philosopher). It is perhaps a law of life that it will also be the case with us, "with you and me," Nietzsche writes. We can, however, derive sustenance and even consolation from the fact that other birds and other spirits will fly further:

This our insight and assurance [*Gläubigkeit*] vies with them in flying up and away; it rises straightaway above our head and beyond its own inadequacy into the heights and looks out from there into the distance, sees the flocks of birds much more powerful than we are, who are striving to get to where we were striving toward and where everything is still sea, sea, sea!—And where, then, do we want to go? Do we want to go *across* the sea? Where is it tearing us toward, this powerful craving that means more to us than any other pleasure? Why precisely in this direction, toward precisely where heretofore all of humanity's suns have *set*? Will it perhaps be said of us

14. As Large points out, these aeronauts are flying an "air-ship" and he suggests that their flying out over the sea indicates "how close is their kinship to their more earthbound, or at least sea-bound mariner-cousins" ("Nietzsche and the Figure of Columbus," 171).

one day that we too, *steering toward the west, hoped to reach an India*—that it was, however, our lot [*Loos*] to shipwreck upon infinity? Or else, my brothers? Or else?—(*D* 575)

In *Ecce Homo* Nietzsche draws attention to the closing of the book (though its search will soon be reopened with *The Joyful Science*, which was initially conceived by Nietzsche as a continuation of *Dawn*) and suggests that it is the only book to close in this manner (*EH* "Why I Write Such Good Books" D1).[15] The "Or else?" is necessary because the question is a genuine one; the search admits of no resolution, at least not until humanity reaches a point of completed knowledge with all suns discovered and thoroughly explored. But this is to speak of an infinitely long *durée* and Nietzsche derives his confidence in the future from this. He will continue in his writings to provide instruction on the sea, on our new infinite, offering both encouragement and warnings (see, for example, *JS* 124–25, 283, 289, 343, 374; *Z* II "On the Blissful Islands").[16]

In the period up to 1878, the standard form Nietzsche adopted for his writings was the essay or pamphlet, in accordance with his professional training as an academic classicist. It is in the texts of the middle period (1878–82) that he explores both a new kind of philosophizing, inspired by the psychological ob-

15. For further insight see ibid. and Ernst Bertram, *Nietzsche: Attempt at a Mythology*, trans. Robert E. Norton (Urbana: University of Illinois Press, 2009), 237: "The moment of this extreme, unsettled inner 'Or?' finds its classical expression perhaps in the last sentences of *Daybreak*, which are also, simultaneously, a classic example of his mastery of the end . . . no matter from which direction we approach him, even Nietzsche's mighty torso always rounds out his intellectual silhouette with a final 'Or?' just as all of his works from the *Birth* to *Ecce* finish in the doubling of such an Or. Hardly any of them, however, do so with such calm pride, such regal surrender, such masterly confidence in the face of all 'Beyonds' as *Dawn*."

16. For further insight into the enigmatic character of the closing of the book and the reference to India, see Karl Löwith, *Nietzsche's Philosophy of the Eternal Recurrence of the Same*, trans. J. Harvey Lomax (Berkeley: University of California Press, 1997), 113.

servations of the French Enlightenment thinkers and his friend
Paul Rée, and a new means of expressing it, equally inspired by
the aphoristic works of the French *moralistes*.[17] Perhaps the most
distinctive feature of Nietzsche's style is the numbered paragraph, which amounts to the essential building block of his
prose style. The Nietzschean paragraph is an extraordinarily
supple unit, ranging in length from a bare line or two to several
pages. The number of genuine aphorisms in his works is relatively small; instead, most of what are called the "aphorisms"
are more substantial paragraphs which exhibit a unified train
of thought frequently encapsulated in a paragraph heading in-
dicating the subject-matter, and it is from these building blocks
that the other, larger structures are built in more or less extended sequences.[18]

For Nietzsche "the will to system" displays a lack of integrity (*TI* "Sayings" 26) and he balks at the idea of constructing
the kind of philosophical edifice in which his philosophical
predecessors so often delighted. He was criticized in his own
time for his lack of scholarly research and his criticisms of
scholarly myopia and asceticism are scathing. Above all he
wants to distinguish himself from the traditions of German
academic philosophy that preceded him, which he finds life-
less and, ultimately, simply boring. He does not simply present
his readers with disquisitions on philosophical topics, such as
truth and knowledge, but rather dramatizes them through a
series of parables, thought experiments, imagined conversations, and the like. His aim is always to energize and enliven

---

17. This and the following paragraphs on Nietzsche's style are borrowed
in part from the introduction to *The Nietzsche Reader*, ed. Keith Ansell-
Pearson and Duncan Large (Malden, MA: Basil Blackwell, 2006).

18. See also Gary Handwerk, afterword to *Human, All Too Human* (Stanford: Stanford University Press, 1997), 377. For insights into Nietzsche's
need to break free from certain literary constraints and search for a proper
textual vehicle, see Richard T. Gray, afterword to *Unpublished Writings
from the Unfashionable Observations* (Stanford: Stanford University Press,
1999), 491–92.

philosophical style through an admixture of aphoristic and poetic — broadly speaking, "literary" — forms. The specificity of Nietzsche's style, then, lies in the fact that it occupies the ground midway between what one might call philosophy and poetry "proper." Perhaps the most appropriate way of describing his style is with reference to its multifarious impropriety, for its lack of scholarly niceties is but the least of its provocations. Nietzsche's favorite lyric poet was Heinrich Heine, whom he praises for possessing "that divine sense of mischief without which I cannot conceive of perfection" (*EH* "Why I am so Clever" 4), and this transgressive "wickedness" is of course a quality he himself assiduously cultivates. His stylistic ideal is, parodying Horace, "*ridendo dicere* severum" ("saying what is *somber* through what is laughable"), and these two modes, the somber and the sunny, are mischievously intertwined in his philosophy, without the reader necessarily being sure which one is uppermost at any one time. His work is an unsettling provocation for both his philosophical antagonists and his readers, especially when his breadth of allusion, and lack of references, the love of impropriety and paradox, are combined with an ideal of concision, as when he declares that his ambition is to say in ten sentences what everyone else says in a book — or does not say in a book (*TI* "Forays" 51). The texture of Nietzsche's work, evident in many parts of *Dawn*, is often very dense and he is under no illusions that it is straightforward to read. When he conjures up his perfect reader it is as a "monster of courage and curiosity," and someone "pliable, crafty, cautious, a born adventurer and discoverer" (*EH* "Why I Write Such Good Books" 3). Nietzsche did not want hurried readers. In the Preface to *Dawn*, he stresses that a book such as this is in no hurry and that he and his book are friends of *lento* or slowness:

> Having been a philologist is not for nothing; perhaps you
> remain one, a teacher, in other words, of slow reading — in
> the long run, you end up writing slowly as well. Nowadays it
> is not only a matter of habit for me, but also one of taste, a

malicious taste perhaps? — To write nothing more that would
not drive to despair every sort of person who is "in a hurry."
(*D* P5)

In an age of *work*, that is, "of unseemly and sweating overhaste that wants at once to be over and done with everything,
even with every old and new book," philology is that "venerable art" that requires that one take one's time, becoming still
and slow: "as a goldsmith's art and connoisseurship of the *word*,
which has nothing but fine, cautious work to take care of and
which achieves nothing if it does not achieve it *lento*."

Dawn is composed of 575 "aphorisms" or short thoughts,
some of only a single line, others running to three pages, and
grouped together in five books (the original plan was for a
work of four books). As Arthur Danto notes, while each component piece has a title of its own none of the five books do,
hence it is unclear "what, if any, principle of organization may
have applied." Further, "the 'thoughts' of one book seldom relate more closely to other thoughts in it than they do to those
in other books," and it is true to say that only occasionally do
we read a suite of thoughts on the same topic, for example,
Mitleid (compassion) from 132 almost to the end of book two.[19]
In aphorism 454, entitled "Interpolation," Nietzsche confides
that the book is not one for reading straight through but for
"cracking open" (*Aufschlagen*) in which he wants the reader to
place his head into it and out again, finding nothing about
him that he is accustomed to. From this Danto infers that the
absence of headings from the individual books of the work,
along with the abrupt shift from topic to topic, "*could* be de-
vices for slowing the reader down."[20] Although this is conjec-
tural, it accords well with what Nietzsche says in his 1886
preface to the book, where he wishes to be the teacher of "slow

19. Arthur C. Danto, *Nietzsche as Philosopher*, expanded ed. (New York:
Columbia University Press, 2005), 246.
20. Ibid., 247.

reading." But it is also the case that in *Dawn* Nietzsche conceives philosophy as a *form of entertainment* (*D* 427), one that takes over a role hitherto assumed by religion, and it may be that in conceiving the book in a nonlinear fashion Nietzsche hoped to keep his readers intrigued by and interested in the problems of self, world, and knowledge he was pursuing and staging. The world is bereft of the consolations of religion and metaphysical philosophy, and our minds need cultivating in new ways; we need new interests and new things to keep us occupied and interested in life.

Concerning Nietzsche's style of writing Danto puts it supremely well when he describes the prose style of the work as "a kind of eroticism of writing," one that requires from its reader a partnership in pleasure and intelligence. The text is characterized by sudden shifts of tone and rhythm, "at one moment lyrical and at the next moment earthy," with moments of "mock distance and then of sudden intimacy," and its "jeers, sneers, jokes and whispers," all contribute to this eroticism.[21] As Danto further notes, while Nietzsche's voice has lost the professorial authority of the early writing it has yet to acquire the "strident conviction of a prophet unheeded" that characterizes the later writings. He is perhaps right to suggest that in none of the books do we get a more palpable sense of spiritual well-being than we do in *Dawn*.

Danto also rightly notes that the psychology in the book is dazzling and precocious. Nietzsche's psychology, he argues, is resolutely anti-Cartesian and has to be inasmuch as his critique of morality entails the view that we do not really know what we are, while Cartesianism is precisely the view that what we essentially are is something immediately present to consciousness, and nothing is true of us psychologically of which we are not directly and noninferentially aware.[22] Here several aphorisms in book two are especially significant. In aphorism 115 on

21. Ibid., 249.
22. Ibid.

the "so-called 'ego'" (*Ich*), Nietzsche draws attention to the prejudices of *language*, noting that they hinder a properly rich and subtle understanding of inner processes and drives. We seem to have words that exist only for the "*superlative* degrees" of these processes and drives: "Wrath, hate, love, compassion, craving, knowing, joy, pain—these are all names for *extreme* states." This would not be important were it not for the fact, Nietzsche thinks, that it is the milder middle degrees, as well as the lower ones, which elude us and yet "collaborate . . . in the formation of our character and destiny." In 116 on the "unknown world of the 'subject,'" Nietzsche startles us with his shocking assertion that from the most distant times of the past to the present day what has been so difficult for us to comprehend is our ignorance of ourselves: "The age old delusion that one knows, knows just exactly in every instance *how human action comes about*, lives on." We superstitiously believe we know what we want, that we are free and can freely assume responsibility for ourselves and hold others responsible for their actions, and so on. He urges us to recognize that actions are never what they appear to be: "It took so much effort for us to learn that external things are not what they appear to us—now then! It is just the same with the inner world!" In this regard it is necessary to work against both metaphysical and moral "realism" (*D* 116; see also *D* 120, 124, 128). It is also necessary to develop knowledge of human drives since in spite of the struggles for self-knowledge, nothing is more incomplete to us than the images of all the drives taken together that constitute our being: "Scarcely can he call the cruder ones by name: their number and strength, their ebb and flow, their play and counterplay, and, above all, the laws of their *alimentation* remain completely unknown to him." Without such knowledge we will continue to live badly, with the "starving and stunting" of some drives and the "overstuffing" of other drives (*D* 119).

Julian Young helpfully describes *Dawn* not as a theoretical treatise but as a "spiritual *resource*," by which he means a book for meditation and rumination rather than instant consumption. He adds that the book does not aim to fulfill this purpose in the manner of Eastern philosophy where the aim is to put the intellect out of action. As he puts it, "the basis for the work is the use, even the passionate use, of reason."[23] Nietzsche's thinking in *Dawn* contains a number of proposals and recommendations of tremendous value to philosophical therapy, including (a) a call for a new honesty or integrity about the human ego and human relations, including relations of self and other and of love, so as to free us from certain delusions;[24] (b) the search for an authentic mode of existence which appreciates the value of solitude and independence; (c) the importance of having a rich and mature taste in order to eschew the fanatical. *Dawn* is a book written for mortal souls: several times in the book Nietzsche draws attention to the fact that a typical life span is seventy years (see, for example, *D* 196, 501). One of the heroes of the book is Epicurus, who sought to demonstrate the mortality of the soul and whose aim was "to free humans from 'the fears of the mind.'"[25] *Dawn* can be read in part, and on an existential or therapeutic level, as an attempt to revitalize for a modern age ancient philosophical concerns,

23. Julian Young, *Friedrich Nietzsche: A Philosophical Biography* (Cambridge: Cambridge University Press, 2010), 297.

24. In *Dawn, Redlichkeit* (honesty or integrity) is said to be mankind's youngest virtue (*D* 456). Nietzsche writes extensively on "integrity" in the notebooks of 1880–81 with several sketches for planned books bearing the title *Die Leidenschaft der Redlichkeit* (see *CW* 13, 6[459]). In *CW* 13, 7[53], he writes: "I am not in a position to acknowledge anything great that is not connected to *integrity toward oneself*; playacting toward oneself fills me with horror." Finally, in *CW* 13, 7[262], he notes a comparison with Pascal: "don't we, like him, have our strength in beating ourselves into submission? He in aid of God, and we in aid of integrity?"

25. Catherine Wilson, *Epicureanism at the Origins of Modernity* (Oxford: Oxford University Press, 2008), 7. See Epicurus, "Letter to Menoeceus," in *The Epicurus Reader*, ed. Brad Inwood and Lloyd P. Gerson (Indianapolis: Hackett, 1994), 29: "For there is nothing fearful in life for one who has grasped that there is nothing fearful in the absence of life . . . the wise man neither rejects life nor fears death."

notably a teaching for mortal souls who wish to be liberated from the fear and anguish of existence, as well as from God, "metaphysical need,"[26] and romantic music,[27] and are able to affirm their mortal conditions of existence. In *Dawn* Epicurus is portrayed as the enemy of the idea of punishments in Hell after death, which was developed by numerous secret cults of the Roman Empire and was taken up by Christianity.[28] For Nietzsche the triumph of Epicurus's teaching resounds most beautifully in the mouth of the somber Roman Lucretius but comes too early. Christianity takes the belief in "subterranean terrors" under its special protection and this foray into heathendom enables it to carry the day over the popularity of the Mithras and Isis cults, winning to its side the rank of the timorous as the most zealous adherents of the new faith (Nietzsche notes that because of the extent of the Jews' attachment to life

26. In a note from the autumn of 1880 Nietzsche maintains that metaphysical need is not the source of religion, as might be supposed, but rather the aftereffect of its decline: the "need" is a result and not an origin (*CW* 13, 6[290]). See also *JS* 151, where Nietzsche makes it clear that he is arguing contra Schopenhauer on this point.

27. The texts of the middle period find Nietzsche seeking to emancipate himself from Wagner and his youthful captivation by his music. In *HAH* 153, he states that the free spirit's intellectual probity is put to the test in moments when it listens to something like Beethoven's Ninth Symphony, which makes him feel that he is hovering above the earth in a dome of stars and with the dream of immortality in his heart: "If he becomes conscious of this state, he no doubt feels a sharp pang deep in his heart and sighs for someone who might lead his lost love, whether we call it religion or metaphysics, back to him."

28. In *D* 202, Nietzsche encourages us to do away with the concepts of "sin" and "punishment": "In future may these banished monsters live somewhere other than among people if they insist on wanting to survive and are not destroyed by their own self-disgust!" In *D* 208, entitled "Question of conscience," he states what he wishes to see changed: "We no longer want to turn the causes into sinners and consequences into executioners." In *D* 53, he notes that it is the most conscientious who suffer so dreadfully from the fears of hell: "Thus, a gloom falls over the lives of precisely those most in need of serenity and pleasant images."

such an idea fell on barren ground). However, the teaching
of Epicurus triumphs anew in the guise of modern science
which has rejected "any other representation of death and
any life beyond" (*D* 72; see also 150). Nietzsche is keen to
encourage human beings to cultivate an attitude toward existence in which they accept their mortality and attain a new
serenity about their dwelling on the earth, to conquer unjustified fears, and to reinstitute the role played by chance and
chance events in the world and in human existence (*D* 13, 33,
36). As Pierre Hadot notes, for the Epicurean sage the world
is the product of chance, not divine intervention, and this
brings with it pleasure and peace of mind, freeing him from
an unreasonable fear of the gods and allowing him to consider each moment as an unexpected miracle.[29]

Not only does Nietzsche subscribe at this time to much of
the teaching of Epicurus on cosmology and philosophy, he
was also inspired by Epicurus's conception of friendship and
ideal of withdrawing from society and cultivating one's own
garden.[30] In a letter to Peter Gast of 3 August 1883 Nietzsche
writes that Epicurus "is the best negative argument in favor of

29. See Pierre Hadot, *Philosophy as a Way of Life: Spiritual Exercises from
Socrates to Foucault*, trans. Michael Chase (Oxford: Blackwell, 1995), 252.

30. In her recent study, Catherine Wilson neatly lays out the central tenets of the Epicurean system. They include the denial of supernatural
agency engaged in the design and maintenance of the world; the view that
self-moving, subvisible particles acting blindly bring about all growth, change,
and decline; and the insistence that the goal of ethical self-discipline, which
involves asceticism, is the minimization of mental and physical suffering
(*Epicureanism* 37). It is on this last point that Nietzsche will come to later
criticize Epicureanism and describe Epicurus as a "*typical decadent*" (*AC* 30).
In the same text Epicurus is once again prized on account of his battle
against "the *underground* cults, the entire latent Christianity," his fight
against the "degradation of the soul through guilt, through the concept of
punishment and immortality" (*AC* 58). For further insight into Nietzsche's
reading of Epicurus, see also Howard Caygill, "The Consolation of Philosophy or 'Neither Dionysus nor the Crucified,'" *Journal of Nietzsche Studies* 7
(1994): 131–51, and, by the same author, "Under Epicurean Skies," *Angelaki*
11, no. 3 (2006): 107–15.

my challenge to all rare spirits to isolate themselves from the mass of their fellows" (*KGB* III:1, 418). If philosophical therapeutics is centered on a concern with the healing of our own lives,[31] so as to return us to the pleasure and joy in existing, then in Nietzsche's texts of his middle period, including *Dawn*, he can be seen to be an heir to this ancient tradition. The difference is that he is developing a therapy for the sicknesses of the soul under peculiarly modern conditions of existence of social control and discipline.

In the book Nietzsche is tracing a history of human fear and self-torment. I think it is his uncovering of this history which for Nietzsche accounted for the gloomy character of the book. His evaluations of our inheritance—of the origins and sources of human identity in fear; of the cruel practices employed by the ancient discipline of customary morality; and of Christianity—are not simply negative but subtle and nuanced (which does not prevent him from making certain key decisions about the future direction of humanity).[32] Nietzsche notes that cultural institutions and mores instill in the passions, and contrary to their nature, a belief in their duration and responsibility for this duration, and gives the example of the institution of marriage which has this effect on the passion of love. While such transformations introduce much hypocrisy and lying into the world they also bring with them "a *superhuman*, human-exalting concept" (*D* 27). On the one hand, and on a wider scale, a "vague fear and reverence" has directed humanity in its consideration of "our higher and more important concerns" and in the process a fearful humanity has prejudged and paralyzed thinking, choosing instead to enslave itself to self-abasement, self-torture, and much torment of body and soul (*D* 107; see also 142). On the other hand, however, it is possible to

31. Hadot, *Philosophy as a Way of Life*, 87.

32. In *D* 18 Nietzsche writes: "Nothing has been purchased more dearly than the little bit of human reason and sense of freedom that make up the sum total of our pride today."

locate in the history of human rituals, including rituals of sacrifice, a "prodigious training ground of the intellect" (*D* 40). As Nietzsche notes, it is not only religions that have been hatched and nurtured on this soil but also the "prehistoric world of science" as well as the poet, the thinker, the physician, and the lawgiver: "The fear of the unintelligible, which, in ambiguous fashion, demanded ceremonies from us, metamorphosed gradually into a fascination with the hardly intelligible, and where one knew not how to explicate, one learned to create" (*D* 40). He goes so far as to claim that it is fear and not love that has furthered the universal knowledge of humanity—where love is deceptive and blind (it harbors a secret impulse to elevate the other as high as possible), fear has a capacity for genuine discernment, for example, discerning the powers and desires of a person or an object (*D* 309).

For Nietzsche we are both heirs to, and continuers of, a history of sacrifice and of the sublime; the difference is that now for us the promise of happiness—which centers on a strengthening and elevation of "the general feeling of human *power*"—seeks to remain true to our mortal dwelling on the earth. Our task is now to take our time in our search; we are no longer looking for a single answer to our questions or some ultimate solution to the riddles of existence. Nietzsche advises us to go slowly and wisely, to administer the means of transforming ourselves in small doses and unremittingly over long periods of time since "What great things can be accomplished at one fell swoop?" (*D* 534). In the course of time we may discover that we have in fact created a new nature for ourselves. For Nietzsche a chief task is to purify ourselves of the origins and sources of our desire for the sublime, since the higher feelings associated with it are bound up with humanity's investment in an imaginary world: an "exalted humanity" is full of self-loathing and this needs to be conquered.[33] The sublime

33. The sublime as a noun is employed in the following aphorisms of the text, with a concentration in book five: 33, 45, 130, 169, 192, 210, 423, 427,

denotes for Nietzsche at this time not simply an aesthetic category but rather humanity's investment in a metaphysical
need of transcendence (see *HAH* 130 for a succinct perspective on the problem). Through knowledge a purified humanity can conquer the fear and anxiety that has captivated
previous humanity and taught it to kneel down before the
incomprehensible. In *Dawn* Nietzsche's concern is with a tran-
sitional humanity that is moving from a heritage of religions
and moralities to something new, in fact, to uncharted conditions of existence. He is keen to militate against the sublime of
dread and terror and to configure the sublime in a more modest and even humbling manner.[34] For Nietzsche the new sublimities of philosophy—addressed in the highly enigmatic
book five—are bound up with a new comportment toward
existence as it now concerns us as searchers of knowledge, and
a new fearlessness is required as we embark on this search free
of "the presumptions of morality." We are in the process of
becoming creatures that exist largely to know and who seek to
conquer the elevation offered by "morality."

As one commentator has noted, in the eyes of many of
his adherents as well as opponents, Nietzsche is an anti-
Enlightenment irrationalist.[35] One of the reasons why a
study of the middle period Nietzsche, including if not especially *Dawn*, is important, and proves so fruitful, is because
it can show this viewpoint to be a caricature, if not an out-
right distortion. Although Nietzsche is hostile to the French

---

435, 449, 459, 461, 542, 553, 570; and notions of elevation and exaltation are
deployed extensively throughout the text.

34. The link between the sublime and terror is, of course, the one made
by Edmund Burke, *A Philosophical Enquiry into the Origin of Our Ideas of
the Sublime and Beautiful* (Oxford: Oxford University Press, 1998), pt. 1, sec.
7, and pt. 2, sec. 2. Compare Immanuel Kant, *Critique of Judgment*, trans.
Werner S. Pluhar (Indianapolis: Hackett, 1987), sec. 28.

35. See Nicholas Martin, *"Aufklärung und Kein Ende*: The Place of Enlightenment in Friedrich Nietzsche's Thought," *German Life and Letters*, 61,
no. 1 (2008): 79–97, 79. See also Handwerk, afterword to *HAH I*, 364.

Revolution, he seeks to sever the link between enlightenment and revolution—because he suspects, or more than suspects, that revolution breeds fanaticism and is a throwback to a lower stage of culture. The sentiments informing revolutionary seizures and overthrows of power are for him so much delusion. As Nicholas Martin notes, Nietzsche takes the Enlightenment very seriously and as a cultural critic of the late nineteenth century he cannot afford to escape it and its legacy.[36] He is an admirer of the critical and rationalist spirit of the Enlightenment, of both the eighteenth-century version, as we find it in the likes of Voltaire and Lessing, and earlier incarnations, such as one finds in Epicurus, Petrarch, and Erasmus. Nietzsche shares many of the ideas and commitments of the modern Enlightenment, including the attack on superstition, religious dogmatism, rigid class structures, outmoded forms of governance and rule, and so on. Its fundamental spirit is one of demystification, of liberation of the human from its chains (see *WS* 350), seeking "to provide the individual with the critical tools to achieve autonomy, to liberate himself from his own unexamined assumptions as well as the dictates of others."[37] Nietzsche is an enlightenment thinker, then, in that his overriding aim is to foster autonomy and maturity in his readers. In this respect Nietzsche is an inheritor of Kant, as he acknowledges in *Dawn*.[38] In fact, he presents himself as being

36. Martin, *"Aufklärung und Kein Ende,"* 80.

37. Ibid.

38. Kant famously defines enlightenment as a human being's emergence from their self-incurred immaturity or the courage to use their own understanding without the guidance of another. See Immanuel Kant, "An Answer to the Question: 'What Is Enlightenment?'" (1784) in Kant, *Political Writings*, ed. Hans Reiss (Cambridge: Cambridge University Press, 1991), 54. For Kant it is "religious immaturity" that is "the most pernicious and dishonourable variety of all" (59). "Laziness and cowardice," Kant writes, "are the reasons why such a large proportion of men, even when nature has long emancipated them from alien guidance . . . nevertheless gladly remain immature for life." Compare the opening to Nietzsche's *Schopenhauer as Educator*. For an instructive comparison of Kant and Nietzsche on enlight-

even more faithful to the rational spirit of enlightenment than Kant was with his incomprehensible residues, such as the thing-in-itself and the categorical imperative (*D* 207). Nietzsche strongly allies himself with progressive forces but insists that social transformation, which is desirable, ought to be pursued gradually and patiently: there is no "miraculous" solution to human ills.

When Nietzsche discusses his favorite authors and books it is usually at the expense of German authors and German philosophy. In *The Wanderer and His Shadow*, for example, he mentions some of his favorite reading, which includes the likes of Montaigne, La Rochefoucauld, Fontenelle, and Chamfort. The works of these authors "form an important link in the great, ongoing chain of the Renaissance" (*WS* 214). What Nietzsche admires about them is that they are above the changes and vagaries of "national taste" and also above the "philosophical coloring" which every modern book radiates as a matter of rule and does so if it wishes to become famous. Moreover, these books "contain more *real ideas* than all the books of German philosophers put together." German philosophy books are characterized by "obscurity" and "exaggeration." Even Schopenhauer, who has affinities in his style of writing with the French moralists, wanders among images of things rather than among the things themselves. What Nietzsche admires about the French writers is their "wittiness of expression" and their "clarity and elegant precision." Moral philosophy, Nietzsche contends, has taken a wrong turn with German thought, notably with Kant's moralism (which, he notes, comes from Rousseau and the reawakened Stoicism of ancient Rome), and the moralism of Schiller too (*WS* 216). Since the beginning of the eighteenth century a "stream of moral awakening has been flowing through Europe" with "virtue" becoming eloquent

---

enment, see David Owen, "The Contest of Enlightenment: An Essay on Critique and Genealogy," *Journal of Nietzsche Studies* 25 (Spring 2003): 35–58.

and teaching human beings to discover "unconstrained gestures of exaltation [*Erhebung*] and emotion." The ultimate
source of this development for Nietzsche is Rousseau, but the
mythical Rousseau, that is, the one constructed out of the impression produced by his writings and confessions. What wor-
ries Nietzsche is that this "moral awakening" has resulted in
"regressive movements for the *knowledge* of moral appear-
ances," or genuinely scientific inquiry into the sources and nature of morality. Against this development he champions the
unfashionable (then and now) likes of Helvétius who sought to
treat morality, like all the other sciences, "founded on experiment, as well as natural philosophy":[39]

> What is all of German moral philosophy, counting from Kant
> onward, . . . ? A half-theological assault upon Helvetius, a
> rejection of the laboriously acquired clear views or indications
> of the right path, which he did in the end articulate and bring
> together well. Up to today, Helvetius is in Germany the most
> abused of all the good moralists and good humans. (*WS* 216)

Nietzsche picks up this theme again in *Dawn* with section
197 being the most important (but see also 190, 193, 207, 481).
The section is entitled "The Germans' hostility to the Enlightenment." In it Nietzsche seeks to take note of the intellectual
contribution Germany, including German philosophers, has
made to culture at large. He sees German philosophy of the
first half of the nineteenth century as a retrogressive force:
"they retreated to the first and oldest level of speculation, for,
like the thinkers of dreamy ages, they found satisfaction in
concepts rather than in explanations—they resuscitated a
pre-scientific type of philosophy" (*D* 197). Nietzsche sees similar retarding forces operating in German history and German
science. In the former, a general concern was to accord honor
upon primitive sensibilities, especially Christianity, but also

---

39. See Claude A. Helvétius, *De L'Esprit or Essays on the Mind and Its
Several Faculties* (Paris: Elibron Classics, 2005), preface.

folk-lore and folk-language, oriental asceticism, and the world
of India. In natural science German scientists have struggled
against the spirit of Newton and Voltaire and, following Goethe
and Schopenhauer, "sought to erect once again the idea of a
divine or demonic nature suffused with its universal ethical
[*ethischen*] and symbolic significance" (*D* 197). Thus, Nietzsche infers, the proclivity of the Germans runs contrary to the
Enlightenment as well as contrary to the revolution in society.
The German spirit is antiquarian: "piety towards everything
then in existence sought to metamorphose into piety towards
everything that once had existed in order that heart and spirit
might once again grow *full* and no longer have any room for
future, innovative goals" (*D* 197). German culture has erected
a cult of feeling at the expense of a cult of reason with German
composers—Nietzsche surely has in mind Wagner amongst
others—being artists of the invisible, of raptures, and of the
fairy-tale. Nietzsche objects to this cultural development, it is
important to note, for one main reason: it serves to retard,
suppress even, knowledge, as in Kant's famous words in the
second edition of the *Critique of Pure Reason* that he has found
it necessary to deny knowledge in order to make room for
faith and thus to draw up the limits of knowledge. Nietzsche
makes it clear that he champions the genuine enlightenment
and argues against all the forces of obscurantism:

> And strange to say: the very spirits that the Germans had so
> eloquently invoked became, in the long run, the most
> injurious for their invokers—history, understanding of origin
> and evolution, sympathy with the past, the newly aroused
> passion for feeling and knowledge, after having for a time
> appeared to be beneficial companions of the spirit of raptur-
> ous obscurantism and reaction, assumed one day a different
> nature and now fly on the widest wings above and beyond
> their earlier invokers as new and stronger geniuses of *that very
> Enlightenment* against which they had been invoked. This
> Enlightenment we now must carry on—unperturbed that

there has existed a "great Revolution" and then again a "great reaction" against it, that indeed both still exist: they are, after all, the mere ripple of waves in comparison to the truly great tide in which *we* surge and want to surge! (*D* 197)

As Mazzino Montinari remarks, a note from the spring of 1881—that is, just prior to the publication of *Dawn*—provides additional clues for deciphering section 197.[40] In it Nietzsche portrays the nineteenth century as one of reaction in which a conservative and preservative frame of mind predominates. The note runs as follows:

19th century, Reaction: people sought the *basic principles* of everything that had *lasted*, and sought to prove it was *true*. Permanence, fruitfulness and good conscience were seen as indices of truth! This was the conservative mentality: they called everything that had not yet been shaken; they had the egoism of the possessors as their strongest objection to the philosophy of the 18th century: for the non-possessors and malcontents there was *still* the church and even the arts (for some highly talented individuals there was also the worship of genius by way of gratitude if they worked for the conservative interests). With *history* [*Geschichte*] (new!!!) people *proved* things, they became *enthusiastic* for the great fruitful complexes called cultures (*nations*!!!). A huge part of the *zeal for research* and of the *sense of worship* was thrown at the past: modern philosophy and natural science *forfeited* this part!— —Now new **backlash**! History [*Historie*] *ultimately* proved something other than what was wanted: it turned out to be the most certain means of destroying those principles. Darwin. On the other hand skeptical historicism as aftereffect, empathy. People became *better* acquainted with the *motivating* forces in history [*Geschichte*], not our "beautiful"

40. Mazzino Montinari, "Enlightenment and Revolution: Nietzsche and the Later Goethe," in Mazzino Montinari, *Reading Nietzsche*, trans. Greg Whitlock (Urbana: University of Illinois Press, 2003), 50–56, 51.

ideas! Socialism has a *historical* foundation, similarly national
wars for historical reasons! (*CW* 13, 10[D88])[41]

For Nietzsche, then, it is history that serves as the means of
destroying the conservative principle, and this history includes
Darwin's theory of evolution. What we need to learn and take
cognizance of are the real forces operating in history and not
our beautiful ideas. Everything that comes into existence—e.g.,
socialism—plants its own foundations in history.[42] As Nietzsche presents it in *Dawn* 197, the basic idea is that the "enlightenment" project we are to further is to make its claim, "not
against but rather beyond a great revolution (socialism) and a
great reaction, *beyond* the conservative frame of mind."[43] It is
thus an error in Nietzsche's account of the story to conceive the
Enlightenment as the cause of the Revolution, a misunderstanding that is the "reaction" itself and it would be equally an
error to conceive the continuing enlightenment as the cause of
socialism. As Montinari notes, the new great reaction in the
form of the conservative mentality consists in this error. As he
further notes, from 1878 onwards, Nietzsche considers a new
enlightenment as the noble task for the free spirit of his own
times. There have been to date two great historical periods in
which an enlightenment has sought to flourish but has been
halted by a paired revolution and reaction: first, the Enlightenment of Italian and European humanism, or the Renaissance
(Petrarch and Erasmus), but followed by the German Reformation and the Counter-Reformation; second, the Enlightenment
of France, notably Voltaire, with the French Revolution and
German romanticism as the corresponding revolution and reaction. In progress now is a third enlightenment, conceived by
Nietzsche as a "new" enlightenment which contrasts itself to
both the great revolution and great reaction of modern times,

41. The note is not translated in Montinari's essay and was prepared for
this Afterword by Duncan Large.
42. Montinari, "Enlightenment and Revolution," 51.
43. Ibid., 52.

socialism and conservatism.[44] Nietzsche notes in *Human, All Too Human* 26, entitled "Reaction as progress," that in the previous two enlightenments the new "free spirited" tendencies were not powerful enough to withstand the appearance of impassioned but backward spirits who conjured up once again a bygone phase of humanity. This is the case with Luther's Reformation in which "all stirrings of the freedom of spirit were still uncertain, delicate, youthful" and "science could not yet raise its head." It is the case in the nineteenth century where Schopenhauer's metaphysics showed "that even now the scientific spirit is not yet strong enough": in spite of the achieved destruction of Christian dogmas in Schopenhauer's doctrine the whole medieval Christian world-view once again celebrated its resurrection. Although there is in Schopenhauer "a strong ring of science," this does not master his thinking; rather, it is the "'metaphysical need'" that does. As Martin notes, Nietzsche wants an "enlightenment of the Enlightenment."[45] Nietzsche sees the task as a never-ending critical process; the problem with Revolution is that it aims at the achievement of an imagined end and this longing for finality and resolution is ultimately seen by Nietzsche as a symptom and defining characteristic of nihilism.[46]

In *Dawn* Nietzsche's revaluation of values is underway insofar as (a) the value of egoistic actions is to be restored and such actions are to be deprived of their evil conscience (*D* 148); and (b) morally motivated actions are acknowledged to exist but the claim is that they rest on erroneous presuppositions (*D* 103). As already noted, Nietzsche states in *Ecce Homo* that his "campaign" against morality begins in earnest with *Dawn*. Much of

44. I borrow this schema of enlightenment in Nietzsche's thought from Montinari, ibid., 52. See also Martin, *"Aufklärung und Kein Ende,"* 89–90.

45. Martin, *"Aufklärung und Kein Ende,"* 89.

46. Ibid., 94. Again, compare Kant, *Political Writings*, 57: "One age cannot enter into an alliance on oath to put the next age in a position where it would be impossible to extend and correct its knowledge . . . or to make any progress whatsoever in enlightenment."

the polemic is directed at what Nietzsche regards as our peculiarly modern conception of morality in terms of the sympathetic affects. Indeed, unifying the different lines of enquiry undertaken by Nietzsche in *Dawn* is his critical concern with the *Vorurtheile* of "morality." The German word, in this context, is better translated as "presumptions" or "presuppositions" or "prejudgments" than "prejudices," as Nietzsche is addressing what morality presumes and doesn't question, not the already decided prejudicial conclusions morality has come to.[47] Within modernity there reigns the presumption that we know "what actually constitutes morality": "it seems *to do* every single person *good* these days to hear that society is on the road to *adapting* the individual to fit the needs of the throng and that the *individual's happiness as well as his sacrifice* consist in feeling himself to be a useful member of the whole . . ." (*D* 132). We can, Nietzsche thinks, explain this development in terms of a movement towards managing more cheaply, safely, and uniformly individuals in terms of "*large bodies and their limbs.*" This, he says, is "*the basic moral current of our age*": "Everything that in some way supports both this drive to form bodies and limbs and its abetting drives is felt to be *good* . . ." (ibid.).

Nietzsche's campaign has to be heard carefully. Although he contests the idea that there is a *single* moral-making morality, he does not contest the idea that morality is necessary or that there are not different ways of being ethical. He is keen, then, to challenge the idea that there is a single, absolute conception of morality. *D* 139 is instructive on this point: "You say that the morality of being compassionate is a higher morality [*Moral*] than that of Stoicism? Prove it! But remember that what is 'higher' and 'lower' in morality is not, in turn to be measured by a moral yardstick: for there is no absolute morality [*Moral*]. So take your rule from somewhere else—and now beware!"

---

47. An alternative to "prejudices" in the translation of the book's subtitle is proposed by Young, *Nietzsche*, 304 note.

In the modern assumption that the essence of the moral is to be defined in terms of purely other-regarding actions there is lacking an appreciation of our ethical complexity and the fact that in any action multiple motives might be in play. For Nietzsche moral motives are epistemically opaque, and on this point he is close to Kant.[48] Kant acknowledges that we can never know with absolute certainty the nature of our motives: we may believe we have performed an action out of respect for the moral law but in fact it may have been performed out of self-love or some other heteronomous inclination. Nietzsche adheres to this view because for him there are many motives informing any single action and these motives are hidden from the agent performing the action. As he indicates in his treatment of *Mitleid*, it may well be that honor, fear, self-defense, or revenge are what moves us to help another although we tell ourselves it was an act performed solely for their well-being (*D* 133). As one commentator notes, for Nietzsche human nature "has depths and obscurities that make it extremely difficult, if not impossible to specify the drives and urges from which our actions stem."[49] We are not transparent to ourselves in Nietzsche's view, and when we rely on introspection or self-consciousness to discover our motives and intentions we are involved in processes of selection and interpretation; that is, we do not simply retrieve so-called mental facts in such acts. Rather, we "impose, form, organize, and categorize our inner experiences just as we do our outer experiences."[50] Nietzsche is arguing against what he sees as Schopenhauer's moral realism, as when Schopenhauer claims that "every one of us is really a competent and perfectly moral judge exhibiting exact knowledge of good and evil, holy in that we love good and abhor evil" (quoted in *D* 116).

48. David E. Cartwright, "Kant, Schopenhauer, and Nietzsche on the Morality of Pity," *Journal of the History of Ideas* 45, no. 1 (Jan.–Mar. 1984): 83–98, 96.

49. Ibid., 96–97.

50. Ibid., 98.

Today, then, the presumption holds sway in Europe that the sympathetic affects and compassion define the moral, as in actions deemed to be congenial, disinterested, of general utility, and so on. Although Nietzsche mentions Schopenhauer and John Stuart Mill as famous teachers of this conception of morality, he holds that they merely echo doctrines that have been sprouting up in both fine and crude forms since the time of the French Revolution (*D* 132).[51] Central to modernity, as Nietzsche perceives it, is the idea that the ego must deny itself and adapt itself to the whole and as a result the "individual" is debilitated and cancelled: "one never tires of enumerating and excoriating everything evil and malicious, prodigal, costly, and extravagant in the prior form of individual existence . . . individual empathy and social sentiment here go hand in hand" (*D* 132). Nietzsche contests this sacrifice of the individual for the sake of the social whole and offers an alternative conception of "self-sacrifice." In contrast to a narrow, petty bourgeois morality, a higher and freer manner of thinking will now look beyond the immediate consequences our actions have for others and seek to further more distant aims. Under some circumstances this will be at the expense of the suffering of others, for example, by furthering genuine knowledge: does not "free thinking" initially plunge people into doubt and distress? In seeking victory over ourselves we need "*to get beyond our compassion*" (*D* 146). Nietzsche too seeks "universal interests"

51. In his sketch of modern European thought since the French Revolution, Nietzsche fails to acknowledge, of course, the extent to which Mill is a champion of individual liberty and autonomy. In the chapter "Individuality, as One of the Elements of Well-Being" in his *On Liberty*, Mill writes: "but the evil, is that individual spontaneity is hardly recognized by the common modes of thinking, as having any intrinsic worth, or deserving any regard on its own account. The majority, being satisfied with the ways of mankind as they now are (for it is they who make them what they are), cannot comprehend why those ways should not be good enough for everybody" (J. S. Mill, *On Liberty*, ed. John Gray [Oxford: Oxford University Press, 1991], 63).

through this cultivation of free-mindedness: "Supposing we went in for self-sacrifice: what would prohibit us from sacrificing our neighbor as well? — just as state and prince have forever done when they sacrificed one citizen to the other 'in the universal public interest,' as they put it. But we too have universal, perhaps more universal interests: why shouldn't some individuals from the current generation be sacrificed for future generations?" (ibid.). The grief, despair, blunderings, and fearful footsteps of individuals may form part of "a new ploughshare" that will "cleave the ground, rendering it fruitful for all . . ." (ibid.).

The morality that humanity has cultivated and dedicated itself to is one of enthusiastic devotion and living for others in which it looks down from sublime heights on the more sober morality of self-control (which is regarded as egotistical). Nietzsche suggests the reason why morality has been developed in this way is owing to the enjoyment of the state of intoxication which has stemmed from the thought that the person is at one with the powerful being to whom it consecrates itself; in this way "the feeling of power" is enjoyed and is confirmed by a sacrifice of the self. For Nietzsche such an overcoming of the "self" is impossible: "In truth you only *seem* to sacrifice yourselves; instead, in your thoughts you transform yourselves to gods and take pleasure in yourselves as such" (*D* 215; see also *D* 269).

Part of Nietzsche's hostility toward "morality" stems from what he regards as the anti-naturalism of moral concepts and thinking, as when he writes that what he wants is to stop making causes into sinners and consequences into executioners (*D* 208).[52] A "moral" interpretation of the body and its affects blocks off the securing of naturalistically informed self-knowledge and generates a psychical suffering peculiar to it, as when Nietzsche writes of Pascal that he construed whatever proceeded from the stomach, entrails, heartbeat, nerves, gall,

---

52. See Carl B. Sachs, "Nietzsche's *Daybreak*: Toward a Naturalized Theory of Autonomy," *Epoché* 13, no. 1 (2008): 81–100, 88.

and the semen—"the whole contingent nature of the machine we know so little!"—as "a moral and religious phenomenon" of which one could ask "whether it contains God or devil, good or evil, salvation or damnation" (*D* 86).

In examining the inflated character of moral language Nietzsche is dealing with a problem that preoccupies him in his middle and late periods: the problem of fanaticism (*D* 57–58, 68, 298, 511; see also *MM* 15; *JS* 347; *BGE* 10).[53] As he notes, such "enthusiasts" will seek to implant the faith in intoxication "as *the* life within life: a terrible faith!" (*D* 50). Such is the extent of Nietzsche's anxiety that he wonders whether humanity as a whole will one day perish by its "spiritual firewaters" and those who keep alive the desire for them. The "strange madness of moral judgments" is bound up with states of exaltation and "the most exalted language" (*D* 189). Nietzsche is advising us to be on our guard, to be vigilant as philosophers against the "half-disturbed, fantastical, fanatical," including so-called human beings of genius who claim to have "visions" and to have seen things others do not see. We are to be cautious, not credulous, when confronted with the claims of visions, that is to say, "of profound mental disturbances!" (*D* 66). The problem with the consolations that have been offered to humanity by religions to date is that they have imparted to life the fundamental character of suffering: "the human being's greatest disease grew

53. At this time Nietzsche is reading Voltaire's *Mahomet* (see *HAH* 221) and recommending to people, including his sister Elisabeth, that they read it (see letter to her dated 13 February 1881, *KGB* III:1, 62). However, we need to read carefully here because there is the danger of turning Nietzsche's championing of the Enlightenment against forces of reaction into an all-too-timely position against Islam. To avoid this requires a careful analysis of Nietzsche's comments on different religions. In *JS* 347, for example, it is not Islam but Christianity and Buddhism that he describes as teaching fanaticism. In *D* 68, Saint Paul is described as a fanatic while in *D* 546 Epictetus is presented as an example of a nonfanatical person. For further insight into Nietzsche on fanaticism, see Bernard Reginster, "What Is a Free Spirit? Nietzsche on Fanaticism," *Archiv für Geschichte der Philosophie* 85 (2003): 51–85.

out of the battle against its diseases, and the apparent remedies have, in the long run, produced something much worse than what they were supposed to eliminate" (*D* 52). Humanity has mistaken "the momentarily effective, anesthetizing, and intoxicating means, the so-called consolations, for the actual remedies" (ibid.). It is under the most "scandalous quackery" that humanity has come to treat its diseases of the soul.

Nietzsche appeals to Epictetus for an example of a non-fanatical mode of living and as a counterweight to modern idealists who are greedy for expansion. Epictetus's ideal human being, lacking all fear of God and believing strictly in reason, "is not a preacher of penitence" (*D* 546). Although this ancient thinker was a slave, the exemplar he invokes is without class and is possible in every class. Nietzsche notes, moreover, that while Christianity was made for a different species of antique slave (one weak in will and mind), Epictetus neither lives in hope nor accepts the best he knows as a gift but "possesses it, he holds it valiantly in his hand, and he would take on the whole world if it tries to rob him of it" (*D* 546). Epictetus is also admired by Nietzsche on account of his dedication to his own ego and for resisting the glorification of thinking and living for others (*D* 131). He serves as a useful contrast to Christian thinkers such as Pascal, who considered the ego (*Ich*) something hateful (*D* 79).[54]

Nietzsche thinks that "morality" serves to suppress genuine individuality and to retard individual self-knowledge. In an aphorism on "pseudo-egotism," he notes how most people do nothing for their ego, but rather live in accordance with the "phantom ego" that has been formed in the opinions of those around them. The result is that we live in a fog of impersonal or half-personal opinions and arbitrary evaluations: "one person always in the head of the other and then again this head in other heads:

54. For further insight into Nietzsche's appreciation of Epictetus, see Thomas Brobjer, "Nietzsche's Reading of Epictetus," *Nietzsche-Studien* 32 (2003): 429–35.

a curious world of phantasms that nonetheless knows how to don such a sensible appearance!" (*D* 105). As Nietzsche notes, this fog of habits and opinions comes to live and grow independently of the people it envelops. Unknown to ourselves we live within the effect of general opinions about the "human being," which is a "bloodless abstraction" and "fiction" (*D* 105).

Even the modern glorification of work and talk of its blessings can be interpreted as a fear of everything individual. The subjection to hard industriousness from early until late serves as "the best policeman" since it keeps everyone in bounds and hinders the development of reason, desire, and the craving for independence. It uses vast amounts of nervous energy which could be given over to reflection, brooding, dreaming, loving and hating and working through our experiences: "a society in which there is continuous hard work will have more security: and security is currently worshipped as the supreme divinity" (*D* 173). Nietzsche claims that it is the moral fashion of a commercial society to value actions aimed at common security and to cultivate above all the sympathetic affections. At work here is a collective drive toward timidity which desires that life be rid of all the dangers it might have once held: "Are we not, with this prodigious intent to grate off all the rough and sharp edges of life, well on the way to turning humanity into *sand*?" (*D* 174). In place of the ruling ethic of sympathy and compassion, which can assume the form of a "tyrannical encroachment," Nietzsche invites individuals to engage in self-fashioning, cultivating a self that the other can behold with pleasure, a "lovely, peaceful, self-enclosed garden . . . with high walls to protect against the dangers and dust of the roadway, but with a hospitable gate as well" (*D* 174).

In Nietzsche's conception of the (ethical) task, self-creation is self-cultivation and not a matter of creating *ex nihilo*.[55] He is

---

55. See Young, *Friedrich Nietzsche*, 306. For further insight into Nietzsche on an ethics of self-cultivation, see Michael Ure, *Nietzsche's Therapy: Self-Cultivation in the Middle Works* (Lanham, Md.: Lexington Books, 2008),

not, it seems clear, advocating the abolition of all possible types or forms of morality. His concern is that "morality" in the forms it has assumed in the greater part of human history, right up to Kant's moral law, has opened up an abundance of sources of displeasure and with every refinement of morals human beings have only become more discontented with themselves, their neighbor, and their lot (*D* 106). The individual in search of happiness, and who wishes to become its own lawgiver, cannot be treated with general prescriptions to the path to happiness simply because individual happiness springs from one's own unknown laws, and external prescriptions only serve to obstruct and hinder it: "The precepts that one labels 'moral' are, in truth, directed against individuals and are in no way aimed at promoting the happiness of individuals" (*D* 108). Up to now, Nietzsche notes, the moral law has been supposed to stand above our personal likes and dislikes; we did not want to impose this law upon ourselves but preferred to take it from somewhere or have it commanded to us. If we assume (a) only those actions performed solely for the sake of another can be called moral; and (b) only those actions performed out of miraculously self-causing free will can be called moral (*D* 148), there can be no moral actions. If we liberate ourselves from these errors a revaluation can take place in which we will discover that we have overestimated the value and importance of free and non-egoistic actions at the expense of unfree and egoistic ones (see also *D* 164).

What, ultimately, is it that drives Nietzsche's project in the texts of his middle period and as we encounter it in *Dawn*? It can perhaps best be summarized as the search for an authentic mode of existence. To have one's own evaluation of things is something exceedingly rare (*D* 104). Our actions can be traced

---

and Horst Hutter, *Shaping the Future: Nietzsche's New Regime of the Soul and Its Ascetic Practices* (Lanham, Md.: Lexington Books, 2006). For insight into the early Nietzsche and "cultivation," see Gray, afterword to *Unpublished Writings from the Unfashionable Observations*, 477–78.

back to our evaluations, which are either "original" or "adopted." It is the latter that is the most common. We adopt them from fear, Nietzsche argues, and pretend that they are our own and accustom ourselves to this pretence and over time this becomes our nature. An "original" evaluation is said to be one in which a thing is assessed according to the extent that it pleases or displeases us alone and nobody else, and this is something rare. We learn as children and then rarely learn to change our views: "most often we are, throughout our lives, the dupe of the way we learned in childhood to judge our neighbors (their intellect, station, morality, exemplarity or reproachability) and to deem it necessary to pay homage to their evaluations" (D 104).

As we have already noted, Nietzsche challenges the idea that there can be a single morality; every code of ethics that affirms itself in an exclusive manner "destroys too much valuable energy and costs humanity much too dearly" (D 164). In the future, Nietzsche hopes, the inventive and fructifying person shall no longer be sacrificed and numerous novel attempts at living life and fashioning society shall be undertaken. When this takes place we will find that an enormous load of guilty conscience has been purged from the world. Humanity has suffered for too long from teachers of morality who wanted too much all at once and sought to lay down precepts for everyone (D 194). In the future the care of truth will need to center on the most personal questions and create time for them (D 196). Small individual questions and experiments are no longer to be viewed with contempt and impatience (D 547). We will grow and become the ones that we are, however, only by experiencing dissatisfaction with ourselves and assuming the risk of experimenting in life, freely taking the journey through our wastelands, quagmires, and icy glaciers. The ones who don't take the risk of life "will never make the journey around the world (that you yourselves are!), but will remain trapped within yourselves like a knot on the log you were born to, a mere happenstance" (D 343).

In *Dawn* Nietzsche makes numerous practical recommendations for how we might go about cultivating and practicing such an authentic existence. When we are tired and fed up with ourselves and require fresh stimulation the best practice is to "*sleep a lot*, literally and figuratively! That way one will also awaken again upon a new morning!" (*D* 376). An essential test to learn is the endurance of solitude (*D* 443). Solitude has the advantage of providing us with the distant perspective we need to think well of things: "on my own I seem to see my friends more clearly and more appealingly than when together with them; and at the time when I loved music most and was most sensitive to it, I loved at a distance from it" (*D* 485). We need solitude "so as not to drink out of everyone's cisterns" for among the many we simply do not think as an "I." Not only is such solitude of benefit to ourselves, it also improves our relation to others; when we turn angry toward people and fear them we need the desert to become good again (*D* 491).

Nietzsche seeks to counsel us in the wisdom of "slow cures" (*D* 462). He notes that chronic diseases of the soul, like those of the body, rarely emerge through one-time large offenses against the rationality of body and soul, but rather through countless undetected little acts of negligence. If this is the case then the cure has to be equally subtle and entail countless little offsetting exercises and the unwitting cultivation of different habits: "Many a person has a cold, malicious word to say for his environment ten times a day and doesn't think anything of it, especially since, after a few years, he has created for himself a *law* of habit that from now on *compels* him ten times every day to sour his environment. But he can also accustom himself to doing it a kindness ten times!" (*D* 462). In *Dawn* the emphasis is on knowing one's circumstances and as a means of knowing one's power: "One ought to think of oneself as a variable quantity whose capacity for accomplishment can perhaps under favorable circumstances match the highest ever." Nietzsche argues that one, therefore, needs to reflect on the circumstances and "spare no diligence" in our contemplation or knowledge of them (*D* 326).

Nietzsche stresses that once you have taken "the decisive step" and entered "on the way one calls one's 'own way [*eigenen Weg*]' a secret suddenly reveals itself to us: even all those with whom we were friendly and intimate—all have imagined themselves superior to us and are offended" (*D* 484). He continues:

> The best among them are lenient with us and wait patiently for us to rediscover the "right way"—they know it, of course! Others make fun and act as if one had gone temporarily batty or else point spitefully to a seducer. The more malicious declare us to be vain fools and attempt to blacken our motives. The worst ones see in us their worst enemy, one who thirsts for revenge after a long period of dependence—and is afraid of us. What's to be done? I advise: we initiate our sovereignty [*Souveränität*] by assuring all our acquaintances a year's amnesty in advance for their sins of every kind.

Nietzsche is not recommending self-withdrawal and isolation as the ultimate cure to one's predicament; rather, these are means or steps on the way to working on oneself so one can become genuinely beneficent toward others. We go wrong when we fail to attend to the needs of the "ego" and flee from it. Nietzsche notes that hitherto fleeing from the ego, hating it even, and living in and for others has been called, "unreflectedly" unegotistical and therefore good (*D* 516).

In a note from autumn 1880, Nietzsche insists that the intellect is the tool of our drives, "it is *never free*." What it does is to sharpen itself in the struggle with various drives and thereby refines the activity of each individual drive. But he also insists that "The will to power [*der Wille nach Macht*], to the infallibility [*Unfehlbarkeit*] of our person, resides in our greatest justice and integrity [*Redlichkeit*]: skepticism just applies to all authority, we do not want to be duped, not even by *our drives*! But what does not *want*? A drive, certainly!" (*CW* 13, 6[130]). At work in Nietzsche we see an ethic of "individualization" which: (a) is a form of perfecting oneself through quite radical independence; (b) entails constant and intense self-observation of the circumstances and situations one finds oneself in.[56]

The focus of an ethics of self-cultivation for Nietzsche needs to be on our drives and not on a metaphysically conceived "self," for there is no self independent of the structuring and organization of the drives. That is, the "self" just is for Nietzsche a site or agent of structuring, ordering, and organizing. If free spirits aspire to a new condition of freedom this is because a new drive, such as the drive to independence and one's own style of existing, has become dominant within them and expresses itself as a "task," which Nietzsche compares to an unconscious pregnancy (*HAH* preface of 1886). The actual "philosophy" one comes up with may itself be nothing other than a sublimation and refinement, even a release, of the drives. Thus, Nietzsche admits in *Dawn* that *his* philosophy is, at bottom, an instinct for a personal diet and hygiene, one that suits a particular taste and for whom it alone is beneficial. This is an instinct that is searching for its own air, its own heights, its own weather, its own type of health, and through the detour of its own head. He writes with astonishing honesty and insight: "There are many other and certainly many loftier sublimities (*höhere Erhabenheiten*) of philosophy and not just those that are more gloomy and more ambitious than mine—perhaps they too are, each and every one, nothing other than intellectual detours for these kinds of personal drives?—" (*D* 553).

Our focus, then, is to be on the cultivation of the drives, and an initial step on the path to self-enlightenment and self-liberation is to know that here we do enjoy a certain, albeit limited, freedom. Contra Schopenhauer's doctrine on the immutability of character, Nietzsche argues that although we are "facts," we are not *fully grown* ones, so here there is room for the cultivation of the shoots of one's drives and affects. Although the exercise may be a minimal one, involving the fash-

---

56. See Sachs, "Nietzsche's *Daybreak*," 91.

ioning of what we might call a "modest egoism"—since we are not the authors of our own selves and need to give up on the Oedipal fantasy, in which we would exist as it were as our own mother and father (see *D* 128)—it is nevertheless an ethical *task* that Nietzsche sets for himself and his readers. Nietzsche conceives the work of self-cultivation in terms of the gardener stylizing nature, which one can do with the good or bad taste of a gardener, and in the French or English, or Dutch or Chinese style (*D* 560).[57]

It is clear that Nietzsche is a thinker of autonomy and his project has some resemblances to that of Kant's, but the differences are ultimately crucial. Nietzsche has something more modest, more "experimental," and more uniquely individual in mind when he thinks the nature of autonomy. Interestingly, in *Dawn*, we find Kant is praised over other moral philosophers, especially Schopenhauer, for esteeming reason over sentiment in ethics and for standing outside the modern movement with its emphasis on defining morality in terms of the sympathetic affects (see *D* 132). The problem, Nietzsche says in *Dawn* 339, is that Kant demands that duty "must *always* be something of a burden," never habit and custom, and in this demand "there is concealed a remnant of ascetic cruelty." So, one of Nietzsche's interests in ethics is that duty should cease being a burden and he has the hope that after long practice it can become instead a "pleasurable inclination" and a need in which the rights of others to whom our duties, and now our inclinations, refer become

57. The ethical task that Nietzsche conceives is much more modest, perhaps, than what we find in Michel Foucault's conception of ethics, which has taken up Nietzsche's invitation that the "self" gives style to its character (*JS* 290). Nietzsche conceives the work of self-cultivation in terms of the gardener stylizing nature, rather than the kind of Baudelairean-inspired idea of unrestricted, open-ended self-invention we arguably encounter in Foucault. On this point see Ure, *Nietzsche's Therapy*, 76–77. For Foucault, see *The Essential Works of Foucault. Volume I: Ethics*, ed. Paul Rabinow (New York: New Press, 1997), especially "On the Genealogy of Ethics: An Overview of Work in Progress," 253–80.

"occasions of pleasant feelings for us." And it is clear that
Nietzsche thinks the ethical task of achieving self-control and
self-mastery will be more appealing to us if we practice it aes-
thetically, for one can take pleasure, even delight, in such an
exercise and use the full range of one's senses and reason.

It goes without saying perhaps that Nietzsche's emphasis on
the individual's self-cultivation entails a corresponding deval-
uation of economics and politics. He considers these to represent a squandering of spirit: "Our age, no matter how much it
talks and talks about economy, is a squanderer: it squanders
what is most precious, spirit" (D 179). Today, he holds, we are
in a state of "colossal and ridiculous lunacy" with everybody
feeling obliged to know what is going on day in and day out
and longing at every instant to be actively involved to the
point of abandoning the work of their own therapy. Here he
has a number of concerns which I shall only briefly mention,
concerns that contemporary readers may find remarkably pre-
scient of our own world. First, he sees emerging within society
a culture whose "soul" is commerce, as the personal contest
was for the Greeks and the war and victory was for the Romans: "Commercial man understands how to assess the value
of everything without having made it and, indeed, to assess it
not according to his own, most personal need, but *according to
consumer need*; 'Who and how many will consume this?' is his
question of questions" (D 175). This mode of appraisal then
gets applied, Nietzsche notes anxiously, to everything, including the productions of the arts and sciences, of thinkers, scholars, artists, statesmen, etc., thereby becoming the character of
an entire culture. Second, we are today creating a society of
"national security" but the price being paid for it is, Nietzsche
thinks, much too high: "the maddest thing of all is, moreover,
that this behavior brings about the very opposite of 'national
security'" (D 179). Third, and finally, in this age of "grand politics" (D 189) we are developing not a politics of food or diges-
tion but one of "intoxication": "Nations are so exceedingly deceived because they are always *seeking* a deceiver, namely a

stimulating wine for their senses. If only they can have *that*, they gladly put up with lousy bread. Intoxication is more important to them than food" (*D* 188).

The final book of *Dawn*, book five, is among the most neglected parts of Nietzsche's oeuvre. And yet it is of vital importance for an appreciation of how Nietzsche conceives philosophy at this time and anticipates what is to become "the joyful science." He has an expectation of new dawns and declares the era of "harmless counterfeiting" to be over; he now looks ahead to the "astronomers of the ideal" who will take over the role of the poets whose task was to be seers who could recount to us "something of the *possible*!" (*D* 551).

Toward the end of the text Nietzsche, in fact, addresses the question of the direction of this new philosophy of the morning: where is it headed with all its detours? (*D* 553). Nietzsche is looking forward to new experiences and new possibilities of life, and he is keen to offer wise counsel concerning the future. He suggests, for example, that we should no longer feel the need to rush knowledge along to some end point (*D* 547). There is no longer the need to approach questions and experiments as if the solutions to them had to correspond to a typical human time span. We are now free to take our time and go slowly. The idea has evolved that there is a riddle to solve for the philosopher and the task is to compress the problem of the world into the simplest riddle-form: "The boundless ambition and jubilation of being the 'unriddler of the world' were the stuff of thinker's dreams" (*D* 547). Under such a conception of the task of thinking, philosophy assumed the guise of being a supreme struggle for the tyrannical rule of spirit reserved for a single individual (Nietzsche thinks that it is Schopenhauer who has most recently fancied himself as such an individual). The lesson to be drawn from this inheritance is that the quest for knowledge has been retarded by the moral narrow-mindedness of its disciples; in the future, Nietzsche declares, "it must be pursued with a higher and *more magnanimous* basic feeling: 'What do I matter!' stands over the door of the future thinker" (*D* 547).

For Nietzsche, philosophy's love of knowledge will now develop as a form of passion that shrinks at no sacrifice. In Aphorism 429 he notes that we moderns fear a possible return to barbarism and not because it would make us unhappier since in all ages barbarians have been happier peoples. Rather, he argues, our drive to knowledge has become so strong for us that we now cannot tolerate the idea of happiness without knowledge. We now honestly believe that "under the pressure and suffering of *this* passion the whole of humanity must believe itself to be more sublime and more consoled than previously, when it had not yet overcome its envy of the cruder pleasure and contentment that result from barbarism" (*D* 429). Nietzsche holds that we feel "more consoled," I think, because of our growth in intellectual strength: we have the chance of knowledge and rendering things comprehensible, and with this there comes a new courage, fearlessness, and serenity (*Heiterkeit*). We even entertain the thought that humanity might perish of its newfound passion for knowledge, though clearly Nietzsche is not an advocate of this. As he notes, such a thought can hold no sway over us. Our evolution is now bound up with this passion, however, and the task is to allow ourselves to be ennobled and elevated by it: "if humanity is not destroyed by a *passion* it will be destroyed by a *weakness*: which does one prefer? This is the main question. Do we desire for humanity an end in fire and light or in sand?" (*D* 429).

In Aphorism 427 Nietzsche addresses what philosophy now means and does in relation to the emerging science (*Wissenschaft*) of knowledge. He draws a comparison with rococo horticulture, which arose from the feeling that nature is ugly, savage, and boring and thus the aim was to beautify it. This is now what philosophy does with science, beautifying what strikes us as ugly, dry, cheerless, and laborious. Philosophy is a species of art and poetry and thus a form of "entertainment": "in keeping with its inherited pride, however, it wants to do this in a more sublime and elevated manner among a group of select spirits" (*D* 427). Nietzsche already has here, then, the conception of the project of the "joyful science" with its mixture of poetry, song, the philosophical aphorism, and dedication to science. Nietzsche himself raises the question whether the philosopher of the morning is really renouncing things or gaining a new cheerfulness or serenity:

> To relinquish the world without knowing it, like a *nun*—that leads to an infertile, perhaps melancholic solitude. This has nothing in common with the solitude of the thinker's *vita contemplativa*: when he elects *it*, he in no way wishes to renounce; on the contrary, it would amount to renunciation, melancholy, downfall of his self for him to have to endure the *vita practica*: he relinquishes the latter because he knows it, knows himself. Thus he leaps into *his* water, thus he attains *his* serenity. (*D* 440)

For the thinker who now has the new dedication to knowledge and can recognize the extent of its future-oriented character—it is such because the discoveries of knowledge always run ahead of a humanity that in time will seek to become equal to it—existence is lived magnanimously. It is this "magnanimity" that characterizes Nietzsche's project in *Dawn* and that he wishes his readers to be equal to. His aim in this text is not to offer his philosophy as if it was a binding institution for the future of humankind—to canonize himself as it were—but rather to suggest and open up new possibilities of life. *Dawn* is a philosophy of experiments that centers on new tasks of knowledge and whose aim is ultimately practical. Our task is to build anew the laws of life and action: "We are experiments: let us also want to be such!" (*D* 453).

Whether one should look in the book for a consistent and fully worked out moral philosophy is a difficult question. It is not that Nietzsche is inconsistent or incoherent; it is rather that the text develops what might be called trains of thought that sometimes lead to decisive insights but which also leaves much for the reader to engage with and to complete (for an excellent example of Nietzsche's use of the ellipsis or aposiopesis see *D* 146). Nietzsche wants his readers to develop an intimate relationship with the text. The text has a sense of the future—that new dawns are about to break—but much is deliberately left open for the reader's rumination.

How, then, is *Dawn* to be best assimilated? It is clear that Nietzsche wants his readers to proceed slowly, to pause and to reflect, and like most of his so-called aphoristic works, they are best read, as Gary Handwerk notes, in the manner they were written, that is, in snatches.[58] Each "aphorism" in the book, whether long or short, has been crafted and written for the reader's careful and intelligent rumination. The insights and "truths" they offer are ones that need to be subject to the test of experience and experiment, which is the only arena where thoughts can become real. *Dawn*, finally, is a new kind of book and in it is a new kind of philosophy: the fact that much of what Nietzsche was attempting is now recognizable by us is surely testimony to its richness, strength, and maturity of spirit.[59]

---

58. Handwerk, afterword to *HAH II*.

59. For valuable feedback on earlier drafts of this Afterword, which have helped me improve it, I am grateful to Gary Handwerk, Alan D. Schrift, and Brittain Smith.

Index of Persons

Subject Index

The Complete Works of Friedrich Nietzsche

IN NINETEEN VOLUMES

Library of Congress Cataloging-in-Publication Data

Nietzsche, Friedrich Wilhelm, 1844–1900, author.
  [Morgenröthe. English]
  Dawn : thoughts on the presumptions of morality / Friedrich
Nietzsche ; translated by Brittain Smith ; afterword by Keith
Ansell-Pearson.
        pages cm — (The complete works of Friedrich Nietzsche ; v. 5)
  "Translated from Friedrich Nietzsche, Sämtliche Werke: Kritische
Studienausgabe, ed. Giorgio Colli and Mazzino Montinari, in 15 vols. This
book corresponds to Vol. 3."
  Includes bibliographical references and index.
  ISBN 978-0-8047-2876-8 (cloth : alk. paper) —
ISBN 978-0-8047-8005-6 (pbk. alk. paper)
  1. Ethics.   I. Smith, Brittain, 1956– translator.   II. Title.   III. Series:
Nietzsche, Friedrich Wilhelm, 1844–1900. Works. English. 1995 ; v. 5.
  B3313.M72E5 2011
  193—dc22

                                                        2011007436

Typeset by Westchester Book Group in 10.5/12 Adobe Garamond